Growth with Equity

THE TAIWAN CASE

A World Bank Research Publication

Growth with Equity

THE TAIWAN CASE

John C. H. Fei
Gustav Ranis
Shirley W. Y. Kuo

with the assistance of
Yu-Yuan Bian
Julia Chang Collins

Published for the World Bank
Oxford University Press

Oxford University Press

NEW YORK OXFORD LONDON GLASGOW
TORONTO MELBOURNE WELLINGTON HONG KONG
TOKYO KUALA LUMPUR SINGAPORE JAKARTA
DELHI BOMBAY CALCUTTA MADRAS KARACHI
NAIROBI DAR ES SALAAM CAPE TOWN

Library of Congress Cataloging in Publication Data

Fei, John C. H.
Growth with equity
Includes bibliographical references and index.

1. Income distribution—Taiwan. 2. Taiwan—Economic conditions. I. Ranis, Gustav, joint author. II. Kuo, Shirley W. Y., 1930– joint author. III. Title.
HC430.5.Z9I5196 339.2′0951′249 79–23354
ISBN 0-19-520115-9
ISBN 0-19-520116-7 pbk.

Foreword

Can governments modify policies to produce a more equitable distribution of the benefits of economic growth? Or must they initiate more drastic structural changes? These questions are at the heart of one of the most debated issues in economic development. Most studies of developing countries indeed show that the rich tend to benefit more than the poor from rises in national income during the early phases of economic growth. The experience of Taiwan thus is of particular interest, because the country has managed to achieve rapid growth with considerable equity.

This study by Fei, Ranis, and Kuo develops an analytical framework that relates changes in family income to the evolution of its several components, which are in turn related to development theory. Application of this method to Taiwan helps to explain the observed changes in income distribution during two decades of rapid growth. Circumstances specific to Taiwan naturally played an important part in this performance. But in speculating about the effects of government intervention and the pattern of growth on changes in equity, the authors identify processes that are relevant both to economic theory and to economic policy. The authors' catalog of findings deserves consideration by pessimists who feel the tradeoff between growth and equity to be inevitable.

This book is one of a series of studies investigating the relations between growth and distribution in the developing countries—a series supported by the research program of the World Bank. Other books in this series include *Income Distribution Policy in Developing Countries: A Case Study of Korea* by Irma Adelman and Sherman Robinson, *Public Expenditure in Malaysia: Who Benefits and Why* by Jacob Meerman, *Who Benefits from Government Expenditure: A Case Study of Colombia* by Marcelo Selowsky, and *Redistribution with Growth* by Hollis Chenery and others. Additional titles forthcoming at this writing include *Models of Growth and Distribution for Brazil* by Lance Taylor and others, *Urban Labor Markets and Income Distribution in Malaysia* by Dipak Mazumdar, and *Inequality and Poverty in Malaysia: Measurement and Decomposition* by Sudhir Anand. As in these other studies, the authors of this book alone are responsible for the findings. It is the Bank's hope that this series will improve understanding of the choices that developing countries have with respect to growth and the distribution of income. Clearly, the method of analysis and findings for Taiwan presented here are important contributions to that understanding.

HOLLIS B. CHENERY
Vice President, Development Policy
The World Bank

Contents

Figures

Tables

Acronyms and Initials

ATP	After the turning point
BTP	Before the turning point
DGBAS	Directorate-General of Budget, Accounting, and Statistics
FID	Family distribution of income
GDP	Gross domestic product
GNP	Gross national product
ICCT	Industrial and Commercial Census of Taiwan
JCRR	Joint Commission for Rural Reconstruction
LDC	Less developed country
NDP	Net domestic product
OECD	Organization for Economic Cooperation and Development

Preface

THIS VOLUME IS DEDICATED to the study of the family distribution of income in the context of growth. Because the empirical application is to Taiwan, we quote at the outset a famous observation Confucius made 2,500 years ago: "Inequality is to be lamented more than scarcity." More recently, Ricardo had this to say in a letter to Malthus: "Political economy, you think, is an enquiry into the nature and causes of wealth—I think it should be called an enquiry into the laws which determine the division of the produce of industries amongst the classes who concur in its formation." Ricardo's sentiment ushered in the classical school's interest in the social problem of income distribution. Although that interest lapsed for some time, few today will deny that the persistence of income gaps between wealthy and poor families probably is the most serious social problem and that such gaps will continue to be a serious problem as long as there is scarcity.

It is curious then, despite such universal recognition of the social importance of the distribution of family income, that modern economists did not devote serious attention to it until really quite late: that is, until the post-Keynesian era after the Second World War. The classical economists focused on the functional distribution of income and attempted to explain the forces that determine the division of the national income into various functional distributive shares. The problem of the equity of income distribution is entirely different. The phenomenon is explained by the pattern of total income received by families. That pattern can be summarized by the degree of inequality of income, as measured by the Gini coefficient or some other index of inequality. The much more complicated nature of this problem, as well as the only recently reawakened interest in the fate of the poorer classes under conditions of growth, were undoubtedly responsible for the delayed rebirth of academic and policy interest in this area.

It is no coincidence that the new concern with the family distribution of income emerged, after a lag, with the revival of interest in the study of economic growth—itself a post-Keynesian, postwar phenomenon. The inequality of the distribution of family income must be traced directly to the inequality in the pattern of family ownership of the primary factors of production. These factors include physical and human assets, as well as their compensation. Because growth theory is primarily concerned with the augmentation of assets—that is, with capital formation, population growth, and the accumulation of human capital—the distributional impact of any change in the pattern of asset ownership can be meaningfully assessed only in the context of growth. The linkage between the family distribution of income and the theory of growth, and the conclusions for theory and policy which can be derived from the inductive examination of the Taiwan experience, thus constitute the focal points of this volume.

We clearly have not solved the problem. Indeed we shall be pleased if it is judged that we have somewhat advanced the cause. Moreover we fully realize that tensions between the political need for action and the scientific need for a better understanding of behavior are perhaps more pronounced in the study of income distribution than in any other area of economics. In fact, researchers are likely to have to defend themselves against a two-front attack. On one front, academic and scientific progress demands the formalism of variables and equations within a deterministic theory based on behavioristic hypotheses. Such formalism is technically difficult to achieve in this field, to say the least. On the second front, action-oriented policymakers demand to know the implications of research findings with an unusually high time preference. Consequently researchers run the risks of having to navigate a narrow course between accusations of sloppy humanitarianism and those of esoteric irrelevance. We nevertheless feel that both charges can and must be met.

Academics surely understand that there often exists a pretheoretical stage in the social sciences—a stage in which inductive evidence is examined to separate the relevant elements of a problem from the irrelevant, the essential from the nonessential. Because of the brief life of research examining the distribution of family income, most contemporary work cannot, we believe, escape from the grip of the pretheoretical stage we are in. The present volume is no exception.

Policymakers, on the other hand, sometimes need to be reminded that good policy is ultimately based on good theory. Although no one expects a moratorium on policy, planning commissions and aid donors have little at their disposal to permit them even to rule out absurdities. Given the many remedies proposed to cure the maldistribution of income, including fiscal reform, poverty relief, public works, and land reform, this volume's aim is to begin to fill the vacuum by specifying some of the things known about the behavioral relations, and consequently the policy relations, between growth and the distribution of income.

In short, we are concerned with developing a theory relating income distribution to growth—a theory which is to be implemented with statistical data, and a theory from which policy recommendations are to be deduced. Given the pioneering nature of this area of inquiry, the task is difficult. The interpretation of results, drawn from imperfect data, suffers from the absence of a recognized standard of international comparison. For example, what is the real significance of, say, a 2 percent drop in the Gini coefficient over a ten-year period? In addition, the deduction of policy recommendations, which always is an art, is particularly difficult at an early phase when the theory still is highly imperfect. We are aware of these shortcomings, and we disclaim any notion that our methodology has been perfected or that definitive policy conclusions can be drawn from it. Our main hope is that this volume may help to open up a new approach to understanding an important social problem.

We also recognize that all researchers concerned with the distribution of income face a conceptual difficulty of a basically philosophical nature. If a Gini coefficient $[G_y]$ is used to measure the degree of inequality of a pattern of income distribution $[Y = (Y_1, Y_2, \ldots, Y_n)]$, the underlying implication always is that perfect equality, $G_y = 0$ or $Y_1 = Y_2 = \ldots = Y_n$, represents the social ideal. This implication is true for all the familiar indexes of inequality which satisfy the axiom of the desirability of transfer: the axiom that any redistribution from rich to poor increases social equity. The conceptual difficulty arises when that axiom is subject to question.

Any modern industrial society, regardless of its organizational structure, requires a pyramid of positions differentiated by earning power. There should, for example, be relatively few positions for doctors and relatively many for unskilled workers. Individuals differentiated by ability, determination, and other characteristics will attempt to occupy positions in the pyramid. As a result, in any rational society, perfect income equality among individuals cannot really prevail. Regardless of how positions are allocated to individuals, the pyramid itself determines a nonzero value for the Gini. This probably explains why a Gini value below 0.30 is seldom found even in the most equitable society.

The ideal criterion of equity should thus be the equality of opportunity to reach for various positions in the pyramid. The major obstacles in the way of such equality of opportunity are, we believe, inherent in the genealogical relations of the family system. Even when markets are perfect and every position is rewarded according to its productive contribution—that is, even when there are no elements of discrimination or distortion—not every member of the new generation has an equal opportunity to reach for these positions. Differences in family background are the reason. The son of a wealthy black family, for example, can be expected to earn more than the son of a poor white family. This inherent inequality of opportunity, whether caused by variations in inherited assets or educational opportunities, probably is the principal cause of individual income inequality. Thus intergenerational, occupational, or class mobility represents the ultimate test of true equity in a rational society. Income equality does not.

In this volume we have chosen to study the family distribution of income as it relates to growth. The choice is based in part on the belief that a more equal distribution of income across families increases the equality of opportunity in each generation. For this reason a lower value or decline in the Gini coefficient will be regarded as a "good thing." We admit this to be an arbitrary value judgment on our part. We are content to leave to others, more competent than we, the unresolved philosophical issues raised in this context.

We would like to thank the World Bank for its financial support and Montek Ahluwalia, Clive Bell, Hollis Chenery, John Duloy, and Graham Pyatt for their substantive comments. We are most grateful for the thorough and perceptive comments of Anthony Atkinson, who acted as the Bank's outside reader. Others whose constructive criticisms were appreciated in the course of this effort include Gary Fields, Mahar Mangahas, and Guy Orcutt. We were beneficiaries of the cooperation of the Economic Planning Council of Taiwan and the Economic Growth Center at Yale. Our thanks also go to M. C. Cheng, M. M. Hsih, T. F. Hsuh, Françoise Le Gall, Regina Liu, and C. M. Tang for their help in preparing the manuscript, and to Cheryl Hunt and Paula Saddler for their patience and expert typing.

Bruce Ross-Larson edited the manuscript for publication. Raphael Blow prepared the charts, Brian J. Svikhart managed production of the book, and Kathryn M. Tidyman indexed the text.

JOHN C. H. FEI
GUSTAV RANIS
SHIRLEY KUO

New Haven, Connecticut
December 1979

INTRODUCTION

An Approach to Growth with Equity

THE INEQUALITY OF THE DISTRIBUTION OF INCOME AND WEALTH in a given society has been of concern to man for a very long time. Economists nevertheless have traditionally focused their attention more on the functional distribution of income and the determination of factor prices and shares in the manner of the classical and Austrian schools. Although the size or family distribution of income (FID) has not been totally neglected—witness the literature on utopian socialism and the use of the Lorenz curve—it probably is fair to say that economists have viewed FID more as a descriptive device. Until quite recently, it was not successfully integrated with the main body of analytical economics.[1]

During the early postwar period, the main social problem everywhere, but especially in the newly independent developing world, was a concern with growth. The 1950s and 1960s have been characterized, if unfairly, as being exclusively oriented to growth. Growth was not quite a religion, but common sense led to one basic assumption: when the pie is small, policies must be geared to increasing its size, at least for the time being. The concept of redistribution could not have much meaning until the pie became much larger.

1. In the first decades of this century, such writers as Cannan and Dalton were concerned with the measurement of the size distribution of income and its integration with mainstream economics. Historical hindsight suggests, however, that their attempt at integration was not very successful. Because the size distribution of income appears to be a growth-related issue, related to the accumulation of human and physical assets, the chance for successful integration became real only with the revival of interest in growth after the Second World War.

In recent years, however, all parties have become increasingly unwilling to accept the "grow now, redistribute later" package. One reason for this is a growing reluctance to be generous only to future generations. But the main reason is the growing skepticism about whether "later" would ever come. Nevertheless most language in currency today still relates to redistribution. How is a better measure of equity to be regained *after* growth has occurred? How much growth is to be sacrificed for the sake of better distribution along the way? This second formulation comes closer to the heart of this volume, with one proviso: we do not accept the notion that there always has to be a sacrifice. Consequently it seems more appropriate to address the extent to which equity can accompany growth from the start, not to constrain the discourse to the achievement of one objective at the expense of the other. Of course, the matter may be as much semantic as it is substantive.

Most economists and policymakers understandably share, at least implicitly, the assumption of the need for tradeoffs having varying degrees of severity. Consider the work of Kuznets, Paukert, and Adelman and Morris.[2] On the basis of cross-country cross-sections, they seem to discern an inverse U-shaped relation between growth and equity. They conclude that, as income increases from low levels in a developing society, the distribution of income must first worsen before it can improve. Two facts support their conclusion. First, today's less developed countries (LDCS) generally have distributions which are less equal than those of the rich countries. Second, accelerated LDC growth has most often been accompanied by a worsening of already unfavorable indexes of equality.

Based on the historical evidence, almost all contemporary LDCS support the general aura of tradeoff pessimism. Taiwan is one exception. According to the best data available, Taiwan's family distribution of income in the 1950s was not very different from the unfavorable levels most LDCS seem to be prey to in the early years of

2. Simon Kuznets, "Economic Growth and Income Inequality," *American Economic Review*, vol. 45, no. 1 (March 1955), pp. 1–28; idem, "Quantitative Aspects of the Economic Growth of Nations: VIII, Distribution of Income by Size," *Economic Development and Cultural Change*, vol. 11, no. 2 (1963), pp. 1–80; Felix Paukert, "Income Distribution at Different Levels of Development: A Survey of Evidence," *International Labour Review*, vol. 108, nos. 2–3 (August and September 1973), pp. 97–124; Irma Adelman and Cynthia Taft Morris, *Economic Growth and Social Equity in Developing Countries* (Stanford, Calif.: Stanford University Press, 1973).

their transition effort. But that distribution has substantially improved during two decades of rapid growth. This "deviant" record should therefore be of interest to academicians and policymakers.

Although no two countries ever are alike, and deviant performance may be based on special circumstances, an examination of the relations between growth and equity in a country exhibiting such a deviant performance can help to isolate the critical elements of that performance. Only then is it possible to judge whether the underlying conditions, which seem to have had the effect of virtually eliminating the usual conflict between these two principal societal objectives in Taiwan, are sufficient elsewhere to permit somewhat greater optimism. Such optimism would not be based on the conclusion that achieving growth with equity is easy. Instead it would be based on the conclusion that some of the obstacles are made by man, not nature, and can thus be removed by changes in policy.

Framework of Analysis

The problem of growth with equity can, we believe, be fruitfully analyzed in the historical context. During the third quarter of this century, the less developed world experienced unprecedented growth, a phenomenon accompanied by a resurgence of interest in the theory of economic development. We therefore felt that a natural way to proceed was to construct a framework of analysis that takes advantage of this new stock of knowledge. In this respect, three dimensions common to many contemporary growth models are points of departure for the work of this volume: historical perspective, subphases of growth, and typological sensitivity.

By historical perspective we mean that the quarter century after the Second World War can be viewed in most LDCs as a period of transition between a long epoch of agrarianism and an epoch of modern growth.[3] There in fact are two periods in the history of

3. Latin American countries, for example, started the transition earlier than most LDCs. For general works on the subject see Simon Kuznets, *Modern Economic Growth* (New Haven: Yale University Press, 1966); John C. H. Fei and Douglas S. Paauw, *The Transition in Open Dualistic Economies: Theory and Southeast Asian Experience* (New Haven: Yale University Press, 1973); and John C. H. Fei and Gustav Ranis, "Economic Development in Historical Perspective," *American Economic Review*, vol. 59, no. 2 (May 1969), pp. 386–400.

economic doctrine when economists have been interested in growth and income distribution. The first period is the age of the classical economists—Smith, Malthus, and Ricardo; it dealt with transition growth in western Europe. The second period is that after the Second World War; it deals with transition growth in the contemporary developing world. This setting of transition growth gives the problem of "growth with equity" its distinctive character. Moreover the economic content of transition growth includes recognition of the dualistic structure of most less developed countries: agricultural and nonagricultural production sectors coexist; the center of gravity gradually shifts from one to the other. The basic phenomena include modernizing agriculture, generating an agricultural surplus, accumulating real capital to provide nonagricultural employment, and reallocating labor from agricultural to nonagricultural pursuits.

It is convenient and substantively important to divide the overall phase of transition growth into subphases. These subphases are related to marked changes in the system's endowment of resources and in the prevailing package of policies—changes which affect relative factor prices and shares, as well as the behavior and performance of the economy. Because the reallocated labor and the accumulated assets are largely owned by individual families, the phenomenon of transition growth clearly has important implications for the distribution of income among families.

To take full advantage of this base of growth theory, an additional dimension particularly relevant to the analysis of FID must be added: the spatial perspective. By spatial perspective we mean that a distinction must be made in the typical LDC between urban families and rural families, depending on their location and occupational pursuits. Urban families live in and near the major population centers and overwhelmingly engage in nonagricultural production. Rural families are spatially dispersed and derive their income from agricultural and nonagricultural production, the relative proportions of which depend upon the locational pattern of industries and services. Thus the separation of rural and urban households is a basic analytical device used in this volume.

We also find it useful to distinguish among various types of factor income accruing to families. Wage income and property income are examples. This separation is essential for our analysis both at the aggregate and the disaggregate levels. At the aggregate or holistic level, such a separation makes it possible to trace the inequality of family income to its various factor components and, in this way, to link that inequality to the theory of development for a dualistic economy. At the disaggregate level, an intensive search into the causes of inequality of particular factor components forms a complementary part of the inquiry.

We must naturally be somewhat selective in choosing the focus for such disaggregate analysis. A case will be made that the causation of the inequality of family wage income can be singled out for more intensive study. The system's labor force usually represents the most important type of capital distributed among families: human capital. Moreover, in the course of development, a functionally specialized modern labor force will gradually be formed out of the more homogeneous unskilled labor force of the agrarian epoch. A differentiated wage structure obtains for this increasingly heterogeneous labor force, which is differentiated by such characteristics as skill, sex, education, and age. In addition, the rules of family formation—or the composition of families with respect to this stratified labor force—also undergo transformation, depending on the propensity of families and society to invest in education. It is evident that the inequality of family wage income, an important component of overall inequality, can in turn be traced to this pattern of family ownership of differentiated labor, as well as to the differentiated wage structure.

A similar disaggregate study could have examined the ownership and accumulation of physical capital by families. The usual classification of assets suggests that capital assets also are highly heterogeneous. The portfolio choice of families appears, however, to be a much more complex problem that perhaps is less relevant to the study of family income inequality than its wage counterpart. In any case, we have not tackled it in this volume.

The role of the public sector also changes in the transition to modern growth. First and foremost, LDC governments must set the policy environment for private economic activity through their actions with respect to foreign exchange, trade, domestic credit, tariffs, and so on. These actions—whether they work through the market by way of indirect controls or circumvent the market by way of direct controls—may be critical for the kind of growth path and the pattern of income distribution generated. Second, governments directly participate, at different times and to a greater or lesser extent, in productive activities through the ownership of public enterprises. Third, governments act through their tax and expenditure policies to affect FID after the fact, after the dust of production has settled. In this volume we attempt to tackle only one of these aspects: taxation.

The organization of this volume should be viewed in the foregoing perspective. We first make an effort to acquaint the reader with the general story of transition growth and distribution in Taiwan, especially for the 1950s—a period for which precise FID data either do not exist or are deficient in quality and sectoral breakdown. Next, we focus on the period after 1964, when reasonably good and comprehensive data become available on income distribution. Our principal attempt is to forge a more precise link at the aggregate level between the family distribution of income and the theory of development in a labor surplus economy. We also attempt to dig more deeply into the causes of the equity or inequity of income distribution from a number of related disaggregate perspectives.

The study of FID still is in a pretheoretical stage in which much of the effort must be directed at examining the empirical evidence. By sorting out the essential from the nonessential and the relevant from the irrelevant, it is to be hoped that the relevant and the essential can then be integrated with the mainstream of economic ideas, especially those related to development theory. The problems of measurement and data, two crucial facets of empirical research, thus receive special attention in this introduction so that readers can maintain their bearings in the rest of the volume.

Problems of Measurement

How is inequality to be measured? The basic problem is the choice of an appropriate index of inequality [$I(Y)$] that can be computed when the pattern of income distribution [$Y = (Y_1, Y_2, \ldots, Y_n)$] is given for n families. Many alternative indexes of inequality are in use, such as the Gini coefficient [G_y], the Theil index, the Atkinson index, the Kuznets index, and the coefficient of variation. All of them are reasonable but arbitrary, because none has a conspicuous advantage over the rest. For reasons spelled out below, we have generally chosen in this volume to use the Gini coefficient.

All measurements are ultimately motivated by certain theoretical considerations—or, more appropriately, theoretical intuitions—in the pretheoretical stage. In our attempt to link the distribution of family income to growth—the growth of human and physical assets over time—it is natural to distinguish several types of assets. An example is the familiar dichotomy between capital [K] and labor [L] in the mainstream of growth theory. Our basic choice of the additive dimension of income is based on the recognition that this is the only way to forge the necessary links to development theory.

The pattern of family income [$Y = (Y_1, Y_2, \ldots, Y_n)$] is thus seen to comprise several additive factor components:

MODEL OF ADDITIVE FACTOR COMPONENTS

$$Y = Y^1 + Y^2 + \ldots + Y^r, \quad \text{where}$$

$$Y^i = (Y^i_1, Y^i_2, \ldots, Y^i_n). \qquad (i = 1, 2, \ldots, r)$$

Each factor income component [Y^i] corresponds to a particular type of asset owned by the n families. The formulation of additive factor-components problems of this type is, with minor exceptions, a central and unifying theme of this volume. For example, in our attempt to link FID to growth theory, the two factor components are property income [Y^1] and wage income [Y^2] for urban households ($r = 2$). Agricultural income [Y^3] is added as a third component for rural households ($r = 3$).[4] By letting $W = (W_1, W_2, \ldots, W_n)$ represent the wage income pattern and $\pi = (\pi_1, \pi_2, \ldots, \pi_n)$ the property income pattern, the pattern of family ownership of the labor force can be traced to certain demographic rules of family formation, and the pattern of family ownership of physical assets can be traced to the rules of saving.

For a more intensive treatment of the wage income component, the labor force can be stratified by age, sex, education, and other characteristics. In the model of additive factor components, Y stands for the pattern of total family wage income; Y^i for the wage income earned by a particular type of labor force, such as adult college-educated females. The observed structure of wages in part reflects labor attributes and in part such noncompetitive elements as nepotism and sex discrimination. Abstractly the problem can again be treated as a problem of additive factor components.[5] In addition to the differences in human capital dictated by market forces, other differences are the result of labor market imperfections caused by government intervention, oligopoly power, and so on. For one such

4. This formulation is used to forge a link to the dualistic growth model in chapter three, Growth and the Family Distribution of Income by Factor Components.

5. This formulation is used in chapter four, The Inequality of Family Wage Income.

intervention, taxation, the total family income before tax [Y] can be viewed as the sum of family income after tax [Y^1] and tax payments [Y^2]. Family income after tax can in turn be seen to comprise various categories of expenditure and savings; tax payments to comprise direct and indirect taxes.[6] Abstractly the problem once again becomes one of additive factor components.

When the pattern of total income is abstractly formulated as comprising additive factor components, a natural way to explain the Gini coefficient of Y [G_y] is to trace it to $G(Y^1)$, $G(Y^2)$, . . . , $G(Y^r)$, the factor Gini coefficients computed for the r factor components. If:

$$\phi_i = (Y_1^i + Y_2^i + \ldots + Y_n^i)/(Y_1 + Y_2 + \ldots + Y_n), \qquad (i = 1, 2 \ldots, r)$$

the values of ϕ_i [$(\phi_1, \phi_2, \ldots, \phi_r)$] correspond to the r factor income shares. It then is tempting to design a decomposition formula of the following type:

$$G_y = \phi_1 G(Y^1) + \phi_2 G(Y^2) + \ldots + \phi_r G(Y^r),$$

which states that total family income inequality [G_y] is the weighted average of the factor Ginis [$G(Y^i)$]. It turns out that this is an approximation relevant only under special conditions. A major theoretical task of this volume is to design exact and approximate decomposition formulas of this type.[7] The Gini coefficient is thus used in this volume not because of its greater familiarity or superior characteristics, but because it has the intrinsic additive property that makes it convenient for the design of decomposition formulas.

The model of additive factor components differentiates among various types or sources of income and represents only one kind of framework for FID analysis. It happens to be the one we find useful for most of the purposes of this volume. There also are other general models, such as those which try to differentiate among various types

6. This formulation is used in chapter six, Taxation and the Inequality of Income and Expenditure.

7. Problems of this type are inherently technical and have therefore been consolidated in the five chapters constituting part two, The Methodology of Gini Coefficient Analysis. When the results of that discourse on methodology are discussed in part one, however, numerical examples and other pedagogical devices are used to enable the less technically inclined reader to follow the argument.

of income recipient or income-receiving family. For such a model the pattern of total family income [Y] is abstractly segmented as follows:

$$Y = (Y_1, Y_2, \ldots, Y_n) = (S_1, S_2, \ldots, S_r), \quad \text{where}$$

$$S_1 = (Y_1, Y_2, \ldots, Y_{r1}), S_2 = (Y_{r1+1}, Y_{r1+2}, \ldots, Y_{r2}), \ldots .$$

Each subvector [S_i ($i = 1, 2, \ldots, r$)] represents a particular class of income recipients. For example, when r is 2, S_1 and S_2 can represent males and females or, what would be more pertinent to our work, agricultural households and nonagricultural households. This classification suggests that all families within each S_i can be referred to as a homogeneous group. Consequently the abstract framework can be referred to as a homogeneous group model—or, mathematically, as a segmentation model. Abstractly an index of inequality can then be defined on all income recipients [$I(Y)$], as well as on each homogeneous group [$I(S_i)$ ($i = 1, 2, \ldots, r$)]. $I(S_i)$ is to be called *intragroup inequality*. If $\bar{Y}_i$ ($i = 1, 2, \ldots, r$) is the mean value of the ith group, the income pattern obtained by replacing every Y_i by its group mean becomes:

$$R = [(\bar{Y}_1, \bar{Y}_1, \ldots, \bar{Y}_1), (\bar{Y}_2, \bar{Y}_2, \ldots, \bar{Y}_2), \ldots, (\bar{Y}_1, \bar{Y}_2, \ldots, \bar{Y}_r)].$$

While suppressing the intragroup inequality, this equation clearly brings out the intergroup inequality. Consequently $I(R)$ is called *intergroup inequality*. In the homogeneous group approach, the purpose of any decomposition formula is to trace $I(Y)$ to the intergroup effect $I(R)$ and the intragroup effect $I(S)$.[8]

Intrinsically the study of family income distribution is a technically complicated matter, precisely because of the concern with patterns of income over families, patterns that are represented by vectors. Because this volume is principally aimed at the general reader, the foregoing explanation has been to help identify the contours of part one, where the methods of analysis are summarized and the empirical

8. This model of homogeneous groups is used only in chapter five, Income Distribution and Economic Structure. The decomposition of $I(Y)$ into intergroup and intragroup effects in essence is the analytical technique used in that chapter, where it also turns out to be more convenient to use the variance as a measure of inequality, not the Gini coefficient.

findings for Taiwan are presented. As noted earlier, the more technical aspects of decomposition are presented in part two. It is recommended that general readers turn to this part only after absorbing the essential ideas in part one.

Problems of Data

In this pretheoretical stage of inquiry, much of the effort must necessarily be inductive. Consequently the availability and quality of data become unusually critical issues. The foregoing discussion of the problem of measurement has already suggested the kind of data needed for the work of this volume. The model of additive factor components requires, for example, data on the total family income pattern $[Y]$ and on the patterns of income components $[Y^i]$ for all families involved. All such data must ultimately be based on household surveys.

For Taiwan in the 1950s, only two surveys gathered data on the overall distribution of income: one was conducted in 1953; the other in 1959–60.[9] In addition, surveys by the Joint Commission on Rural Reconstruction (JCRR) for 1952, 1957, 1962, and 1967 contain information only on farm family incomes.[10] Both sets deal with the total income of these families, not with factor income components; neither set is of good quality. In 1964, however, the Directorate-General of Budget, Accounting, and Statistics (DGBAS) began to conduct household surveys which included information on factor components, as well as total family incomes.[11] In 1966 the DGBAS

9. Kowie Chang, "An Estimate of Taiwan Personal Income Distribution in 1953–Pareto's Formula Discussed and Applied," *Journal of Social Science*, vol. 7 (August 1956); National Taiwan University, College of Law, "Report on Pilot Study of Personal Income and Consumption in Taiwan" (prepared under the sponsorship of a working group of National Income Statistics, Directorate-General of Budget, Accounting, and Statistics (DGBAS); processed in Chinese).

10. See Y. C. Tsui and S. C. Hsieh, "Farm Income in Taiwan in 1952," *Economic Digest Series*, no. 4 (Taipei: Joint Council on Rural Reconstruction (JCRR), 1954) and JCRR, Rural Economics Division, "Taiwan Farm Income Survey of 1967—with a Brief Comparison with 1952, 1957, and 1962," *Economic Digest Series*, no. 20 (Taipei: JCRR, 1970).

11. DGBAS, *Report on the Survey of Family Income and Expenditure, Taiwan Province, Republic of China*, 1964 and subsequent years (Taipei: DGBAS).

broadened the classification to distinguish between rural and urban households. These data represent the principal data source for the formal analysis of this volume. The decomposition analysis could thus be carried out only for the years beginning with 1964; the separation of urban and rural households, for the years beginning with 1966.[12]

Even when good household surveys became available after 1964, specific dimensions of the data needed to be recognized and addressed. There are problems associated with the randomness of sampling and the biased nonresponses among sample returns. There are problems associated with differences between primary and published data—problems which cause the appearance of a "consolidation error." There are problems associated with data interpretation, especially in relation to the imputation of the functional shares and the spatial characteristics of economic activities. Although these by no means exhaust all the data problems in this field of inquiry, they are the ones directly relevant to the theoretical focus of the analysis in this volume.[13]

Data quality

For surveys the DGBAS began to conduct in 1964, a sharp distinction must be made between the published data and the primary data contained in the original questionnaires. Only the published data are available to the public; what is published obviously is severely constrained by what is viewed as the effective consumer demand for particular combinations of primary information. As it is, a typical DGBAS volume contains more than 700 pages of tables, but will nevertheless disappoint many prospective data users. To illustrate this point, suppose that workers are classified by sex (male and female), education (primary, junior high, senior high, professional

12. The city of Taipei originally was part of Taiwan Province and was included in the overall DGBAS surveys. Since 1968 Taipei has been reclassified as a special municipality; the Taipei City government, not DGBAS which is a provincial organization, has accordingly carried out the same household surveys. For comparability we have merged the two sets of data by adding, for each income bracket, both the families and incomes of those living in the city of Taipei.

13. For example, the issues of life-cycle income and family lineage are among the dimensions of FID analysis not addressed. To have formally treated these issues would have raised even more severe problems of data constraints.

school, and college), and age (subdivided into nine age groups). These three characteristics alone imply the existence of 90 kinds of labor—180 if rural and urban households are distinguished. Such an exhaustive cross-listing can be conveniently preserved only in coded tapes, not in published data.[14]

There is no question in our minds that the DGBAS surveys were based on competently drawn and stratified random samples. Even when samples are random, however, a frequent problem is the underresponse of certain groups, such as wealthier families. The conscientiousness of DGBAS personnel and the good attitude of respondents to questionnaire surveys nevertheless give us a high degree of confidence.[15] In addition, we know of no reason to suspect differences in the quality of the data over time. We are, moreover, mainly concerned with interpreting the *changes* rather than the precise *levels* of, say, the Gini coefficients.

It should also be noted that even if the information reported by the households is perfect, the data may not give the functional income distribution as the economist would like to have it. In urban family enterprises, for example, it is difficult to differentiate between the entrepreneurial income of an owner-operator and his income as a skilled laborer. The problem is even more serious in a family farm, where there is less functional specialization. For the urban sector, DGBAS made its best effort to "impute" family income to the proper functional share, leaving only a small unallocated "mixed income" category. For the agricultural income of the rural families, no such imputation was made by the DGBAS or us. Consequently agricultural income is a mixed category that includes all property and wage income. For the spatial dimension, which also is important in the study of FID, the DGBAS data give the breakdown by "farm" and "nonfarm" households. We have taken these respective categories to

14. Published DGBAS data are used in chapters two, three, and five; coded DGBAS data in chapters four and six. Because a complete description of the data available to us should also focus on the design of questionnaires, the years of availability, and the absolute and relative sizes of samples, we discuss these matters in an appendix to chapter four, where the original coded data are used for the first time. The use of published DGBAS data is discussed as it is deployed.

15. For analysis of this issue see Shirley W. Y. Kuo, "Income Distribution by Size in Taiwan Area—Changes and Causes," in *Income Distribution, Employment, and Economic Development in Southeast and East Asia*, 2 vols. (Tokyo: Japan Economic Research Center, 1975), vol. 1, pp. 80–146.

be proxies for "spatially dispersed rural households" and "spatially concentrated urban households."[16]

The quality of data must be judged in the context of the problems indicated. The inferences we derive from the data must be open to the criticism that conclusions should not be sensitive to small variations. On the whole, we feel that the quality of data in Taiwan favorably compares with that in other LDCs; we are quite confident that our findings are robust in this sense. We nevertheless recognize that the quality of data of this kind is such that stronger statements are not admissible. We therefore refrained from applying refined econometric tests in any of our applications.

Data aggregation

Another problem is the consolidation issue associated with published data. Suppose there are $n = 5{,}000$ families. The published tabulation of the pattern of total family income $[(Y_1, Y_2, \ldots, Y_n)]$ must then be in the form of decile or other income groups. By using such a tabulation, FID analysis tends to underestimate the degree of income inequality, because some intragroup inequality is inevitably suppressed. In the published DGBAS data, the number of income classes varies between 23 and 32; that represents a high degree of consolidation of sample survey returns for 3,000 to 6,000 families. Moreover the demand for international comparability required a somewhat higher degree of consolidation.[17] Because of this consolidation, trends in the Gini coefficients over time once again become more meaningful than the absolute magnitudes.

16. One survey year, 1968, contains in addition to the farm and nonfarm breakdown a locational breakdown into urban, semiurban, and rural residence. Because we are basically interested in the broad locational distinctions of urban residence in relation to rural residence, semiurban workers can thus belong to either the urban type of household or the rural. For 1968 the breakdown shows that about 80 percent of nonfarm households and more than 95 percent of farm households directly correspond to our urban (nonfarm) and rural (farm) sectors (households). In the absence of ideal data, we thus have confidence that the results of our empirical research give a relatively accurate picture of the effect of growth on FID in a dualistic economy.

17. In chapter three we tried to preserve the possibility for international comparisons by reprocessing our data to conform to the decile grouping convention of the World Bank. See for example Shail Jain, *Size Distribution of Income* (Washington, D.C.: World Bank, 1975).

Using grouped data for the analysis of additive factor components is a new and important problem. It is new in its application to the particular methodology used by us and thus is not dealt with in the existing literature.[18] It is important because everyone is using grouped data and the international comparisons based on those data. We admit that this volume raises these and associated problems without being able to resolve them. They are shared by virtually all researchers now investigating income distribution, and this gives us some comfort. The fact that we lean heavily on the interpretation of changes in Ginis over time, not on the interpretation of the absolute levels of Ginis at different times, gives us additional comfort. Consequently our quantitative conclusions, like those of others, must be read with these qualifications in mind.

We should add, moreover, that these problems are being tackled on at least two fronts. On the theoretical front, considerable progress is being made by Graham Pyatt at the World Bank, Fei and Ranis at Yale, and Chow and Chen at the Academia Sinica in Taiwan. On the statistical front, ungrouped or computerized data are now becoming available in Taiwan—data which will enable us to implement the theory and determine just how much difference the extent of aggregation makes to the results. We believe this to be an exciting new area of future research, but one that will take considerable time to sort out.[19]

Data interpretation

The effort to tackle the relations between equity and growth, the main objective of this volume, involves matters of theory and the use of data to implement the theory. For the theory we have, in the main, chosen to introduce a method of decomposition by additive factor components. For the data we have used the Gini coefficient to describe the level and changes in the pattern of equity. In any such formulation, there always is the problem of interpreting "significant" or "insignificant" changes in magnitudes. Neither the theoretical formulations nor the data provide a firm basis for such judgments.

18. See for example Joseph L. Gastwirth, "The Estimation of the Lorenz Curve and Gini Index," *Review of Economics and Statistics*, vol. 54, no. 3 (August 1972), pp. 306–16.

19. The outline of these issues is fully presented in chapter twelve.

These judgments can be arrived at only in reference to some consensual convention or standard derived over many years of research and observation. Such a consensus exists, say, for per capita income and population growth; it does not yet exist for measures of the equity of income distribution. The experience with international and intertemporal comparisons on national income and population growth does permit judgments about the significance or insignificance of changes to be made with some confidence. In the realm of the Gini, however, we do not yet have a similar experience. Our description of change thus reflects more of our own judgments, which cannot as yet be checked against an agreed-upon convention.[20] As more empirical work, especially in international comparisons, accumulates in this relatively new field, we will be in a better position to make qualitative statements. Meanwhile the reader is asked to take our own judgments about the significance of quantitative results with a grain of salt.

20. We especially wish to thank Tony Atkinson for bringing this point home to us.

PART ONE

The Case of Taiwan

IN CONTEMPORARY LDCS the issue of growth with equity must be viewed in the historical context of attempts by these countries to make the transition from their agrarian heritage to the epoch of modern growth. In analyzing equity during this transition, a framework is developed to link the distribution of family income to the store of growth theory which has been accumulating over the last quarter of a century. Central to this framework is a decomposition technique which makes it possible to trace the inequality of family income to various components of factor income and to various groups of income recipients. This approach, we believe, reflects the needs of the current pretheoretical stage of analysis and permits the systematic processing of data accumulated in recent years.

Chapters one and two outline the case of Taiwan in the context of transition growth in the open, dualistic, labor-surplus economy. The crucial phenomenon for focus is the relatedness between the reallocation of domestic labor from agricultural to nonagricultural activities and the pattern of foreign trade. Upon examination, postwar development seems to be marked off by well-defined subphases of transition growth: a subphase of primary import substitution in the 1950s and a subphase of primary export substitution in the 1960s. Toward the end of the 1960s, the condition of labor surplus seems to have become gradually exhausted, as marked by substantial increases in unskilled real wages. Analysis of the family distribution of income (FID) over the entire period of transition must be related to this background. Chapter two concentrates on an analysis of distribution during the subphase of import substitution, for which the inadequacy of data on income distribution does not permit a fully rigorous analysis. Subsequent chapters analyze the distribution of income during the 1964–72 period, for which the data are much better.

In chapter three a dualistic model is used; it contains rural and urban sectors, each with a number of households. With such a model, the impact of growth on the equity of FID over time is measured by the Gini coefficient [G_y] and analyzed by a method of additive factor Gini decomposition. According to this method, the impact of growth on the equity of FID is traced, both quantitatively and qualitatively, to three causal factors: a reallocation effect, a functional distribution effect, and a factor Gini effect. Each effect is explained and related as closely as possible to the theory of development. The functional distribution effect captures changes in the functional distribution of income—that is, the relative shares accruing to capital and labor. The reallocation effect captures changes in the share of agriculture in total income and the extent to which the center of gravity in the dualistic economy has, or has not, shifted. The factor Gini effect captures the impact of changes in the inequality of factor income—that is, the inequality of wage income [G_w], property income [G_π], and agricultural income [G_a] taken separately. Development theory within the context of the dualistic economy can adequately explain only the impact of the reallocation effect and the functional distribution effect on G_y over time. To increase understanding of the factor Gini effect, which the empirical work of this volume indicates may be quantitatively important, a fuller inquiry into the causation of the inequality of particular important factor incomes is required.

Chapter four accordingly concentrates on the causation of the inequality of family wage income, which is the largest component of family income. At least two nonconventional aspects of modernization or development enter into this analysis. First, the formation of a modern labor force leads to recognition of the growing importance of labor heterogeneity as workers are stratified by such attributes as age, sex, and educational attainment. Second, the rules of family formation regulate the composition of family ownership of various types and qualities of labor. In this effort at disaggregate analysis, the competitive and discriminatory elements in the wage structure are analyzed by means of a multiple correlation analysis. On the basis of this information, as well as that relating to family membership and formation, a first-cut determination of the basic causes of wage income inequality among families is attempted. The model of additive factor components is used in this chapter as well.

Chapter five further analyzes the inequality of total family income, but disregards the functional additive components of family income and classifies the income-receiving families by various criteria. For example, (Y_1^1, Y_2^1, Y_3^1), $(Y_1^2, Y_2^2, Y_3^2, Y_4^2)$, (Y_1^3, Y_2^3, Y_3^3) represents the classification of ten families into three homogeneous subgroups. Whenever such a classification or segmentation is attempted, the inequality of total family income can be traced to an intergroup inequality effect and an intragroup inequality effect. Substantively three explanatory classifications are used: farm and nonfarm families; the degree of urbanization of the families; and characteristics of the head of household, such as age, sex, and educational standard. This chapter thus attempts to throw additional light on the causes of income inequality by pointing to differences in family attributes as causation factors.

Chapter six examines inequality in the disposition of family income. If $Y = (Y_1, Y_2, \ldots, Y_n)$ is the pattern of family incomes before tax, then the family income pattern after tax $[V = (V_1, V_2, \ldots, V_n)]$ will be different because of the payments of direct tax $[(T_1^d, T_2^d, \ldots, T_n^d)]$ and indirect tax $[(T_1^i, T_2^i, \ldots, T_n^i)]$. The degree of inequality of family income before tax $[G_y]$ and after tax $[G_v]$ may also be different, depending upon the progressiveness of direct and indirect taxes. One issue with very obvious policy implications is the impact of taxation on the equality of FID after taxes. The pattern of family income after tax $[V]$ is after all only a means to family economic welfare. That income will in turn be disposed of by the families in various ways, leading to various patterns of family consumption $[C^i = (C_1^i, C_2^i, \ldots, C_n^i)]$ and saving $[S = (S_1, S_2, \ldots, S_n)]$. The inequality of family income after tax $[G_v]$ will thus lead to inequality of family savings and family expenditure on education and other consumption categories, depending on the ways in which incomes are disposed of. A second issue studied in this chapter is the relation of the inequality of expenditure $[G(C^i)]$ and saving $[G_s]$ to the inequality of family income after tax $[G_v]$. The inequality of family investment in physical and human capital may be regarded as the primary causes of the persistence of family income inequality over the longer run. Persistence of the inequality of family consumption in particular consumption categories, such as housing or other items of conspicuous consumption, indicates the existence of class distinctions and points to possible targets for additional consumption taxation calculated to reduce the social impact created by family income inequality. The model of additive factors components is again used in this chapter.

Chapter seven summarizes the principal analytical findings and presents the policy conclusions that can be derived from these findings. As stated earlier, a fully deterministic theory of the distribution of income—one that is behaviorally specified—frankly is still beyond reach. We nevertheless believe that we have pointed out some directions that future work might take at the aggregate and disaggregate levels. Meanwhile there is no possibility of a moratorium on policy for those wanting to ameliorate existing or potential conflicts between strategies for growth and equity. Thus, although our analysis is by no means complete or comprehensive, we feel it important at this stage to try to derive the main conclusions for policy.

Part two is devoted to a systematic derivation of the various decomposition formulas and equations used in part one. There are two reasons for postponing the discussion of technical issues. First, by gathering most such matters into one part, it is easier for the interested reader to appreciate the relatedness of the various methods used in this volume, to each other and to other contributions in the literature. Second, the less technically inclined reader can absorb the main argument of the early chapters without the periodic intrusion of an undue amount of technical detail.

CHAPTER 1

Historical Perspective

THE BROAD OUTLINES of Taiwan's social and economic development during the postwar period are relatively well known. Although there is no unanimity concerning the transferability of this experience to other nations, there is general agreement that Taiwan's success is rare among less developed countries (LDCS). Two of Taiwan's achievements in the years after 1953 are particularly notable: extremely rapid rates of economic growth were accompanied by improvements in the family distribution of income; unemployment, or underemployment, was virtually eliminated by the end of the 1960s. This success may in part be attributed to the legacy of the Japanese colonial era. The Japanese left behind an excellent physical and human infrastructure upon which Taiwan could later build growth in agriculture and industry. Moreover the influx of high-level manpower from the mainland more than compensated for the withdrawal of Japanese human resources after the war. As a result of these and other factors facilitating reconstruction, all output indicators in 1953 were roughly back to their prewar levels. The difference was that the economy, poised for takeoff, was engaged in purposive national development.

The Colonial Legacy

Patterns of colonial investment and resource flows in Taiwan had features recognizable in most LDCS: the colony supplied the colonizing country with primary products, in this case sugar and rice; in return, the colonizing country supplied the colony with manufactured consumer goods.[1] Until the Second World War altered Japanese priorities, there was little encouragement of domestic industry beyond the processing of agricultural goods for export and the construction and operation of utilities required to support this processing. Somewhat less typical, however, was that Japanese colonial activity in Taiwan focused on food production. This focus led to the maintenance and expansion of an extensive, well-distributed irrigation system and to the organization of an islandwide network of farmers' associations and cooperatives.

The Japanese, in their occupation of Taiwan from 1895 to 1945, sought to develop the colony into an agricultural supplier for Japan. All government activities during this period were directed toward this goal. At the same time Taiwan received a substantial inflow of physical, human, and institutional capital from Japan, and economic growth was considerable. Between 1910 and 1945 the population increased by 58 percent, net domestic product by 178 percent, agricultural production by 133 percent, industrial production by 267 percent, and export volume by 361 percent. Agriculture, which dominated the economy, was in turn dominated by rice and sugar cane. During 1935–37 rice accounted for 53 percent of the total value of agricultural output; sugar cane for 15 percent. The Japanese strongly encouraged the production of both crops, which together constituted 72.7 percent of Taiwan's total exports during 1930–39. During 1906–40 the production of rice grew at an annual rate of 2.7 percent; the production of sugar cane, at 4.5 percent.

To encourage agricultural production the Japanese undertook a variety of projects to develop the physical, human, and institutional infrastructure of rural areas. They built an efficient and inexpensive system of railroads and rural roads to facilitate the transport of rural production. They brought in massive quantities of fertilizer from Japan and introduced new farming techniques to increase the productivity of the land. They constructed an extensive irrigation system: between 1910 and 1942 the area of land under irrigation increased from 227,000 hectares to 545,000 hectares; the total area under cultivation increased from 519,000 hectares to 837,000 hectares. Even with that increase in the total area under cultivation,

1. Discussion of the colonial period is largely based on Samuel P. S. Ho, *Economic Development in Taiwan: 1860–1970* (New Haven: Yale University Press, 1978).

Table 1.1. *Distribution of Land and Owner-Cultivator Households, by Size of Holding, 1920, 1932, and 1939*

Size of holding (chia)[a]	Distribution of owner-cultivator households (percent) 1920	1932	1939	Distribution of land (percent) 1920	Average size of holding (chia) 1920
0–0.5	42.7	38.4	43.2	5.7	0.24
0.5–1	21.4	20.9	20.9	8.7	0.72
1–2	17.5	18.7	17.2	13.9	1.42
2–3	7.1	8.1	7.4	9.7	2.45
3–5	5.7	6.7	5.6	12.3	3.81
5–10	3.7	4.5	3.7	14.1	15.50 (5–10 and Over 10)
Over 10	2.1	2.7	2.0	35.8	
Total (chia)	405,181[b]	340,674	431,366	721,252	—

— Not applicable.

Source: Samuel P. S. Ho, *Economic Development in Taiwan: 1860–1970* (New Haven: Yale University Press, 1978).

a. One chia is equal to 0.97 hectare or 2.47 acres.

b. Because of the poor quality of the survey for 1920, this figure is generally considered to be too high.

the index of multiple cropping rose from 115.1 for 1911–15 to 125.3 for 1941–45. The Japanese also set up farmers' associations to give farmers advice on modern agricultural practices and rural credit cooperatives to provide agricultural finance. Health and education received considerable attention as well: the average life span rose significantly during the colonial period; the literacy rate rose from 1 percent in 1905 to 27 percent in 1940.

The distribution of farm families and farmland by size of holding did not change very much in the twenty years before the Second World War (table 1.1). Nor did the distribution of families and land by type of cultivator change very much (table 1.2). It may thus be inferred that the distribution of land in 1945, when Japanese rule came to an end, probably was not very different from that during 1920–39. The poorest 40 percent of households (with less than 0.5 chia) owned less than a tenth of the land; the wealthiest 2 percent (with more than 10 chia) owned more than a third of

Table 1.2. *Distribution of Farm Families and Agricultural Land, by Type of Cultivator, 1920–22, 1927–30, and 1939–40*

Item and type of cultivator	*1920–22*	*1927–30*	*1939–40*
Total farm families	385,277	411,377	429,939
Distribution of families (percent)			
Owner	30.3	29.1	32.0
Part-owner	28.9	30.7	31.2
Tenant	40.8	40.2	36.8
Distribution of land (percent)			
Owner	41.9	43.8	43.7
Tenant	58.2	56.2	56.3
Total agricultural land (hectares)[a]	670,567	762,289	827,886

Source: Ho, *Economic Development in Taiwan.*
a. Total area surveyed.

the land. The pattern of tenancy reveals further inequity: about 40 percent of households were landless tenant households; they worked almost 60 percent of the cultivated land.

Industrial activity during the colonial period also deviated from the typical colonial pattern. First, rather than serving mainly to facilitate primary exports to Japan, industry in Taiwan focused heavily on industries which either used the output of the agricultural sector or provided inputs to that sector. A survey of industrial activity in 1930 indicates that food processing accounted for 64 percent of registered factories, 55 percent of factory employment, and 76 percent of gross value of factory production. Sugar was by far the most important commodity; its share in total factory production during the 1930s was about 50 percent. The chemical and ceramic industries accounted for about 10 percent of total production. Both industries used raw materials readily available in Taiwan and were linked to the agricultural sector, which used by-products of sugar processing. Most of Taiwan's colonial industry thus was a direct extension of agriculture.

In 1940 Taiwan had 8,940 factories which employed 128,000

workers. The vast majority of factories employed fewer than five workers and were establishments processing food, primarily rice. The capitalization of firms reflects the same pattern of small-scale operations: in 1936 the six largest firms accounted for 80 percent of paid-up capital. There was, in addition, a sizable handicraft sector, which accounted for 25 percent of manufacturing employment. To meet the power demands of the infant industrial sector, the Japanese invested heavily in power generation. Between 1926 and 1941 the capacity for power generation increased by 700 percent to levels that were reached again only in 1954 after the reconstruction of wartime damage.

The Japanese controlled most of this infant industrial sector in Taiwan, partly because of initially restrictive regulations regarding capital ownership and partly because of the lack of accumulated wealth by Taiwanese. In 1929 the Japanese owned three-fourths of all paid-up capital in industry. The larger joint-stock companies engaged in manufacturing accounted for 60 percent of total paid-up capital. The Japanese also owned sizable shares of commerce, mining, and unspecified limited partnerships. In contrast, Taiwanese capital was concentrated in traditional industries based on agriculture; these industries accounted for only 3 percent of total paid-up capital. Taiwanese ownership of businesses not based on agriculture was mainly in handicrafts, commerce, and traditional transport. Most of these businesses, such as rice mills and noodle factories, were small-scale operations. In all, the Taiwanese owned less than 10 percent of the joint stock in larger scale operations and 22 percent of the paid-up capital in industry.

The objectives and actions of Japanese colonial rule in Taiwan were similar to those applied in most other colonies. The Japanese implanted a typical triangular mode of operation and segmented the domestic economy into two distinct sectors: a modern sector oriented toward exports, and a large, backward sector oriented toward traditional agriculture. For most colonies such segmentation led to the formation of two mutually exclusive enclaves having little or no interaction. But this pattern did not evolve in Taiwan for three reasons. First, the export commodities were agricultural in origin and were produced by the land-based peasant class. Second, modernization of the agricultural sector occurred without the introduction of the plantation system. Third, industrialization had its roots in agriculture, and the linkages between the industrial and agricultural sectors were extensive and close. This high degree of integration and interaction between the economy's two domestic sectors greatly facilitated postcolonial development in Taiwan.

Primary Import Substitution, 1953–61

The beginning of a country's effort to make the transition from colonialism to modern growth is customarily assigned to the year of its political independence. Taiwan became independent of Japan in 1945 and mainland China in 1949, but 1953 is more appropriately regarded as the initial year of its transition. An economic system independent of the mainland economy did not begin to emerge until late 1949. The Taiwanese economy did not recover from the damage caused by allied bombing during the Second World War, or from the cutoff of such vital agricultural inputs as fertilizer, until about 1951. Nevertheless the influx of talented officials, managers, and entrepreneurs from the mainland minimized problems associated with replacing the Japanese colonial presence. By the time government promulgated the first four-year plan in 1953, Taiwan possessed an unusually good physical and institutional infrastructure, especially in agriculture. It also had a solid base of human resources to go along with the more common features of a surplus of labor on limited arable land.

The first subphase of transition growth, common to virtually all developing countries, is primary, or first-stage, import substitution. It is characterized by the diversion of traditional export proceeds away from further expansion of the colonial enclave and toward investment intended to replace previously imported industrial consumer goods by domestically produced consumer goods. Primary import substitution proceeded at a rapid pace in Taiwan. It was aided by the customary package of diverse policies aimed at encouraging the emergence of a class of industrial entrepreneurs and by a good dosage of natural import substitution made necessary by the severe disruption of Taiwan's traditional trading channels. Whether defined in horizontal or vertical terms, this subphase came to an end in Taiwan by the late 1950s or early 1960s (figure 1.1).

The policies Taiwan chose during the 1950s to effect the desired redirection of resources seem quite standard. Deficit financing by government and substantial rates of inflation accompanied the

Figure 1.1. *Ratios of Imports of Nondurable Consumer Goods to Total Imports and Total Supply, 1953–72*

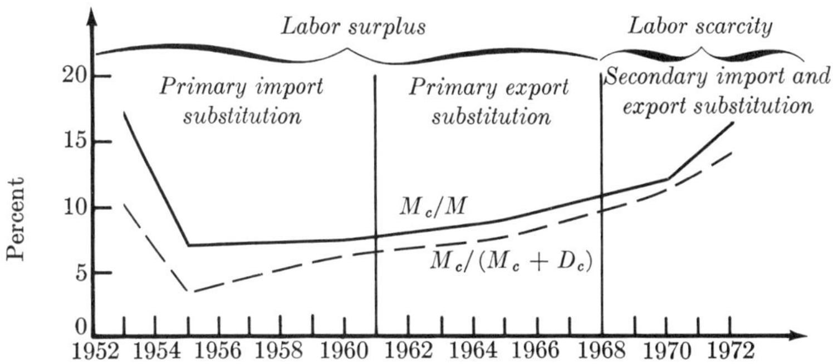

M_c = *imports of nondurable consumer goods*

M = *total imports*

$M_c + D_c$ = *total supply*

Source: Kuo-shu Liang and Ching-ing Hou Liang, "Exports and Employment in Taiwan" (paper read at Conference on Population and Economic Development in Taiwan, December 29, 1975–January 3, 1976, Academia Sinica, Institute of Economics, Taipei; processed).

classic syndrome of overvalued exchange rates and import licensing. Close examination nevertheless reveals substantial differences from the classic syndrome, and these differences suggest that Taiwan's primary import substitution was mild in relation to that in other countries. Although agriculture was squeezed both directly and by way of international trade to help finance industrialization, it was not as relatively disadvantaged as is normal. The agricultural sector received favorable attention during the 1950s, primarily through major land reforms and the allocation of additional investment to rural infrastructure. Agriculture's terms of trade never dropped below 96 (1952 = 100) in the 1950s. This accomplishment is remarkable by any standard. Even interest rates, which normally are very low or negative in real terms during this subphase, were reasonably high after a reform in the mid-1950s. Interest rates, in addition to generating savings, thus performed an allocative function.

Taiwan's overall economic growth was good during the 1950s

Figure 1.2. *Growth Rate of Real Gross National Product per Capita, 1953–72*

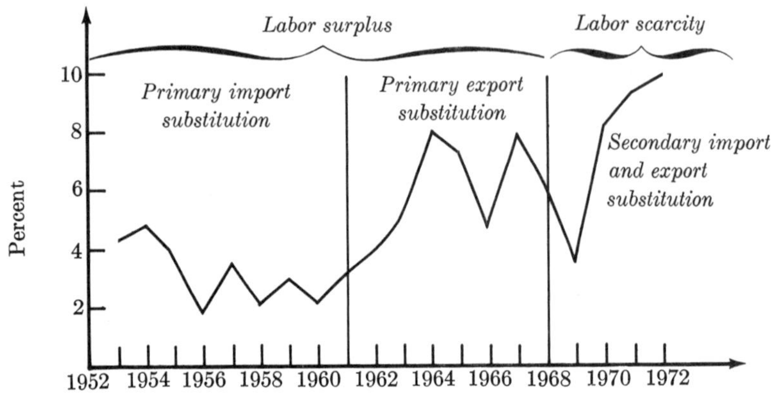

Sources: Directorate-General of Budget, Accounting, and Statistics (DGBAS), *National Income of the Republic of China* (Taipei, 1975); Economic Planning Council, *Taiwan Statistical Data Book* (Taipei, 1975).

(figures 1.2 and 1.3). Despite formidable pressures of population growth, real per capita income rose at an average rate of almost 3 percent a year. As would be expected, the growth of nonagricultural output was rapid—8.7 percent a year. Although a high rate of increase of agricultural output would not be expected, that output in Taiwan grew at the average rate of 5.5 percent a year during this decade. Saving rates, fluctuating in the vicinity of 10 percent, were also respectable. In addition, the pattern of industrial growth, featuring technological choices that were compatible with Taiwan's comparative advantage and output mixes that were abnormally intensive in labor, led to annual rates of nonagricultural labor absorption of more than 3 percent. Foreign capital, mainly U.S. aid, also was important. It initially helped to stabilize the economy and subsequently enabled purchases of overhead capital and industrial producer goods beyond those procurable with Taiwan's earnings from primary exports alone.

Much of Taiwan's initial success can be attributed to the relative mildness and flexibility of its regime of primary import substitution. This subphase inevitably runs out of steam as domestic markets

Figure 1.3. *Ratios of Savings and Investment to Gross National Product, 1953–72*

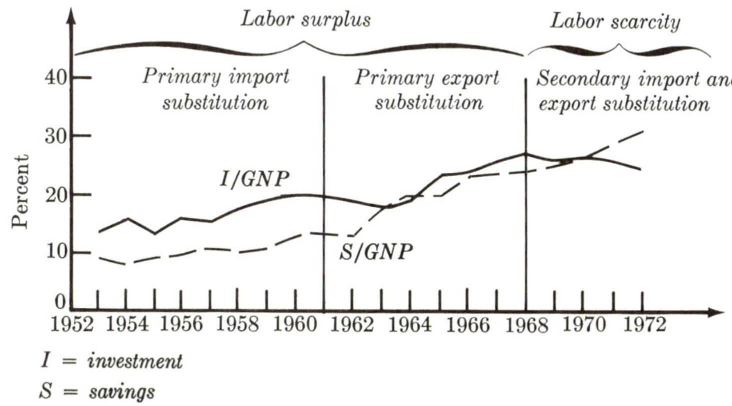

Source: DGBAS, *National Income of the Republic of China* (Taipei, 1975).

for nondurable consumer goods are exhausted. Domestic markets in Taiwan reached that point of exhaustion by the late 1950s. Taiwan did not, however, move into secondary or backward-linkage types of import substitution, as is typical. Instead Taiwan shifted the strategy for industrial development from the domestic market to international markets. The economy's industrial entrepreneurs were of good quality to start with. By cutting their teeth in the domestic market, they matured sufficiently to compete abroad and to find new markets for their labor-intensive industrial consumer goods.

The story of the policy reforms adopted in Taiwan to accommodate export-led industrial expansion during the late 1950s and early 1960s is well documented. Chief among these reforms were the move toward a unified and realistic exchange rate, the relaxation of exchange controls, the reduction in the rate of effective protection, and the continuing modification of interest rates. Government promulgated nineteen major reforms in 1960 alone.[2] Intended to increase production, liberalize trade, and establish a more realistic

2. For a detailed account see Neil H. Jacoby, *U.S. Aid to Taiwan* (New York: Frederick A. Praeger, 1966), pp. 85–103.

set of relative factor prices, these reforms helped to usher in a radically different pattern of resource allocation during the second subphase of economic transition: primary export substitution.

Export Substitution, 1961–72

Several indicators reflect the change in direction of resource flows in Taiwan and the ensuing change in the structure of production. During the subphase of primary import substitution, the system continued to rely mainly on its land-based primary exports, supplemented by foreign aid, to finance industrial growth. But the reversal was dramatic as industrial exports based on unskilled labor increasingly substituted traditional primary exports. By 1972 they accounted for more than 80 percent of total exports, compared with 10 percent in 1952 and 50 percent in 1962 (figure 1.4). Equally

Figure 1.4. *Ratios of Exports of Primary Goods and Industrial Goods to Total Exports, 1953–72*

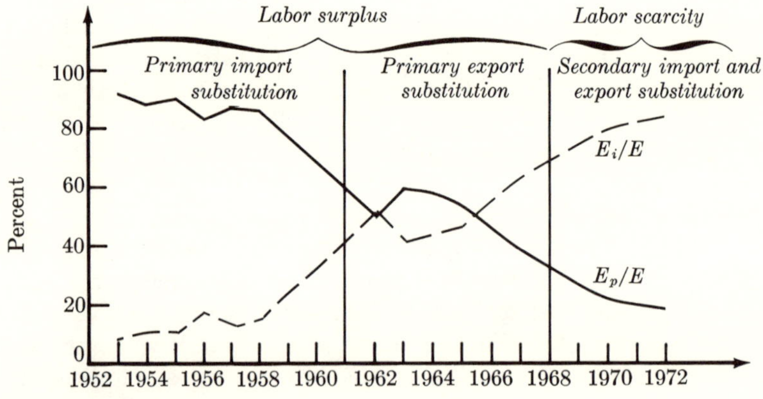

E_i = *exports of industrial goods*

E_p = *exports of primary goods*

E = *total exports*

Source: Economic Planning Council, *Taiwan Statistical Data Book* (Taipei, 1975).

Figure 1.5. *Ratio of Exports to Gross National Product, 1953–72*

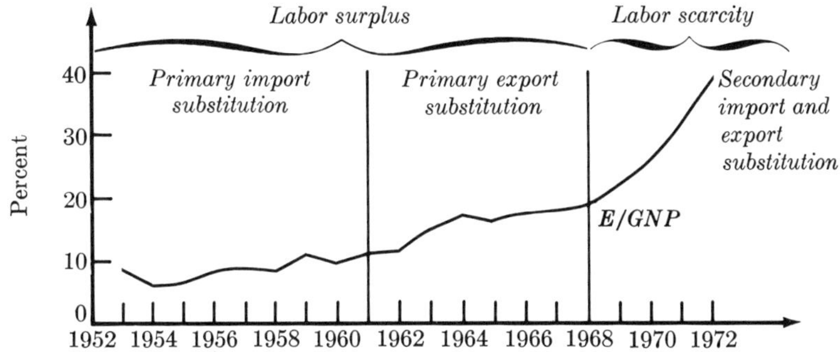

E = *exports*

Sources: Same as for figure 1.2.

dramatic was the increase in the trade orientation of this relatively small, open economy. With exports growing at rates of more than 30 percent by the end of the 1961–72 period, the export ratio advanced to nearly 40 percent (figure 1.5). Nor has it since slowed down: Taiwan's export ratio today is more than 50 percent, one of the highest in the world. Furthermore the industries that grew fastest during the 1960s were such light consumer goods as textiles and such intermediate goods as electronics. Both were internationally competitive because of the use of technologies extremely intensive in unskilled labor. Concurrently the productivity of agricultural labor—supported by earlier investments in rural infrastructure, an increasingly favorable policy environment, and new technologies and crops—increased at 6.6 percent a year during the 1960s, compared with 4.9 percent during the 1950s. These gains kept the prices of foodstuffs low, despite the pattern of rapid industrialization, and prevented a premature sharp rise in real wages.

Because of all these developments, rates of absorption of nonagricultural labor doubled from 3 percent in the 1950s to more than 6 percent in the 1960s. Despite high, if declining, rates of population growth, the reserve of surplus labor in Taiwan was virtually exhausted by the end of the 1960s. As would be expected, the proportion of the labor force in agriculture continuously declined during the 1950s and 1960s. But even the absolute size of the agricultural

Figure 1.6. *Ratios of Agricultural and Nonagricultural Employment to Total Employment, 1953–72*

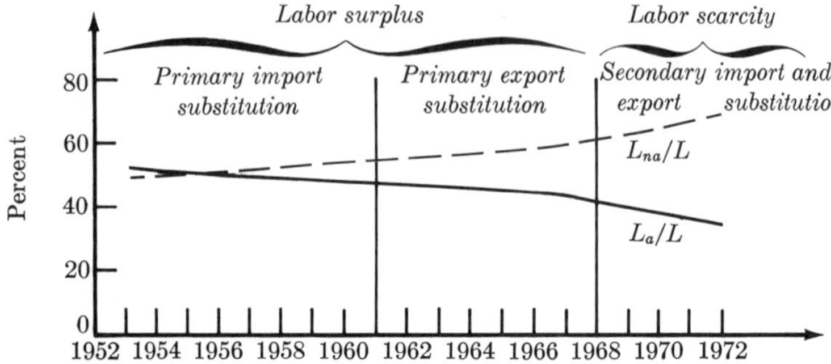

L_{na} = *nonagricultural employment*

L_a = *agricultural employment*

L = *total employment*

Source: Shirley W. Y. Kuo, "A Study of Factors Contributing to Labor Absorption in Taiwan, 1954–71" (paper read at Conference on Population and Economic Development in Taiwan, December 29, 1975–January 3, 1976, Academia Sinica, Institute of Economics, Taipei; processed).

work force began to decline after 1965 (figure 1.6). By about 1968 the rapid pace of labor reallocation had led to the end of labor surplus and the beginning of labor scarcity. The rapid rise in real wages of unskilled workers, most closely proxied by the wage series for female textile workers, indicates this transition (figures 1.7, 1.8, and 1.9).

By returning to the aggregate indicators of performance, it can be seen that per capita growth rates, which were respectable during the subphase of primary import substitution, accelerated to new levels and reached almost 10 percent during the subphase of primary export substitution (see figure 1.2). This performance was achieved despite the virtual termination of concessional foreign assistance and its only partial replacement by private capital from abroad. Booming industrial exports, along with continuing and expanding agricultural surpluses, provided ample fuel for the economy's rapid progress. The domestic saving rate also indicates a regime of substantially more rapid growth during the 1960s (see figure 1.3). The

Figure 1.7. *Index Numbers of Real Wages of Males and Females in Manufacturing, 1953–72*
(1964 = 100)

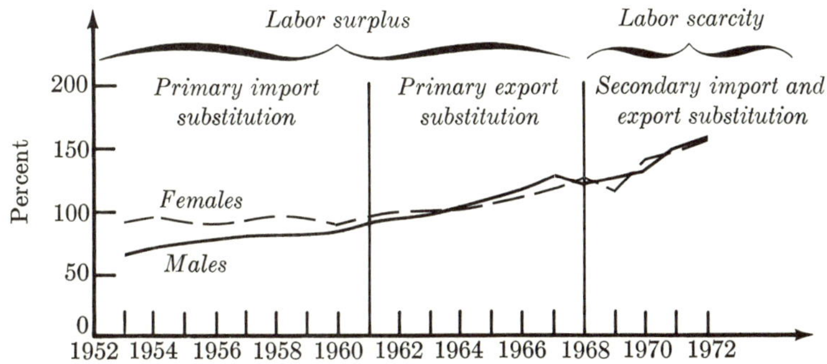

Sources: Taiwan Provincial Government, Department of Reconstruction, *Report of Taiwan Labour Statistics*, 1958, 1963, 1969, and 1973.

Figure 1.8. *Index Numbers of Real Wages of Males and Females in Textiles, 1953–72*
(1964 = 100)

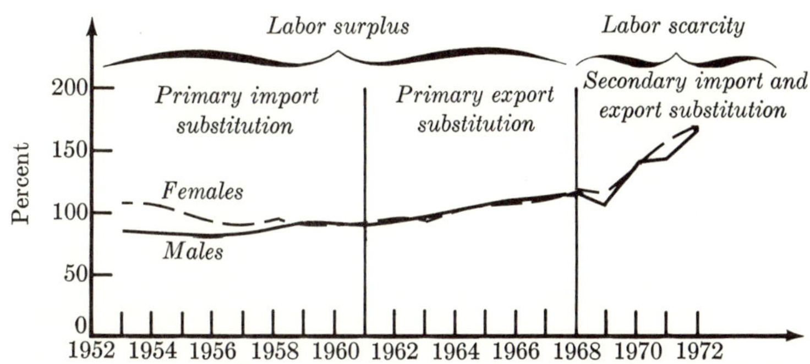

Sources: Same as for figure 1.7.

Figure 1.9. *Index Numbers of Real Wages of Males and Females in Transport and Communications, 1953–72*
(1964 = 100)

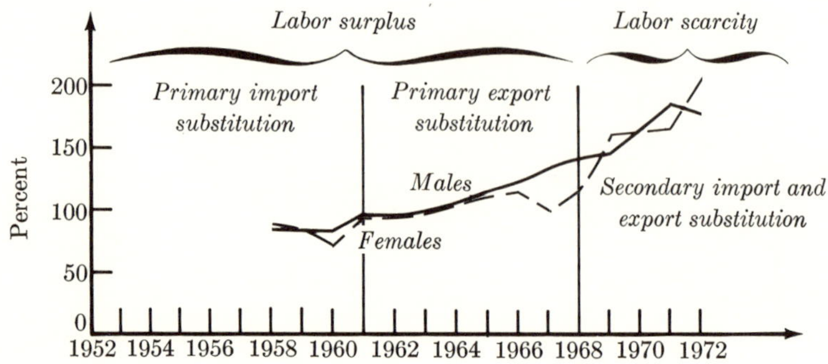

Sources: Same as for figure 1.7.

rate virtually doubled between the 1950s and the 1960s and reached a prodigious 30 percent in 1972 to make Taiwan a net exporter of capital. Such effective functioning of financial, commodity, and labor markets during the 1960s was in part the result of the stabilization achieved with the help of policy reforms adopted early in that decade.[3]

The scarcity of unskilled labor after 1968 indicates that Taiwan's economic development was heading into a new subphase characterized by the need for higher levels of skills and greater capital intensity. But that subphase—which might be called secondary import and export substitution and which Taiwan had fully entered by 1973—is part of another story.[4] This volume is mainly concerned with a developing economy's pattern of income distribution as it

3. Note the contrast between a 9 percent average annual rise in the consumer price index (CPI) during the 1950s and a modest 2 percent average annual rise during the 1960s.

4. Because of the substantial cyclical noise in the data for 1973 and subsequent years, the statistical series and the analysis in this book generally have been terminated in 1972, the last year of the fifth four-year plan. Extreme inflation accompanied the economic boom of 1973; inflation persisted during the international recession of 1974 and most of 1975.

Figure 1.10. *Gini Coefficients, 1953–72*

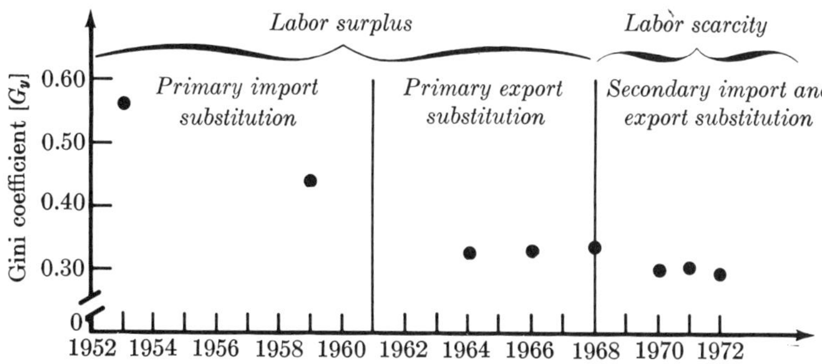

Source: Shirley W. Y. Kuo, "Income Distribution by Size in Taiwan Area—Changes and Causes," in *Income Distribution, Employment, and Economic Development in Southeast and East Asia.* 2 vols. (Tokyo: Japan Economic Research Center, 1975), vol. 1, pp. 80–146.

makes its way to the turning point when accelerated labor-intensive growth has mopped up underemployment.

The pattern of income distribution in Taiwan for the 1953–72 period is summarized by Gini coefficients in figure 1.10.[5] Although the observations for 1953 and 1959 are based on a small sample of low quality, the overall pattern indicates that the reduction of income inequality was substantial. Even if the two observations for the decade of import substitution are disregarded, the low levels of the Gini coefficient after 1964, when the data become much more reliable, and the generally downward trend between 1964 and 1972 are both striking. The distribution of income appears to have improved over the entire 1964–72 period, as it very clearly does after the advent of labor scarcity in about 1968. The pattern after 1968 would be consistent with the views of Lewis and the findings of Kuznets, Adelman, and Morris that equity can be expected to

5. The purpose here is to present a brief overview of trends in the distribution of income in Taiwan. Detailed analysis of this pattern, especially for the 1964–72 period, is a principal subject of this volume and is reserved for subsequent chapters, particularly chapter three.

improve along with growth once real wages rise in a sustained fashion after commercialization. The really interesting question raised by the relations between growth and equity in Taiwan is this: Why was the Gini coefficient virtually constant during the period of extremely rapid growth *before* commercialization began in 1968? The answer clearly could be of great interest to other LDCs because most of them still are a long way from conditions of labor scarcity. Two problems are of greatest policy relevance to them: whether the conflict between growth and equity can be eliminated, or at least mitigated, before basic conditions of labor surplus can be brought to an end; and how this conflict might best be eliminated or mitigated. It would be small comfort for policymakers in these countries to have to conclude that economic growth is compatible with an improved distribution of income only after real wages have begun to rise consistently for neoclassical reasons.

CHAPTER 2

Economic Growth and Income Distribution, 1953–64

DESPITE CONSIDERABLE WARTIME DESTRUCTION, the physical and institutional infrastructure established under colonial rule in Taiwan was instrumental in the rapid growth of agriculture during the 1950s. The irrigation system, which extended over more than half of Taiwan's cultivated area, proved valuable in ensuring the equitable distribution of benefits of green-revolution technology. Linkages between agriculture and the rural-based food-processing industry led to a marked spatial dispersion of economic growth. This pattern later enabled the provision of substantial nonagricultural employment to farmers. Progress in public health and education during the colonial period provided the basis for a highly productive labor force in both agriculture and industry. In addition, the overwhelmingly Japanese ownership of manufacturing enterprises contributed to a more equal distribution of income in two ways: it reduced the concentration of industrial assets in private Taiwanese hands in the period immediately after independence; and it provided a source of industrial assets that could be distributed as compensation to landowners under the program of land reform. The preconditions for rapid economic growth and an improved distribution of income thus were considerably more favorable in Taiwan than in the typical developing country.

This chapter probes the reasons for the apparent absence of a conflict between growth and equity in Taiwan, especially during the 1950s. Even if the level of the Gini coefficient, based on poor data for the 1950s, must be viewed with several grains of salt, it probably is true, contrary to the experience in most LDCS, that the family distribution of income (FID) substantially improved during the subphase of primary import substitution in Taiwan.[1] The following sections examine the distribution of assets and the conditions of production during this period, first in agriculture, then to a limited extent in nonagriculture. The chapter concludes with a discussion of inferences about the course of FID in the 1950s and early 1960s. In subsequent chapters the superior detailed data available after 1964 enable more rigorous analysis of the interplay of economic growth and FID during the subphase of export substitution, both before and after commercialization.

Land Reform

The land reform that government instituted between 1949 and 1953 probably was the most important factor in improving the distribution of income before the beginning of the subphase of export substitution in the early 1960s.[2] Although much of the reform took place before 1952, the year for which sample data on the distribution of income first exist, it continued to have its impact well into the 1950s. The reform thus remained an important factor in explaining improvements in FID during that decade.

Land reform was initiated for several reasons. Although the Japanese had developed a substantial agricultural infrastructure in Taiwan, they paid relatively little attention to the distribution of land (see tables 1.1 and 1.2 in chapter one). Given the large class of tenants, competition for the scarce land was so fierce that the average lease was less than one year. As a result, rents often were equal to 50 percent of the anticipated harvest, especially in the

1. Kowie Chang, "An Estimate of Taiwan Personal Income Distribution in 1953—Pareto's Formula Discussed and Applied," *Journal of Social Science*, vol. 7 (August 1956); National Taiwan University, College of Law, "Report on Pilot Study of Personal Income and Consumption in Taiwan" (prepared under the sponsorship of a working group of National Income Statistics, DGBAS; processed in Chinese).

2. Discussion of land reform draws heavily on Samuel P. S. Ho, *Economic Development in Taiwan: 1860–1970* (New Haven: Yale University Press, 1978) and Chao-Chen Chen, "Land Reform and Agricultural Development in Taiwan" (paper read at Conference on Economic Development of Taiwan, June 19–28, 1967, Taipei; processed).

more fertile regions. Contracts frequently were oral; rent payments had to be made in advance; no adjustments were made for crop failures. These conditions and practices left the typical tenant helpless in any dispute with his landlord. The record of landlord abuse and the need to meet the food demands of postwar Taiwan—which, in addition to its own increased population, included hundreds of thousands of mainland Chinese—laid the groundwork for reform.[3] In addition, the principle of land ownership by the tiller, although never receiving much attention, had always been part of the ideology of the Chinese Nationalists. The loss of the mainland and the social unrest threatening in Taiwan made the redistribution of wealth a particularly important issue for government. Land reform was also considered to be an essential ingredient of agricultural growth and economic recovery. Moreover, it could be imposed by a government free of obligations and ties to the landowning class.

Government's conception of land reform was broad. Strengthening farmers' associations and other elements of organizational and financial infrastructure in rural areas was considered to be important. Moreover the repair of physical infrastructure, started as soon as Taiwan was retroceded to China and almost completed by 1952, increased the effect of land reform on both growth and equity. But the main component of the successful reorganization of the agricultural sector clearly was the three-pronged package of land reform: the program to reduce farm rents, the sale of public lands, and the land-to-the-tiller program.

The first step taken to promote agricultural incentives and output was to reduce farm rents and thereby to increase the share of tenant farmers in crop yields. Promulgated in 1949, this program had five basic provisions: first, farm rents could be fixed at no more than 37.5 percent of the anticipated annual yield of the main crops; second, if crops failed because of natural forces, tenant farmers could apply to local farm-tenancy committees for a further reduction; third, tenant farmers no longer had to pay their rent in advance; fourth, written contracts and fixed leases of three to six years had to be registered; fifth, tenants had the first option to purchase land from its owners. The reform affected about 43 percent of the 660,000 farm families, 75 percent of the 410,000 part

3. In 1945 and 1946, 640,000 mainlanders moved to Taiwan. Kuang Lu, "Population and Employment," in *Economic Development of Taiwan,* ed. Kowie Chang (Taipei: Cheng Chung Books, 1968), p. 532.

owners and tenants, and 40 percent of the 650,000 hectares of private farmland. Prices of farmland immediately dropped: paddy field prices by 20 percent; dry field prices by more than 40 percent by December 1949 and a further 66 percent by 1952.[4] Equally important, the requirement for written contracts and the fixing of standard reduced rents enabled tenants to benefit from their own increased efforts for the first time. This incentive was a primary ingredient of the sustained increase in Taiwan's agricultural productivity during the early 1950s. With higher yields and lower rents, the average income of tenant farmers rose by 81 percent between 1949 and 1952.[5] These rising incomes enabled tenants to purchase land put up for sale by their landlords; about 6 percent of private farmland changed hands.

Given the success of the program to reduce farm rents, government decided to accelerate the program initiated in 1948 to sell public land to tenant farmers. Formerly owned by the Japanese, about 170,000 hectares of public land, or about 25 percent of Taiwan's arable land, were suitable for cultivation. Taiwan Sugar Corporation owned most of this land and leased part of it to tenant farmers. The program gave priority in land purchases to cultivators of public land and landless tenants. The size of parcels was limited according to predetermined fertility grades, and the average size was 1 chia. Selling prices were 2.5 times the value of the annual yield of the main crops; payments in kind were set to coincide with the harvest season over a ten-year period. In all, 35 percent of Taiwan's arable public land was sold during 1948–53; 43 percent during 1953–58.

With government setting the example of returning land to the tiller, the stage was set for the most dramatic component of the three-pronged package: the compulsory sale of land by landlords. This program stipulated that privately owned land in excess of specified amounts per landowner had to be sold to government, which would resell that land to tenants.[6] The purchase price was set at 2.5 times the annual yield of the main crops. Landlords were paid 70 percent of the purchase price in land bonds denominated

4. Chen Cheng, *Land Reform in Taiwan* (Taipei: China Publishing, 1961), p. 310.

5. Cheng, *Land Reform in Taiwan*, p. 309.

6. Individual landowners were allowed to retain three chia of medium-grade land. Anthony Y. C. Koo, *The Role of Land Reform in Economic Development—A Case Study of Taiwan* (New York: Frederick A. Praeger, 1968), p. 38.

in kind and 30 percent in industrial stock of four public enterprises previously owned by the Japanese. The selling prices and conditions of repayment were the same as those provided in the sale of public lands. This third program had a dual objective. The new owner-cultivators were encouraged to work harder because they would benefit from any increases in agricultural output. The landlords, deprived of the privilege of living comfortably off the land, were encouraged to participate in the industrial development of Taiwan through ownership of four large-scale industrial enterprises. Between May and December of 1953, tenant households acquired 244,000 hectares of farmland, or 16.4 percent of the total area cultivated in Taiwan during 1951–55.

Effects of land reform on the distribution of assets

Tables 2.1, 2.2, and 2.3 summarize the extent of land reform and its importance for the redistribution of wealth in Taiwan. Because

Table 2.1. *Area and Households Affected by Land Reform, by Type of Reform*

	Type of reform			
Item	*Reduction of farm rents*	*Sale of public land*	*Land-to-the-tiller program*	*Total redistribution*[a]
Area affected (thousands of chia)	256.9	71.7	193.6	215.2
Farm households affected (thousands)	302.3	139.7	194.9	334.3
Ratio of cultivated area affected to total area[b] (percent)	29.2	8.1	16.4	24.6
Ratio of farm households affected to total farm households (percent)	43.3	20.0	27.9	47.9

Note: Figures may not reconcile because of rounding.
Source: Samuel P. S. Ho, *Economic Development in Taiwan: 1860–1970* (New Haven: Yale University Press, 1978), p. 163.
a. Comprises land distributed under the sale of public land and the land-to-the-tiller program.
b. Total area is the total area cultivated in 1951–55.

Table 2.2. *Distribution of Land and Owner-Cultivator Households, by Size of Holding, 1952 and 1960*

Size of holding (chia)[a]	*Distribution of owner-cultivator households (percent)*		*Distribution of land (percent)*		*Average size of holding (chia)*	
	1952	*1960*[b]	*1952*	*1960*[b]	*1952*	*1960*[b]
0–0.5	47.3	20.7	9.9	5.2	0.23	0.30
0.5–1	23.3	45.9	15.1	30.5	0.72	0.81
1–2	16.9	15.3	21.1	19.3	1.39	4.58
2–3	5.7	14.8	12.3	30.3	2.42	2.50
3–5	3.9	2.7	13.2	10.2	3.79	4.58
Over 5	3.4	0.6	28.4	4.6	10.14	9.10
Total (chia)	611,193	776,002	681,154	948,738	—	—

— Not applicable.
Note: Table 1.1 in chapter one gives comparable figures for the prewar period.
Source: Ho, *Economic Development in Taiwan.*
a. One chia is equal to 0.97 hectare or 2.47 acres.
b. Includes only individual farm households; excludes public and private commercial farms, which all are larger than 10 chia and account for about 6 percent of total land and less than 0.1 percent of the number of holdings.

of the reform, the distribution of land holdings dramatically changed between 1952 and 1960. The rising share of families owning medium-sized plots of land ranging from 0.5 to 3 chia reflects this change: their share increased from 46 percent in 1952 to 76 percent in 1960. The largest rise was in the share of families owning between 0.5 and 1 chia. What is even more dramatic, the average size of holdings in all categories of less than 5 chia increased. The combined share in total land of families owning less than 3 chia increased from 58 percent in 1952 to 85 percent in 1960. The proportion of land cultivated by tenants fell from 44 percent in 1948 to 17 percent in 1959. The proportion of tenant farmers in farm families fell from 38 percent in 1950 to 15 percent in 1960.

Although government compensated landlords for the land they were forced to give up, this compensation was only 2.5 times the standard annual yield; market values of land ranged between 5 and

Table 2.3. *Distribution of Farm Families and Agricultural Land, by Type of Cultivator, 1948–60*

Item and type of cultivator	*1948*	*1950*	*1953*	*1955–56*	*1959–60*
Total farm families	n.a.	638,062	n.a.	732,555	785,592
Distribution of families (percent)					
Owner	n.a.	36.0	n.a.	59.0	64.0
Part-owner	n.a.	26.0	n.a.	24.0	21.0
Tenant	n.a.	38.0	n.a.	17.0	15.0
Distribution of land (percent)					
Owner	55.9	n.a.	82.9	84.9	85.6
Tenant	44.1	n.a.	17.1	15.1	14.4

n.a. Not available.

Note: Table 1.2 in chapter one gives comparable figures for the prewar period.

Sources: Family distribution from Ho, *Economic Development in Taiwan;* land distribution from Chen Cheng, *Land Reform in Taiwan* (Taipei: China Publishing, 1961).

8 times the annual yield. The exercise thus represented a substantial redistribution of wealth. The total value of wealth redistributed as a result of this price difference was equivalent to about 13 percent of Taiwan's gross domestic product (GDP) in 1952.[7] Furthermore bonds used to reimburse landowners paid an interest rate of only 4 percent, substantially less than the prevailing market rates. Because of the landlords' lack of experience in nonagricultural matters, most landlords did not place much value on the 30 percent of their compensation received as industrial stocks. They promptly sold the stocks at prices far below value. Most of their proceeds went to consumption; some went to investments in small businesses. The majority of landlords thus ended up being not much better off than the new owner-cultivators.[8]

7. Ho, *Economic Development in Taiwan,* p. 166.

8. T. Martin Yang, *Socio-Economic Results of Land Reform in Taiwan* (Honolulu: East-West Center, 1970).

Table 2.4. *Distribution of Agricultural Income, by Factor, 1941–56* (percent)

Year	*Property*		
	Land	*Capital*	*Labor*
Before land reform			
1941	52.20	11.48	36.32
1942	51.99	11.44	36.57
1943	45.65	10.04	44.31
After land reform			
1953	37.39	8.23	54.38
1954	38.05	8.37	53.58
1955	38.19	8.40	53.41
1956	36.28	7.98	55.74

Source: S. C. Hsieh and T. H. Lee, "Agricultural Development and Its Contributions to Economic Growth in Taiwan," *Economic Digest Series*, no. 17 (Taipei: JCRR, 1966).

Through the reduction of rents and the redistribution of assets, the land reform had a marked effect on the functional distribution of income. Between 1941 and 1956 the combined share of property in total agricultural income fell from 63.7 percent to 44.3 percent (table 2.4). The sharp reduction in the share of property income was thus accompanied by a broader distribution of that income. Two investigators estimated the shares of farm income by recipient before the land reform, using the 1936–40 average, and after the land reform, using the 1956–60 average.[9] According to these estimates, the share of cultivators in farm income increased from 67 percent to 82 percent; the share of government and public institutions, which received repayments from new landowners, increased from 8 percent to 12 percent; but the share of landlords and moneylenders declined from 25 percent to 6 percent.

9. T. H. Lee and T. H. Shen, "Agriculture as a Base for Socio-Economic Development," in *Agriculture's Place in the Strategy of Development*, ed. T. H. Shen (Taipei: JCRR, 1974), p. 300.

Reorganization of institutional infrastructure

The institutional infrastructure of Taiwan's agriculture was extensively reorganized and improved during the 1950s. The farmers' associations and credit cooperatives, set up by the Japanese to facilitate agricultural extension programs and rice procurement, were top-down institutions dominated by landlords and nonfarmers. As a result, most farmers did not directly benefit from them. In 1952 government consolidated those institutions in multipurpose farmers' associations restricted to farmers and serving their interests. In addition to the original function of agricultural extension, the activities of farmers' associations expanded to include a credit department, which accepted deposits from farmers and made loans to them, and to provide facilities for purchasing, marketing, warehousing, and processing.[10] The associations thus became clearinghouses for farmers, who controlled and maintained them and viewed them as their own creatures.

The other major institutional reform affecting agriculture during the 1950s was the establishment of the Joint Commission on Rural Reconstruction (JCRR) by the U.S. Congress in 1948. Its main functions were to allocate U.S. aid, provide technical assistance, and help the Taiwanese government plan and coordinate programs for agricultural extension, research, and experimentation. Thus, while the farmers' associations provided the much-needed organizational structure at local levels and facilitated the efficient flow of agricultural surpluses to the industrial sector, the JCRR was a major catalyst. It funded and initiated many innovations in farming techniques, and it introduced new crops and new markets. For

10. Deposits of the credit divisions of farmers' associations increased from about NT$100 million to NT$2,700 million by the end of 1965. Loans increased commensurately. (At the time of writing, the new Taiwan dollar was equal to about US$0.025.) Wen-Fu Hsu, "The Role of Agricultural Organizations in Agricultural Development" (paper read at Conference on Economic Development of Taiwan, June 19–28, 1967, Taipei; processed). Also during this period, credit became available to farmers from the JCRR, government-owned banks, and government agencies and monopolies. Between 1949 and 1960 the proportion of farm loans provided through the organized money market rose from 17 percent to 57 percent. Ho, *Economic Development in Taiwan,* pp. 179–80.

example, the JCRR was behind the introduction of asparagus and mushroom cultivation, which led to the highly successful production and export performance of those commodities in the 1960s.

Agricultural Development during the 1950s

Land reform alone could not solve the primary constraint facing Taiwan's agriculture: the shortage of land for a rapidly growing agricultural population. Although an ever-increasing number of farmers left agriculture to live and work in Taiwan's expanding urban areas, the population pressure on farmland was severe, especially during the early 1950s. The agricultural population rose from 4.3 million in 1952 to 5.8 million in 1964, an increase of 33 percent. During the same period the total area of cultivated land remained nearly fixed, culminating in a decline of the average size of holding from 1.29 hectares per family to 1.06 hectares (table 2.5). Taiwan

Table 2.5. *Parameters and Indexes of Agricultural Employment, Production, and Development, 1952–64*

Item	*1952*	*1956*	*1960*	*1964*
Agricultural population (thousands)	4,257	4,699	5,373	5,649
Agricultural employment (thousands)	1,792	1,806	1,877	2,010
Cultivated land (thousands of hectares)	876	876	869	882
Cropped land (thousands of hectares)	1,506	1,537	1,595	1,658
Percentage of agricultural population in total population	52.4	50.0	49.8	46.1
Hectares of cultivated land				
Per farm family	1.29	1.17	1.11	1.06
Per capita on farm	0.21	0.19	0.16	0.16
Per agricultural employee	0.49	0.48	0.46	0.44

Table 2.5 (*Continued*)

Item	*1952*	*1956*	*1960*	*1964*
Indexes				
Agricultural population	100.0	110.4	126.2	132.7
Agricultural employment	100.0	100.1	104.7	112.2
Total agricultural production	100.0	121.0	142.8	178.7
Agricultural crop production[a]	100.0	116.8	132.1	159.7
Output of crops and livestock	100.0	121.4	139.1	168.5
Agricultural crop production per worker	100.0	115.4	126.1	142.4
Man-days of labor	100.0	104.1	111.5	116.9
Agricultural crop production to man-days of labor	100.0	112.2	118.8	136.6
Man-days of labor to employment	100.0	104.0	106.5	104.2
Fixed capital	100.0	107.5	116.6	133.6
Working capital	100.0	151.5	169.7	240.2
Multiple cropping	171.9	175.5	183.6	188.0
Diversification[b]	3.54	4.07	4.01	5.75

Sources: Parameters of land and population and indexes of production from Economic Planning Council, *Taiwan Statistical Data Book, 1975*, pp. 47–51; indexes of labor man-days, output of crops and livestock, working capital, and fixed capital from Ho, *Economic Development in Taiwan*, p. 245; index of diversification from Shirley W. Y. Kuo, "Effects of Land Reform, Agricultural Pricing Policy, and Economic Growth on Multiple Crop Diversification in Taiwan," in *Economic Essays*, vol. 4 (Taipei: National Taiwan University, Graduate Institute of Economics, November 1973); other indexes from calculations by the authors.

a. Excludes forestry, fishing, and livestock.

b. The diversification index is calculated for 181 different crops by the formula: $1/\Sigma$ (value of each product/value of total products)^2.

overcame these pressures in three ways: by the achievement of substantial increases in agricultural productivity at the intensive margin; by the diversification of agricultural production into more profitable crops; and by the part-time reallocation of labor to nonagricultural activities, including off-farm employment for many members of agricultural families.

The growth of the agricultural sector during the 1950s was impressive. The real net domestic product (NDP) by agricultural origin increased by about 80 percent during the 1952–64 period, or at an average rate of 5 percent a year, even though agriculture's share in NDP declined, from 36 percent to 28 percent. Because the agricultural population increased by only a third, an agricultural surplus was assured. Although this 5 percent annual increase in net output during the subphase of import substitution is considerably smaller than that of the industrial sector, it still is an impressive figure by any international standard of comparison. It is even more impressive when two additional factors are considered: the natural fertility of the soil is low; the land frontier on the mountainous island already had essentially been reached. The growth in agricultural output could only be called dramatic. Between 1952 and 1964 total agricultural production, including forestry, fishing, and livestock, rose by 78 percent, with the production of crops alone rising by 59.7 percent (see table 2.5). These production increases were primarily the result of increased yields in traditional crops, but they were also the result of the introduction of new crops. While the yields of such traditional crops as rice increased 50 percent, the yields of relatively new specialty crops, such as cotton and fruits, increased more than 100 percent.[11]

Fixed capital in agriculture expanded by about 34 percent between 1952 and 1964 (see table 2.5). Much of this expansion was in irrigation and flood control facilities, which deteriorated during the war and were rebuilt and expanded during the 1950s. Farm buildings and other structures were added to and improved. The water buffalo was gradually replaced by small tillers and other small mechanical devices. Working capital increased even more dramatically than fixed capital, growing by 140 percent between 1952 and 1964 (see table 2.5). The continuous introduction of new seed varieties, responsive to intensive fertilizer applications, and the gradual reduction in fertilizer prices and government restrictions enabled Taiwan's total fertilizer use to grow by 91 percent over the same period.[12] As livestock production grew by nearly 120 percent, more and more commercial feeds were imported. Further increases in working capital included widespread use of pesticides, a major postwar innovation which helped to reduce high losses caused by disease and insects.

11. Economic Planning Council, *Taiwan Statistical Data Book, 1975* (Taipei, 1975), pp. 48, 53–55.

12. *Taiwan Statistical Data Book, 1975*, p. 58.

Technology change, introduced mainly by such government-supported research agencies as the JCRR, clearly was a significant factor in generating the increased agricultural output.[13] In 1960 Taiwan had 79 agricultural research workers for every 100,000 persons active in agriculture, compared with 60 in Japan, 4.7 in Thailand, 1.6 in the Philippines, and 1.2 in India.[14] The research agencies successfully introduced new strains of rice and sugar and such new crops as asparagus and mushrooms, as well as pesticides, insecticides, and new agricultural tools and machinery. In the Hayami-Ruttan terminology, most of the technology change was of the chemical variety, not the mechanical.[15]

Taiwan's impressive success in agriculture can thus be attributed to many factors. Although the purpose of this volume is not to analyze these factors in detail, their relation to the distribution of income nevertheless is relevant to the argument here. Given the physical and organizational improvement of the environmental infrastructure and the pervasive package of land reform, farmers had the incentives and the tools to improve their situation during the subphase of primary import substitution, which usually discriminates against agriculture. Moreover the technology change seemed to be of a type that generally used labor and saved land and capital. Although the number of persons employed in agriculture increased by 12 percent between 1952 and 1964, the number of man-days increased by 17 percent (see table 2.5). Consequently the number of working days per worker steadily increased. In 1965 the average worker had 156 days of farm employment, compared with 90 days in 1946 and 134 days in 1952.[16] As a result, the number of working days per hectare of land increased from approximately 170 in 1948–50 to about 260 in 1963–65.[17]

13. Ho estimated that 44.9 percent of the growth of agricultural output during 1951–60 can be attributed to changes in total factor productivity, 10.3 percent to increases in crop area, and 34.7 percent to increases in working capital. Ho, *Economic Development in Taiwan*, pp. 147–85.

14. Ho, *Economic Development in Taiwan*, p. 178.

15. Yujiro Hayami and Vernon W. Ruttan, *Agricultural Development in International Perspective* (Baltimore: Johns Hopkins University Press, 1971), passim.

16. You-tsao Wang, "Agricultural Development," in *Economic Development of Taiwan*, ed. Kowie Chang, p. 176.

17. W. H. Lai, "Trend of Agricultural Employment in Post-war Taiwan" (paper read at Conference on Manpower in Taiwan, 1972, Taipei; processed).

Larger labor inputs to the cultivation of traditional crops and the diversification into new crops resulted in more intensive cultivation of land. Between 1952 and 1964 the multiple-cropping index increased from 171.9 to 188; the diversification index increased from 3.54 to 5.75 (see table 2.5). The shift toward such labor-intensive crops as vegetables and away from the complete dominance of the traditional crops of rice and sugar was continuous. As an indication of the labor intensity of vegetable cultivation, the cultivation of one hectare of asparagus requires 2,900 times the labor input of the cultivation of one hectare of rice.

Despite the substantial increase in the absorption of labor in agriculture between 1952 and 1964, rural underemployment continued during the 1950s and has been estimated at about 40 percent.[18] The smaller, poorer farms were especially unable to generate sufficient income or to keep the entire family fully employed. This pattern led to a small amount of net physical migration out of the agricultural sector, estimated at less than one percent annually during the 1950s. Mostly, however, farmers increasingly sought off-farm employment in the rapidly growing rural industrial sector. Consequently underemployment did not develop into as serious a problem as in most other LDCS.[19] The pattern of agricultural growth and the participation in that growth by rich and poor farmers were the basic ingredients of the dramatic improvement in the distribution of income in Taiwan during the 1950s.

The Distribution of Assets and Industrial Growth

What can be said about the distribution of assets outside agriculture during this period? Obviously much less, but broad patterns nevertheless are indicative. The 56.6 percent share of the public sector in industrial output in 1952 characterized the Taiwanese economy in the early 1950s (table 2.6). This pattern was mainly

18. The estimation difficulties here are well known, and the authors do not place much confidence in these numbers.

19. Ho, *Economic Development in Taiwan*, p. 158. Ho derived his figures from S. F. Liu, "Disguised Unemployment in Taiwan Agriculture" (Ph.D. dissertation, University of Illinois, 1966) and Paul K. C. Liu, "Economic Development and Population in Taiwan since 1895: An Overview," in *Essays on the Population of Taiwan* (Taipei: Academia Sinica, Institute of Economics, 1973).

Table 2.6. *Distribution of Industrial Production, by Public and Private Ownership, 1952–64*
(percent)

	Total		*Manufacturing*		*Mining*		*Electricity, gas, and water*
Year	*Public*	*Private*	*Public*	*Private*	*Public*	*Private*	*Public*
1952	56.6	43.4	56.2	43.8	28.3	71.7	100.0
1953	55.9	44.1	55.9	44.1	24.4	75.6	100.0
1954	52.7	47.3	49.7	50.3	32.5	67.5	100.0
1955	51.1	48.9	48.7	51.3	28.5	71.5	100.0
1956	51.0	49.0	48.3	51.7	26.5	73.5	100.0
1957	51.3	48.7	48.7	51.3	26.3	73.7	100.0
1958	50.0	50.0	47.2	52.8	24.2	75.8	100.0
1959	48.7	51.3	45.2	54.8	22.6	77.4	100.0
1960	47.9	52.1	43.8	56.2	24.2	75.8	100.0
1961	48.2	51.8	45.3	54.7	18.8	81.2	99.9
1962	46.2	53.8	42.3	57.7	19.6	80.4	98.6
1963	44.8	55.2	40.6	59.4	19.1	80.4	99.7
1964	43.7	56.3	38.9	61.1	20.5	79.5	98.8

Source: Economic Planning Council, *Taiwan Statistical Data Book, 1975*, p. 75.

a consequence of the Chinese takeover of Japanese assets at the end of the Second World War. In addition, before the evacuation from the mainland, the Nationalist government dismantled and shipped industrial equipment, such as textile spindles, and in some cases entire enterprises to Taiwan. Firms under public ownership were initially plagued with typical problems: inefficiency, overstaffing, rigid pay structures, and bureaucratic interference. Meanwhile small firms and simple equipment characterized the private sector. As late as 1961, 31 percent of all manufacturing establishments employed fewer than ten workers.[20] All industry was hampered by the shortage of foreign exchange.[21]

This situation undoubtedly was favorable to the equity of the

20. Ho, *Economic Development in Taiwan*, p. 597.
21. Council on U.S. Aid, *Industry of Free China*, vol. 1, no. 4 (1954).

initial distribution of industrial assets. Because private ownership of capital was not on a large scale, entrepreneurs generally were not in a position to gain monopolistic control of industries or to accumulate great wealth from property income. In the private sector the small size and labor intensity of firms was favorable to the share of workers. Profits of the larger, more capital-intensive firms went to government, not to private entrepreneurs.

During the early 1950s government began transfering the four public enterprises under its control to private ownership: Taiwan Cement Corporation, Taiwan Pulp and Paper Corporation, Taiwan Industrial and Mining Corporation, and Taiwan Agriculture and Forestry Development Corporation. This transfer was not easily accomplished. Government had difficulty finding buyers because of the lack of accumulated private wealth and entrepreneurial expertise and because of the poor track records of these enterprises. In 1953 a large portion of government assets was nevertheless transferred as partial payment to landlords under the land-to-the-tiller program. As a result of this transfer and such other factors as the increasingly rapid growth of private industry, the government-owned share of total industrial production fell to 43.7 percent in 1964 (see table 2.6). Industries remaining in the public sector included utilities, railroads, shipbuilding, and iron and steel. Thus, despite the substantial drop in government ownership, the public control of assets continued to be important, particularly in the most capital-intensive industries, in which growth is least favorable to the distribution of income.

Taiwan's industrial growth during 1952–64 was impressive: NDP grew at the average annual rate of 7 percent; the industrial sector at the average annual rate of 11 percent. By 1964 the real NDP of the industrial sector was more than 250 percent higher than in 1952; that sector's share in total NDP rose from 18 percent to 28 percent. Most of this growth was the result of the emergence of the manufacturing subsector: its share in NDP grew from only 11 percent in 1952 to more than 20 percent in 1964.[22] The concentration on food processing and textiles, as well as on other industries that typically predominate during the subphase of primary import substitution, continued to be heavy.

22. *Taiwan Statistical Data Book, 1975*, p. 28.

The reorientation of industrial output between the late 1950s and early 1960s is also reflected in the changing composition of imports and exports. Although total imports in constant prices more than doubled during the 1952–64 period, the share of imports of consumption goods in total imports rapidly declined from 20 percent to 6 percent. In constant prices those imports in 1964 were slightly below their 1952 level. Imports of raw materials for agriculture and industry kept pace with the growth of total imports. But imports of capital goods, such as machinery and electrical and transport equipment, almost quadrupled. This growth reflected the twin efforts to shift industrial activity away from the narrow domestic market toward wider international markets and to provide the physical infrastructure needed for that shift. Even though government policy was to reduce imports in the 1950s, total imports doubled during 1952–64. This expansion reflected the need to fuel import substitution during the 1950s, as is evidenced by the growth of imports of capital goods by about 20 percent a year before 1960.[23] Imports of raw materials, which were growing steadily at 8 percent a year during the 1950s, started to grow at 11 percent a year in response to the new opportunities of the export-substitution era. This policy of accelerated imports of raw materials, combined with the use of unskilled labor, was at the heart of the drive that followed for expanding labor-intensive industrial exports.

As would be expected in any developing economy, imports continued to outstrip exports throughout the 1952–64 period in Taiwan. Exports in constant prices nevertheless quadrupled. Moreover, as noted earlier, industrial exports increased by a phenomenal 2,800 percent and dramatically changed the composition of exports. The share in total exports of agricultural and related exports declined from 92 percent to less than 60 percent in only twelve years; the share of industrial exports went up fivefold, from 8 percent to 40 percent. Industrial production and export growth during this period was concentrated in the textile, leather, and wood and paper industries. Most of the increase occurred between 1960 and 1964: that is, after changes in policies and factor endowment ushered in the subphase of export substitution.

23. See Carlos F. Diaz-Alejandro, "On the Import Intensity of Import Substitution," *Kyklos*, vol. 18, no. 3 (1965).

Effects of Growth on Equity

Information about the family distribution of income (FID) in Taiwan is meager before 1964, when the Directorate-General of Budget, Accounting, and Statistics (DGBAS) began to conduct regular surveys. One investigator conducted sample surveys of overall income distribution for 1953 and 1959.[24] The JCRR conducted sample surveys of the income of farm families in 1952, 1957, 1962, and 1967.[25] The Economic Planning Council conducted surveys of a very limited sample of urban wage and salary workers in 1955 and 1959.[26]

Rural FID

Farm families have three types of income: the income from agricultural activities [Y_a], a merged return to property (mainly land) and labor, is preponderant; it is augmented by wage income [Y_w] and property income [Y_π] from rural industry and services. Table 2.7 gives the Gini coefficients of total income and factor income and the distributive shares of factor income components for 1952, 1957, 1962, and 1967.[27] In the following analysis, average farm-size groupings are used as a proxy for average income-size groupings, which are not available. Because the data are grouped into only a few intervals based on farm size, the resulting Gini coefficients undoubtedly are lower than if there had been more intervals. Never-

24. Chang, "Estimate of Personal Income Distribution in 1953;" National Taiwan University, "Report on Pilot Study."

25. JCRR, "Taiwan Farm Income Survey of 1967—with a Brief Comparison with 1952, 1957, and 1962," *Economic Digest Series*, no. 20 (Taipei: JCRR, 1970).

26. Economic Planning Council, "Family Income and Expenditure Survey of Wages and Salaries by Income Class, Taiwan Province" (Taipei, n.d.; processed in Chinese); idem, "Family Income and Expenditure Survey of City Consumers, Taiwan Province" (Taipei, n.d.; processed in Chinese).

27. The following notation will be adhered to throughout this volume in tables and text: the Gini coefficient of income from all sources is G_y; the Gini coefficients for (merged) agricultural income, rural industry wage income, and rural industry property income respectively are G_a, G_w, and G_π; the distributive shares, or weights, of these kinds of income accruing to farm families respectively are ϕ_a, ϕ_w, and ϕ_π.

Table 2.7. *Gini Decomposition Analysis Based on Farm Family Income Stratified by Size of Farm, 1952–67*

Item	1952	1957	1962	1967	Percentage change[a] 1952–57	1957–62	1962–67
Gini coefficients							
Wage income [G_w]	n.a.	0.0631	0.0862	0.0823	n.a.	37	−6
Property income [G_π]	n.a.	0.1662	0.0604	0.1116	n.a.	−64	31
Agricultural income [G_a]	n.a.	0.3499	0.3641	0.3225	n.a.	4	−12
Total income [G_y]	0.2860	0.2335	0.2126	0.1790	−18	−9	−14
Distributive shares							
Wage income [ϕ_w]	0.0580	0.2339	0.1969	0.2522	303	−16	24
Property income [ϕ_π]	0.1630	0.1342	0.2124	0.1639	−18	58	−36
Agricultural income [ϕ_a]	0.7790	0.6320	0.5908	0.5840	−19	−7	−1

n.a. Not available.

Sources: 1952 from Y. C. Tsui and S. C. Hsieh, "Farm Income in Taiwan in 1952," *Economic Digest Series,* no. 4 (Taipei: JCRR, 1954); 1957, 1962, and 1967 from JCRR, "Taiwan Farm Income Survey of 1967—with a Brief Comparison with 1952, 1957, and 1962," *Economic Digest Series,* no. 20 (Taipei: JCRR, 1970).

a. For 1952–67 the change in G_y was −37 percent, of which 1952–57 accounted for −18 percent, 1957–62 for −7 percent, and 1962–67 for −12 percent; the changes in distributive shares were 335 percent for wage income, 0.6 percent for property income, and −25 percent for agricultural income.

theless it still is possible to observe significant trends in movements of the Gini coefficient of total income after 1952 and the Gini coefficients of factor income after 1957.[28]

Throughout the 1952–67 period the Gini coefficient of total income [G_y] declined by a remarkable 37 percent; it declined by 18

28. To the extent that the ranking of family income differs from, and is poorly proxied by, the ranking of family farm size, the Gini coefficient in table 2.7 tends to underestimate the true inequality of income. The authors have no way of checking the degree of this underestimation. The other issue addressed basically is the error introduced when families are grouped by income ranges, a problem fully discussed in chapter twelve.

percent during 1952–57 alone, the heart of the subphase of import substitution. As import substitution ran out of steam because of the limitations of domestic markets, the pace of decline slowed down; the decline for 1957–62 was only 7 percent. Interestingly enough, the decline of the Gini coefficient picked up speed again after the policy reforms of 1960–61 got the new era of export substitution under way. The decline for 1962–67 was 12 percent. This figure is similar to the decline of 11 percent for 1964–68 obtained from superior DGBAS data. Hence, the trend of these results, if not the magnitude, would seem to be fairly reliable.

The data for factor income components indicate that the distribution of agricultural income and wage income worsened between 1957 and 1962; that of property income improved. After export substitution got under way, however, the distribution of property income worsened; that of agricultural and wage income improved. What are the reasons for these patterns of the Gini coefficients of factor income over time?

One reason is the increase in multiple cropping. The multiple-cropping index of farms smaller than 0.5 chia was about 25 percent higher than that for farms larger than 2 chia (table 2.8). This inverse relation between farm size and multiple cropping indicates that the poorer families cultivated their land more intensively,

Table 2.8. *Multiple Cropping, by Size of Farm, 1952 and 1967*
(single cropping = 100)

Size of farm (*chia*)	*Index of multiple cropping*	
	1952	*1967*
Less than 0.5	227	216
0.5–1	214	206
1–1.5	204[a]	197
1.5–2	204[a]	193
2–3	184[b]	190
More than 3	184[b]	161
Average	198	197

Sources: Same as for table 2.7.
a. The 1952 average for farms of 1–2 chia applies to both categories.
b. The 1952 average for farms larger than 2 chia applies to both categories.

either by introducing additional harvests in rice or adding high-valued, and usually more labor-intensive, secondary crops. The marked decline of the agricultural Gini [G_a] between 1962 and 1967 coincides with the introduction of mushrooms, asparagus, and other important secondary crops. This pattern implies that poorer farmers could take more advantage of this type of product-oriented technology change in agriculture.

A second reason is that the high distributive share of agricultural income significantly declined, from 78 percent in 1952 to 58 percent in 1967; the share of nonagricultural income increased from 22 percent to 42 percent (see table 2.7). The increase in the share of wage income from 6 percent to about 25 percent is particularly noteworthy. These figures testify to a rapid reallocation of labor from agricultural to nonagricultural sources of income for the average farm family. The speed of this reallocation may be explained in a variety of ways. First, the phenomenon is closely associated with the pattern of industrial dispersion, which is an important feature of industrialization in Taiwan. The rapid increase in the share of wage income may thus be traced to the rapid growth of rural industries, which provided employment to members of rural families. Second, associated with transition growth are certain institutional changes germane to commercialization and the functional specialization of tasks traditionally performed by members of farm households under family farming. For example, the replacement of the son as farm-to-market transporter by a transport firm, which hires the same son as a wage earner, reduces agricultural income and increases wage income. Much functional specialization of this type must have taken place during the transition, especially because of the spatial dispersion of nonagricultural production activities. But to adduce more about this important problem would require a different set of data and a more refined analytical design.

A third reason for the movements in the Gini coefficients of factor income is the greater importance of off-farm wage income to poorer families than to wealthier families, at least when farm size is used as a proxy for income class (tables 2.9, 2.10, and 2.11). As the size of the farm increases, the share of nonagricultural income decreases. This pattern reflects the greater ability of poorer farmers to take advantage of nonagricultural income opportunities. For example, farm families holding less than 0.5 chia in 1957 earned a remarkable 61.9 percent of their income from nonagricultural activities; wage income accounted for 41.4 percent of their total income. In contrast,

Table 2.9. *Average Income of Farm Families, by Size of Farm, 1952–67*
(1952 N.T. dollars)

	Average income				
Year and type of income	*0–0.5 chia*	*0.5–1 chia*	*1–2 chia*	*2–4 chia*	*Average size farm*
1952					
Total income	3,765	5,097	8,010	14,653	7,361
Wage income	n.a.	n.a.	n.a.	n.a.	427
Property income	n.a.	n.a.	n.a.	n.a.	1,200
Agricultural income	n.a.	n.a.	n.a.	n.a.	5,734
1957					
Total income	5,015	6,873	9,481	16,606	8,613
Wage income	2,278	1,940	1,695	2,146	2,011
Property income	825	1,140	1,021	2,030	1,160
Agricultural income	1,912	3,793	6,765	12,430	5,443
1962					
Total income	5,655	7,937	11,144	17,629	9,682
Wage income	2,355	1,890	1,565	1,775	1,906
Property income	1,835	1,883	2,229	2,462	2,056
Agricultural income	1,465	4,163	7,351	13,392	5,720
1967					
Total income	9,920	10,754	15,302	24,962	13,727
Wage income	4,247	3,369	2,928	3,061	3,475
Property income	2,262	1,643	2,426	3,218	2,262
Agricultural income	3,411	5,742	9,946	18,684	7,990

n.a. Not available.

Note: At the time of writing, the new Taiwan dollar was equal to about US$0.025.

Sources: Same as for table 2.7.

the shares of nonagricultural income in total income were 44.8 percent for families holding 0.5 to 1 chia, 28.7 percent for families holding 1 to 2 chia, and 25.2 percent for families holding more than 2 chia. For these families the shares of wages in total income respectively were 28.2 percent, 17.9 percent, and 12.9 percent. Thus off-farm income, particularly wage income, clearly was an important

Table 2.10. *Distribution of Factor Shares, by Size of Farm, 1952–67*

Year and type of income	Factor share				
	0–0.5 chia	0.5–1 chia	1–2 chia	2–4 chia	Average size farm
1952					
Wage income	n.a.	n.a.	n.a.	n.a.	0.0580
Property income	n.a.	n.a.	n.a.	n.a.	0.1630
Net agricultural income	n.a.	n.a.	n.a.	n.a.	0.7789
1957					
Wage income	0.4142	0.2823	0.1788	0.1292	0.2338
Property income	0.2045	0.1658	0.1077	0.1223	0.1342
Net agricultural income	0.3813	0.5519	0.7135	0.7485	0.6320
1962					
Wage income	0.4164	0.2381	0.1404	0.1007	0.1969
Property income	0.3245	0.2373	0.2000	0.1397	0.2123
Net agricultural income	0.2591	0.5246	0.6596	0.7597	0.5908
1967					
Wage income	0.4281	0.3133	0.1913	0.1226	0.2522
Property income	0.2280	0.1528	0.1586	0.1289	0.1638
Net agricultural income	0.3438	0.5339	0.6501	0.7485	0.5840

Note: For each size category in each year, the sum of the shares of wage, property, and net agricultural income is 1.0000.
Sources: Same as for table 2.7.

FID equalizer because it constituted a greater share of total income for the poorer farm families.

Data on the extent of off-farm activity by farm families in 1960 give further support to this notion (table 2.12). Less than 50 percent of farm households engaged in full-time farming in 1960. What is more relevant, the percentage engaged in full-time farming generally increased with farm size. Among farm families with less than 0.5 hectares, only 30 percent engaged in full-time farming, and 35

Table 2.11. *Distribution of Farm Households, Income, and Factor Shares, by Size of Farm, 1952–67*

Item	*0–0.5 chia*	*0.5–1 chia*	*1–2 chia*	*2–4 chia*
1952				
Total income	0.1535	0.1869	0.2367	0.4229
Households	0.3000	0.2700	0.2176	0.2124
1957				
Total income	0.1752	0.2134	0.2936	0.3177
Wage income	0.3410	0.2581	0.2249	0.1759
Property income	0.2140	0.2629	0.2348	0.2884
Agricultural income	0.1057	0.1864	0.3316	0.3763
Households	0.3010	0.2675	0.2668	0.1648
1962				
Total income	0.1596	0.2358	0.3352	0.2693
Wage income	0.3377	0.2853	0.2392	0.1378
Property income	0.2438	0.2634	0.3158	0.1770
Agricultural income	0.0700	0.2094	0.3743	0.3463
Households	0.2732	0.2876	0.2912	0.1479
1967				
Total income	0.2193	0.2269	0.2943	0.2595
Wage income	0.3710	0.2808	0.2224	0.1257
Property income	0.3036	0.2104	0.2830	0.2030
Agricultural income	0.1296	0.2081	0.3286	0.3337
Households	0.3037	0.2896	0.2640	0.1427

Note: For each row the sum of the entries is 1.0000.
Sources: Same as for table 2.7.

percent had some kind of side income. In contrast, among farm families with more than 5 hectares, 61 percent were full-time farmers, and fewer than 10 percent had side incomes.[29]

29. The greater capacity of the richest farmers—that is, those with the largest holdings—to engage in nonagricultural rural activities as investors might explain why they again had somewhat higher nonagricultural participation rates; the greater necessity of the poorest farmers—that is, those with the smallest holdings—to take advantage of opportunities by offering their labor services probably explains their high participation.

Table 2.12. *Off-farm Activity of Farm Families, by Size of Farm, 1960*
(percent)

Size of farm (hectares)	*Farming as only activity*	*Farming as main activity*	*Sideline as main activity*	*Farm workers with sidelines*
Less than 0.5	30.1	26.7	43.2	34.8
0.5–1	55.6	35.4	9.0	17.9
1–2	65.2	31.7	3.1	11.9
2–3	67.3	30.8	1.9	9.3
3–5	66.5	31.5	2.0	8.5
More than 5	61.4	35.9	2.7	8.6
Total	49.3	30.9	19.8	20.0

Source: Ho, *Economic Development in Taiwan,* p. 157.

A 1963 study by the JCRR examined the character of such off-farm employment (table 2.13). This study found that 61 percent of men who found employment off their own farms were seasonal workers; of these, nearly 80 percent worked in farming, presumably at harvest times. This study also found that 23.5 percent of men who found employment off their farms were commuters who lived on farms but held regular off-farm jobs. Of these commuters, 41 percent held jobs in factories or mining; most of the rest worked in small enterprises, in communication and transport, or as public officials and teachers. The remaining 15.5 percent of men finding off-farm work were long-term employees, living away from the farm but retaining a close budgetary connection with their farm homes. Long-term workers held roughly the same kinds of job as commuters, but more worked as clerks and in factories, and fewer worked in mining. Of women finding off-farm work, a greater percentage worked as commuters and long-term employees; fewer were seasonal workers. Employment patterns were roughly the same for women as for men, but a somewhat higher percentage of women worked in factories and handicrafts. The study also found that off-farm employment varied considerably from region to region, depending upon the proximity of industrial areas and the availability of factory work, other nonfarm employment, and jobs in the service trades. Industry grew not only in the big cities, but in

Table 2.13. *Composition of Off-farm Employment of "Moved-out" Workers, by Type of Work, 1963*
(percent)

Type of work	Commuters[a]		Seasonal workers[b]		Long-term employees[c]	
	Male	*Female*	*Male*	*Female*	*Male*	*Female*
Farming	1.6	2.1	79.6	80.1	2.5	2.0
Mining	14.4	10.5	3.9	3.5	2.1	1.5
Factory labor	27.1	31.9	3.1	4.2	30.5	29.1
Small enterprise	9.0	6.8	—	—	6.6	5.2
Clerks	1.1	2.1	—	—	12.8	11.9
Public officials and teachers	27.5	24.1	—	—	21.1	18.0
Communication and transport	7.6	6.0	—	—	7.9	5.8
Handicrafts	1.6	7.0	0.9	1.3	5.0	5.5
Carpenters and plasterers	4.4	3.3	3.4	2.8	4.1	2.9
Other	5.7	6.2	9.1	8.1	7.4	18.1
All workers surveyed	23.5	35.0	61.0	41.1	15.5	23.9

— Not applicable.

Source: Y. C. Tsui and T. L. Lin, "A Study on Rural Labor Mobility in Relation to Industrialization and Urbanization in Taiwan," *Economic Digest Series*, no. 16 (Taipei: JCRR, 1964), pp. 12–16.

a. Commuters are persons regularly traveling back and forth from their farm home and receiving a monthly salary.

b. Seasonal workers are persons temporarily working for others during their leisure time and receiving daily wages.

c. Long-term employees are persons who leave their farm home and work rather permanently in cities or other places. They nevertheless have close connections with their farm home—for example, by remitting earnings. For convenience, students living away from home, military servicemen, and dependents of long-term employees are included in this category.

previously rural areas as well. At times, rural roadbuilding and other construction projects were important sources of off-farm employment in many areas.[30]

Table 2.14 shows the distribution of the growth of establishments

30. JCRR, *Rural Progress in Taiwan* (Taipei: JCRR, 1955), pp. 83–85.

Table 2.14. *Establishments in Taiwan, by Location, 1951 and 1961*

Location[a]	Number of establishments, 1951	Growth in number of establishments, 1951–61[b] (percent)	Percentage distribution of establishments	
			1951	1961
Cities	2,959	419.8	24.2	21.5
Semiurban cities	1,235	395.2	10.1	8.5
Semiurban prefectures	2,876	490.1	23.6	24.4
Rural prefectures	2,024	562.2	21.5	25.6
Mixed urban, semiurban, and rural prefectures	2,517	458.0	20.6	20.0
All Taiwan	12,211	472.3	100.0	100.0

Note: See table 3.9 in chapter three for figures to 1971.
Source: Industrial and Commercial Census of Taiwan (ICCT), *General Report, 1971 Industrial and Commercial Census of Taiwan and Fukien Area,* 7 (?) vols. (Taipei: ICCT, 1972), vol. 1, table 6.
a. Based on DGBAS definitions in 1964.
b. Based on number in operation at the end of the year.

in urban, semiurban, and rural areas, based on 1964 DGBAS definitions. Although some semiurban areas may have been rural in 1951, this table nevertheless gives an idea of the spatial distribution and growth of industrial establishments. It reveals that the distribution of establishments in Taiwan was fairly well dispersed in the early 1950s and that the growth of establishments was fairly uniform into the 1960s. Throughout the 1951–71 period the distribution of establishments did not become concentrated in any one area, especially in such large urban centers as Taipei City and Kaohsiung City, where heavy concentrations might have been expected. This spatially dispersed growth pattern enabled farm families almost anywhere in Taiwan to move easily into rural industries that were intensive in labor.

What are the conclusions to be drawn? As a result of rapidly increasing agricultural productivity, Taiwan was able to feed itself and to finance a policy of import substitution on its way to rapid industrialization and successful export substitution. There were

Table 2.15. *Gini Coefficients and Factor Shares Based on Income of Urban Wage and Salary Workers, 1955 and 1959*

Item	*1955*	*1959*
Gini coefficients		
Total income [G_y]	0.3964	0.3960
Wage income [G_w]	0.4210	0.4176
Other income [G_o]	0.3162	0.2958
Distributive shares		
Wage income [ϕ_w]	0.7637	0.8196
Other income [ϕ_o]	0.2363	0.1804

Sources: 1955 from Economic Planning Council, "Family Income and Expenditure Survey of Wages and Salaries by Income Class, Taiwan Province" (Taipei, n.d.; processed in Chinese); 1959 from idem, "Family Income and Expenditure Survey of City Consumers, Taiwan Province" (Taipei, n.d.; processed in Chinese).

three main reasons for this success: the early initiation of land reform, government's subsequent support of agriculture, and the dispersed pattern of nonagricultural growth. The distribution of the income of farm families thus improved as a combined result of the initial distribution of assets and the availability of off-farm employment for poorer rural families, particularly the employment opportunities that stemmed from the policy reforms instituted around 1960.

Urban FID

Evidence on the distribution of income for nonfarm or urban families during 1953–64 is much sketchier than that for rural families. Hence the results necessarily are less conclusive. Only two studies investigated the distribution of urban wage income alone during the 1950s, and these give some indication of a slight improvement. The first is a study of wage and salary income for 1955; the second, a study of city consumers for 1959.[31] If it is assumed that the wage and salary class and the city consumers are roughly comparable categories, comparison of the Gini coefficients derived from

31. Economic Planning Council, "Family Income and Expenditure Survey of Wages and Salaries by Income Class, Taiwan Province;" idem, "Family Income and Expenditure Survey of City Consumers, Taiwan Province."

these two surveys may be attempted (table 2.15). The basic conclusion, drawn mainly from the more reliable figures on wage income, must be that the urban FID changed very little. At best it improved only slightly, but it certainly contributed much less than rural FID to the overall increase in equity.

Overall FID

The pattern of overall FID for 1953, 1959, and 1964 shows a striking improvement by almost every measure (table 2.16). In 1953 the Gini coefficient was 0.56, which is comparable to patterns of income distribution now prevailing in Brazil and Mexico. By 1964 the Gini coefficient dropped to 0.33, a level comparable to that of the best performers anywhere.[32] This substantial decline in overall

32. The quality of the data, particularly for the 1950s, is suspect. Calculation of total personal income in 1953, by aggregating the product of average family income and the number of households in each income group, gives a figure 20 percent lower than that of the national accounts data. A similar calculation found that the 1953 data underestimated the total family income given in the national accounts data by 16.7 percent, but that the 1959 data overestimated total family income by 15.3 percent. The 1964 DGBAS data were found to underestimate total family income by only about 5 percent.

Although more than half of Taiwan's population in 1953 was in agriculture, 84 percent of the 1953 sample group came from the more urbanized and industrialized areas; 58 percent of that group lived in Taiwan's four largest cities. If rural income was better distributed than urban income, as was seen earlier, any overweighting of urban income may have resulted in a low estimate of total personal income and a high estimate of the Gini coefficient. In turn, although DGBAS data for 1964 did not include an appropriate number of families with income exceeding NT$200,000, the downward bias in the Gini probably is too small to be of much importance. Nevertheless the survey results for the 1950s must be accepted with caution.

With respect to the underestimation of FID inequality—the 1964 Gini coefficient based on decile groups is 0.328—households with income exceeding NT$200,000 accounted for only 0.1 percent of the population and 1.15 percent of total income. Even if the income share of these households is increased by 1 percentage point, which almost doubles their income share, and if the 1 percent loss is equally assigned to the first nine decile groups, the Gini coefficient increases by only 3.1 percent to 0.3307. The increase really is not that large. To give an idea of the effect of the underestimation of the Gini coefficient, again for the 1964 data, suppose the income share of the top decile group to be increased by 2, 3, and 4 percentage points. Then the Gini coefficients respectively rise by 6.2 percent, 9.3 percent, and 12.4 percent to 0.3406, 0.3505, and 0.3604. Thus the smaller the population, income share, underestimation of the wealthiest households, or any combination of these elements, the smaller the downward bias of the Gini coefficient.

Table 2.16. *Measures of the Equity of the Family Distribution of Income, 1953, 1959, and 1964*

Item	*1953*[a]	*1959*[b]	*1964*[c]
Distribution of income by percentile of households (percent)			
0–20	3.0	5.7	7.7
21–40	8.3	9.7	12.6
41–60	9.1	13.9	16.6
61–80	18.2	19.7	22.1
81–95	28.8	26.3	24.8
96–100	32.6	24.7	16.2
Mean income per household (N.T. dollars in 1972 prices)	22,681	31,814	32,452
Per capita GNP in market prices (N.T. dollars in 1972 prices)	6,994	8,629	10,875
Ratio of income share of top 10 percent to that of bottom 10 percent	30.40	13.72	8.63
Gini coefficient	0.5580	0.4400	0.3280

Sources: 1953 from Kowie Chang, "An Estimate of Taiwan Personal Income Distribution in 1953—Pareto's Formula Discussed and Applied," *Journal of Social Science,* vol. 7 (August 1956), p. 260; 1959 from National Taiwan University, College of Law, "Report on Pilot Study of Personal Income and Consumption in Taiwan" (prepared under the sponsorship of a working group of National Income Statistics, DGBAS; processed in Chinese), table A, p. 23; 1964 from DGBAS, *Report on the Survey of Family Income Expenditure, 1964* (Taipei: DGBAS, 1966); Shirley W. Y. Kuo, "Income Distribution by Size in Taiwan Area—Changes and Causes," in *Income Distribution, Employment, and Economic Development in Southeast and East Asia,* 2 vols. (Tokyo: Japan Economic Research Center, 1975), vol. 1, pp. 80–146.

a. Data are based on a sample of 301 families, or a sample fraction of 2/1,000.

b. Data are based on a sample of 812 families, or a sample fraction of 4/1,000.

c. Data are based on a sample size of 3,000 families, or a sample fraction of 14.6/1,000.

FID during the 1950s can be traced primarily to the rapidly improving rural FID, as noted earlier, and secondarily to the distribution of nonagricultural income, which probably did not worsen and may even have slightly improved.

As will be more fully and rigorously explained in chapter three, the pattern of industrial growth can affect the family distribution of income through changes in the functional distribution of income. For example, if the wage share goes up because of the adoption of a labor-intensive growth path, the distribution of income will improve, assuming that wage income is better distributed than property income, which it generally is. If the wage share declines because of technological changes that save labor and deepen capital, the distribution of family income will worsen. Between 1951 and 1954, the early period of import substitution, the share of wage income in total income sharply increased from 40.7 percent to 46.2 percent (table 2.17). In ensuing years that share was fairly stable, at least until the onset of policies of export substitution again increased the wage share in the 1960s, especially after commercialization. Given the distortion of relative prices usually accompanying import substitution, Taiwan's achievement of a stable wage share is significant. The chief reasons for this performance are that factor prices were more distorted before 1954 than subsequently and that import substitution policies were relatively mild.

If a stable or improving wage share is one precondition for the improved distribution of nonagricultural income, the adoption of a labor-intensive growth path is another. Table 2.18 shows the distribution and growth of the branches of manufacturing in which most nonagricultural growth took place. The data indicate that growth in Taiwan during the 1950s was not focused on the highly capital-intensive industries, as is typical in many LDCs. In fact, the most labor-intensive branches of industry grew at rates well above average. The share in total industrial value added of the seven industries most intensive in labor rose from 10.9 percent in 1954 to 17.6 percent in 1961. The large textile and apparel industry, which still was more labor-intensive than the average for all industry, grew at a slower rate; the tobacco industry, the least labor-intensive, became smaller. In addition, manufacturing in Taiwan was much more labor intensive than in the typical LDC, such as West Pakistan.

The labor-intensive bias of manufacturing, the good distribution of industrial assets, the pattern of growth and spatial dispersion of the more labor-intensive industries, the relatively mild price distortions—all these factors served to improve the overall distribution of nonagricultural income, or at least prevent its worsening. This performance, together with the rapidly improving rural FID, paved the way for the substantial decline observed in overall FID during

Table 2.17. *Distribution of National Income, by Factor Share, 1951–72*

Year	*National income*	*Wage income*[a]	*Property income*[b]	*Agricultural income*
	(hundreds of thousands of N.T. dollars)			
1951	10,527	4,287	2,636	2,980
1952	14,653	6,250	3,470	4,208
1953	19,542	7,911	4,789	6,096
1954	20,761	9,600	5,240	5,171
1955	24,684	11,309	5,816	6,374
1956	28,079	13,188	6,147	6,961
1957	32,409	14,903	7,490	7,957
1958	35,921	16,614	8,353	8,585
1959	41,592	18,781	10,248	9,684
1960	50,828	23,107	11,083	12,969
1961	57,012	26,089	13,178	14,061
1962	61,524	29,182	14,756	14,114
1963	70,603	32,918	18,028	14,688
1964	84,570	39,085	19,803	18,555
1965	91,559	44,036	20,809	19,385
1966	101,967	49,642	24,069	20,373
1967	118,046	58,873	29,647	20,241
1968	136,074	69,770	32,817	21,231
1969	152,795	79,564	37,119	20,484
1970	179,195	93,534	45,763	22,269
1971	204,816	112,115	54,592	21,421
1972	241,320	132,416	61,323	23,688

Note: Although nonagricultural income is functionally classified into wage and property income, agricultural income is not. This explains why the shares here and later in this volume may add up to something slightly less than one and reflects the unimputed mixed income of urban family unincorporated enterprises and professionals. The consistent decline of the share of agricultural income throughout these years reflects a familiar type of structural change in the transition and will be more formally analyzed in chapter three. The reversal from the trend during 1954 and 1955 is a short, noncyclical phenomenon related to the slack in the economy immediately after the Korean War.

Sources: DGBAS, *National Income of the Republic of China*, 1969 and 1974.

a. Wages, salaries, and income of professions.

b. Property income and income of other incorporated enterprises.

Distributive shares of national income			*Relative share of wage and property income*	
Wage income [ϕ_w]	*Property income* [ϕ_π]	*Agricultural income* [ϕ_a]	[ϕ_w/ϕ_π]	*Year*
0.4072	0.2504	0.2841	1.627	1951
0.4265	0.2368	0.2872	1.740	1952
0.4048	0.2451	0.2153	1.652	1953
0.4624	0.2524	0.2491	1.832	1954
0.4582	0.2356	0.2582	1.944	1955
0.4697	0.2189	0.2479	2.146	1956
0.4598	0.2311	0.2455	1.990	1957
0.4625	0.2325	0.2390	1.989	1958
0.4516	0.2464	0.2320	2.072	1959
0.4546	0.2180	0.2552	2.085	1960
0.4576	0.2311	0.2466	1.980	1961
0.4743	0.2398	0.2294	1.978	1962
0.4662	0.2553	0.2080	1.826	1963
0.4622	0.2342	0.2194	1.974	1964
0.4810	0.2273	0.2117	2.116	1965
0.4868	0.2360	0.1998	2.063	1966
0.4987	0.2511	0.1715	1.986	1967
0.5127	0.2411	0.1560	2.127	1968
0.5207	0.2429	0.1341	2.144	1969
0.5249	0.2568	0.1250	2.044	1970
0.5421	0.2640	0.1036	2.053	1971
0.5487	0.2541	0.0982	2.159	1972

the 1950s. It is not possible to say more than this. The meager quantity and quality of data for the 1950s, especially for factor income, preclude formal decomposition analysis of the type undertaken in subsequent chapters. Instead the estimates should be viewed as orders of magnitude that might explain the marked tendency for the value of the Gini coefficient to decline between 1953 and 1964. But even if the magnitude of FID levels and changes must

Table 2.18. *Gross Domestic Product, Employment, Share of Wages in Value Added, and Labor Intensity, by Industry, Various Years*

Industry[a]	Percentage distribution of GDP in manufacturing 1954	Percentage distribution of GDP in manufacturing 1961	Real GDP in 1961 (1954 = 100)	Percentage distribution of employment 1954	Percentage distribution of employment 1961	Employment in 1961 (1954 = 100)
Furniture	0.85	1.14	249.3	2.01	2.63	187.9
Metal products	1.36	3.06	416.9	4.64	4.53	140.8
Transport equipment	1.70	2.84	311.4	5.92	6.29	153.0
Electrical machinery	1.36	2.26	307.6	1.67	2.93	252.2
Printing	3.22	4.41	255.2	3.39	2.94	124.6
Machinery	1.36	2.72	371.1	4.21	3.71	126.6
Rubber	0.91	1.19	244.0	1.74	1.51	124.9
Leather	0.30	0.29	177.0	0.47	0.33	100.0
Wood	3.91	4.88	231.8	5.75	5.91	147.8
Nonmetallic mineral products	5.88	8.10	256.2	9.65	8.82	131.5
Textiles and apparel	24.26	14.86	114.0	21.92	20.91	137.2
Food	26.84	26.51	183.8	20.66	19.86	138.2
Basic metals	1.94	4.14	396.7	2.06	2.45	171.0
Chemicals	10.98	9.27	158.5	5.74	6.97	174.9
Beverages	0.39	0.58	273.0	1.25	1.99	228.7
Paper	2.59	3.53	264.4	2.11	3.04	206.6
Petroleum	3.73	6.16	307.3	1.10	1.24	162.5
Tobacco	6.00	2.69	83.5	1.58	1.21	110.1
Total manufacturing[c]	100.00	100.00	186.5	100.00	100.00	143.2

n.a. Not available.

Sources: GDP figures from DGBAS, *National Income of the Republic of China, 1969;* employment and labor intensity figures from ICCT, *1961 Industrial and Commercial Census;* wage figures from Mo-huan Hsing, *Taiwan and the Philippines—Industrialization and Trade Policies* (London: Oxford University Press for the OECD Development Centre, 1971).

a. Ranked by labor intensity in 1954.

b. Number of employees per hundred thousand N.T. dollars.

c. Includes a miscellaneous category equal to 2 percent of total manufacturing.

be taken with a grain of salt, the evidence that a substantial improvement occurred during the 1950s is conclusive. This improvement occurred against the background of an unusually good initial

Share of wages in value added						
Taiwan			*West Pakistan,*	*Labor intensity*		
1952	*1957–60*	*1965–68*	*1967–68*	*in 1954*[b]	*Industry*[a]	
n.a.	n.a.	n.a.	n.a.	165.95	Furniture	
81.7	63.4	60.7	31.1	122.10	Metal products	
n.a.	n.a.	n.a.	n.a.	84.66	Transport equipment	
58.3	70.7	49.0	29.3	79.18	Electrical machinery	
n.a.	n.a.	n.a.	n.a.	77.82	Printing	
n.a.	n.a.	n.a.	n.a.	59.96	Machinery	
n.a.	n.a.	n.a.	n.a.	57.64	Rubber	
n.a.	n.a.	n.a.	n.a.	55.96	Leather	
71.1	63.7	80.9	43.6	55.39	Wood	
61.2	60.6	56.0	19.9	49.00	Nonmetallic mineral products	
63.1	53.8	51.3	34.6	44.53	Textiles and apparel	
81.1	43.5	58.4	19.1	28.97	Food	
n.a.	n.a.	n.a.	n.a.	22.90	Basic metals	
55.4	49.6	42.6	19.0	19.76	Chemicals	
n.a.	n.a.	n.a.	n.a.	18.35	Beverages	
70.3	58.1	60.0	52.4	13.48	Paper	
n.a.	n.a.	n.a.	n.a.	9.44	Petroleum	
n.a.	n.a.	n.a.	n.a.	7.57	Tobacco	
n.a.	n.a.	n.a.	n.a.	35.91	Total manufacturing[c]	

distribution of assets, the relatively mild regime of import substitution, the efficient use of abundant labor, and the early attention to the rural sector—all of which must have contributed to equity. Furthermore the general liberalization of the economy under the reforms of the early 1960s could only serve to reinforce these trends. More precise analysis linking growth and income distribution nevertheless had to await the superior data that began to become available in 1964.

CHAPTER 3

Growth and the Family Distribution of Income by Factor Components

THE DETAILED HOUSEHOLD SURVEY DATA available after 1964 make it possible to move beyond the descriptive treatment of the 1950s and early 1960s to a more analytical assessment of the relations between growth and the family distribution of income (FID) for the 1964–72 period. As mentioned earlier, the total income pattern of n families [$Y = (Y_1, Y_2, \ldots, Y_n)$] has a finite number [$r$] of factor income components [$W^i = (W_1^i, W_2^i, \ldots, W_n^i)$ $(i = 1, 2, \ldots, r)$]. Total income [Y] is the vector sum of such factor income components [W^i] as wage, property, and transfer income. When the labor force is heterogeneous—differentiated by age, sex, skill, and level of education—the wage component is in turn the additive sum of a number of homogeneous wage-income components. If some index of the inequality of total income is adopted—say, the Gini coefficient [G_y]—it is possible, in addition, to adopt factor Gini coefficients [G_i] that describe the inequality of distribution of factor income. That index of inequality of total income [G_y] can be decomposed into indexes of the inequality of various factor income components [G_i] and traced to them.

These factor income components can be of several types, depending on the way their inequality relates to and influences the inequality of total income. One type of income, what we label as type one income, is distributed less equally than total income; its share increases as the total income of families increases. Another type of factor income, type two income, is distributed more equally than total income; its share decreases as the total income of families increases. A third type of income, type three income, decreases *absolutely* in magnitude as the total income of families increases; this is unlike type one and type two incomes, which increase *absolutely* as the total income of families increases. Property income typically is a type one income; wage income a type two income; and transfer income a type three income. Because transfer income is insignificant in Taiwan, the empirical analysis of this chapter focuses only on the first two types of income. It should be emphasized that decomposition of income inequality by source or type of income considerably differs from decomposition by type of income recipient, which is far more common.

The purpose here is to introduce a basic decomposition equation that links the inequality of total income [G_y] to the inequality of factor incomes [G_i] and to their shares in total income [ϕ_i]. In essence that equation states that the inequality of total family income is the weighted sum of the inequalities of the factor incomes, with one proviso—that negative signs are attached to the type three incomes. The reason is that type three income contributes not to inequality, but to equality. Because type three income does not enter into the analysis of this chapter, the basic decomposition equation is of the following form: $G_y = \phi_1 G_1 + \phi_2 G_2 + \ldots + \phi_r G_r$. That equation is then applied to the substantive problem of this chapter: analyzing the relations between growth and FID.[1]

Two recognizable phenomena accompany the successful develop-

1. For a systematic derivation of the decomposition equations used in this chapter, see chapter ten of part two. A self-contained derivation of the same set of equations is in the appendix to John C. H. Fei, Gustav Ranis, and Shirley Kuo, "Growth and the Family Distribution of Income," *Quarterly Journal of Economics*, vol. 92, no. 1 (February 1978), pp. 17–53. Other decomposition efforts in the literature include the following: N. Bhattacharya and B. Mahalanobis, "Regional Disparities in Household Consumption in India," *Journal of the American Statistical Association*, vol. 62, no. 317 (March 1967), pp. 143–61; V. M. Rao, "Two Decompositions of Concentration Ratio," *Journal of the Royal Statistical Society*, series A, vol. 132, pt. 3 (1969), pp. 418–25; F. Mehran, "Decomposition of the Gini Index: A Statistical Analysis of Income Inequality," (Geneva: International Labour Organisation, n.d.; processed); Mahar Mangahas, "Income Inequality in the Philippines: A Decomposition Analysis," World Employment Programme Working Papers, *Population and Employment Working Paper, no. 12* (Geneva: International Labour Organisation, 1975); and Graham Pyatt, "On the Interpretation and Disaggregation of Gini Coefficients," *Economic Journal*, vol. 86 (June 1976), pp. 243–55. With the exception of Rao, these articles deal with decomposition by homogeneous groups, not by additive income components.

ment of a dualistic developing economy: labor is gradually reallocated from agricultural to nonagricultural activities; changes in technology and the accumulation of capital affect the absorption of labor and the functional distribution of income. Within this developmental framework the disaggregation of total income [Y] into agricultural and nonagricultural income [Y_a and Y_x] and the disaggregation of nonagricultural income into wage and property income [Y_w and Y_π] enable analysis of the relations between growth and FID. Changes in the inequality of total income [G_y] over time can thus be examined in relation to changing patterns of growth. Specifically the decomposition equation introduced in this chapter enables attributing the changes in G_y over time to three effects: a reallocation effect, a functional distribution effect, and a factor Gini effect.

The reallocation effect captures the change in the inequality of income caused by changes in the share of agricultural income in total income. A declining share of agricultural income indicates the shift from agricultural to nonagricultural activities—that is, the extent to which the center of gravity has shifted in a dualistic economy. How does this shift affect the distribution of income? It depends, of course, on whether agricultural income is distributed more equally or less equally than total income. If agricultural income is a type one income, less equally distributed than total income, its declining share would contribute to the equality of total income. If it is a type two income, its declining share would contribute to the inequality of total income. The functional distribution effect captures the change in the inequality of income caused by changes in the relative share of wage and property income. Because wage income typically is a type two income, more equally distributed than total income, it would be expected that any increase in labor's relative share would contribute to the equality of total income. Analogously an increase in the share of the less equally distributed property income would contribute to the inequality of total income. The factor Gini effect captures the change in the inequality of total income caused by changes in the inequality of the various factor income components. In essence the equality of total income increases when the equality of a type one or type two factor income component increases. The opposite is true for a type three component.

The first section of this chapter summarizes the technique for decomposing total income inequality into factor income inequality. The second section uses this technique to formulate the problem of the effects of growth on FID. The third section presents historical data for the 1964–72 period in Taiwan. The fourth and fifth sections respectively trace the quantitative and qualitative effects of growth on FID.

Income Inequality and Its Factor Components

At first glance it may seem intuitively appealing to regard total income inequality [G_y] as the sum of the weighted factor Ginis [$\phi_i G_i$] where the weights [ϕ_i] are the distributive shares of factor income in total income. Such a decomposition nevertheless is likely to be misleading. For example, if transfer income [Y_N] is concentrated among poor families, and especially if the welfare budget is large, the distribution of Y_N will contribute to the equality of total income, not to its inequality. In addition, other components of factor income can differ in other ways in their relation to the overall distribution of income. The methodological contribution of this chapter centers on the design of a correct decomposition equation that is sensitive to different types of factor income components and that enables tracing changes in G_y over time to changing shares of factor income components. This equation is rigorously developed in chapter ten.

Let the pattern of total income of n families [Y] be the sum of r nonnegative factor income components [W^i]:

(3.1a) $$Y = (Y_1, Y_2, \ldots, Y_n);$$

(3.1b) $$Y = W^1 + W^2 + \ldots + W^r;$$

(3.1c) $$W^i = (W_1^i, W_2^i, \ldots, W_n^i) \geq 0; \qquad (i = 1, 2, \ldots, r)$$

(3.1d) $$\phi_i = \bar{W}^i/\bar{Y}, \quad \text{where} \qquad (i = 1, 2, \ldots, r)$$

(3.1e) $$\bar{Y} = (Y_1 + Y_2 + \ldots + Y_n)/n,$$

(3.1f) $$\bar{W}^i = (W_1^i + W_2^i + \ldots + W_n^i)/n, \quad \text{and}$$

(3.1g) $$\phi_1 + \phi_2 + \ldots + \phi_r = 1.$$

The values of ϕ_i are the distributive shares of the factor income components in national income.

In the numerical example given in table 3.1, where $n = 5$ and $r = 3$, the three factor income components are wage income [W_j], property income [π_j], and transfer or welfare income [N_j]. Notice

Table 3.1. *Numerical Example with Three Factor Income Components and with Total Income Arranged in a Monotonically Nondecreasing Order*

Item	*Wage income*[a]	*Property income*[a]	*Transfer income*[a]	*Total income*[a]
Income pattern[b]	W_j	π_j	N_j	Y_j
Family 1	3 (2)	0 (1)	8 (4)	11 (1)
Family 2	1 (1)	0 (2)	12 (5)	13 (2)
Family 3	17 (5)	2 (3)	0 (3)	19 (3)
Family 4	15 (4)	8 (4)	0 (2)	23 (4)
Family 5	9 (3)	25 (5)	0 (1)	34 (5)
Total factor income	45	35	20	100
Factor share [ϕ_i]	0.45	0.35	0.20	1.00
Factor or total Gini [G_i]	0.3912	0.6628	0.6400	0.2239
Estimated income pattern[c]	$\hat{W}_j$	$\hat{\pi}_j$	$\hat{N}_j$	$\hat{Y}_j$
Family 1	5.79 (1)	−2.96 (1)	8.18 (5)	11.00 (1)
Family 2	6.50 (2)	−0.75 (2)	7.25 (4)	13.00 (2)
Family 3	8.64 (3)	5.89 (3)	4.46 (3)	19.00 (3)
Family 4	10.07 (4)	10.32 (4)	2.61 (2)	23.00 (4)
Family 5	14.00 (5)	22.50 (5)	−2.50 (1)	34.00 (5)
Total factor income	45	35	20	100
Factor share [ϕ_i]	0.45	0.35	0.20	1.00
Factor or total Gini [G_i]	0.1777	0.7083	0.5202	0.2239

Source: Constructed by the authors.
a. The ranks of families are indicated in parentheses.
b. From original data.
c. Estimated by linear approximation.

in this table that total family income [Y_j] is arranged in a monotonically nondecreasing order, satisfying:

$$0 \leq Y_1 \leq Y_2 \leq \ldots \leq Y_n \qquad (n = 5) \tag{3.2}$$

and that the rank index of each factor income component is given.

A highly positive rank correlation is assumed between total income and property income; a highly negative rank correlation between total income and transfer income. This pattern gives rise to an intuitive notion: although the unequal distribution of property income contributes to the inequality of total income, the unequal distribution of transfer income contributes to the equality of total income. The typological distinction among income components is emphasized in this section.

Heuristically the total Gini coefficient defined on Y can be estimated in the following manner[2]:

(3.3a) $$G_y = \hat{G}_y - \theta, \quad \text{where}$$

$$[0.2239 = 0.2800 - 0.0561]$$

(3.3b) $$\hat{G}_y = \phi_w G_w + \phi_\pi G_\pi - \phi_N G_N.$$

$$[0.2800 = (0.45)(0.39) + (0.35)(0.66) - (0.20)(0.64)]$$

The estimator Gini $[\hat{G}_y]$ is the weighted average of the factor Gini coefficients; the distributive shares $[\phi_i]$ defined in equation (3.1d) constitute the system of weights. Notice that a negative sign is assigned to the transfer income term $[\phi_N G_N]$. This assignment conforms to the idea that certain components of income—those having a large distributive share (ϕ_N in this case) and a distribution that is more unequal than that of total income (G_N in this case)—contribute to the equality of overall Y and reduce the value of $\hat{G}_y$.[3] In the numerical example the error of estimation $[\theta]$ is 0.0561, and the degree of overestimation $[\theta/G_y]$ is about 20 percent. Notice that if a negative sign had not been attached to transfer income—that is, if the following alternative estimator $[\hat{\hat{G}}_y]$ had been used—the error of estimation would have been larger:

(3.4a) $$G_y = \hat{\hat{G}}_y + E, \quad \text{where}$$

$$[0.2239 = 0.5360 - 0.3121]$$

2. The numbers in brackets under equations (3.3a) and (3.3b) are based on the numerical example in table 3.1.

3. The rule about whether a plus or minus sign should be attached to certain types of factor income is presented below. As can readily be seen from the numerical example, the intuitive idea is that a minus sign should be attached to the transfer income because it has a negative rank correlation with total income. The more formal analysis of rank correlations is presented in chapter nine of part two.

$$\hat{\hat{G}}_y = \phi_w G_w + \phi_\pi G_\pi + \phi_N G_N. \tag{3.4b}$$

$$[0.5360 = (0.45)(0.39) + (0.35)(0.66) + (0.20)(0.64)]$$

For the numerical example the error of estimation associated with $\hat{\hat{G}}_y$ is 0.3121, and the degree of overestimation $[E/G_y]$ is more than 100 percent in this case.

Return to the general case of equation (3.1) and fit a system of r linear equations to the original data by the method of least squares:

$$W^i = b_i + a_i Y, \quad \text{where} \qquad (i = 1, 2, \ldots, r) \tag{3.5a}$$

$$b_1 + b_2 + \ldots + b_r = 0 \quad \text{and} \tag{3.5b}$$

$$a_1 + a_2 + \ldots + a_r = 1. \tag{3.5c}$$

These linear approximations give this chapter its methodological character.[4] Applying them to the numerical example gives:

$$\pi = -15.143 + 1.1071Y; \tag{3.6a}$$

[*property income on Y*]

$$W = 1.857 + 0.3571Y; \tag{3.6b}$$

[*wage income on Y*]

$$N = 13.286 - 0.4643Y. \tag{3.6c}$$

[*transfer income on Y*]

The factor income components can then be classified into types by the signs of the regression coefficients $[a_i]$ and the regression constants $[b_i]$.[5]

For type one income:

$$a_i \geq 0, b_i < 0; \qquad (a_\pi = 1.1071, b_\pi = -15.143) \tag{3.7a}$$

for type two income:

$$a_i \geq 0, b_i \geq 0; \qquad (a_w = 0.3571, b_w = 1.875) \tag{3.7b}$$

4. It should be emphasized that these regression relations are used for purely descriptive purposes; they are devoid of the usual behavioristic connotations associated with regression lines in economics. Notice that the combination of equation (3.1b) with the ordinary least-squares method directly implies equations (3.5b) and (3.5c).

5. Because the n pairs (W_1^i, Y_1), (W_2^i, Y_2), . . . , (W_n^i, Y_n) are nonnegative, a_i and b_i cannot both be negative.

for type three income:

(3.7c) $a_i < 0, b_i \geq 0.$ $(a_N = -0.4643, b_N = 13.286).$

As will be shown below, type one income is distributed less equally than total income and concentrated among rich families; type two income is distributed more equally than total income. The distinguishing characteristic of type three income (typically welfare income) is that it decreases absolutely as the family is wealthier. This explains why a minus sign is assigned to the transfer income term $[\phi_N G_N]$ in the decomposition of the estimator Gini $[\hat{G}_y]$ in equation (3.3b). Transfer income is a type three income and may be viewed as an income distribution equalizer.

A generalization of equation (3.3b) is the basic decomposition equation used in this chapter:

(3.8a) $G_y = \hat{G}_y - \theta,$ where

(3.8b) $\hat{G}_y = H_1 + H_2 - H_3,$ where

(3.8c) $H_1 = \phi_1 G_1 + \phi_2 G_2 + \ldots + \phi_{r_1} G_{r_1},$

(summation over r_1 type one incomes)

(3.8d) $H_2 = \phi_{r_1+1} G_{r_1+2} + \ldots + \phi_{r_2} G_{r_2},$ and

(summation over $r_2 - r_1$ type two incomes)

(3.8e) $H_3 = \phi_{r_2+1} G_{r_2+2} + \ldots + \phi_r G_r.$

(summation over $r - r_2$ type three incomes)

The usefulness of equation (3.8b) clearly depends on the small size of the error term $[\theta]$. To investigate θ, first decompose Y into r factor income components constructed with the aid of the linear regression lines of equation (3.5a):

(3.9a) $Y = \hat{W}^1 + \hat{W}^2 + \ldots + \hat{W}^r;$

(3.9b) $\hat{W}^i = (\hat{W}^i_1, \hat{W}^i_2, \ldots, \hat{W}^i_n);$ $(i = 1, 2, \ldots, r)$

(3.9c) $\hat{W}^i_j = b_i + a_i Y_j;$ $(i = 1, 2, \ldots, r;\ \ j = 1, 2, \ldots, n)$

(3.9d) $\phi_i = (\hat{W}^i_1 + \hat{W}^i_2 + \ldots + \hat{W}^i_n)/n\bar{Y}.$

$= (W^i_1 + W^i_2 + \ldots W^i_n)/n\bar{Y} = \bar{W}^i/\bar{Y}$

[see equations (3.1e) and (3.1f)]

The decomposition of Y into estimated patterns of factor income is shown in the bottom part of table 3.1. [Notice that the values of ϕ_i remain unchanged, which verifies equation (3.9d).] Applying the approximation equation (3.8) to the estimated patterns of factor income gives:

(3.10a) $G_y = \hat{G}_y - \theta$, where

$$[0.2239 = 0.2239 - 0]$$

(3.10b) $\theta = 0$ and

(3.10c) $\hat{G}_y = \phi_w G_{\hat{w}} + \phi_\pi G_{\hat{\pi}} - \phi_N G_{\hat{N}}.$

$$[0.2239 = (0.45)(0.178) + (0.35)(0.708) - (0.20)(0.520)]$$

Thus the error term [θ] in equation (3.8a) vanishes when the linear relation between total income [Y] and each factor income component [W^i] is perfect: that is, when equation (3.5) is satisfied. The following theorem can now be stated:

THEOREM 3.1. $G_y = \hat{H}_1 + \hat{H}_2 - \hat{H}_3$, *where*

(*a*) $\hat{H}_1 = \phi_1 G(\hat{W}^1) + \ldots + \phi_{r_1} G(\hat{W}^{r_1}),$

(*b*) $\hat{H}_2 = \phi_{r_1+1} G(\hat{W}^{r_1+1}) + \ldots + \phi_{r_2} G(\hat{W}^{r_2}),$ *and*

(*c*) $\hat{H}_3 = \phi_{r_2+1} G(\hat{W}^{r_2+1}) + \ldots + \phi_r G(\hat{W}^r).$

Comparing equation (3.8) and theorem 3.1 shows that the error term [θ] in equation (3.8) can be interpreted as a nonlinearity error. It tends to be small or negligible when the linear correlations between total income [Y] and the factor income components [W^i] are nearly perfect: that is, when the correlation coefficients for type one income and type two income approach one and those for type three income approach minus one. In fact the existence of such high correlations is sufficient for the applicability of the basic decomposition equation (3.8). The major task remaining in this section is to show how theorem 3.1 can be derived. We begin with the following theorem, which is rigorously proved in chapter ten:

THEOREM 3.2. *For type one income and type two income*:

(*a*) $G(\hat{W}^i) = (a_i/\phi_i) G_y = (a_i \bar{Y}/\bar{W}^i) G_y,$

and for type three income:

(*b*) $G(\hat{W}^i) = -(a_i/\phi_i) G_y = -(a_i \bar{Y}/\bar{W}^i) G_y.$

The theorem states that the Gini coefficients of the estimated patterns of factor income can be obtained by multiplying the Gini coefficient of total income by the elasticity of the regression lines of equation (3.5) at their mean points. The term a_i/ϕ_i is the elasticity of the regression lines of equation (3.5) at their mean points $[\bar{Y}, \bar{W}^i]$ as defined in equations (3.1e) and (3.1f). Notice that for type three income a negative sign is assigned to the right-hand side of theorem 3.2(b) because the Gini coefficients of estimated factor income $[G(\hat{W}^i)]$ and of total income $[G_y]$ and the shares of estimated factor income in total income $[\phi_i]$ are nonnegative. Theorem 3.2 can be verified by substituting values from the numerical example.

For property income:

$$(3.11a) \qquad 0.708 = (1.107/0.35)0.2239, \quad \text{which implies that}$$

$$a_\pi G_y = \phi_\pi G(\hat{\pi}) \quad \text{or} \quad (1.107)(0.2239) = (0.35)(0.708);$$

for wage income:

$$(3.11b) \qquad 0.178 = (0.357/0.45)0.2239, \quad \text{which implies that}$$

$$a_w G_y = \phi_w G(\hat{W}) \quad \text{or} \quad (0.357)(0.2239) = (0.45)(0.178);$$

and for transfer income:

$$(3.11c) \qquad 0.520 = (-0.464/0.20)0.2239, \quad \text{which implies that}$$

$$a_N G_y = -\phi_\pi G(\hat{N}) \quad \text{or} \quad (-0.464)(0.2239) = -(0.20)(0.520).$$

Now use theorem 3.2 to prove theorem 3.1. When the implied equalities of equations (3.11a), (3.11b), and (3.11c) are added, equation (3.10c) is obtained by using equation (3.5c). Thus theorem 3.1 is obtained in the general case when all r terms $a_i G_y$ are added. This result shows that theorem 3.1 follows from equation (3.11). Theorem 3.2 can now help to illuminate the difference between type one income and type two income. Making use of the relation, $\bar{W}^i = b_i + a_i\bar{Y}$, rewrite theorem 3.2(a) as follows:

For type one income:

$$(3.12a) \quad G(W^i) = \frac{a_i\bar{Y}}{b_i + a_i\bar{Y}} G_y, \quad \text{which implies that } G(W^i) > G_y,$$

because $a_i > 0$ and $b_i < 0$;

for type two income:

$$(3.12b)\quad G(W^i) = \frac{a_i\bar{Y}}{b_i + a_i\bar{Y}} G_y\,, \quad \text{which implies that } G(W^i) < G_y,$$

because $a_i > 0$ and $b_i > 0$.

Thus type one income is distributed less equally than total income, and type two income is distributed more equally than total income, as can be readily verified by equations (4.9a) and (4.9b). This pattern is borne out by comparison of the factor Gini coefficients in the numerical example with the overall Gini coefficient of 0.224: the factor Gini of property income, a type one income, is 0.708; that of wage income, a type two income, is 0.178. Furthermore equation (3.5a) shows that the share of income attributable to the *i*th factor is:

$$(3.13)\qquad W^i/Y = b_i/Y + a_i\,.$$

Because the regression constants for type one income are less than zero ($b_i < 0$), the share of factor income increases with total income. Similarly, because the regression constants for type two income are greater than zero ($b_i > 0$), the share of factor income decreases with total income. Property income typically is type one income: wealthier families have absolutely and relatively more of such income than poorer families. Wage income typically is type two income: wealthier families have absolutely more but relatively less of such income than poorer families. Type one, two, and three incomes, as summarized in the summation terms [H_1, H_2, and H_3] in equation (3.8), thus represent decreasing contributions to inequality.

When there is no type three income—that is when r equals r_2—equation (3.8) has a special case:

$$(3.14a)\qquad G_y = \phi_1 G_1 + \phi_2 G_2 + \ldots + \phi_r G_r - \theta;$$

$$(3.14b)\qquad \theta \geq 0.$$

As is shown in chapter ten, the nonlinearity term [θ] always is nonnegative—that is, the estimator Gini [$\hat{G}_y$] always slightly overestimates the true Gini [G_y]. In the empirical application of these formulations to Taiwan, only this case is used because of the virtual absence of type three income. The general case of equation (3.8) nevertheless is methodologically more interesting than this special case because it can take into account factor incomes that contribute to the equality of FID, as well as those that contribute to its inequality.

Growth and the Distribution of Income

Students of income distribution of course are interested in the forces determining the inequality of income [G_y] at any given time, but even more in what may occasion changes in G_y over time. The approximation equation (3.14a) derived in the preceding section can be used to analyze two types of forces that affect the value of G_y over time, assuming that there is no type three income and that the nonlinearity error is small. First assume a simple one-sector economy in which the two factor income components ($r = 2$) are capital [K] and labor [L] and the respective distributive shares of those components are ϕ_π and ϕ_w. This simple version of equation (3.8) then reduces to:

(3.15a) $$G_y = \phi_\pi G_\pi + \phi_w G_w, \quad \text{where}$$

(3.15b) $$\phi_w + \phi_\pi = 1.$$

Differentiating equation (3.15a) with respect to time t gives:

(3.16a) $$dG_y/dt = D + B, \quad \text{where}$$

(3.16b) $$D = (G_w - G_\pi)d\phi_w/dt \quad \text{and}$$

[*functional distribution effect*]

(3.16c) $$B = \phi_\pi(dG_\pi/dt) + \phi_w(dG_w/dt).$$

[*factor Gini effect*]

Equation (3.16a) attributes the causation of changes in G_y over time to two distinct types of growth-relevant effects. The functional distribution effect [D] describes the change in G_y caused by changes in the relative shares of capital and labor. The factor Gini effect [B] describes the change in G_y caused by the net effect of favorable or unfavorable changes in the factor Gini coefficients. In this simple world the change in G_y may thus be traced in part to changes in the functional distribution of income and in part to changes in the patterns of family ownership of labor, capital, land, and so on.

Examination of equation (3.16b) reveals that when wage income is distributed more equally than property income (that is, when $G_w < G_\pi$) a change in the functional distribution in favor of labor, indicated by a rise in the distributive share of wage income in total income [ϕ_w], will always serve to improve FID. In fact this relation establishes the necessary condition for the notion, usually accepted uncritically, that any change in favor of labor's share in income necessarily improves FID.

This analysis of the direction of change in the distributive shares of factor income components can be integrated with development theory. In a developing economy such as Taiwan's, two historical periods can be distinguished in addition to the periods of primary import substitution and primary export substitution: the period before commercialization when labor still was in excess supply; the period after commercialization, or the turning point, when surplus labor has been fully absorbed into productive employment. For these two periods the following relations help to link FID directly to the forces of growth:

RELATION 3.1. *Before the turning point, when the real wage approaches constancy, ϕ_w increases only when the degree of the labor-using bias of innovation (in the manner of Hicks) overwhelms the innovation-intensity effect.*[6]

RELATION 3.2. *After the turning point, when the real wage is flexible, ϕ_w increases only when there is capital deepening or when innovations are biased in a labor-using direction.*

The growth equation relevant to analyzing the direction of change of the distributive share of wage income [ϕ_w] after the turning point is:

$$\eta_{\phi_w} = (1 - \phi_w)\eta_{K/L}\left(\frac{1}{\epsilon} - 1\right) + B_L . \tag{3.17}$$

The term η_x denotes the rate of change of any x per unit of time. The term ϵ is the elasticity of substitution; K/L is the capital-labor ratio; B_L is the degree of Hicksian labor-using bias of innovation. This equation can be derived from normal analysis of aggregative production functions.[7]

6. John R. Hicks, *Theory of Wages* (New York: St. Martin's Press, 1963), ch. 5.

7. For a fuller exposition and derivation of both these equations, see chapter three (especially table 1 and the appendix to that chapter) in John C. H. Fei and Gustav Ranis, *Development of the Labor Surplus Economy: Theory and Policy* (Homewood, Illinois: Richard D. Irwin, 1964). The term ϵ used in this chapter coincides with the more conventional definition in the literature, but is the reciprocal of the definition used in the volume just mentioned.

If equation (3.17) is substituted in equation (3.16b), the functional distribution effect becomes:

$$(3.18a)\qquad D = [\phi_w(G_w - G_\pi)d\phi_w/dt]/\phi_w \qquad (= \phi_w(G_w - G_\pi)\eta_{\phi_w})$$

$$(3.18b)\qquad = \phi_w(G_w - G_\pi)[(1 - \phi_w)\left(\frac{1}{\epsilon} - 1\right)\eta_{K/L} + B_L].$$

Equation (3.18b) shows that, when wages are upwardly flexible after the turning point, FID improves under two conditions: when technology change is biased in a labor-using direction (that is, when B_L is greater than zero); when there is overall capital deepening (that is, when $\eta_{K/L}$ is greater than zero). The reason is that the functional distribution effect definitely is favorable ($D < 0$) only under these conditions. These conditions are the necessary conditions for an improvement in labor's share (see equation [3.17]).[8]

Nevertheless, as long as the supply of labor still is unlimited and the real wage consequently is nearly constant, equation (3.17) reduces to the following special form[9]:

$$(3.19a)\qquad \eta_{\phi_w} = B_L\epsilon - J(1 - \epsilon), \quad \text{which implies that}$$

8. This statement is true for the "normal" case of production complementarity—that is, when $\epsilon < 1$. For the case of production substitutability—that is, when $\epsilon > 1$—it is true when there is capital shallowing ($\eta_{K/L} < 0$) instead of capital deepening.

9. When η_w is zero, the rate of labor absorption is:

$$\eta_L = \eta_K + (B_L + J/\epsilon_{LL})$$

(see Fei and Ranis, *Development of the Labor Surplus Economy*, ch. 3). Substituting:

$$\eta_{K/L} = -(B_L + J)/\epsilon_{LL}$$

in equation (3.17) gives:

$$\eta_{\phi w} = -(\phi_\pi/\epsilon_{LL})\left(\frac{1 - \epsilon}{\epsilon}\right)(B_L + J) + B_L,$$

which can be reduced to equation (3.18) with the help of $\epsilon = \phi/\epsilon_{LL}$ (see page 85 in the work just cited). By comparing equations (3.18) and (3.20) it can be seen that the behavior of ϕ_w is caused by different types of forces before and after the turning point. This difference is traced basically to the fact that employment before the turning point is causally determined by capital accumulation through labor absorption. After the turning point, capital and labor are symmetrical, and the real wage is endogenously determined.

$$(3.19b) \quad \eta_{\phi_w} > 0 \quad \text{if and only if} \quad B_L > J\left(\frac{1}{\epsilon} - 1\right), \quad \text{with } \frac{1}{\epsilon} - 1 > 0.$$

Combining equation (3.19a) with equation (3.16b) gives the following form to the functional distribution effect before the turning point:

$$(3.20) \qquad D = \phi_w(G_w - G_\pi)[B_L\epsilon - J(1 - \epsilon)].$$

Consequently, as long as labor is unlimited, FID is improved and G_y is reduced when equation (3.19) holds: that is, when technology change in the commercialized sector is sufficiently biased in a labor-using direction to overcome J, the innovation-intensity effect.[10]

Thus, for a labor surplus economy, a high innovation-intensity effect [J] and a high degree of Hicksian labor-using bias of innovation [B_L] always contribute to the elimination of unemployment and the coming of the turning point. The distribution of income may nevertheless get worse when the intensity effect [$J(1/\epsilon - 1)$] overwhelms B_L. This result would be reflected in a decline in the distributive share of wage income [ϕ_w] and a rise in the inequality of total income [G_y]. After the turning point a higher value of B_L, combined with capital deepening, contributes to the improvement of FID. This result would be reflected in a decline in G_y, an increase in B_L, and an increase in $\eta_{K/L}$, the rate of capital deepening. Whether these conditions are met determines whether the Kuznets hypothesis about the inverse U-shaped time path of G_y is valid. In summary:

RELATION 3.3 *When* $d\phi_w/dt > 0$, *the functional distribution effect is favorable to* FID ($D < 0$) *if and only if* $G_w < G_\pi$.

What about the factor Gini effect [B]? A negative B, which would contribute to growing FID equity, can be caused by a change in the patterns of asset ownership of capital, labor, or both. The

10. In the normal case of production complementarity, a high innovation intensity leads to more labor absorption and a lower K/L ratio, decreasing labor's share. Thus a high B_L contributes both to employment objectives and FID objectives; a high J contributes to the first objective, but not the second. In the "less normal" case of production substitutability, a high J *and* a high B_L would contribute both to the elimination of unemployment and to the improvement of FID.

pattern of family ownership of capital becomes more equal over time (that is, dG_π/dt is less than zero) when lower income families acquire capital assets faster than wealthier families do, as might occur because of higher saving rates or favorable inheritance laws or because of land or capital reform. The pattern of family ownership of labor becomes more equal over time (that is, dG_w/dt is less than zero) when lower income families acquire more skilled labor because of their expenditure on education or because of government's provision of education to them. In summary:

RELATION 3.4. *The factor Gini effect is favorable to* FID $(B < 0)$ *when there is a net improvement in the equity of the distribution of any factor income (other than a type three income).*

One additional source of real-world complexity must be accommodated when the foregoing relations are applied to a dualistic LDC, such as Taiwan. This complexity can be traced to the dualistic locational aspect of families and production activities and to the importance of agricultural income. Urban families primarily receive income from nonagricultural production, that is, from wage and property income from urban industry and services. Rural families usually receive income from both agriculture and nonagriculture, that is, merged wage and property income from agriculture and wage and property income from rural industry and services. This additional complexity in the real world is the motivation for treating the whole economy in accord with three models: urban households, rural households, and all households. The decomposition equation (3.16) can be directly applied to urban households. But because the models of all households and rural households also have the additional and important source of agricultural income, the analysis of these two groups must be modified. It is substantially enriched in the process.

For nonagricultural production the functional distributive shares of wage and property income will be explicitly treated as above; income from agriculture will not, however, be functionally distinguished. This treatment is based on two considerations, the first practical, the second theoretical. First, in the farm-family type of agricultural activity, property and wage income can be disentangled only by using highly artificial procedures of imputation. Second, the essence of development in the dualistic economy is the gradual reallocation of resources, particularly labor, from agricultural to nonagricultural activities. A declining distributive share of agricultural income in total income [ϕ_a] is a proxy for this reallocation. Now modify equation (3.15a):

(3.21a) $G_y = \phi_x G_x + \phi_a G_a$, where $\phi_x = \phi_w + \phi_\pi$; $\phi_x + \phi_a = 1$;

(3.21b) $G_x = \phi'_w G_w + \phi'_\pi G_\pi$,

where $\phi'_w = \phi_w/\phi_x$; $\phi'_\pi = \phi_\pi/\phi_x$; $\phi'_w + \phi'_\pi = 1$.

The two functional distributive shares in the nonagricultural sector are ϕ'_w and ϕ'_π; the Gini coefficient of all nonagricultural income is G_x. Differentiating the inequality of total income [G_y] with respect to time t gives:

(3.22a) $dG_y/dt = R + D + B$, where

(3.22b) $R = (G_a - G_x)d\phi_a/dt$;

[*reallocation effect*]

(3.22c) $D = (G_w - G_\pi)(d\phi'_w/dt)\phi_x$; and

[*functional distribution effect*]

(3.22d) $B = (dG_a/dt)\phi_a + (dG_w/dt)\phi_w + (dG_\pi/dt)\phi_\pi$.

[*factor Gini effect*]

The functional distribution effect, which reflects the importance of capital intensity and technology change, can now be summarized by using the shares of wage and profit income from all nonagricultural activity [ϕ'_w and ϕ'_π]. Equation (3.21b) indicates that these shares move in the same direction as the distributive share of wage income [ϕ_w] in total income. Thus the entire foregoing discussion of the one-sector case continues to hold in the more complex case. The factor Gini effect remains unchanged, but it now includes agricultural income. What is new is the addition of the reallocation effect [R], which reflects the continuous shift of the economy's center of gravity from agriculture to nonagriculture. A decline in the distributive share of agricultural income in total income is a proxy for this shift. Notice that when such reallocation takes place over time, the distributive share of agricultural income in total income declines over time ($d\phi_a/dt$ is less than zero). Thus the impact of the reallocation effect on the equity of distribution of total income [G_y] in equation (3.22b) depends upon the sign of the term, $G_a - G_x$: that is, on whether the inequality of agricultural income is greater or less than the inequality of nonagricultural income. When agricultural income is a type two income—that is, when the inequality of agricultural income [G_a] is less than the inequality of total income [G_y]—the inequality of nonagricultural income [G_x] must be greater than G_y. Hence the term, $G_a - G_x$, would be negative. As a result, R would be greater than zero, which means that the reallocation effect would cause the overall equity of income distribution to worsen. Conversely, when agricultural income is a type one income—that is, when the inequality of agricultural income [G_a] is greater than the inequality of total income [G_y]—it is more of a disequalizer of FID than nonagricultural income. Hence, the term, $G_a - G_x$, would be positive. As a result, R would be less than zero, which means that the reallocation effect would help to improve overall FID. In summary:

RELATION 3.5. *When* $d\phi_a/dt < 0$, *the reallocation effect is favorable to* FID ($R < 0$) *if and only if* $G_a > G_x$.

Changes in the inequality of total income [G_y] may thus be traced to three forces. The first is the continuous reallocation of labor from agricultural to nonagricultural activities, proxied by the decline of the share of agricultural income in total income as the economic center of gravity shifts from agriculture to nonagriculture. The second is the changing impact of the functional distribution of income as traced to such factors as capital accumulation, technology change, and population growth. The third is the impact of changes in factor income distribution as traced to abrupt changes in asset structure arising from land reform and inheritance laws and to gradual changes arising from different patterns of private and public saving for the formation of physical and human capital. For the first two forces the link of growth theory to FID is quite direct. For the third force the relation of traditional economic analysis to FID is more indirect and complicated.

Decomposition equation (3.22), by capturing the effects of these three forces, provides a framework for analyzing the impact of growth on FID in a typical developing economy. It enables us to make qualitative statements about the direction of the impact of a selected pattern of growth on the distribution of income. Moreover it enables us to make quantitative statements about the relative importance of various effects as they contribute to changes in income inequality over time.

Empirical Application to Taiwan

Sample survey data on household income in Taiwan—collected by the Directorate-General of Budget, Accounting, and Statistics (DGBAS) for 1964, 1966, 1968, 1970, 1971, and 1972—have been processed in accord with the analytical framework presented in the foregoing section.[11] The following assumptions were made in transforming the raw data into a simplifying three-model framework. First, a category of unallocable miscellaneous income was ignored, as was the agricultural income of urban families. Both were quantitatively small. Second, no account was taken of intersectoral payments, such as the inclusion in rural wage income of the urban income of farmers' daughters. Isolating such payments in the data was impossible. Third, as pointed out before, agricultural income [Y_a] was not functionally disaggregated into wage and property shares. For farm-family agriculture, such a separation would have entailed a rather arbitrary imputation procedure.

Table 3.2 summarizes the results for all households, urban households, and rural households. Figures 3.1 and 3.2 provide a graphic depiction of these time series. Table 3.3 gives the results of linear regressions for the three models.[12] Comparison of factor shares emanating from the DGBAS surveys and the national income accounts shows that differences generally are quite small: around 2.5 percent (table 3.4). Consequently the survey data used here are fairly reliable as a source of data on income distribution.

The regression coefficients [a_i] and constants [b_i] indicate the following findings:

FINDING 3.1a. *For all three models property income was a type one income and wage income was a type two income.*[13] *Hence* $G_w < G_y < G_\pi$.

11. DGBAS, *Report on the Survey of Family Income and Expenditure,* 1964, 1966, 1968, 1970, 1971, and 1972.

12. For reasons already cited, the values of a_i do not quite add up to 1; the values of b_i to zero. Regressions are based on grouped data classified into decile population groups.

13. The exception is property income of rural households in 1968: when using deciles, it marginally was a type two income; when using more intervals, it was a type one income.

Figure 3.1. *Gini Coefficients of Total and Factor Incomes, by Model, 1964–72*

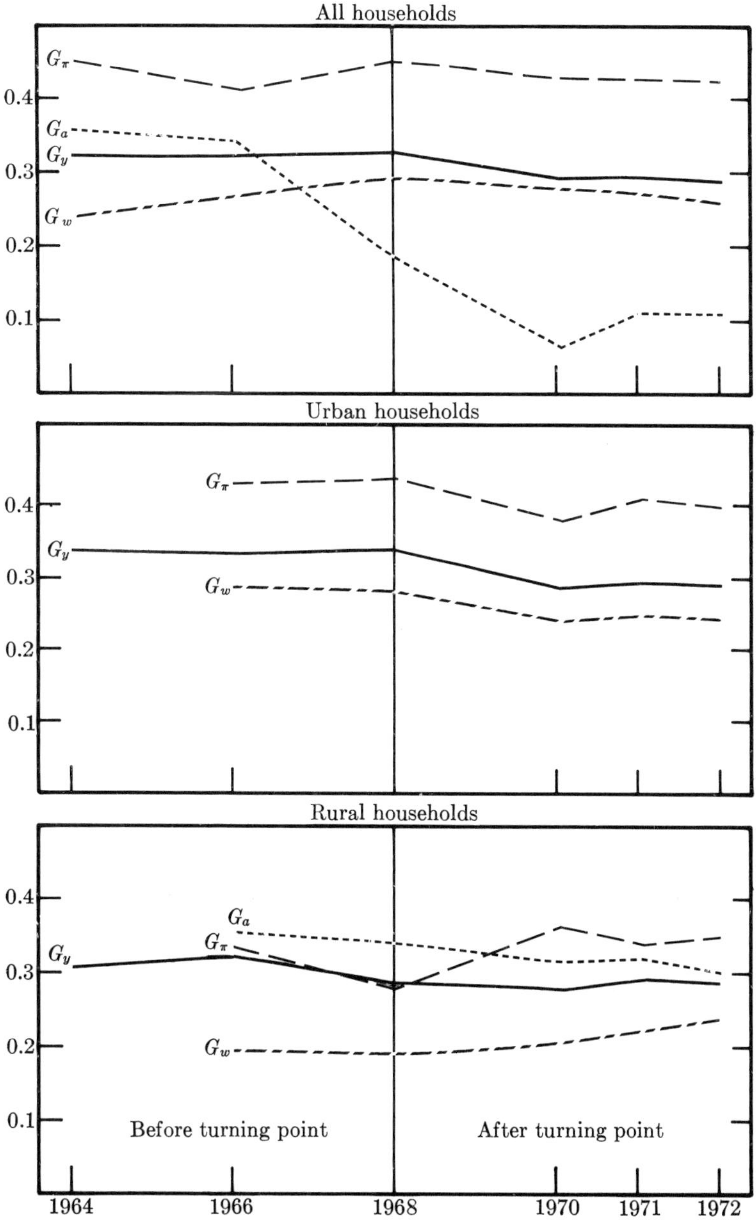

—— *Total income* — —*Property income* - - - *Wage income* - - - - *Agricultural income*

Source: Table 3.2.

Table 3.2. *Gini Decomposition by Additive Factor Components, 1964–72*

Model and variable	*Notation*	*1964*	*1966*	*1968*
All households				
Total Gini	G_y	0.3208	0.3226	0.3260
Wage Gini	G_w	0.2365	0.2697	0.2932
Property Gini	G_π	0.4487	0.4104	0.4598
Agricultural Gini	G_a	0.3543	0.3410	0.1817
Wage share[a]	ϕ_w	0.4324	0.4760	0.5066
Property share	ϕ_π	0.2401	0.2557	0.2777
Agricultural share	ϕ_a	0.2754	0.2118	0.1523
Estimated total Gini	$\hat{G}_y$	0.3218	0.3230	0.3278
Nonlinearity error	$\theta = \hat{G}_y - G_y$	0.0009	0.0004	0.0019
Degree of overestimation	$D_y = \theta/G_y$	0.0029	0.0013	0.0058
Urban households				
Total Gini	G_y	0.3288	0.3236	0.3296
Wage Gini	G_w	n.a.	0.2797	0.2732
Property Gini	G_π	n.a.	0.4193	0.4246
Wage share[a]	ϕ_w	0.5729	0.5925	0.5673
Property share	ϕ_π	0.3225	0.3218	0.3366
Agricultural share	ϕ_a	0.0374	0.0217	0.0288
Estimated total Gini	$\hat{G}_y$	n.a.	0.3244	0.3304
Nonlinearity error	$\theta = \hat{G}_y - G_y$	n.a.	0.0008	0.0009
Degree of overestimation	$D_y = \theta/G_y$	n.a.	0.0026	0.0026
Rural households				
Total Gini	G_y	0.3080	0.3200	0.2842
Wage Gini	G_w	n.a.	0.1933	0.1880
Property Gini	G_π	n.a.	0.3344	0.2775
Agricultural Gini	G_a	n.a.	0.3534	0.3372
Wage share[a]	ϕ_w	0.2134	0.2016	0.3227
Property share	ϕ_π	0.1115	0.1000	0.0994
Agricultural share	ϕ_a	0.6468	0.6595	0.5263
Estimated total Gini	$\hat{G}_y$	n.a.	0.3221	0.2862
Nonlinearity error	$\theta = \hat{G}_y - G_y$	n.a.	0.0021	0.0020
Degree of overestimation	$D_y = \theta/G_y$	n.a.	0.0065	0.0069

n.a. Not available.

Sources: Calculated from DGBAS, *Report on the Survey of Family Income and Expenditure*, 1964, 1966, 1968, 1970, 1971, and 1972.

a. The relative shares do not quite add up to 1 because the merged category of

1970	*1971*	*1972*	*Notation*	*Model and variable*
				All households
0.2928	0.2950	0.2897	G_y	Total Gini
0.2775	0.2730	0.2604	G_w	Wage Gini
0.4278	0.4268	0.4235	G_π	Property Gini
0.0655	0.1109	0.1105	G_a	Agricultural Gini
0.5454	0.5974	0.5895	ϕ_w	Wage share[a]
0.2558	0.2417	0.2577	ϕ_π	Property share
0.1307	0.1015	0.1027	ϕ_a	Agricultural share
0.2939	0.2961	0.2907	$\hat{G}_y$	Estimated total Gini
0.0011	0.0011	0.0010	$\theta = \hat{G}_y - G_y$	Nonlinearity error
0.0036	0.0036	0.0033	$D_y = \theta/G_y$	Degree of overestimation
				Urban households
0.2794	0.2794	0.2813	G_y	Total Gini
0.2328	0.2403	0.2349	G_w	Wage Gini
0.3689	0.3992	0.3874	G_π	Property Gini
0.6016	0.6500	0.6335	ϕ_w	Wage share[a]
0.3022	0.2680	0.2975	ϕ_π	Property share
0.0292	0.0262	0.0235	ϕ_a	Agricultural share
0.2803	0.2865	0.2832	$\hat{G}_y$	Estimated total Gini
0.0009	0.0017	0.0019	$\theta = \hat{G}_y - G_y$	Nonlinearity error
0.0034	0.0059	0.0068	$D_y = \theta/G_y$	Degree of overestimation
				Rural households
0.2772	0.2907	0.2844	G_y	Total Gini
0.2042	0.2207	0.2378	G_w	Wage Gini
0.3607	0.3370	0.3477	G_π	Property Gini
0.3138	0.3178	0.2983	G_a	Agricultural Gini
0.3602	0.3572	0.4226	ϕ_w	Wage share[a]
0.1029	0.1224	0.1072	ϕ_π	Property share
0.4869	0.4523	0.4230	ϕ_a	Agricultural share
0.2789	0.2917	0.2847	$\hat{G}_y$	Estimated total Gini
0.0017	0.0010	0.0003	$\theta = \hat{G}_y - G_y$	Nonlinearity error
0.0063	0.0035	0.0009	$D_y = \theta/G_y$	Degree of overestimation

mixed incomes, which constitute less than 10 percent of the total, was neglected. In addition, the share of agricultural income in the total income of nonfarm households is uniformly small, which conforms to the assumption about the income of urban households.

Table 3.3. *Regression Results for Decile Income Groups, 1964–72*

Model and variable	*Notation*	*1964*	*1966*	*1968*
All households				
Slope	a_w	0.292	0.375	0.435
	a_π	0.364	0.344	0.411
	a_a	0.296	0.215	0.070
Constant	b_w	4.191	3.382	2.907
	b_π	−3.694	−2.971	−5.415
	b_a	−0.608	−0.098	3.358
Correlation coefficient	r_w	0.979	0.992	0.995
	r_π	0.988	0.992	0.993
	r_a	0.992	0.991	0.902
Urban households				
Slope	a_w	n.a.	0.474	0.452
	a_π	n.a.	0.440	0.440
Constant	b_w	n.a.	4.038	5.139
	b_π	n.a.	−4.033	−4.590
Correlation coefficient	r_w	n.a.	0.987	0.994
	r_π	n.a.	0.993	0.998
Rural households				
Slope	a_w	n.a.	0.123	0.183
	a_π	n.a.	0.107	0.099
	a_a	n.a.	0.712	0.637
Constant	b_w	n.a.	2.538	4.469
	b_π	n.a.	−0.224	0.005
	b_a	n.a.	−1.688	−3.552
Correlation coefficient	r_w	n.a.	0.974	0.918
	r_π	n.a.	0.989	0.996
	r_a	n.a.	0.998	0.997

n.a. Not available.
Sources: Same as for table 3.2.

FINDING 3.1b. *For rural households agricultural income was a type one income. Hence* $G_a > G_y$.

FINDING 3.1c. *For all households agricultural income was a type one*

1970	*1971*	*1972*	*Notation*	*Model and variable*
				All households
0.495	0.524	0.511	a_w	Slope
0.391	0.369	0.387	a_π	
0.025	0.035	0.035	a_a	
2.326	3.829	4.722	b_w	Constant
−6.333	−6.729	−7.922	b_π	
4.987	3.508	4.094	b_a	
0.995	0.992	0.996	r_w	Correlation coefficient
0.995	0.992	0.996	r_π	
0.828	0.950	0.951	r_a	
				Urban households
0.474	0.525	0.518	a_w	Slope
0.422	0.394	0.417	a_π	
6.605	7.025	7.478	b_w	Constant
−6.168	−7.108	−7.682	b_π	
0.988	0.993	0.997	r_w	Correlation coefficient
0.991	0.992	0.999	r_π	
				Rural households
0.238	0.234	0.321	a_w	Slope
0.149	0.149	0.146	a_π	
0.551	0.503	0.448	a_a	
4.318	5.043	5.021	b_w	Constant
−1.629	−1.083	−1.894	b_π	
−2.276	−2.078	−1.250	b_a	
0.960	0.928	0.973	r_w	Correlation coefficient
0.958	0.991	0.974	r_π	
0.998	0.993	0.998	r_a	

income before 1968 ($G_a > G_y$) *and a type two income after 1968* ($G_a < G_y$).[14]

14. This reversal of type is a complicated phenomenon related to the rapid decline of the relative importance of the merged agricultural income and the very rapid decline of the Gini coefficient of agricultural income.

Figure 3.2. *Factor Shares, by Model, 1964–72*

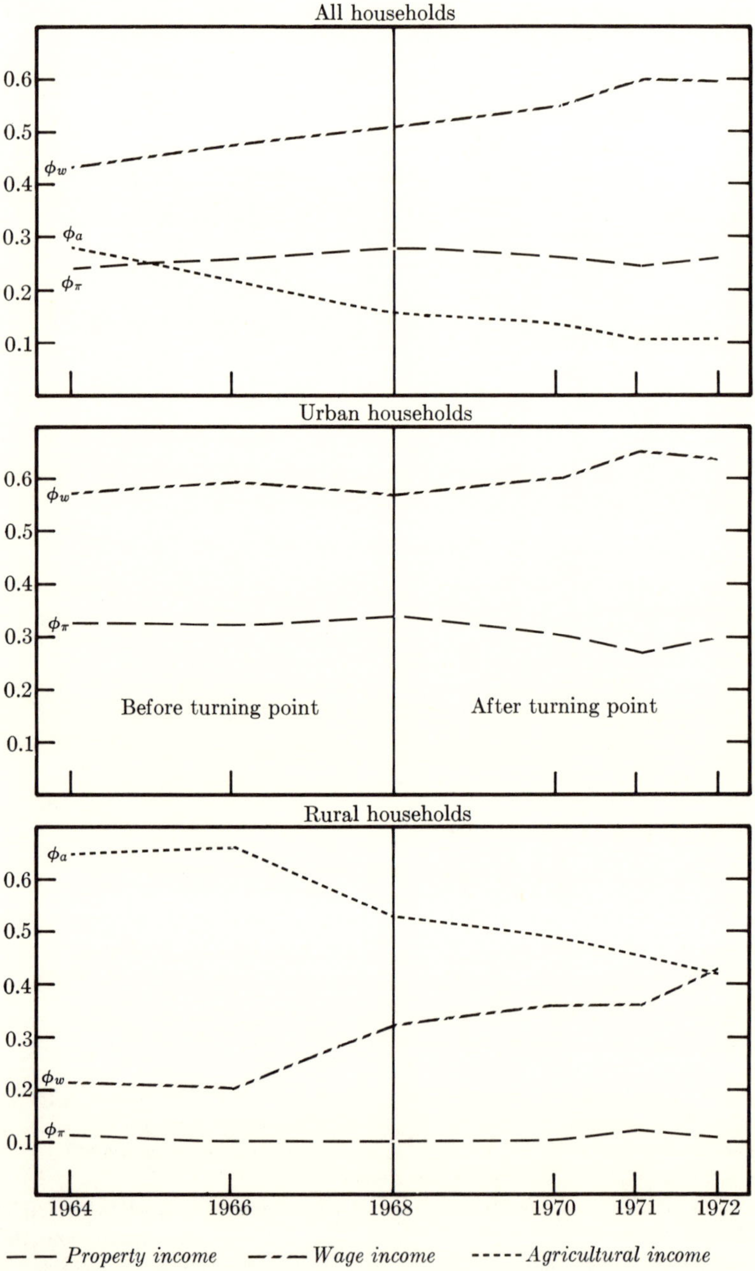

Source: Table 3.2.

Table 3.4. *Comparison of Factor Shares from National Accounts and Household Surveys, 1952–72*

	Share of wage income		*Share of property income*		*Share of agricultural income*	
Year	*Household surveys*	*National accounts*	*Household surveys*	*National accounts*	*Household surveys*	*National accounts*
1952	n.a.	0.4488	n.a.	0.2491	n.a.	0.3021
1957	n.a.	0.4910	n.a.	0.2468	n.a.	0.2622
1962	n.a.	0.5027	n.a.	0.2542	n.a.	0.2431
1964	0.4561	0.5047	0.2532	0.2557	0.2905	0.2396
1966	0.5045	0.5276	0.2710	0.2558	0.2245	0.2165
1968	0.5409	0.5635	0.2965	0.2650	0.1626	0.1715
1970	0.5860	0.5789	0.2738	0.2832	0.1403	0.1378
1971	0.6350	0.5960	0.2570	0.2902	0.1079	0.1139
1972	0.6205	0.6090	0.2713	0.2820	0.1082	0.1089

n.a. Not available.

Note: Because of differences in definitions, the category of transfers and miscellaneous income has a different meaning for the two sources. To facilitate comparability of the factor shares for wage, property, and agricultural income, the shares in this table are based on a total income that excludes this category.

Sources: Calculated from DGBAS, *National Income of the Republic of China,* 1967 and 1974; and idem, *Report on the Survey of Family Income and Expenditure,* 1964, 1966, 1968, 1970, 1971, and 1972.

FINDING 3.1d. *For all three models there was no type three income.*[15] *(Notice that this finding follows from findings 3.1a, b, and c.)*

Thus the special case equation (3.14a) may be used rather than the general case equation (3.8) for all three models. Notice also that the error term [θ] in table 3.2 always is nonnegative, verifying expression (3.14b), and that the degree of overestimation [D_y]

15. To be precise, a category of so-called transfers, small enough to be neglected, does show up, but it does not decrease absolutely with total family income, as is required for a type three income. This is not to claim that a negligible volume of type three income could not be detected at some more disaggregated level.

never exceeds 1 percent in any of the three models.[16] Consequently the nonlinearity error can safely be ignored in the empirical analysis.

As would be expected, the Gini coefficient of property income is larger than the Gini coefficient of total income; the Gini coefficient of wage income is smaller than the Gini coefficient of total income. Furthermore finding 3.1a implies that, as households get wealthier, the share of wage income decreases and the share of property income increases [see equation (3.13)]. This pattern leads to the generally consistent straddling of the total Gini curve by the two factor Gini curves in figure 3.1.[17]

Findings 3.1b and 3.1c imply that the curve for the agricultural Gini income lies above the curve for the total Gini for rural households; the opposite generally is true for all households (figure 3.1). Thus the share of agricultural income in the total income of rural households increased with total family income: that is, it was a type one income. Consequently income from nonagricultural rural sources, such as rural industry and services, served as an important FID equalizer because it constituted a larger share of the income of poor rural families than of rich rural families [see equation (3.13)]. The same relation was true for all households before 1968. But for all households after 1968 the share of agricultural income began to decrease with total family income: that is, it became a type two income. Wealthier families began to derive a larger proportion of their income from property income than from agricultural income (see finding 3.1a). Consequently agricultural income became an income equalizer: any decline in its distributive share would have resulted in a worsening of FID. The comparative magnitudes of the factor Gini coefficients of findings 3.1a, 3.1b, and 3.1c then lead to the following conclusions:

FINDING 3.2a. *The functional distribution effect: In all models a change in the functional distribution of income in favor of labor—that is,* $d\phi_w/dt > 0$ *equivalent to* $d\phi'_w/dt > 0$*—improved the equity of overall* FID *(see relation 3.3 and finding 3.1a).*

16. This supports the linearity specification.

17. The reader might recall that this relation was established for the expected, not the actual, pattern of factor income. But in view of the almost uniformly high correlation coefficients in table 3.3, a high degree of linearity is indicated, and the relation $G_w \leq G_y \leq G_\pi$ is seen to be valid for the actual factor Ginis as well.

FINDING 3.2b. *The reallocation effect: A decrease in the share of agricultural income—that is,* $d\phi_a/dt < 0$*—contributed to the greater equity of* FID *for:*

- *rural households before and after 1968 (see relation 3.5 and finding 3.1b)*
- *all households before 1968 (see relation 3.5 and finding 3.1c).*

It contributed to the greater inequity of FID *for all households after 1968 (see relation 3.5 and finding 3.1c).*

These findings considerably simplify the analytical task in the next section.

Impact of Growth on FID: Quantitative Aspects

With GNP growing at more than 10 percent a year, the 1960s were a period of extremely rapid growth in Taiwan. In addition, the levels of the overall Gini coefficient were unusually low. They held in the 0.30 range between 1964 and 1968 and substantially declined thereafter. The substantial decline, particularly in percentage terms, of the Gini coefficient after the turning point when wages began to rise markedly thus seems to reinforce our independent finding that Taiwan reached the end of its labor surplus condition around 1968.[18] Such a pattern is consistent with the views of Lewis, Kuznets, and others. But what is much more interesting and not in keeping with the conventional wisdom, the Kuznets effect was almost completely avoided during the period of rapid growth before 1968.

The analytical tools developed earlier in this chapter are used here to assess the reasons for the quantitative behavior of the Gini coefficients for rural, urban, and all households. In other words, the general decomposition equation (3.22) is used to trace changes in the Gini coefficients over time to three "causative" factors: the reallocation effect, the functional distribution effect, and the factor Gini effect. Tables 3.5, 3.6, and 3.7 in this section summarize the results. Because of the natural break apparent in the direction of changes in the Gini coefficients around 1968, that year divides the 1964–72 period into two subphases: before the turning point (BTP),

18. John C. H. Fei and Gustav Ranis, "A Model of Growth and Employment in the Open Dualistic Economy: The Cases of Korea and Taiwan," *Journal of Development Studies*, vol. 11, no. 2 (January 1975), pp. 32–63.

Figure 3.3. *Gini Coefficient of Total Income, by Model, 1964–72*

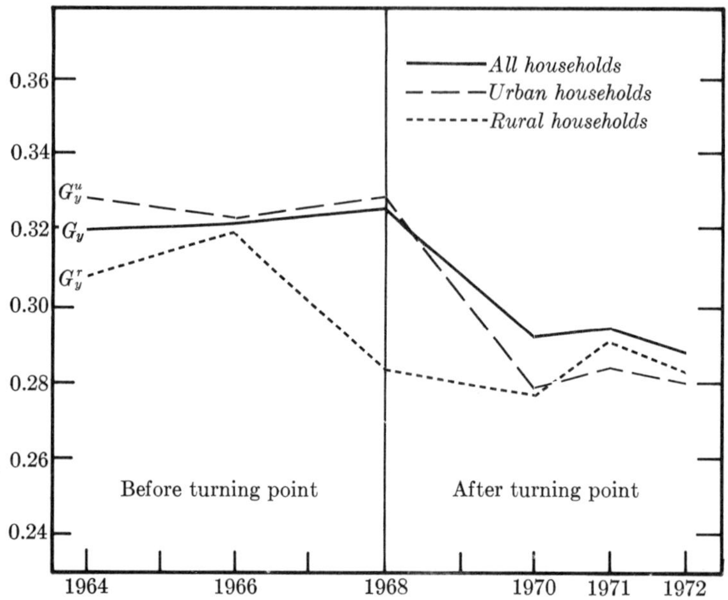

Source: Table 3.2.

and after the turning point (ATP). The magnitudes and percentages of change in the Gini coefficients are shown for each of the three models, as are the estimated total changes in G_y based on decomposition equations (3.16) and (3.22). These results make it possible to deduce the relative quantitative contributions of the reallocation effect [R], the functional distribution effect [D], and the factor Gini effect [B]. For a graphic summary see figures 3.3 and 3.4, and 3.5 and 3.6 in the next section.

FINDING 3.3a *For all households there was a moderate deterioration of* FID *before 1968 (+0.0052 or +1.6 percent for 1964–68) and a significant improvement after 1968 (−0.0363* or *−11.1 percent for 1968–72).*[19]

19. In this section, all percentage changes of Ginis refer to actual changes; all percentage changes of effects refer to their percentage contributions toward the total estimated changes in G_y.

Figure 3.4. *Gini Coefficients of Wage and Property Income, by Model, 1964–72*

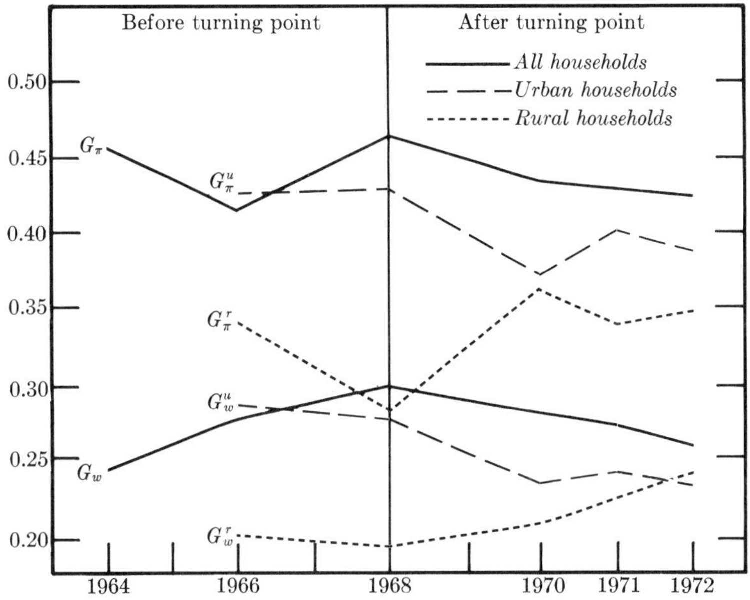

Source: Table 3.2.

FINDING 3.3b *For rural households there was a significant improvement of* FID *before 1968 (−0.0358 or −11.2 percent for 1966–68) and virtually no deterioration after 1968 (+0.0002 or +0.1 percent for 1968–72).*

FINDING 3.3c. *For urban households there was virtually no deterioration in* FID *before 1968 (+0.0060 or +1.9 percent for 1966–68) and a significant improvement after 1968 (−0.0480 or −14.6 percent for 1968–72).*

The absolute magnitude of a "significant" change is about ten times larger than a "moderate change," as is apparent in figure 3.1. For a "significant" change the quantitatively dominant causative factors are to be determined. For a "moderate" change it is to be determined whether that change is the result of the stability of all causa-

Table 3.5. *Changes in the Family Distribution of Income and Their Decomposition, All-households Model, 1964–72*

Variable	Notation	Total change[a] 1964–68	Total change[a] 1968–72	Percentage change[a] 1964–68	Percentage change[a] 1968–72
Total Gini	G_y	0.0052	−0.0363	1.6	−11.1
Reallocation effect	R	—	—	—	—
Functional distribution effect	D	—	—	—	—
Factor Gini effect	B	—	—	—	—
Agricultural Gini	G_a	−0.1726	−0.0712	−48.7	−39.2
Nonagricultural Gini	G_x	0.0389	−0.0422	12.8	−12.0
Property Gini	G_π	0.0111	−0.0363	2.5	−7.9
Wage Gini	G_w	0.0567	−0.0328	24.0	−11.2

— Not applicable. See note a.

Source: Calculated from table 3.2.

a. Actual changes in G_y, G_a, G_x, G_π, and G_w. The changes do not equal the sum of the three effects for three reasons: decomposition equations (3.16) and (3.22) do not include the quantitatively small, unallocable category of miscellaneous income (for urban households a small amount of agricultural income is also neglected); there is a small nonlinearity error there is a need to make discrete approximations to continuous changes.

tive factors or the result of the offsetting effects of positive and negative causative factors. Concentrating first on the all-households model in table 3.5, the major quantitative finding is:

FINDING 3.4. *For all households the (net) factor Gini effect was the dominant causative factor of change in total G_y both before and after 1968.*

- *Before 1968 the highly favorable agricultural Gini effect (−0.0475 or −183 percent) overwhelmed the highly unfavorable nonagricultural Gini effect (+0.0272 or +105 percent) to cause the slight worsening of G_y (+0.0052 or +1.6 percent for 1964–68).*
- *After 1968 the still favorable agricultural Gini effect (−0.0108 or −30 percent) reinforced the newly favorable nonagricultural Gini effect (−0.0267 or −75 percent) to cause the significant improvement of G_y (−0.0363 or −11.1 percent for 1968–72).*

Total estimated change[b]		*Percentage distribution of estimated change*[b]		*Notation*	*Variable*
1964–68	*1968–72*	*1964–68*	*1968–72*		
−0.0259[c]	−0.0356[c]	100[c]	100[c]	G_y	Total Gini
−0.0052	0.0084	−20	24	R	Reallocation effect
−0.0004	−0.0065	−2	−18	D	Functional distribution effect
−0.0203[d]	−0.0375[d]	−78[d]	−105[d]	B	Factor Gini effect
−0.0475	−0.0108	−183	−30	G_a	Agricultural Gini
0.0272[e]	−0.0267[e]	105[e]	−75[e]	G_x	Nonagricultural Gini
0.0027	−0.0101	10	−28	G_π	Property Gini
0.0245	−0.0166	95	−47	G_w	Wage Gini

b. Based on decomposition equations (3.16) and (3.22). Consequently the values generally differ slightly from those for actual changes and in rare instances may even change sign.
c. Equal to the sum of the three effects.
d. Equal to the sum of changes in the agricultural and nonagricultural Ginis.
e. Equal to the sum of changes in the property and wage Ginis.

Investigation of the possible causes for the pattern of changes in the overall Gini coefficient leads to the conclusion that the nonagricultural Gini [G_x] followed a pronounced inverse U-shaped pattern. That is, the actual G_x rose by 12.8 percent in the four years before the turning point and declined by 12 percent in the four years after the turning point. It nevertheless was consistently overwhelmed by the combination of a highly favorable agricultural Gini effect, a moderately favorable reallocation effect, and a slightly favorable functional distribution effect. The result was that the Gini coefficient of total income [G_y] increased by a mere 1.6 percent before 1968. After the turning point that signaled the end of the labor surplus condition, the nonagricultural Gini effect became highly favorable and was reinforced by the still highly favorable agricultural Gini effect and an even more favorable functional distribution effect. These effects overwhelmingly offset the unfavorable reallocation effect. The reason is that once a lot of labor had been reallocated

Table 3.6. *Changes in the Family Distribution of Income and Their Decomposition, Rural-households Model, 1966–72*

Variable	Notation	Total change[a] 1966–68	Total change[a] 1968–72	Percentage change[a] 1966–68	Percentage change[a] 1968–72
Total Gini	G_y	−0.0358[c]	0.0002	−11.2[c]	0.1
Reallocation effect	R	—	—	—	—
Functional distribution effect	D	—	—	—	—
Factor Gini effect	B	—	—	—	—
Agricultural Gini	G_a	−0.0162	−0.0389	−4.1	−11.5
Nonagricultural Gini	G_x	−0.0310	0.0509	−12.9	24.3
Property Gini	G_π	−0.0569	0.0702	−17.0	25.3
Wage Gini	G_w	−0.0053	0.0498	−2.7	26.5

— Not applicable. See note a to table 3.5.

Note: It should be recalled that the data do not permit a detailed factor decomposition for rural households for 1964. Consequently the decomposition results are for 1966 onward.

Source: Calculated from table 3.2.

a. See note a to table 3.5.

by 1968, agricultural income switched from being a type one income for all households to a type two income. Consequently the weight of agriculture was reduced, and it no longer served as an FID equalizer. The result was that FID showed a highly significant improvement: the overall G_y declined by 11.1 percent in the short span of four years. The combination of these effects led to the very mild Kuznets effect observed for the overall time pattern of G_y.

All this evidence implies that the Kuznets effect is a complex phenomenon that needs to be disaggregated. In its extreme form, it really is relevant only to the nonagricultural sector. In countries where agricultural activity is important—as it is in Taiwan and in most LDCs—growth does not necessarily conflict with equity, even before the turning point has been reached.[20]

20. This observed, mild, overall Kuznets effect could also be examined in relation to the partially offsetting time patterns of the Ginis, taken separately, of urban and rural households (see figure 3.3 below). Before the turning point

Total estimated change[b]		*Percentage distribution of estimated change*[b]		*Notation*	*Variable*
1966–68	*1968–72*	*1966–68*	*1968–72*		
−0.0367[d]	−0.0120[d]	100[d]	100[d]	G_y	Total Gini
−0.0151	−0.0133	−41	−111	R	Reallocation effect
−0.0041	−0.0013	−11	−11	D	Functional distribution effect
−0.0175[e]	0.0026[e]	−48[e]	22[e]	B	Factor Gini effect
−0.0107	−0.0205	−29	−171	G_a	Agricultural Gini
−0.0068[f]	0.0231[f]	−19[f]	193[f]	G_x	Nonagricultural Gini
−0.0057	0.0070	−16	59	G_π	Property Gini
−0.0011	0.0161	−3	134	G_w	Wage Gini

b. See note b to table 3.5.
c. Comparable figures for 1964–68 are −0.0238 and −7.7 percent.
d. Equal to the sum of the three effects.
e. Equal to the sum of changes in the agricultural and nonagricultural Ginis.
f. Equal to the sum of changes in the property and wage Ginis.

FINDING 3.5. *For rural households the favorable reallocation effect had a quantitative significance almost equal to or greater than that of the factor Gini effect.*

- *Before 1968 the favorable reallocation effect (−41 percent) reinforced the favorable factor Gini effect (−48 percent) to cause the significant improvement of G_y^r (−0.0358 or −11.2 percent for 1966–68).*
- *After 1968 the highly favorable reallocation effect (−111 percent) overwhelmed the unfavorable factor Gini effect (+22 percent) to cause the very modest deterioration of G_y^r (+0.0002 or −0.1 percent for 1968–72).*

---

the favorable FID trend for rural households tends to offset the slightly unfavorable FID trend for urban households; after the turning point the opposite is true. This approach relates more to the method of segmentation of total family income by homogeneous groups, as suggested by Theil—a method which is more difficult to link directly to growth-related phenomena. Henri Theil, *Statistical Decomposition Analysis* (Amsterdam: North-Holland, 1972).

Table 3.7. *Changes in the Family Distribution of Income and Their Decomposition, Urban-households Model, 1966–72*

Variable	Notation	Total change[a] 1966–68	Total change[a] 1968–72	Percentage change[a] 1966–68	Percentage change[a] 1968–72
Total Gini	G_y	0.0060[c]	−0.0480	1.9[c]	−14.6
Reallocation effect	R	—	—	—	—
Functional distribution effect	D	—	—	—	—
Factor Gini effect	B	—	—	—	—
Agricultural Gini	G_a	—	—	—	—
Nonagricultural Gini	G_x	−0.0007	−0.0460	−0.2	−14.0
Property Gini	G_π	0.0053	−0.0372	1.3	−8.8
Wage Gini	G_w	−0.0065	−0.0383	−2.3	−14.0

— Not applicable. See note a to table 3.5.

Note: It should be recalled that the data do not permit a detailed factor decomposition for urban households for 1964. Consequently the decomposition results are for 1966 onward.

Source: Calculated from table 3.2.

Thus the reallocation effect is quantitatively most important for rural households simply because of the greater share of agricultural income in the total income of those households. The favorable impact of the reallocation effect (−41 percent) before the turning point was consistently reinforced by the factor Gini effect (−48 percent) and the functional distribution effect (−11 percent). The consistently favorable impact of all three effects thus gave rise to a substantial improvement in rural FID before the turning point: the inequality of rural income [G_y^r] declined by 11.2 percent during 1966–68. For the 1968–72 period after the turning point, the nonagricultural Gini increased by 24.3 percent; the agricultural Gini declined by 11.5 percent. This pattern reduced the importance of the factor Gini effect to 22 percent, but by this time it was unfavorable to FID. It nevertheless was overwhelmed by the increased importance of the still favorable reallocation effect (−111 percent) and the still favorable functional distribution effect (−11 percent). Consequently there was almost no worsening of rural FID. The inequality of rural income (G_y^r) increased by only 0.1 percent.

Estimated change[b]		*Percentage distribution of estimated change*[b]			
1966–68	*1968–72*	*1966–68*	*1968–72*	*Notation*	*Variable*
0.0013[d]	−0.0442[d]	100[d]	100[d]	G_y	Total Gini
—	—	—	—	R	Reallocation effect
0.0035	−0.0100	269	−23	D	Functional distribution effect
−0.0022[e]	−0.0342[e]	−169[e]	−77[e]	B	Factor Gini effect
—	—	—	—	G_a	Agricultural Gini
−0.0022[f]	−0.0342[f]	−169[f]	−77[f]	G_x	Nonagricultural Gini
0.0017	−0.0125	131	−28	G_π	Property Gini
−0.0039	−0.0217	−300	−49	G_w	Wage Gini

a. See note a to table 3.5.
b. See note b to table 3.5.
c. Comparable figures for 1964–68 are −0.0008 and 0.2 percent.
d. Equal to the sum of the two effects.
e. Equal to the nonagricultural Gini.
f. Equal to the sum of changes in the property and wage Ginis.

FINDING 3.6. *For urban households the functional distribution effect had a quantitative significance greater than or almost equal to that of the factor Gini effect.*

- *Before 1968 the highly unfavorable functional distribution effect (+269 percent) overwhelmed the moderately favorable factor Gini effect (−169 percent) to cause the moderate worsening of* G_y^u *(+0.0060 or +1.9 percent for 1966–68).*
- *After 1968 the moderately favorable functional distribution effect (−23 percent) reinforced the favorable factor Gini effect (−77 percent) to cause the significant improvement of* G_y^u *(−0.0480 or −14.6 percent for 1968–72).*

Analysis of the pattern of urban FID alone shows that the time pattern of the functional distribution effect reflects the time pattern of the inequality of urban income [G_y^u]. The functional distribution effect is important to the pattern of distribution of urban household income because, as seen in the foregoing discussion, the main forces affecting changes in the share of nonagricultural income in the total income of urban households are capital deepening and technology bias and intensity. The highly unfavorable functional distribution effect before the turning point was softened by the very favorable factor Gini effect, which moderated any worsening of urban FID. The net result was that the inequality of urban income [G_y^u] increased by only 1.9 percent during 1966–68. With the exhaustion of surplus labor after the turning point, the functional distribution effect became favorable to urban FID. The newly dominant and still favorable factor Gini effect (−77 percent) reinforced the newly favorable functional distribution effect (−23 percent). Consequently urban FID tremendously improved. The inequality of urban income [G_y^u] declined by 14.6 percent. These time trends lead to a time pattern of urban FID that is slightly inverse U-shaped.

The reader may have noted some diffidence in the interpretation of the empirical evidence in this section. The reasons are these: Slight changes in the magnitude of the Gini coefficient do not warrant stronger statements in the absence of statistically designed tests of significance. In the pioneering field of analyzing the distribution of income, reliable methods for assessing the significance of variations in data do not yet exist. It must thus be candidly admitted that quantitative findings rely for some of their strength on qualitative findings based on heuristic judgments about their significance in relation to growth.

Impact of Growth on FID: Qualitative Aspects

In this section the findings about the impact of growth on FID are further analyzed and interpreted in relation to the reallocation effect, the functional distribution effect, and the factor Gini effect. First the changes in the total and sectoral Gini coefficients are described. Then the impact of the reallocation effect, functional distribution effect, and factor Gini effect on these underlying phenomena are further analyzed on the basis of findings in the preceding section. The theoretical underpinnings of this analysis are discussed in chapter eleven.

The pattern of Gini coefficients over time

The following statements can be made about the behavior of the Gini coefficients for all households, rural households, and urban households during the 1964–72 period:

FINDING 3.7a. *For all households G_y increased slightly between 1964 and 1968, but consistently and markedly declined thereafter.*

FINDING 3.7b. *For urban households G_y^u showed the same time pattern as that for all households, but was slightly more pronounced.*

FINDING 3.7c. *For rural households G_y^r significantly declined between 1964 and 1968, but remained relatively constant thereafter.*

These observations underscore the arrival of the turning point in the family distribution of income at some time around 1968. We consider this conclusion to be highly significant in the light of our previous work on Taiwan: as was indicated in chapter one, the period around 1968 was independently established as something of a landmark in Taiwan's development path.[21] That year marked the end of labor surplus and the beginning of labor scarcity. It is interesting to note, for all households and urban households, that the distribution of income improved once conditions of labor scarcity arrived and real wages began to rise sharply. Of greater importance, however, is the observation that FID did not worsen very much for any of the three models, even during the period of unusually rapid growth in the early and mid-1960s. As already noted, the Kuznets effect is a complex phenomenon mainly relevant to the nonagricultural sector. Examination of the comparative magnitudes of the urban and rural Gini coefficients provides additional insights about this phenomenon.

The comparative magnitudes of total and sectoral Gini coefficients

How do the sectoral Gini coefficients for rural and urban households compare with the total Gini coefficient for all households?

FINDING 3.8a. *Before the turning point the urban Gini [G_y^u] was greater than the overall Gini [G_y], which was greater than the rural Gini [G_y^r].*

21. See Fei and Ranis, "Model of Growth and Employment," and Mo-huan Hsing, *Industrialization and Trade Policies: The Case of Taiwan* (London: Oxford University Press for the OECD Development Centre, 1971).

FINDING 3.8b. *After the turning point the overall Gini* [G_y] *was greater than the rural Gini* [G_y^r], *which generally was greater than the urban Gini* [G_y^u].

Finding 3.8a implies that industrialization was more rapid in urban centers. Consequently the extent of urban dualism was greater than its rural counterpart before the turning point: the concentration of assets was more substantial; the variations in the scale of production and heterogeneity of labor were wider. Furthermore, despite the substantial inequality of the distribution of agricultural income among rural households, the inequality of rural income [G_y^r] was less than the inequality of urban income [G_y^u]. This pattern suggests that modernization and nonagricultural activity had not yet reached rural areas in a big way.

After the turning point—that is, by 1971—the inequality of rural income [G_y^r] became larger than the inequality of urban income [G_y^u] (see figure 3.3a). Finding 4.17 thus implies that rural areas caught up with urban areas in their degree of modernization and their concomitant rise in structural dualism and FID inequality just when the effect of urban dualism on FID was declining.[22]

Additional data on the inequality of income [G_y] for all households in 1964 and 1968, broken down by urban, semiurban, and rural location, can be used to explore further this issue of how and when modernization occurred (table 3.8).[23] For all households in both years, the results show that the inequality of urban income was greater than the inequality of semiurban income which, in turn, was greater than the inequality of rural income. In addition, the inequality of nonfarm income in the three locations was greater than the inequality of farm income. This evidence implies that, in

22. Because the sectoral Ginis in figure 3.3 are smaller than the total Gini, intrasectoral income inequality is less than intersectoral inequality. In the terminology of the Theil index, the large G_y is the result of the strength of intergroup income variations, not intragroup income variations. See Theil, *Statistical Decomposition Analysis*.

23. The rural and urban breakdowns, available only for these two years, refer to the precise location of households and therefore are not exact equivalents of the "rural" and "urban" categories, which earlier were used generally and which include small amounts of semiurban dwellers. The urban households are almost exclusively nonfarm households, as are the great majority of semiurban households. Most rural households are farm households. Also see finding 3.2.

Table 3.8. *Gini Coefficients Based on Decile Population Groups for Urban, Semiurban, and Rural Households, 1964 and 1968*

Category of household	Share of households 1964	Share of households 1968	Share of income 1964	Share of income 1968	Gini coefficient 1964	Gini coefficient 1968	Percentage change in Gini coefficient, 1964–68
Nonfarm and farm households							
All households	1.0000	1.0000	1.0000	1.0000	0.3208	0.3259	1.59
Urban households	0.3000	0.3243	0.3473	0.4348	0.3185	0.3230	1.41
Semiurban households	0.3435	0.3245	0.3381	0.2852	0.3175	0.3119	1.76
Rural households	0.3565	0.3332	0.3146	0.2800	0.3115	0.2940	−5.62
Nonfarm households							
All households	1.0000	1.0000	1.0000	1.0000	0.3288	0.3296	0.24
Urban households	n.a.	0.4819	n.a.	0.5625	n.a.	0.3259	n.a.
Semiurban households	n.a.	0.3119	n.a.	0.2732	n.a.	0.3135	n.a.
Rural households	n.a.	0.2063	n.a.	0.1643	n.a.	0.3022	n.a.
Farm households							
All households	1.0000	1.0000	1.0000	1.0000	0.3080	0.2842	−7.73
Urban households	n.a.	n.a.	n.a.	n.a.	n.a.	n.a.	n.a.
Semiurban households	n.a.	0.3519	n.a.	0.3214	n.a.	0.2817	n.a.
Rural households	n.a.	0.6088	n.a.	0.6303	n.a.	0.2863	n.a.

n.a. Not available.

Note: The urban, semiurban, and rural categories of household are based on the classification used by the DBGAS in its household surveys. The categories are not to be confused with the categories "urban" and "rural" (which include semiurban dwellings) used elsewhere in this volume.

Sources: Calculated from DGBAS, *Report on the Survey of Family Income and Expenditure,* 1964 and 1968.

moving from urban to semiurban to rural areas, the degree of modernization and the inequality of FID decrease. Thus modernization probably occurs first in the largest urban centers and then slowly permeates semiurban and rural areas.

Because the original urban-households model includes a small proportion of semiurban and rural households, the results given in table 3.8, disaggregated into urban, semiurban, and rural households, can also be used to refine the test of the relevance of the Kuznets hypothesis to the nonagricultural sector. Between 1964 and 1968 the G_y for urban households worsened; that of rural households improved. Further comparison shows that the change in the G_y for urban households, which earned all their income from nonagricultural sources, was much larger than that for all nonfarm households. Thus the observed worsening of the overall G_y was mostly the result of the Kuznets effect of modern urban nonagricultural activity on FID. Nevertheless, even where FID worsened because of the Kuznets effect, that worsening was so mild as to be insignificant. The nonfarm Gini increased by 0.24 percent; the purely nonagricultural urban Gini increased by 1.41 percent. But this worsening of urban FID was ameliorated by corresponding improvements in the semiurban Gini and the rural Gini. Consequently the Kuznets effect on the overall G_y was very mild. This pattern suggests two conclusions. First, the more that nonagricultural activity is urban-centered, the more the Kuznets effect is significant. Second, where agricultural activity is important and industrialization is decentralized, as they are in Taiwan, growth need not conflict with FID, even before the turning point.

Throughout the eight years under observation, the level of the Gini coefficient is unusually favorable, certainly by LDC standards, and it appears that things really do not have to get worse before they can get better. Because this result flies in the face of much general empirical evidence for postwar LDCs, as well as the theoretical arguments of Lewis, Kuznets, and others, it should be of considerable interest to see what emerges from an attempt to dig a little deeper into the causation of changes in FID with the help of tools developed earlier in this chapter. In summary, our evidence does support the existence of a close relation between growth and FID, with marked improvements in FID after the turning point, as we might have suspected, but without any marked deterioration before, as we might not have suspected. We will now explore these issues further, with particular attention to the three types of effects we have identified.[24]

24. The mildness of the Kuznets effect, coupled with the low level of G_y by international standards, was a major motivation for this study. See for example Hollis Chenery and others, *Redistribution with Growth* (London: Oxford University Press, 1974).

The reallocation effect

As already noted, the shift of the economic center of gravity from agricultural to nonagricultural activities, a reallocation effect proxied by the declining share of agricultural income in total income, clearly is a critical feature of development in the dualistic economy.

FINDING 3.9. *For rural households and all households the distributive share of agricultural income [ϕ_a] consistently declined throughout the entire period.*

The speed of this shift, whether measured by income generated or labor force, accelerated during the phase of export substitution that began in about 1961.[25] During the 1960s Taiwan's nonagricultural labor force increased by a remarkable 80 percent, compared with a rise of 35 percent during the 1950s. The agricultural labor force increased by only 5 percent during the 1950s and 4 percent during the 1960s. In the latter decade the agricultural labor force was partly reallocated to (absorbed by) labor-intensive, export-oriented industries and services in the cities, but partly also to spatially dispersed rural industries and services, which rapidly emerged as an additional source of income for rural families.

By the end of the 1960s the share of agricultural labor in the labor force had declined from about a half to only a third. In addition, and of considerable importance, those remaining in the agricultural labor force spent more and more of their time on nonagricultural activities. By 1964, when the DGBAS surveys began, rural industries and services already were important sources of rural family income. They subsequently assumed an even larger role. In 1964 the combined share of rural wage and property income [$\phi_w^r + \phi_\pi^r$] in the total income of rural families [Y^r] was 33 percent; in 1972 it was 53 percent.[26]

25. Such labor reallocation is well proxied by ϕ_a. Although the agricultural labor force has not substantially increased since the beginning of the 1950s, the increase in the total labor force caused the share of the agricultural labor force to decline tremendously. See Shirley W. Y. Kuo, "A Study of Factors Contributing to Labor Absorption in Taiwan, 1954–1971" (paper read at the Conference on Population and Economic Development in Taiwan, December 29, 1975–January 2, 1976; processed).

26. This increase is quite remarkable by any international LDC standard. The relative importance of nonagricultural rural activity can also be seen in its value

The steady rise in the nonfarm income of farm families began in the 1950s. The JCRR surveys of farm-family income conducted between 1952 and 1967 show a continuous rise in the distributive share of nonfarm income in total family income from 22 percent in 1952 to 37 percent in 1957, 41 percent in 1962, and 42 percent in 1967.[27] Moreover the proportion of farm families who considered themselves to be part-time farmers rose from 52 percent in 1960 to 68 percent in 1965 and 72 percent in 1970.[28] By 1968 rural by-employment had become the dominant form of rural labor reallocation and the dominant source of rural family income. Although the total agricultural labor force remained relatively constant, the share of agricultural income in total income continued to decline rapidly.

Even during the 1950s this steady rise of the share of nonfarm income had considerable importance as an equalizer of rural FID. The surveys of farm-family income conducted by the JCRR show that the poorest families, proxied by those with the least land (less than 0.5 chia), earned 62 percent of their total income from nonfarm sources in 1957, 74 percent in 1962, and 66 percent in 1967. Corresponding figures for the wealthiest families, proxied by those with the most land (more than 2 chia), were 25 percent in 1957, 25 percent in 1962, and 26 percent in 1967.[29] In addition, cross-sectional evidence for 1967 indicates that the proportion of families who considered themselves to be part-time farmers increased as farm

added, which averaged about 20 percent of that of urban industry during the period. See International Labour Organisation (ILO), "Sharing in Development: A Programme of Employment, Equity and Growth for the Philippines," in *Special Paper no. 9 on Medium-Scale and Small-Scale Industry* (Geneva: ILO, 1974), pp. 539–68.

27. JCRR, "Taiwan Farm Income Survey of 1967—with a Brief Comparison with 1952, 1957, and 1962," *Economic Digest Series*, no. 20 (Taipei; JCRR, 1970); idem, "A Summary Report of Farm Income of Taiwan in 1957 in Comparison with 1952," *Economic Digest Series*, no. 13 (Taipei: JCRR, 1959). Because of differences in definitions, the values of the shares differ somewhat from those of the DGBAS household surveys for the nearest years, 1966 and 1967. The trend nevertheless is unmistakable.

28. Taipei Provincial Government, Committee on the Census of Agriculture, *Report of the Census of Agriculture*, 1960, 1965, and 1970.

29. Further disaggregation also shows for poorer families that relatively more of that nonfarm income is wage income, not property income. See below for more on the functional distribution of nonagricultural income. JCRR, "Taiwan Farm Income Survey of 1967."

size decreased—from 51 percent of families having more than 2 chia to 84 percent of families having less than 0.5 chia.[30]

The seeds for this rapid shift in the economic center of gravity were planted in the 1950s, when locationally dispersed rural industries began to grow and meet the need and desire for supplementary farm income. Table 3.9 shows the growth and distribution of the number of establishments between 1951 and 1971 grouped into cities, semiurban cities, semiurban prefectures, rural prefectures, and prefectures that are a mixture of urban, semiurban, and rural according to definitions adopted by the DGBAS for the household survey in 1964. This table reveals not only that the initial distribution of nonagricultural establishments was remarkably dispersed in Taiwan, but that growth rates also were quite evenly distributed from 1951 onward.[31] This table also shows that rural areas enjoyed the highest growth rate over the entire period, a remarkable contrast with the performance of most LDCs.

Male labor in rural infrastructure and female labor in home-based handicrafts oriented toward the domestic market exemplified the early forms of nonfarm income. But with the accelerated growth and industrialization of the urban sector and with the new export orientation of government policies in the 1960s, modernization slowly permeated the rural sector. The previously unorganized small handicrafts were organized into small factories, which increasingly modernized in response to export demand.[32] This industrialization of the rural sector was accompanied by substantial growth in agricultural productivity, especially when high-yielding varieties were superimposed on an already productive and research-oriented agricultural sector. With agricultural productivity rising, farmers could spend more time on nonagricultural activities. Taiwan's experience thus shows that fostering a spatially dispersed industrialization pattern, in addition to being beneficial for growth, is a practical way to improve FID for rural households.

30. Derived from the JCRR farm-family income in Y. H. Yu, "Economic Analysis of Full-time and Part-time Farms in Taiwan" (Taiwan Provincial Chung Hsing University, 1969; processed).

31. For example, the three largest cities combined went from 24 percent to 26 percent of total establishments over the twenty-year period. This is in sharp contrast with the growth of establishments in Thailand or the Philippines.

32. Mo-huan Hsing, *Relationship between Agricultural and Industrial Development in Taiwan during 1950–59* (Taipei: JCRR, 1960); Edward S. Kirby, *Rural Progress in Taiwan* (Taipei: JCRR, 1955).

Table 3.9. *Establishments in Taiwan, by Location, 1951–71*

Location[a]	Number of establishments 1951	Growth in number of establishments[b] (percent) 1951–61	1961–68	1968–71	1951–71
Cities	2,959	419.8	854.2	1,164.3	2,438.3
Semiurban cities	1,235	395.2	755.7	903.4	2,054.3
Semiurban prefectures	2,876	490.1	877.0	861.1	2,228.2
Rural prefectures	2,024	562.2	1,063.6	915.6	2,541.4
Mixed urban, semiurban, and rural prefectures	2,517	458.0	804.7	766.8	2,029.5
All Taiwan	12,211	472.3	884.5	931.0	2,287.8

Source: Industrial and Commercial Census of Taiwan (ICCT), *General Report, 1971 Industrial and Commercial Census of Taiwan and Fukien Area,* 7 (?) vols. (Taipei: ICCT, 1972), vol. 1, table 6.

a. Based on DGBAS definitions in 1964.

b. Based on number in operation at the end of the year.

What, then, can be concluded about the reallocation effect?

FINDING 3.10a. *For rural households the reallocation of labor from agricultural activity to rural industries and services improved* FID *equity throughout the entire period (see finding 3.2b, finding 3.5, and relation 3.5).*

FINDING 3.10b. *For all households the reallocation of labor from agricultural to nonagricultural production improved* FID *equity before the turning point and worsened* FID *equity after the turning point (see finding 3.2b, finding 3.4, and relation 3.5).*

The functional distribution effect

Turn now to the functional distribution effect, which is caused by variations in the ratio of the wage share in nonagricultural production to the property share $[\phi_w/\phi_\pi]$ and hence is a proxy for labor intensity. The time paths of that ratio for all three models are given in figure 3.5.

FINDING 3.11a. *The relative share ratio* $[\phi_w/\phi_\pi]$ *was higher for rural industries than for urban industries.*

Distribution of establishments (percent)				
1951	*1961*	*1968*	*1971*	*Location*[a]
24.2	21.5	22.8	25.8	Cities
10.1	8.5	8.6	9.1	Semiurban cities
23.6	24.4	23.7	22.9	Semiurban prefectures
21.5	25.6	25.7	23.9	Rural prefectures
20.6	20.0	19.2	18.3	Mixed urban, semiurban and rural prefectures
100.0	100.0	100.0	100.0	All Taiwan

Figure 3.5. *Ratio of the Wage Share in Nonagricultural Production to the Property Share, by Model, 1964–72*

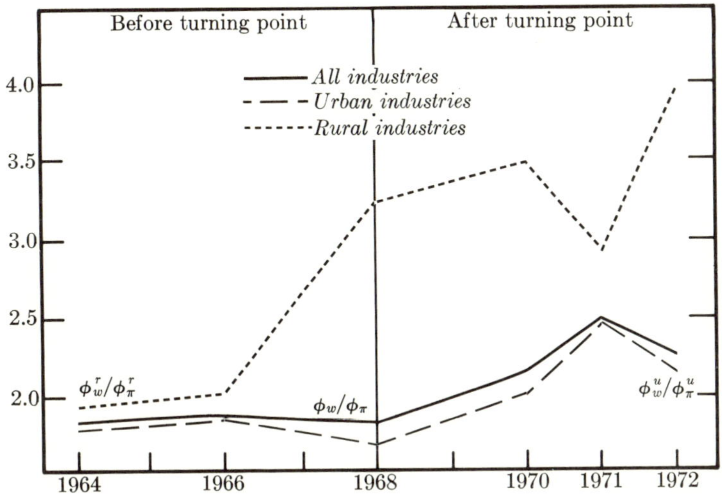

Source: Calculated from table 3.2.

Figure 3.6. *Ratio of Average Urban Income to Average Rural Income for Wage and Property Income, 1964–72*

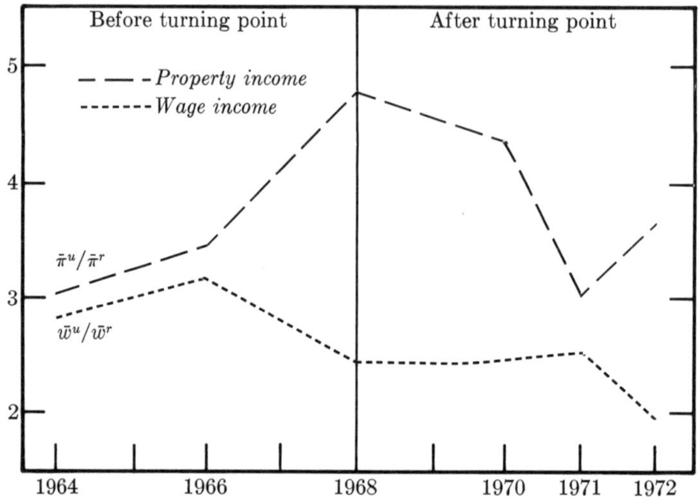

Source: Calculated from table 3.2.

FINDING 3.11b. *In both rural and urban industries ϕ_w exceeded ϕ_π—that is, $\phi_w^r/\phi_\pi^r > \phi_w^u/\phi_\pi^u > 1$.*

Finding 3.11a implies that industrial and service activities, under normal conditions of substitution-inelastic production functions, are more capital intensive in urban areas than in rural areas.[33] Figures compiled from the 1961 and 1971 censuses of industry and commerce substantiate the thesis that the ratio ϕ_w/ϕ_π is a good proxy for labor intensity (table 3.10). The results indicate, for almost

33. If p is the wage-profit or factor-price ratio applying to both sectors—that is, there are no factor-price distortions—and if K_r^* and K_u^* respectively are the capital-labor ratios for rural and urban nonagriculture, the inequality in finding 3.11a implies that $p/K_r^* > p/K_u^*$ or $K_u^* > K_r^*$. That is, for the same p, the capital per worker in urban industries is larger, which is the conventional definition of relatively high capital intensity.

Table 3.10. *Capital Intensity, by Region and Sector, 1961 and 1971*

Year and sector	*Fixed assets per employee (thousands of N.T. dollars)* All Taiwan	Five largest cities[a]	Rural prefectures[b]	Ratio of all Taiwan to rural prefectures	Ratio of five largest cities to rural prefectures
1961					
Manufacturing	48.35	45.13	49.97	0.97	0.90
Construction	37.64	58.65	19.93	1.89	2.95
Utilities	629.94	618.34	664.28	0.95	0.93
Trade	28.85	40.15	21.08	1.37	1.91
Services	61.91	98.00	26.30	2.95	4.67
1971					
Manufacturing	96.09	124.57	63.71	1.51	1.96
Construction	32.43	52.99	11.45	2.83	4.62
Utilities	1,865.79	2,149.79	388.96	4.80	5.52
Trade	66.70	79.47	50.71	1.32	1.57
Services	127.27	180.57	43.43	2.93	4.58

Sources: ICCT, *General Report, Industrial and Commercial Census of Taiwan,* 1961 and 1971; figures for 1971 were compiled by Samuel Ho, *Economic Development of Taiwan: 1860–1970* (New Haven: Yale University Press, 1978).

a. The five cities are Taipei, Taichiung, Kaoshiung, Keelung, and Tainan.

b. The rural prefectures are Miaoli, Taichiung, Changhwa, Nantou, Yunlin, Chiayi, Tainan, Kaoshiung, and Pengtung.

every category of nonagricultural activity in both years, that the capital per employee was higher for urban areas (the five largest cities) than for all Taiwan and for rural areas. Moreover the two marginal exceptions, manufacturing and utilities in 1961, can be easily explained. First, sugar refining, which is large in scale, intensive in capital, and located in rural areas, played a substantial role in total manufacturing in 1961. If that and other such processing are excluded from manufacturing, the general pattern holds. Second, the capital intensity of utilities in 1961 was apparently affected by the installation of the country's largest power plant in rural Nantou Prefecture in that year.

Finding 4.22 indicates that the Gini coefficient of wage income [G_w] always received a heavier weight than that of property income [G_π] (see figure 3.5). Moreover:

FINDING 3.12a. *For urban industries and services, the time path of*

ϕ^u_w/ϕ^u_π was mildly U-shaped—that is, it decreased before the turning point in 1968 and increased thereafter.

FINDING 3.12b. *For rural industries and services, the time path of ϕ^r_w/ϕ^r_π increased, except for one year.*

The explanation of these findings can be based on growth theory (see relations 3.1 and 3.2). Given the relative stability of real wages before 1968, relation 3.1 implies that small-scale rural industries and services responded more to the stimulation of low wages in the adoption of labor-using technology than did the large-scale urban industries and services, which tend to concentrate on a higher intensity of innovation (see the growing divergence in figure 3.5). Thus, contrary to the arguments of Lewis and others, labor's share [ϕ_w] can rise because of rapid increases in the total number of employees and the number of hours worked per employee, even during the phase when labor supply is unlimited and wages are more or less constant. This conclusion also implies that the more active promotion of labor-using technology could lead to a more favorable impact of growth on FID, even on urban FID, before the turning point.

After the turning point, the ratio of the wage share to the property share [ϕ_w/ϕ_π] generally increased in both sectors. According to relation 3.2, rapidly rising real wages accompanied by capital deepening caused that increase, which was somewhat more pronounced in the urban sector. In summary, the impact of the functional distribution effect on FID can be stated as follows:

FINDING 3.13a. *Before the turning point the strong labor-using bias of technology change in rural industries contributed to FID equity for rural households, and the weak labor-using bias of technology change in urban industries made a modest contribution to FID equity for urban households.*

FINDING 3.13b. *After the turning point capital deepening and the labor-using bias both contributed to FID equity for all three models.*

The factor Gini effect

The factor Gini effect, defined in equations (3.16c) and (3.22d), captures the impact of changes in the factor Gini coefficients of wage, property, and agricultural income on the overall Gini coefficient [G_y]. What are the comparative magnitudes of the factor Gini coefficients in each of the three models? What are the longer term or trend characteristics of these Gini coefficients? What are the shorter term or transition characteristics of these Gini coefficients and their impact on G_y? The findings related to these questions will be discussed first for wage and property income, then for agricultural income.

In general:

FINDING 3.14a. *Every Gini in the set* $(G_w, G_w^u, G_w^r) <$ *any Gini in the set* $(G_\pi, G_\pi^u, G_\pi^r)$.

FINDING 3.14b. *In the set* (G_w, G_w^u, G_w^r), $G_w^u < G_w$ *and* $G_w^r < G_w$; *in the set* $(G_\pi, G_\pi^u, G_\pi^r)$, $G_\pi^u < G_\pi$ *and* $G_\pi^r < G_\pi$.

FINDING 3.14c. $G_w^r < G_w^u$ *and* $G_\pi^r < G_\pi^u$.

The economic significance of finding 3.14a—that every wage Gini generally was less than every property Gini—is that it strengthens the intrasectoral conclusion of finding 3.1a. Not only was the inequality of wage income [G_w] less than the inequality of property income [G_π]; the inequality of rural wage income [G_w^r] was less than that of rural property income [G_π^r], and the inequality of urban wage income [G_w^u] was less than that of urban property income [G_π^u]. Thus it again is evident, more concretely now, that the unequal distribution of property ownership contributed far more to FID inequality than its small distributive share might imply; wage income, which had by far the largest distributive share, contributed less to FID inequality than its share might imply. This conclusion can be further illustrated by figures 3.7, 3.8, and 3.9, which show the relative income shares of the highest 10 percent of the population to the lowest 10 percent. The results indicate that the ratio of property shares was about double the ratio of total incomes and treble the ratio of wage shares.

The economic explanation of finding 3.14b—that sectoral Gini coefficients for wage and property income were less than total Gini coefficients for wage and property income—resides in the substantial gap in average wage and profit income between the rich and poor groups of a segmented population. A numerical example can illuminate this gap. Suppose in the extreme that the incomes of three low-income rural families and three high-income urban families are $(Y^r, Y^u) = (1, 1, 1)\ (10, 10, 10)$. Then the Gini coefficients for both rural households and urban households are zero, but the Gini coefficient for all households is very large. Thus the inequality for

Figure 3.7. *Ratio of the Total Income Share of the Top 10 Percent to That of the Bottom 10 Percent, by Model, 1964–72*

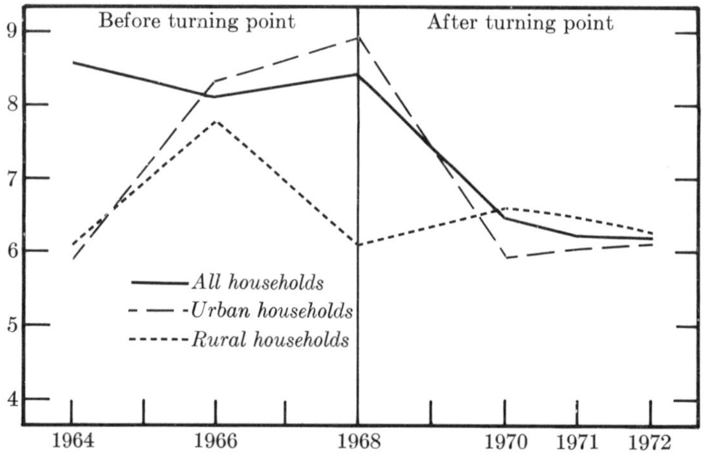

Source: Calculated from DGBAS, *Report on the Survey of Family Income and Expenditure,* 1964–72.

all households necessarily is greater than the inequality for urban and rural households alone. This pattern is also illustrated in figures 3.8 and 3.9, where the ratios of relative income shares of property and wage income generally are less for urban households and rural households than for all households.

The economic explanation of finding 3.14c—that rural Gini coefficients of wage and property income were less than urban Gini coefficients of wage and property income—is this: during most of the 1964–72 period, urban structural dualism, with its more substantial concentration of assets and wider variation in the scale of production, was more pronounced than its rural counterpart. Moreover the degree of labor force heterogeneity, based on education, skill, age, and sex, was greater in urban areas than in rural areas. This pattern led to a more unequal distribution of wage income in urban areas than in rural areas. By 1972, however, the urban wage Gini fell below the rural wage Gini, implying two patterns demonstrated earlier in this section. First, rural dualism related to the gradual modernization of rural industry may have been catching up

Figure 3.8. *Ratio of the Wage Income Share of the Top 10 Percent to That of the Bottom 10 Percent, by Model, 1964–72*

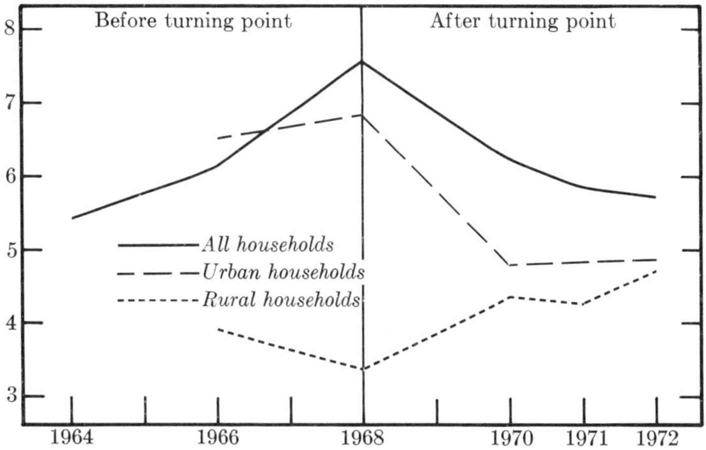

Source: Same as for figure 3.7.

with urban dualism just when urban dualism was beginning to decline. Second, modernization may thus be said to have penetrated the larger urban centers first and to a greater extent and to have permeated the smaller towns and rural areas only later.

The foregoing findings also provide an insight into the time patterns of the wage and property Gini coefficients of rural and urban households after the turning point (see figure 3.4):

FINDING 3.15a. *The gap between the total wage Gini* [G_w] *and the sectoral wage Ginis* [G_w^u *and* G_w^r] *tended to narrow, as did the gap between the total property Gini* [G_π] *and the sectoral property Ginis* [G_π^u *and* G_π^r].

FINDING 3.15b. *The gap between* G_w^r *and* G_w^u *tended to narrow, as did the gap between* G_π^r *and* G_π^u.

FINDING 3.15c. *Thus* (G_π, G_π^u, G_π^r) *tended to converge to a higher "limiting value" than* (G_w, G_w^u, G_w^r), *which also were converging (see findings 3.14a, 3.15a, and 3.15b).*

Figure 3.9. *Ratio of the Property Income Share of the Top 10 Percent to That of the Bottom 10 Percent, by Model, 1964–72*

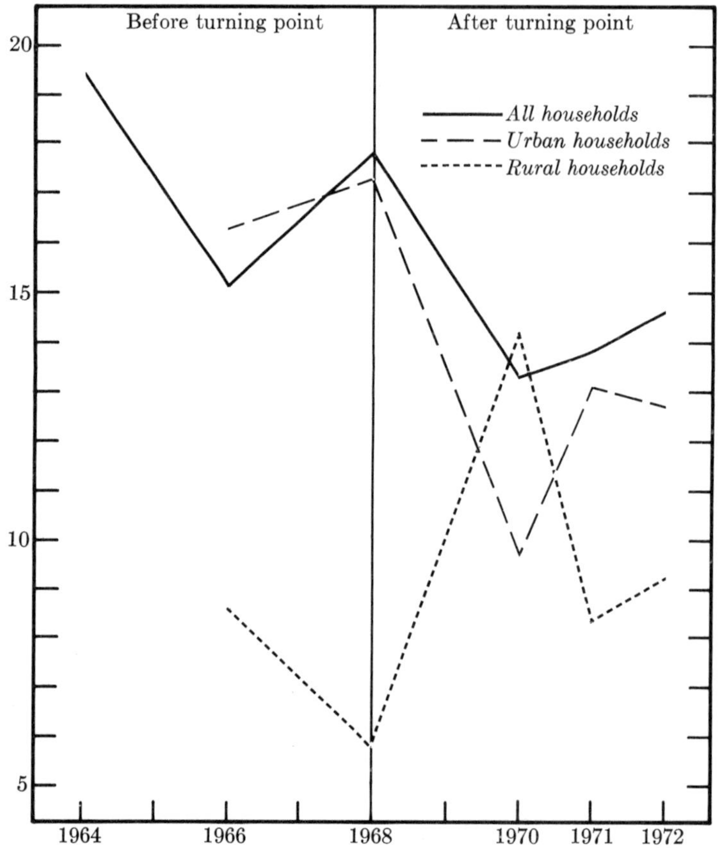

Source: Same as for figure 3.7.

The pattern of intersectoral gaps described in findings 3.15a and 3.15b reinforces the notion expressed in finding 3.14c that the difference in the economic forces affecting rural and urban industries tends to become less significant after the turning point, however pronounced that difference may have been earlier. That is, there is

Figure 3.10. *Ratio of the Agricultural Income Share of the Top 10 Percent to That of the Bottom 10 Percent, by Model, 1964–72*

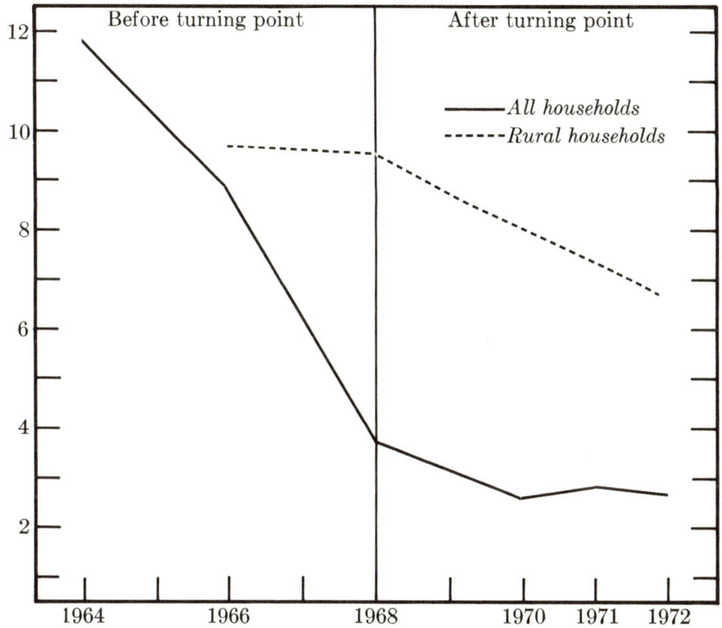

Source: Same as for figure 3.7.

a tendency toward convergence as rural industrialization catches up with urban industrialization. Consequently these gaps are transitional characteristics encountered in the earlier stages of transition growth. Finding 3.15c nevertheless suggests that the gap between the property Gini and the wage Gini, identified in finding 3.14c, tends to persist after the turning point. This pattern suggests that such a gap is a permanent feature of any economy.

FINDING 3.16. *There was a consistency between the patterns of wage and property Ginis both before and after 1968.*

FINDING 3.16a. *For rural households there was an overall U-shaped pattern: G^r_w and G^r_π slightly declined before 1968 and significantly increased thereafter.*

FINDING 3.16b. *For urban households there was an overall mildly inverse* U*-shaped pattern:* G^u_w *and* G^u_π *stayed constant or slightly increased before 1968 and consistently declined thereafter.*

FINDING 3.16c. *For all households there was an overall inverse* U*-shaped pattern:* G_w *and* G_π *slightly rose before 1968 and consistently declined thereafter.*

This consistency of behavior of the Gini coefficients of wage income and property income for each model is, in the opinion of the authors, the result of intrasectoral structural dualism. That is, in both urban and rural industries, some large-scale units hiring higher quality labor and receiving higher rates of return coexist with smaller scale units hiring unskilled labor and receiving lower rates of return. The more pronounced this structural dualism is, the higher are the values for the Gini coefficients of wage income and property income. If the time pattern of these Gini coefficients is inverse U-shaped, as it is for urban industries and for the whole economy (findings 3.16b and 3.16c), an initial increase in structural dualism in both gives way to its gradual elimination after the turning point. Finding 3.16a implies that dualism in rural industries initially is less pronounced than, and only later catches up with, the dualism in urban industries.

Findings 3.16a, 3.16b, and 3.16c facilitate the following summary statement about the impact of the nonagricultural factor Gini effect—that is, the factor Gini coefficient of wage and property income combined [G_x]—on G_y for the three models (also see tables 3.5, 3.6, and 3.7):

	Impact of nonagricultural Gini on:	*Before 1968*	*After 1968*
FINDING 3.17a.	G_y *for all households*	*Very unfavorable*	*Very favorable*
FINDING 3.17b.	G_y *for rural households*	*Slightly favorable*	*Very unfavorable*
FINDING 3.17c.	G_y *for urban households*	*Slightly favorable*	*Very favorable*

Finally, in examining the agricultural Gini effect traced by the curve of the Gini coefficient of agricultural income [G_a], it can be concluded that:

FINDING 3.18. *The factor Gini effect caused by agricultural income was always favorable—that is, it was favorable for the rural-households and all-households models both before and after 1968 (see table 3.8).*

Thus the distribution of agricultural income among rural families was consistently becoming more equal over time and favorably contributing to overall FID.

Summary and Conclusions

In this chapter a technique for the decomposition of Gini coefficients was developed to enable forging causal links between growth and the distribution of income in a developing country. It was shown that distribution, as measured by the Gini coefficient [G_y], is very much affected by the particular forces of growth that a country experiences. In Taiwan, for example, the turning point signifying the exhaustion of surplus labor brought about a marked difference in the behavior of the Gini coefficient. In analyzing the causation of the change in G_y and attempting to relate that change to growth, it helps to recognize that family income has a number of factor components which differ in type and in their impact on overall equity. The time path of G_y, affected by growth, can then be analyzed to determine the quantitative and qualitative impacts of three main effects: the reallocation effect, which captures changes in the share of agricultural income in total income; the functional distribution effect, which captures changes in the relative shares of property income and wage income; and the factor Gini effect, which captures changes in the inequality of factor income components. The quantitative and qualitative findings emerging from such analysis seem to support the notion that historical subphases of growth are relevant to the distribution of income as well.

It is self-evident that governments of most LDCS, despite their limited fiscal capacity, can directly affect the distribution of income through taxes and transfers. But the main inference to be drawn from the findings here is that a change in the growth path is likely to be the most effective method of tackling the maldistribution of income. The experience of Taiwan—with unusually low levels of Gini coefficients, with an unusually mild Kuznets effect over time, and with no significant transfers through welfare payments—bears out our conviction that significant and sustained changes in FID equity are mainly achievable through the modification of the basic forces underlying the pattern of growth—at least in the nonsocialist mixed economy. The findings for Taiwan also enable us to draw a number of more specific conclusions.

For all households the findings demonstrate that the Kuznets effect, whatever trace of it remained, was caused mainly by the nonagricultural factor Gini effect—an effect which nevertheless can be substantially, if not totally, overcome by other forces. It is not surprising that reaching the turning point unambiguously benefits the overall distribution of income along with the objective of growth. What is surprising and important, the functional distribution of income, even before the turning point, does not necessarily make things worse, and the agricultural factor Gini effect substantially contributes to making things better. Early concentration on agricultural productivity thus provides additional income to rural families, encourages nonagricultural activity in rural areas, and increases the capacity of agriculture to equalize FID. At the same time, labor's share can rise because of increases in labor intensity, not because of rapidly rising wages. Under such conditions, the conflict between growth and the distribution of income can be eliminated, even before the turning point.

For urban households equity probably cannot substantially improve until after the turning point, when the unfavorable impact of the functional distribution effect is reversed. The reason for this is that urban FID reflects the overall Kuznets pattern, but does not benefit from the ameliorating effects of agricultural income. The most dependable way to ensure consistency between growth and distribution for urban households is to advance the coming of the turning point by instituting vigorous programs for balanced growth and reallocation. Even before the turning point, much can be accomplished by selecting a relatively labor-intensive path for urban industry.

For rural households the favorable trend of FID before the turning point is essentially derived from two sources. One is the beneficial contribution of the agricultural Gini coefficient, which shows a consistent and sustained pattern of decline. The other is the unusually dispersed pattern of the location of Taiwanese industry, a pattern which benefits the relatively poor rural families. As members of rural families, particularly poor rural families, shift to rural industries, the share of wage income rapidly rises and the share of agricultural income rapidly declines.

Especially surprising is the finding of a rising wage share before the turning point for rural households and all households. It runs counter to the experience of most contemporary LDCs and to the arguments of Lewis, Kuznets, and Marxist and dependency theorists.[34] All these observers share one view: As growth really begins to get under way, distribution must worsen as the shares of rent and profit income rise. The presumed reasons are that the rich in both sectors accumulate more assets than the poor and that the shift from rural to urban activities increases the relative size of the sector demonstrating the more unequal distribution of income. This argument apparently neglects the possibility, demonstrated by Taiwan, that rent reductions in agriculture and a change in the relative position of workers can simultaneously occur and enable FID to be improved by the combination of a rising functional distribution of wage income and a falling agricultural income Gini overcoming all else. Consequently the Kuznets effect applies not at all to rural households in Taiwan and only slightly to urban households and all households.

The analysis of this chapter clearly indicates the need to focus more attention on the wage share and the causes for its pattern of distribution. Although the reallocation effect and the functional distribution effect can be linked to certain familiar notions in growth theory, that level of formal analysis does not exist to guide attempts to explain the important factor Gini effect. Efforts to link the factor Gini effect more fully to growth, by examining the causes of the heterogeneity of human and physical capital, would thus seem to deserve a higher priority. Our effort to examine causes of the heterogeneity of human capital is described in chapter four.

34. See William R. Cline, "Distribution and Development," *Journal of Development Economics*, vol. 1 no. 4 (February 1975), pp. 359–400.

CHAPTER 4

The Inequality of Family Wage Income

THREE INTERRELATED FORCES associated with economic development are the primary causes of the inequality of family wage income: the industrialization of economic activity, the differentiation of the labor force, and the alteration of rules governing family formation. The distribution of wage income, the largest component of national income and family income, is thus influenced by forces quite different from those influencing the distribution of property and transfer income. As capital is accumulated and technology becomes more advanced, the structure of industry rapidly changes. One aspect of this changing structure is the growing demand for a more diversified labor force. Industry not only becomes more sensitive to the distinction between skilled and unskilled labor; it demands a wider variety of workers having different attributes. At one end of the spectrum industry requires accountants, managers, lawyers, and doctors; at the other end, uneducated female workers. Consequently, when an LDC economy modernizes, the labor force is differentiated into various homogeneous groups which can be identified by the different combinations of labor attributes they embody. The attributes of sex, age, and education are the most prominent.

The differentiation of the labor force thus is largely a response to changing industrial demand. That demand, coupled with the supply of labor in various homogeneous groups, determines the structure of wage rates at any given time. But the pricing of labor is both rational and irrational. Market forces operate to reward workers according to their productive contributions—that is, according to their respective marginal productivities. Concomitantly institutions discriminate against women and favor the members of wealthier families to reward workers of the same age and educational qualifications differently. Thus different wage rates prevail for different homogeneous groups of workers for both rational and irrational reasons.

For societies in which the family is the basic labor-owning unit, the basic determinants of the structure of total family wage income are the size of the family and the labor attributes of its members. These determinants are in turn influenced by such factors as fertility patterns, family decisions to invest in education, and the transition from extended to nuclear families. Population growth, in addition to resulting in a larger and increasingly heterogeneous labor force, influences and is influenced by these same determinants. In the process of economic development, then, economic forces determine the wage rates of workers as individuals; demographic and sociological forces determine the grouping of these workers into families. The impact of economic development on demographic variables thus manifests itself in the patterns of family formation, patterns which naturally affect family wage income.

To describe the heterogeneity of Taiwan's labor force, empirical data for 1966 is presented in this chapter.[1] That presentation includes descriptions of the wage structure, the classification of labor attributes, and the frequency distribution of workers according to that classification. The data are then analyzed at three levels. The first level investigates the extent to which the inequality of wage rates can be explained by various labor attributes. The second examines the causes of inequality of wage income for groups of individual wage earners. The third studies the causes of inequality of the distribution of wage income among families. Certain statistical techniques are used at each level of analysis. At the first level the statistical technique is the familiar linear regression method. At the

1. In the introduction a sharp distinction was drawn between published and unpublished DGBAS data. In this chapter use is made of the original unpublished data. For this reason the procedures adopted in the course of processing and coding the data from the original household survey are explained in detail in appendix 4.1 to this chapter. Only one year, 1966, has been singled out for intensive study: it is a high-quality early year; the emphasis here is essentially cross-sectional; and the requirements of manual coding and computerization are very substantial.

second and third levels the technique is based on decomposition equations for the model of additive factor components. But unlike the preceding chapter, which used linear approximations for purposes of decomposition, the general case of an exact decomposition is used here. Although these equations are mathematically derived in part two of this volume, their meaning and applicability are explained in this chapter for the benefit of the general reader who may not be mathematically inclined.

Empirical Data

The labor force in a developing country typically is rather homogeneous before the transition to modern growth gets under way. During the transition the labor force tends to become more and more differentiated and heterogeneous. Although this heterogeneity has many facets, only the five most important characteristics, or variables, are examined here: sex, age, education, job location, and occupation. The sex variable has two values: female and male. The age variable has four values: under 25, 25–45, 45–60, and over 60. The education variable has five values: primary school or less, junior high school, senior high school, technical school, and university or more. The location variable has three values: rural, town, and city. The occupation variable has six values: public employee or serviceman, specialist or professional, service employee, commercial self-employee, manual laborer, and agricultural employee. When labor is classified according to the foregoing criteria, there result 720 types of labor or homogeneous groups. The purpose here is to analyze the impact of this heterogeneity of the labor force upon the degree of wage income inequality. Thus the data inputs required for this analysis consist of the wage rates and frequency distributions of the workers in each homogeneous group. Based on a sample survey of 2,777 workers for 1966, the average annual wage rate and the frequency distribution of workers are presented in tables 4.20–4.23 in an appendix to this chapter. In addition, these tables have been disaggregated to show separately the wage rates and frequency for rural workers in table 4.24, town workers in table 4.25, city workers in table 4.26, and all workers in table 4.27.

The complexity and multidimensionality of issues associated with the inequality of wage income are evident even when only five labor characteristics are selected for analysis. Furthermore such a cross-listing of data, essential for applying the model of additive factor components, seldom is available in published form. And because the pattern of family ownership of the heterogeneous labor force underlies the inequality of family wage income, the family affiliation of workers is needed in addition. To provide a sense of the order of magnitudes associated with each labor characteristic, the sex, education, and age characteristics will be described for the whole economy by suppressing the location dimension. Relevant to all locations, these will be referred to as overall characteristics. The sex, education, and age characteristics will also be separately described for each location—that is, for rural areas, towns, and cities.

Overall characteristics

Of the 2,777 workers covered in the 1966 survey, about 75 percent had completed only their primary education (table 4.1). Junior and senior high school graduates accounted for another 20 percent. With respect to sex, the completion of primary school significantly demarked the educational attributes of workers. Although the female percentage of graduates was higher than the male percentage for the lowest educational group, it was lower than the corresponding male percentage for all other educational groups. The figures reveal the expected pattern: fewer female workers than male workers received higher education. Because shortages of technical workers are generally regarded as a bottleneck for economic development, the low proportion, only 1.3 percent, of graduates of technical schools should also be noted.

When the wage rate of each educational group is expressed as a multiple of that of the primary school group, it is seen that junior high school and university were the most important steps for upgrading the earning power of workers. Three years of junior high school brought about a more than doubling of the wage rate; three additional years of senior high school brought about practically no further improvement. The wage index for junior high school was 2.2 (primary school = 1); that for senior high school was 2.32. Another two years of technical school led to an improvement in the wage index to 2.95. But university education brought about a really significant improvement to 4.18. It seems that solid economic reasoning justified both the strong pressure on high school graduates to pass the college entrance examination and the popular feeling that those who did not enter college were failures.

Table 4.1. *Relative Wage Rates and Frequency Distribution of Labor, by Education, Sex, and Job Location, 1966*
(percent)

Item	*Primary school*	*Junior high school*	*Senior high school*	*Technical school*	*University or over*	*Total*
All workers						
Percentage distribution	73.93	8.46	12.45	1.33	3.83	100.00
Female	82.59	7.10	8.50	0.97	0.84	100.00
Male	70.90	8.94	13.84	1.46	4.86	100.00
Relative wage rate (primary school = 1.00)	1.00	2.22	2.32	2.95	4.18	1.85
Rural workers						
Percentage distribution	89.20	4.65	5.15	0.50	0.50	100.00
Relative wage rate (rural areas = 1.00)	1.00	1.00	1.00	1.00	1.00	1.00
Town workers						
Percentage distribution	70.40	9.81	14.80	1.06	3.93	100.00
Relative wage rate (rural areas = 1.00)	1.54	1.01	1.08	0.91	1.21	1.71
City workers						
Percentage distribution	63.59	10.29	16.36	2.64	7.12	100.00
Relative wage rate (rural areas = 1.00)	2.64	2.74	1.39	0.97	1.80	2.98

Sources: Tables 4.20–4.27 appended to this chapter.

More than half the workers were in the 25–45 age group (table 4.2). The under-25 age group accounted for a quarter of workers; the rest were mainly allocated to the 45–60 age group. When the corresponding percentages of female and male workers are compared, the contrast between the lowest group—that is, the under-25 group—and the other groups once again shows the significance of the influence of the sex characteristic. Although the percentage of female workers was much higher than the percentage of males in the youngest group, it was lower than that for males in all the other age groups. As would be expected, female workers retire from the labor force at a much earlier age than their male counterparts because of their role in the family.

Table 4.2. *Relative Wage Rates and Frequency Distribution of Labor, by Age, Sex, and Job Location, 1966*

Item	*Under 25 years*	*25–45 years*	*45–60 years*	*Over 60 years*	*Total*
All workers					
Percentage distribution	24.70	53.84	19.30	2.16	100.00
Female	44.71	44.71	9.75	0.84	100.00
Male	17.73	57.02	22.63	2.62	100.00
Relative wage rate (under 25 = 1.00)	1.00	2.24	2.79	2.13	2.04
Rural workers					
Percentage distribution	28.14	55.15	15.20	1.51	100.00
Relative wage rate (rural areas = 1.00)	1.00	1.00	1.00	1.00	1.00
Town workers					
Percentage distribution	22.32	55.10	18.48	2.45	100.00
Relative wage rate (rural areas = 1.00)	1.36	1.68	2.03	1.06	1.71
City workers					
Percentage distribution	24.93	50.40	22.30	2.37	100.00
Relative wage rate (rural areas = 1.00)	1.79	3.14	3.11	3.10	2.98

Sources: Tables 4.20–4.27 appended to this chapter.

When the wage rate of each age group is expressed as a multiple of that of the youngest group, it is seen that the gain in the wage rate was most significant for those in the 25–45 age group and much less significant for the 45–60 age group. The wage index for the 25–45 age group was 2.24 (under 25 = 1); that for the 45–60 age group was 2.79; that for the over-60 age group was 2.13. The reward for experience therefore manifested a strong trend toward diminishing return. The probable reasons for this are that "age" is a poor proxy for experience and that the advantage of experience gained with

Table 4.3. *Wage Parity of Female Workers, by Age and Education, 1966*
(male wage rate = 1)

Level of education	*Under 25*	*25–45*	*45–60*	*Over 60*	*Total*
Primary school	0.7099	0.4077	0.3779	0.4937	0.4235
Junior high school	0.7903	0.5272	0.5307	—	0.4638
Senior high school	0.9304	0.7958	1.0115	—	0.7215
Technical school	1.4468	0.7533	—	—	0.7253
University or over	1.0292	0.6372	0.5651	—	0.5798
All levels	0.7688	0.4244	0.4228	0.2984	0.4170

— Not applicable.
Source: Table 4.27 appended to this chapter.

higher age is offset by other disadvantages of "aging" for workers over 60.

The foregoing data reveal that female workers were heavily allocated to age and educational groups that received low pay. The concentration of females in low-paying jobs may have been the result of their free choice to join and to leave the labor force early. There may also have been institutional discrimination in the availability of jobs for female workers. Wage discrimination is less disputable (table 4.3). For all groups the wage rate for females was substantially less than half that for males. Female workers were at a disadvantage in every educational group. Moreover discrimination was higher for the low educational categories, which absorbed almost 90 percent of female workers. The wage rate for females having primary education was 42 percent of that of their male counterparts; that for females having junior high school education, 46 percent. Discrimination against female workers also prevailed for every age group, and the severity of discrimination increased with age. Consequently, elderly women with little education were apt to be most disadvantaged; young women with higher education, least disadvantaged.

Locational characteristics

The concentration of less educated workers in the rural sector was high (see table 4.1). Primary school education significantly demarked the job-location characteristic. The proportion of this group was highest in the rural areas and lowest in cities—89.2 percent compared with 63.6 percent. For all other educational categories the opposite was true: the proportion of high-education graduates was greatest for the cities and lowest for the rural areas. In educational attainment, labor in a tradition-bound rural economy is an inferior homogeneous group. With the rural areas, towns, and cities respectively characterized by increasing degrees of modernization and urbanization, modernization brought about labor heterogeneity in a particular sense: the formation of a superior homogeneous educational group. Although this conclusion is based upon a cross-sectional study, it can and should be verified by the analysis of time series in the future.

When the wage rate of each locational group is expressed as a multiple of the rural wage rate for each educational group, the most significant gaps prevail between city workers on the one hand and town and rural workers on the other. For the two lowest educational groups, the wage rate for city workers was almost three times that of rural workers. For higher educational groups, the wage disparities were less. For the technical school groups, city workers had practically no advantage.

Turning to the age characteristic, it can be seen that the rural sector provided more employment opportunities for younger workers than cities did. The proportions of rural workers in the under-25 and 25–45 age groups respectively were 28.1 percent and 55.2 percent; those of urban workers, 24.9 percent and 50.4 percent. For workers over 45 the town and city offered increasingly greater opportunities. Modernization therefore seems to lengthen the working life. Because older workers had a higher earning power than their younger counterparts, modernization appears to lead to the formation of a superior wage-earning group much in the manner that education does (see table 4.2).

For all age groups, workers in towns and cities received higher wage rates than rural workers. But this disparity was not as great for young workers as it was for all other age groups. For those in the under-25 age group, the wage indexes of town and city workers respectively were 1.36 and 1.79 (rural workers = 1). The reason for this pattern may be that young rural workers were more willing than old workers to migrate to large cities, a propensity that would result in a smaller wage gap in the youngest age group.

Job location thus represents a significant dimension for the analysis of inequality in the distribution of wage income. For this reason the three locations are separately treated in the remainder of this chapter.

Analytical Framework

The analysis of the inequality of wage income thus comprises three distinct types, or levels, of problems: at the first level the problem is to determine the impact of labor heterogeneity on the wage rate; at the second, the causes of the inequality of wage income among homogeneous groups of individual workers; at the third, the causes of the inequality of family wage income. It should be perfectly clear that the focus of this chapter, indeed this entire volume, is the inequality of family wage income. Although the first two levels of analysis may be of interest in their own right, they are discussed in this chapter primarily to lay the foundation and constitute the input for the third level of analysis.

The association of various dimensions of labor heterogeneity with the magnitude of the wage rate perhaps is one of the most popular methods for studying the inequality of wage income. For example, the familiar earnings-function approach uses a linear regression model in which the wage rate is regressed on various labor force characteristics, which are represented by natural and dummy variables.[2] The purpose of this technique is to estimate regression coefficients that can be interpreted as quantified causes of the inequality of the wage rate. The regression coefficients of the wage rate on such characteristics as age, sex, and educational attainment represent the premiums associated with these characteristics—that is, the extra wage income additively accruing to workers having different combinations of values for these characteristics.

This earnings-function technique has nothing to do with the inequality of wage income in the sense used in this volume. Inequality here refers to the degree of inequality of income for a group of income recipients [$W = (W_1, W_2, \ldots, W_n)$] as measured by the Gini

2. See Jacob Mincer, *Schooling, Experience, and Earnings* (New York: National Bureau of Economic Research, distributed by Columbia University Press, 1974) and Sherwin Rosen, "Human Capital: A Survey of Empirical Research," in *Research in Labor Economics*, ed. Ronald G. Ehrenberg (Greenwich, Ct.: JAI Press, 1977), vol. 1, pp. 3–39.

coefficient [G_w]. The earnings-function technique is concerned neither with the pattern of wage income [W] nor with its degree of inequality [G_w]. Nevertheless the earnings function used at the first level of analysis provides certain research inputs required at the second and third levels. With this technique such demographic characteristics of labor as sex, age, and educational attainment can be additively associated with such economic magnitudes as wage income. Given the basic purpose of this chapter, which is primarily directed at the analysis of wage income inequality for homogeneous groups of individual workers and for families, only a rather naive version of such an earnings function is used here. It can clearly be improved as an input to this work. Methodologically, however, it should be obvious that the primary interest here is with the way an earnings-function technique can be combined with the additive factor-components technique, not with the perfectibility of the earnings function itself. The analytical design used in combining these two techniques is discussed more fully in an appendix to this chapter.

At the second level of analysis workers are treated as individuals and all information on their family affiliation is still suppressed. Given the pattern of wage income of individual workers [$W = (W_1, W_2, \ldots, W_n)$] and the degree of wage income inequality [G_w], the crucial analytical task at the second level is to determine the extent to which each of the labor characteristics accounts for G_w. At the first level of analysis the wage-rate inequality attributable, for example, to the sex characteristic is traced to such rational forces as differences in worker productivity and to such irrational forces as sex discrimination. The second level of analysis addresses the same set of socioeconomic forces, but attempts to assess their impact on the degree of inequality of wage income [G_w], not on the wage rate. This analysis will be formulated as an additive factor-components problem and make use of the earnings-function results from the first level of analysis.

Analysis of the inequality of family wage income at the third level requires information on the family affiliation of workers. The technique for this analysis can be illustrated with a simple model examining two labor characteristics, sex and education (table 4.4). The data in this table correspond to the cross-listing of information on the wage rate and frequency distribution of workers in appendix tables 4.20–4.23; they also provide all the information needed for analysis at the second level. For analysis at the third level, the ten workers in table 4.4 are classified into five families to show total

Table 4.4. *Numerical Example Corresponding to the Cross-listing of Information on the Wage Rate and Frequency Distribution of Workers in Tables 4.20–4.27, by Sex and Level of Education*

Item	*Low education*	*Intermediate education*	*High education*
Wage Rate			
Female workers	2	5	10
Male workers	3	7	15
Number of Workers			
Female	1	4	1
Male	2	1	1

Note: $W = (2, 3, 3, 5, 5, 5, 5, 7, 10, 15)$
Source: Constructed by the authors.

family wage income $[Y]$ and to trace the wage income components to the membership composition of families (table 4.5). The six grades of labor in this table correspond to those in table 4.4. The pattern of total family wage income $[Y = (5, 8, 10, 15, 22)]$ results in a Gini coefficient $[G_y]$ of 0.2733. This illustrative numerical example indicates the way the analysis of G_y will be formulated as an additive factor-components problem at the third level.

The total family wage income obviously depends on family size—that is, on the number of wage earners owned by the family—as well as membership structure. A column in table 4.5 describes the pattern by which workers of a particular grade are distributed among the families. It is apparent that the unevenness of this distribution can be a major cause of the inequality of family wage income. A family with high wage income would be expected to "own" more high-grade workers, such as college-educated males, than would a family with low wage income. In addition, the membership composition of families, described by the sex, age, and educational attainment of their members, is determined by the rules of family formation. These rules are affected by a host of sociodemographic factors, including the institution of marriage, the patterns of reproduction, and the properties of nuclear families in transition. Thus the third level of analysis encounters wholly new factors which are

Table 4.5. *Numerical Example Classifying Workers into Five Families and Tracing Wage Income Components to the Membership Composition of Those Families*

Family	Total wage income	Low education		Intermediate education		High education	
		Female	Male	Female	Male	Female	Male
Family 1	5	0	0	5	0	0	0
Family 2	8	2	6	0	0	0	0
Family 3	10	0	0	0	0	10	0
Family 4	15	0	0	15	0	0	0
Family 5	22	0	0	0	7	0	15

Note: The pattern of family wage income is given by $Y = (5, 8, 10, 15, 22)$, and the resulting Gini coefficient is 0.2733.

Source: Constructed by the authors with data from the numerical example of table 4.4.

not encountered at the first two levels of analysis and which are traditionally treated by such other disciplines as sociology and demography. Because this area of inquiry is relatively new for economists, we will be content to speculate about the way the problem can be formulated in future research efforts.

Labor Heterogeneity and the Wage Rate: First-level Analysis

Multiple regression analysis is used to analyze the impact of labor heterogeneity on the wage rate. Let W be the wage rate, and let $x_1, x_2, \ldots, x_r$ be the explanatory variables. A regression equation can then be specified as follows:

$$W = a_o + a_1x_1 + a_2x_2 + \ldots + a_rx_r + \delta, \tag{4.1}$$

where δ is a random error term. The r explanatory variables $[x_i]$ represent the various characteristics that define the heterogeneity of the labor force. The purpose of the regression analysis is to estimate the coefficients $[a_i]$ that measure the quantitative impact of each labor dimension upon the wage rate under the assumption of independence.

In applying the regression analysis to the data for 1966 (see appendix tables 4.20–4.23), the regression equation is specified as:

$$W = a_o + a_1x_1 + a_2x_2 + a_3x_3 + a_4x_4 + \delta. \quad (4.2)$$

In addition to the variables representing sex [x_1], education [x_2], and age [x_3], an additional variable [x_4] represents the total income of the family to which a given wage earner belongs.[3] The reason for using such a variable is to determine whether a wealthy family can exercise undue influence to secure a higher wage rate for its members. Equation (4.2) will be applied separately to each of three job locations: rural areas, towns, and cities.

The explanatory variables [x_i] can be assigned a range of values. The sex variable [x_1] takes on the value of zero for females and 1 for males; the coefficient a_1 thus measures the male premium. The education variable [x_2] takes on values that correspond to the years of formal education completed (6, 9, 12, 14, or 16). The coefficient a_2 thus measures the education premium and corresponds to the market value of one additional year of formal education. The age variable [x_3] takes on values that correspond to an ordinal ranking of age as a proxy for the contribution of experience to wage-earning power (1, 2, 3, or 3).[4] The coefficient a_3 thus measures the age premium and corresponds to the value of experience in earning power. Total family income [x_4] is measured in thousands of new Taiwan dollars.[5] The coefficient a_4 thus measures the nepotism premium associated with undue family influence on the earning power of its members.

This model was applied to the primary data in appendix tables 4.20–4.23. It is apparent from the sample sizes that the regression coefficients are very significant (table 4.6). In cities, where the average wage rate in 1966 was NT$19,831, the male premium was

3. See schedule 4.5 in appendix 4.1 to this chapter for the coded form used to assemble data on total family income.

4. Notice that the over-60 age group is assigned a rank of 3, or the same as that assigned to the 45–60 age group. This choice was made after experimentation with several alternative rankings for the four age groups: (1, 2, 3, 1.5), (1, 2, 3, 2), (1, 2, 3, 2.5), and (1, 2, 3, 3). The last ranking was selected because it leads to the highest value of the coefficient of determination (R_2 = 0.5).

5. At the time of writing, the new Taiwan dollar was equal to about US$0.025.

Table 4.6. *Regression Coefficients of Four Explanatory Variables, by Job Location, 1966*

Item	*Notation*	*Regression coefficient*		
		Rural area	*Town*	*City*
Constant	a_o	−10.8977 (−12.2398)	−12.1360 (−12.2728)	−18.8349 (12.2333)
Sex	a_1	3.3770 (8.4366)	5.2287 (9.0333)	7.3493 (7.3777)
Education	a_2	1.4522 (12.9158)	1.5537 (17.7580)	1.5089 (11.3366)
Age	a_3	1.7635 (6.2578)	2.8801 (7.6676)	6.2734 (10.4305)
Total family income	a_4	0.0841 (7.1972)	0.0800 (6.9843)	0.1757 (9.3398)
Sample size		796	1,223	758

Note: Values in parentheses are *t* scores. The following values have been assigned to characteristics:

X_1 = (female, male) = (0, 1)
X_2 = (primary school, junior high school, senior high school, technical school, university) = (6, 9, 12, 14, 16)
X_3 = (under 25, 25–45, 45–60, over 60) = (1, 2, 3, 3)
X_4 = (total family income in thousands of N.T. dollars)

Source: Calculated from tables 4.20–4.27 appended to this chapter.

NT$7,349, the age premium was NT$6,273, and the education premium was NT$1,509. For earning power, one year of formal education was therefore equivalent to about four to five years of informal education or experience, as measured by a simple gain in age. Being female was equivalent to the disadvantage of having almost five years less formal education.

The locational specifications of rural area, town, and city represent an increasing degree of penetration by the forces of modernization into socioeconomic life. It appears, moreover, that the attributes of labor were probably evaluated (priced) with more sensitivity

Table 4.7. *Influence of Total Family Income on Wage Rates, by Sex and Age, 1966*
(thousands of N.T. dollars)

	Female		*Male*	
Item	*25–45 years*	*45–60 years*	*25–45 years*	*45–60 years*
Without family income effect[a]				
Senior high school	11.8187	18.0921	19.1680	25.4414
Technical school	14.8365	21.1099	22.1858	28.4592
University or over	17.8543	24.1277	25.2063	31.4770
With family income effect				
Senior high school	13.5757	19.8491	20.9250	27.1984
	(29.3887)	(35.6621)	(36.7380)	(43.0114)
Technical school	16.5935	22.8669	23.9428	30.2162
	(32.4065)	(38.6799)	(39.7558)	(46.1292)
University or over	19.6113	25.8847	26.9606	33.2340
	(35.4243)	(41.6977)	(42.7736)	(49.0470)
Ratio of the wage rate influenced by high family income to that influenced by low family income[b]				
Senior high school	2.1611	1.7967	1.7557	1.5814
Technical school	1.9530	1.6915	1.6604	1.5233
University or over	1.8063	1.6109	1.5865	1.4758

Note: Values in parentheses are *t* scores. Higher education is taken to be a proxy for higher wage income.

Source: Calculated from tables 4.20–4.27 appended to this chapter.

a. Computed from equation (4.2) by setting the variable for total family income equal to zero.

b. Values for total family income of NT$100,000 and NT$10,000 were substituted into equation (4.2) to examine the effects of family income on the wage rate.

in the commercialized milieu of large cities than in the traditional rural communities. The male premium of 7.35 in cities was more than double that of 3.38 in rural areas. Either male workers in cities had a higher productive power or, more likely, the discrimination against women was greater. For the age characteristic the difference between cities and rural areas was even greater. The age

Table 4.8. *Distribution of Families, by Job Location and Total Family Income, 1966*

Total family income (N.T. dollars)	*Number of families*		
	Rural area	*Town*	*City*
Less than 10,000	28	46	7
10,000–15,000	70	94	28
15,000–20,000	85	133	46
20,000–25,000	68	114	65
25,000–30,000	48	94	64
30,000–40,000	52	104	87
40,000–50,000	30	51	59
50,000–60,000	8	35	29
60,000–70,000	13	16	23
70,000–80,000	6	11	6
80,000–100,000	7	8	10
More than 100,000	2	6	8

Source: Tables 4.20–4.27 appended to this chapter.

premium of 6.27 in cities was more than triple that of 1.76 in rural areas. For the education characteristic the difference between cities and rural areas was not significant. It would appear that rural areas are less sensitive than cities in their pricing of age and sex attributes of workers, but equally sensitive in pricing educational attributes.

In a society in which families have a long tradition of playing a prominent social role, family influence would be expected to be significant in securing better paid positions for its members. The nepotism coefficient [a_4] measures the extent of the influence of total family income on the wage rates of family members. The nepotism premium of 0.18 in cities was more than double that of 0.08 in towns and rural areas. A better view of the quantitative significance of nepotism in cities can be provided by examining higher wage-income groups, proxied by educational attainment, for which family influence would be expected to be strong (table 4.7). The values in the first part of this table do not take into account the influence of family income; they were computed from equation (4.2) by setting the variable for total family income [x_4]

equal to zero. The values in the second part of this table do take into account the influence of family income. Because the vast majority of city families receive total income ranging from NT$10,000 to NT$100,000 (table 4.8), these two values were substituted into equation (4.2) to examine the effects of family income on the wage rate. The ratios of the wage rate influenced by high family income to the wage rates influenced by low family income are given in the third part of table 4.7. It can be seen that the wage rates a very wealthy family can secure for its members are at least 50 percent higher than those a very poor family can secure for its members. Given the value of the regression coefficient a_4 of 0.1757, the nepotism premium was worth approximately NT$1,800 a year, or NT$150 a month, for every increase of NT$10,000 in total family income.

Inequality of Income of Individual Wage Earners: Second-level Analysis

The regression analysis revealed the impact of various dimensions of labor quality on the wage rate. This section investigates causes of the degree of inequality of wage income for a group of individual wage earners. The method of analysis is based on the application of the following decomposition equation to the data for 1966:

$$G_w = \phi_1 R_1 G_1 + \phi_2 R_2 G_2 + \ldots + \phi_r R_r G_r + \Delta. \tag{4.3}$$

In this equation the Gini coefficient of the wage rate [G_w], or the wage Gini, measures the degree of inequality of wage income. Notice when the wage rate is calculated on an annual basis that the wage rate is the same as wage income. The r terms on the right side represent the various dimensions of labor quality. In this analysis r is equal to 4. The four terms stand for sex, education, age, and total family income and correspond to the four variables of regression equation (4.2). The aim of the decomposition analysis is to assess the quantitative impact, or contribution, of the various labor characteristics on G_w. The term Δ will be referred to as the rank-weighted error term.

Every term $\phi_i R_i G_i$ in equation (4.3) is the product of three factors. The factor G_i measures the degree of inequality of a particular attribute or characteristic and will be called the labor characteristic Gini. The factor ϕ_i measures the share of inequality contributed by a characteristic and will be called the labor characteristic weight. The factor R_i measures the correlation between the values of labor characteristics and wage income and will be called the labor correlation characteristic. Before the empirical analysis, each factor will be precisely defined and given an economic interpretation with the aid of a numerical example.[6]

Labor characteristic Gini

Suppose that five wage earners have wage income $[w_i]$ as shown in the numerical example of table 4.9. The sex, educational attainment, and wage income of these workers constitute the primary data in this numerical example.[7] The sex variable $[x_1]$ takes on the value of zero for females and 1 for males. The education variable $[x_2]$ takes on the value of 1 for low education, 2 for intermediary education, and 3 for high education (the terms low, intermediary, and high conform to usage in Taiwan). Wage income is measured in thousands of new Taiwan dollars. When there are n families, this data can be summarized by vector notation:

(4.4a) $$W = \text{col}(w_1, w_2, \ldots, w_n) \quad \text{and}$$

[*wage pattern*]

(4.4b) $$X_i = \text{col}(x_{i1}, x_{i2}, \ldots, x_{in}). \qquad (i = 1, 2, \ldots, r)$$

[*labor characteristic pattern*]

For any nonnegative column vector $[Y = \text{col}(Y_1, Y_2, \ldots, Y_n)]$ the Gini coefficient $[G_y]$ can then be computed from the following equation[8]:

(4.5a) $$0 \leq Y_1 \leq Y_2 \leq \ldots \leq Y_n;$$

(4.5b) $$G_y = \alpha u_y - \beta;$$

(4.5c) $$\alpha = 2/n; \beta = (n + 1)/n;$$

6. See equation (12.13) and the accompanying discussion in chapter twelve of part two.

7. It is evident that the columns for primary data on sex and education in table 4.9 provide all the information for the frequency distribution that is essential for analysis at the second level (see table 4.5).

8. See chapter eight in part two for a fuller exposition.

Table 4.9. *Numerical Example of Regression Analysis for Five Wage Earners and Two Explanatory Variables*

	Primary data		
	Wage income	*Sex*	*Education*
Item	$[W]$	$[x_1]$[a]	$[x_2]$[a]
Wage earner 1	$w_1 = 2.01$	$x_{11} = 0$	$x_{21} = 1$
Wage earner 2	$w_2 = 4.98$	$x_{12} = 0$	$x_{22} = 2$
Wage earner 3	$w_3 = 7.01$	$x_{13} = 1$	$x_{23} = 2$
Wage earner 4	$w_4 = 7.97$	$x_{14} = 0$	$x_{24} = 3$
Wage earner 5	$w_5 = 10.03$	$x_{15} = 1$	$x_{25} = 3$
Vector notation	W	X_1	X_2
Mean value	$\bar{W} = 6.04$	$\bar{X}_1 = 0.4$	$\bar{X}_2 = 2.2$
Labor characteristic weight	—	—	—
Labor characteristic Gini	—	$G_1 = 0.6000$	$G_2 = 0.1818$
Correlation characteristic [b,c]	—	$R_1 = 0.666$	$R_2 = 1.000$
Rank-weighted error term [d]	—	—	—
Wage Gini [e]	$G_w = 0.2379$	—	—

— Not applicable.
Source: Constructed by the authors.
a. See the text for the assignment of values to these variables.
b. $R_1 = \bar{G}_1/G_1$, where $\bar{G}_1 = 2/5(1 \times 0 + 2 \times 0 + 3 \times \frac{1}{2} + 4 \times \frac{1}{2}) - 6/5 = 0.2$
c. $R_2 = \bar{G}_2/G_2$, where $\bar{G}_2 = 2/5(1 \times 1/11 + 2 \times 2/11 + 3 \times 3/11 + 4 \times 4/11 + 5 \times 5/11)$
d. $\Delta = [1/15 \times (0.01) + 2/15 \times (-0.02) + 3/15 \times (0.01) + 4/15 \times (0.03) + 5/15 \times (0.03)]/6.4 = 0.004688$
e. $G_w = \phi_1 R_1 G_1 + \phi_2 R_2 G_2 = 0.125 \times 0.666 \times 0.600 + 1.03125 \times 1 \times 0.1818 + 0.04688 = 0.2379$

(4.5d) $$u_y = \lambda_1 y_1 + \lambda_2 y_2 + \ldots + \lambda_n y_n;$$

(4.5e) $$\lambda_1 = 1,\ \lambda_2 = 2,\ \ldots,\ \lambda_n = n;$$

(4.5f) $$y_i = Y_i/S_y; \qquad (i = 1, 2, \ldots, n)$$

(4.5g) $$S_y = Y_1 + Y_2 + \ldots + Y_n.$$

Regression analysis				
Regression coefficient			*Estimated wage income* $[W]$	*Regression error* $[\delta c]$
$a_o = -1$ $[a_o]$	$a_1 = 2$ $[a_1x_1]$	$a_2 = 3$ $[a_2x_2]$		
-1	0	3	$\hat{w}_1 = 2$	$\delta_1 = 0.01$
-1	0	6	$\hat{w}_2 = 5$	$\delta_2 = -0.02$
-1	2	6	$\hat{w}_3 = 7$	$\delta_3 = 0.01$
-1	0	9	$\hat{w}_4 = 8$	$\delta_4 = -0.03$
-1	2	9	$\hat{w}_5 = 10$	$\delta_5 = 0.03$
a_c $\bar{a}_c = -1$	a_1x_1 $a_1\bar{x}_1 = 0.8$	a_2x_2 $a_2\bar{x}_2 = 6.6$	$\hat{W}$ $W = 6.4$	δ_c $\bar{\delta}_c = 0$
—	$\phi_1 = 0.125$	$\phi_2 = 1.03125$	—	—
—	—	—	—	—
—	—	—	—	—
—	—	—	—	0.004688
—	—	—	—	—

Expression (4.5a) emphasizes that all values of Y_i must be rearranged in a monotonically nondecreasing order to compute G_y. Then λ_i is the rank of Y_i, and y_i is the fraction of Y_i in total income $[Y]$. When this formula is applied to the wage pattern $[W]$ in equation (4.4a), the wage Gini $[G_w]$ is obtained to measure the degree of inequality of the wage pattern $[W]$. When the same formula is applied to the labor characteristic patterns $[X_i]$ in equation (4.4b), the various labor characteristic Ginis $[G_i]$ are obtained. In the numerical example the wage Gini $[G_w]$ is 0.24, the sex Gini $[G_1]$ is 0.60, and the education Gini $[G_2]$ is 0.18.

The notion of the labor characteristic Gini $[G_i]$ is meaningful only when the values of a characteristic variable indicate wage-earning power, at least in the ordinal sense. To illustrate: The values of the sex variable $[x_1]$ of zero for females and 1 for males presume that a male worker has higher earning power than a female worker.

If all workers are male, the sex Gini [G_1] is zero. Extreme equality means that the group of workers is completely homogeneous with respect to sex. If all workers have completed only primary education, the education Gini [G_2] would also be zero, indicating that the group of workers is homogeneous with respect to education. In these extreme cases, sex and education obviously cannot cause wage income inequality because the terms $\phi_1 R_1 G_1$ and $\phi_2 R_2 G_2$ would both be equal to zero in equation (4.3).

What is the common-sense meaning of the value of the labor characteristic Gini [G_i]? Consider a numerical example with eight workers, where 1 stands for primary education or less and 2 stands for secondary education. The education structures of the eight workers are given by the row vectors of the labor characteristic patterns in the top part of table 4.10. Starting with the homogeneous group of uneducated workers in a traditional economy, the group of workers is slowly transformed into a homogeneous group of educated workers in a modernizing economy. During this transformation the education Gini first increases to a maximum value of 0.1705 and then decreases as the fraction of poorly educated or inferior workers declines, resulting in an inverse U-shaped pattern. Now consider a numerical example, again with eight workers, where 1 stands for primary education or less and 3 stands for university education or more. The education structures are given by the row vectors in the bottom part of table 4.10. During the transformation of the homogeneous group of uneducated workers to the homogeneous group of university-educated workers, the inverse U-shaped pattern is again produced. But with a maximum value for G_i of 0.2679, the amplitude of fluctuation is much greater.[9]

The same numerical example can be used, in reverse, to illustrate the formation of a new inferior group. Suppose that 1 represents female and 2 represents male and read upward from the last row of the first part of table 4.10. Starting with the all-male labor force of a traditional economy, female participation gradually increases. Thus an inverse U-shaped pattern of the labor characteristic Gini is observable over time, whether the splinter group formed is super-

9. This inverse U-shaped pattern is independent of the index of inequality chosen. The same pattern is seen when the standard deviation or mean deviation is used as the index of inequality (see the last two columns of table 4.10).

Table 4.10. *Numerical Example of the Formation of New Homogeneous Groups with Eight Workers*

Labor characteristic pattern[a]	*Fraction in inferior group*	*Gini coefficient*	*Standard deviation*	*Mean deviation*
(1,1,1,1,1,1,1,1)	1.000	0.0000	0.0000	0.0000
(1,1,1,1,1,1,1,2)	0.875	0.0972	0.3308	0.2188
(1,1,1,1,1,1,2,2)	0.750	0.1500	0.4330	0.3750
(1,1,1,1,1,2,2,2)	0.625	0.1705	0.4841	0.4688
(1,1,1,1,2,2,2,2)	0.500	0.1677	0.5000	0.5000
(1,1,1,2,2,2,2,2)	0.375	0.1442	0.4841	0.4688
(1,1,2,2,2,2,2,2)	0.250	0.1071	0.4330	0.3750
(1,2,2,2,2,2,2,2)	0.125	0.0583	0.3308	0.2188
(2,2,2,2,2,2,2,2)	0.000	0.0000	0.0000	0.0000
(1,1,1,1,1,1,1,1)	1.000	0.0000	0.0000	0.0000
(1,1,1,1,1,1,1,3)	0.875	0.1750	0.6614	0.4375
(1,1,1,1,1,1,3,3)	0.750	0.2500	0.8660	0.7500
(1,1,1,1,1,3,3,3)	0.625	0.2679	0.9682	0.9375
(1,1,1,1,3,3,3,3)	0.500	0.2500	1.0000	1.0000
(1,1,1,3,3,3,3,3)	0.375	0.2083	0.9682	0.9375
(1,1,3,3,3,3,3,3)	0.250	0.1500	0.8660	0.7500
(1,3,3,3,3,3,3,3)	0.125	0.0795	0.6614	0.4375
(3,3,3,3,3,3,3,3)	0.000	0.0000	0.0000	0.0000

Source: Constructed by the authors.
a. 1 = primary education or less; 2 = secondary education; 3 = university education or more.

ior or inferior. This is reminiscent of the Kuznets hypothesis that income distribution will worsen before it gets better.

The foregoing ideas can be formulated more rigorously. Suppose that a given labor characteristic has two values, V_1 and V_2, and that V_1 is less than V_2. The value for the privileged group is V_2; that for the less privileged group is V_1. Suppose further that there are n_1 workers in the less privileged group and n_2 workers in the privileged group. The Gini coefficient of this labor characteristic for all workers (n_1 plus n_2) is[10]:

(4.6a) $$G = \frac{n_1 n_2 (V_2 - V_1)}{(n_1 V_1 + n_2 V_2)(n_1 + n_2)} \quad \text{or}$$

(4.6b) $$G = \frac{\Theta_1 \Theta_2 \, s}{\Theta_1 V_1^* + \Theta_2 V_2^*}, \quad \text{where}$$

(4.6c) $$\Theta_1 = n_1/(n_1 + n_2), \quad \Theta_2 = n_2/(n_1 + n_2),$$
$$V_1^* = V_1/(V_1 + V_2), \quad V_2^* = V_2/(V_1 + V_2);$$

(4.6d) $$s = V_2^* - V_1^* \quad \text{with} \quad 0 \leq s \leq 1;$$

(4.6e) $$\Theta_1 + \Theta_2 = 1; \quad \text{and}$$

(4.6f) $$V_1^* + V_2^* = 1.$$

The term Θ_1 is the fraction of labor in the first group, and V_1^* is the relative value of the characteristic for that group. The term Θ_2 is the fraction of labor in the second group, and V_2^* is the relative value of the characteristic for that group. The term s is the gap between V_1^* and V_2^*. Using equations (4.6e) and (4.6f), rewrite equation (4.6b) as:

(4.6g) $$G = \frac{2s(\Theta_1 - \Theta_1^2)}{1 + s - 2s\Theta_1}.$$

This equation makes G a function of s and Θ_1. To determine the impact of the variation of Θ_1 on G, partially differentiate equation (4.6g) with respect to Θ_1:

(4.7a) $$\frac{\partial G}{\partial \Theta_1} = \frac{(1 + s - 2s\Theta_1) - (1 - 2\Theta_1) - (\Theta_1 - \Theta_1^2)(-2s)}{(1 + s - 2s\Theta_1)^2/2s}$$

Thus:

(4.7b) $$\frac{\partial G}{\partial \Theta_1} = 0 \quad \text{if and only if} \quad (\Theta_1 - \alpha_1)(\Theta_2 - \alpha_2) = 0, \quad \text{where}$$

(4.7c) $$\alpha_1 = (1 + s - \sqrt{1 - s^2})/2s,$$

(4.7d) $$\alpha_2 = (1 + s + \sqrt{1 - s^2})/2s, \quad \text{and}$$

(4.7e) $$0 < \alpha_1 < 1 < \alpha_2.$$

10. See theorem 8.2 in chapter eight of part two.

Figure 4.1. *The Emergence of Splinter Groups*

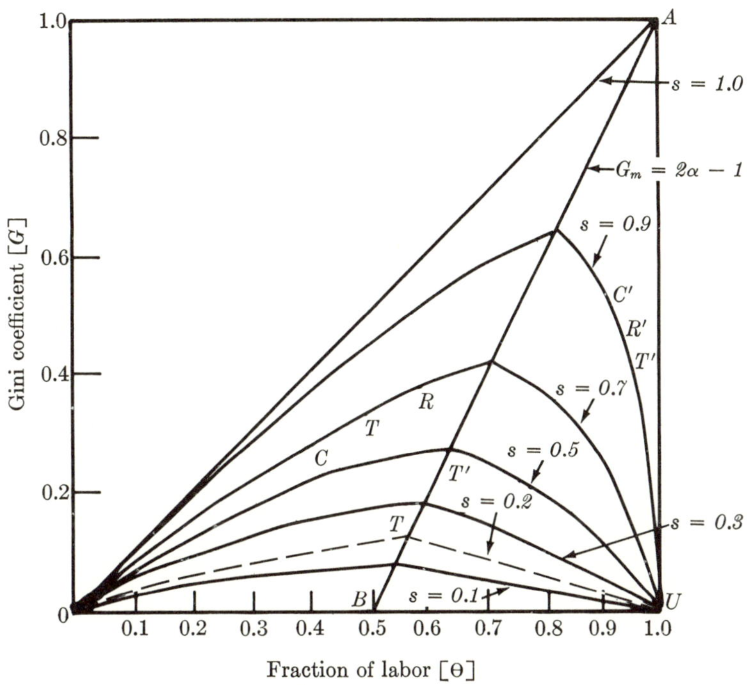

Source: Constructed by the authors.

Hence:

(4.7f) $$\partial G/\partial \Theta_1 > 0 \quad \text{for} \quad 0 < \Theta_1 < \alpha_1 \quad \text{and}$$

(4.7g) $$\partial G/\partial \Theta_1 < 0 \quad \text{for} \quad \alpha_1 < \Theta_1 < 1.$$

When plotted against Θ_1, G is an inverse U-shaped curve that takes on a maximum value of α_1 at Θ_1 (figure 4.1). Therefore α_1 is the critical value of Θ_1 marking off the two phases of G. The maximum value of G, when Θ_1 is equal to α_1, is given by:

(4.8) $$G = 2\alpha - 1.$$

In figure 4.1 the emergence of a privileged splinter group out of a homogeneous labor force is represented by movement along one

Table 4.11. *Numerical Example of the Gap between the Relative Value of the Education Characteristic for a Privileged Group and That for a Less Privileged Group*
(values of s)[a]

V_1 for less privileged group	V_2 for privileged group: Six years (primary school)	Nine years (junior high school)	Twelve years (senior high school)	Fourteen years (technical school)	Sixteen years (university or over)
Six years (primary school)	0	0.200	0.333	0.400	0.455
Nine years (junior high school)	—	0	0.143	0.217	0.280
Twelve years (senior high school)	—	—	0	0.077	0.143
Fourteen years (technical school)	—	—	—	0	0.666
Sixteen years (university or over)	—	—	—	—	0

— Not applicable.
Source: Constructed by the authors.
a. $s = V_2^* - V_1^*$.

of the curves from the point U, where Θ_1 is equal to 1, to the left toward the origin, where Θ_1 is equal to zero. This movement indicates that the fraction of labor in the underprivileged group $[\Theta_1]$ is declining. Consider the level of education as an illustration. The value of s between two education characteristics is given in table 4.11, where the years of education are indicated in the headings. For example, the value of s is 0.2 between junior high school, for which V_2 is 9, and primary school, for which V_1 is 6. Starting from the point U in the curve relevant to an s of 0.2 in figure 4.1, a turning point is reached at point T. Thus popularization of junior high school education will first cause the inequality $[G_i]$ to increase to a maximum of 0.10, at which point the proportion of workers with junior high school education has increased to about 45 percent. Notice when the value of s is higher—such as the s of 0.45 between university and primary education—that popularization of higher education will raise the labor characteristic Gini much faster—in this example to a peak value of 0.24 at point T'. But the turning point [T'] will arrive sooner, when about 38 percent of workers have university education.

The emergence of an underprivileged splinter group out of a homogeneous labor force is represented by movement along one of the curves from the origin, where Θ_1 is equal to zero, to the right toward the point U, where Θ_1 is equal to 1. This movement indicates that the fraction of labor in the underprivileged group is increasing. The entry into the labor force of females and young workers under 25 are typical instances of this pattern. When such an inferior group is formed, inequality precedes equality, just as for the formation of a superior group. But when an inferior group is formed, a higher value of s will not only cause the labor characteristic Gini to increase faster, but will also postpone the turning point to a higher value of Θ_1. The skewness of these curves shows the basic asymmetry between the formation of privileged and underprivileged groups.

Notice when the value of the sex characteristic is indexed by zero for females and by 1 for males that the value of s for sex is the maximum—that is, it is equal to 1. Equation (4.6g) then is reduced to a limiting and special case in which G is equal to Θ_1, a relation represented by the 45° line $0A$. Therefore the sex Gini is precisely the fraction of female workers in the labor force; it continuously increases with increasing rates of female participation.

It can be seen from the foregoing discussion that the labor characteristic Gini [G_i] measures inequality in a special sense. Whether a homogeneous group is inferior or superior, a low value of G_i means that the number of workers in that group is either very small and socially insignificant or very large and common. The first instance would be indicated by a small Θ_1; the second by a large Θ_1. A low G_i also means that the superiority or inferiority of the homogeneous group is not very pronounced, which would be indicated by a small s. Vague as it might seem, the values of G_i consequently measure certain properties of a group of workers—properties which common sense would regard as underlying causes of inequality.

Labor characteristic weight

The labor characteristic Gini [G_i] measures the degree of nonhomogeneity of labor. Whether G_i is a principal cause of inequality of wage income depends upon the influence of that characteristic on the wage rate. Suppose that the male premium $[a_1]$ is zero—that is, there is no difference between the male and female wage rates. Then sex cannot be a principal cause of inequality of wage income, regardless of the magnitude of G_i. The labor characteristic weight $[\phi_1]$ measures the relative wage-earning power associated with a labor characteristic. Notice that the regression coefficients $[a_i]$ of equation (4.1) are computed from the primary data for the wage pattern $[W]$ and the labor characteristic pattern $[X_i]$ of equation (4.4). The primary data for the wage pattern $[W]$, the sex characteristic pattern $[X_1]$, and the education characteristic pattern $[X_2]$ in table 4.9 lead to the following regression equation:

$$W = a_o + a_1x_1 + a_2x_2 + \delta, \quad \text{where} \tag{4.9a}$$

$$a_o = -1, \quad a_1 = 2, \quad \text{and} \quad a_2 = 3. \tag{4.9b}$$

When the r values of X_i are substituted into the regression equation (4.1), a column of error terms $[\delta_c = \text{col}(\delta_1, \delta_2, \ldots, \delta_n)]$ is determined.

$$W = a_o + a_1x_1 + a_2x_2 + \ldots + a_rx_r + \delta_c, \quad \text{where} \tag{4.10a}$$

$$a_o = \text{col}(a_o, a_o, \ldots, a_o) \quad \text{and} \tag{4.10b}$$

$$\delta_1 + \delta_2 + \ldots + \delta_n = 0 \tag{4.10c}$$

The computation of δ_c for the numerical example in table 4.9 appears in the right-hand columns. Notice when the regression coefficients are estimated by the method of least squares that the sum of all values of δ_i is zero (see equation [4.10c]). Because of this property the mean values of all column vectors in equation (4.10a) have the following relations:

$$\bar{W} = a_o + a_1\bar{x}_1 + a_2\bar{x}_2 + \ldots + a_r\bar{x}_r, \quad \text{where} \tag{4.11a}$$

$$\bar{W} = (W_1 + W_2 + \ldots + W_n)/n \quad \text{and} \tag{4.11b}$$

$$\bar{x}_i = (x_{i1} + x_{i2} + x_{i3} + \ldots + x_{in})/n, \quad \text{and} \tag{4.11c}$$

$$1 = \frac{a_o}{\bar{w}} + \phi_1 + \phi_2 \ldots + \phi_r, \quad \text{where} \tag{4.11d}$$

$$\phi_i = a_i\bar{x}_i/\bar{w}. \qquad (i = 1, 2, \ldots, r) \tag{4.11e}$$

In equation (4.11b) $\bar{W}$ is the mean wage income; in equation (4.11c) $\bar{x}_i$ is the mean value of the ith characteristic. For example, if x_2 is measured in years of formal education, then $\bar{X}_2$ is the average years of education for the n workers. The labor characteristic weights $[\phi_i]$ are defined in equation (4.11e). Because the product of the education premium and the average years of education $[a_i\bar{x}_i]$ represents the average contribution of education to the wage rate, the education characteristic weight is a measure of this contribution as a fraction of the average wage rate. For a typical term $\phi_i R_i G_i$ in equation (4.3), it can thus be seen that a labor characteristic Gini $[G_i]$ cannot make a heavy contribution to the inequality of wage income unless the labor characteristic weight $[\phi_i]$ is large.[11]

The values of the labor characteristic weights are given in table 4.9: ϕ_1 is 0.125; ϕ_2 is 1.03125. When a higher value of a variable $[x_i]$ corresponds to higher earning power, the regression coefficient $[a_i]$ is positive. Consequently the values of ϕ_i are nonnegative. It can nevertheless be seen from equation (4.11d) that the r values of ϕ_i do not form a system of weights unless the regression constant $[a_o]$ is equal to zero. Because a_o is negative in the numerical example, the values of ϕ_i add up to more than 1. The rank-weighted error term $[\Delta]$ in equation (4.3) is defined as follows:

(4.12a) $\Delta = (j_1\delta_1 + j_2\delta_2 + \ldots + j_n\delta_n)/\bar{w}$, where

(4.12b) $j_i = i/(1 + 2 + \ldots + n)$ and $(i = 1, 2, \ldots, n)$

(4.12c) $j_1 + j_2 + \ldots + j_n = 1.$

The values of j_i in equation (4.12b) are relative ranks used as a system of weights. Therefore Δ is the rank-weighted error expressed as a fraction of the average wage $[\bar{W}]$. It measures the importance of the error term in equation (4.3). In view of equation (4.10c) Δ can be positive or negative. The computation of Δ as being equal to 0.0047 is shown in table 4.9.

Labor correlation characteristic

The contribution of a labor characteristic, such as education or sex, to the inequality of wage income depends not only on the labor characteristic weight $[\phi_i]$ and the labor characteristic Gini $[G_i]$,

11. Notice that $(\bar{X}_i, \bar{W})$ is a mean point on the regression line. Thus ϕ_i is the elasticity of w with respect to X_i at the mean point. To illustrate: ϕ_2 for education is the percentage increase in the average wage rate when the average number of years of education increases by 1 percent.

but also on the extent to which the values of a characteristic are correlated with wage income. Assume that the pattern of wage income of five workers is $W = \text{col}(10, 12, 18, 25, 30)$ and the years of formal education are given by two alternatives, $X_2^1 = \text{col}(6, 6, 9, 12, 14)$ and $X_2^2 = \text{col}(14, 9, 12, 6, 6)$. For the first alternative, workers with higher income receive a higher education—that is, W and X_2^1 are highly and positively correlated. For the second alternative, the opposite is true. Workers with higher income receive a lower education—that is, W and X_2^2 are negatively correlated. The higher income in the second alternative is the result of such other labor characteristics as sex and age; education in fact contributes to the equality of wage income, not to its inequality.

Observe that the value of the labor characteristic Gini [G_i] is the same for X_2^1 and X_2^2. Thus the impact of education on the inequality of wage income depends not only on the labor characteristic Gini [G_i], but also on the correlation characteristic [R_i]. Other things being equal, a high positive value of R_i indicates that the ith characteristic contributes more to the inequality of wage income than to its equality. If R_i is negative, the ith characteristic contributes to equality, not to inequality [see equation (4.3)].

When the primary data are given for a particular labor characteristic according to equations (4.4a) and (4.4b), the labor correlation characteristic is computed as follows:

(4.13a) $R_i = R_i(W, x_i) = \bar{G}_i/G_i$, where

(4.13b) $\bar{G}_i = 2\bar{u}_i/n - (n + 1)/n$, where

(4.13c) $\bar{u}_i = r_1(x_{i1}/s_i) + r_2(x_{i2}/s_i) + \ldots + r_n(x_{in}/s_i)$, where

(4.13d) $s_i = x_{i1} + x_{i2} + \ldots + x_{in}$

and r_i is the wage income rank of the ith worker. The computation or R_1 and R_2 is indicated in table 4.9. Note that the education characteristic has a perfect rank correlation with wage income, giving R_2 a value of 1. In general the labor correlation characteristic [R_i] is that fraction of the labor characteristic Gini [G_i] which can be explained by the variation of wage income or the correlation characteristic between W and X_i.[12]

12. In part two $\bar{G}_i$ is referred to as the pseudo Gini coefficient, and R_i is the ratio of the pseudo Gini coefficient to the Gini coefficient. See chapters eight and nine in part two.

Empirical analysis

Decomposition equation (4.3) was applied to the data for 1966 (table 4.12). The decomposition was carried out separately for rural areas, towns, and cities to yield the labor characteristic weights [ϕ_i], the labor characteristic Ginis [G_i], and the correlation charac-

Table 4.12. *Decomposition Analysis of the Inequality of the Wage Rate, by Location and Labor Characteristic, 1966*

Variable	*Notation*	*Rural area*	*Town*	*City*
Labor characteristic weight				
Sex	ϕ_1	0.3536	0.3486	0.3123
Education	ϕ_2	1.4952	1.1167	0.6564
Age	ϕ_3	0.5025	0.5360	0.7092
Family income	ϕ_4	0.1979	0.1421	0.2151
Labor characteristic Gini				
Sex	G_1	0.3304	0.2363	0.2190
Education	G_2	0.8092	0.5584	0.5506
Age	G_3	0.5816	0.5798	0.5622
Family income	G_4	0.5020	0.4820	0.4404
Labor correlation characteristic				
Sex	R_1	0.6338	0.8819	0.6932
Education	R_2	0.1036	0.3281	0.3382
Age	R_3	0.1850	0.4129	0.3131
Family income	R_4	0.9693	0.5477	0.4301
Contribution term				
Sex	$\phi_1 R_1 G_1$	0.0740	0.0726	0.0474
Education	$\phi_2 R_2 G_2$	0.1253	0.2046	0.1222
Age	$\phi_3 R_3 G_3$	0.0541	0.1283	0.1248
Family income	$\phi_4 R_4 G_4$	0.0963	0.0375	0.0407
Wage Gini	G_w	0.6108	0.5434	0.4876
Explained wage Gini	$\hat{G}_w$	0.3497	0.4430	0.3351
Rank-weighted error term	Δ	0.2611	0.1004	0.1525

Sources: Calculated from tables 4.20–4.27 appended to this chapter.

Figure 4.2. *The Wage Gini and the Explained Portion of the Wage Gini, by Location, 1966*

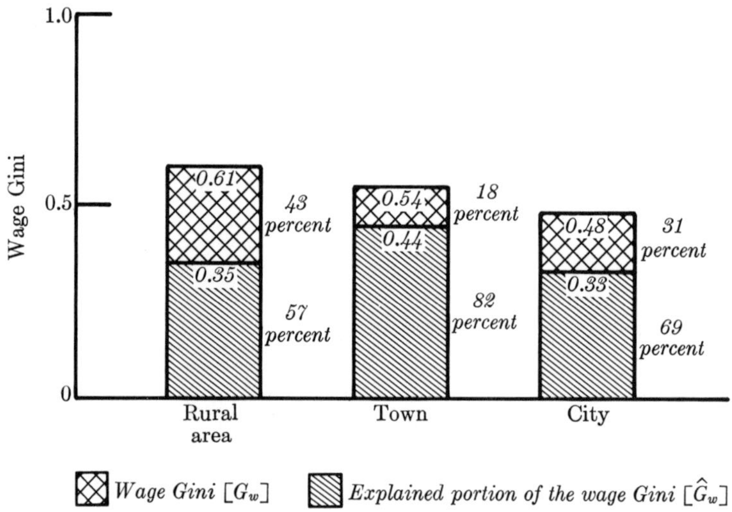

Source: Table 4.12.

teristics [R_i]. The factor contribution terms [$\phi_i R_i G_i$] measure the contribution of various labor attributes to the degree of inequality of wage rates. At the bottom of table 4.12 are shown the Gini coefficient of the wage rate [G_w], the sum of the four factor contribution terms [$\hat{G}_i$], and the rank-weighted error term [Δ] which is equal to G_w minus $\hat{G}_w$. Figures 4.2 and 4.3 graphically summarize the essential information in this table.

The shaded areas in figure 4.2 represent the explained wage Gini [$\hat{G}_w$]—that is, that portion of the wage Gini that can be explained by the four characteristics traced in this analysis. The shaded and unshaded areas together represent the wage Gini [G_w]. It can be seen that the inequality of the wage rate [G_w] consistently declines from 0.61 for traditional rural areas to 0.54 for semimodern and semirural towns and 0.49 for modern cities. These magnitudes indicate, at least for 1966, that modernization was not accompanied by the increased wage inequality which the Kuznets hypothesis would suggest. The explained wage Gini [$\hat{G}_w$] accounted for 57 percent of the wage Gini [G_w] for rural areas, 82 percent of that for towns, and 69 percent of that for cities. The rank-weighted error terms respectively accounted for 43 percent, 18 percent, and 31 percent of the wage Gini. In other words, the influence of sex, education, age, and family income can explain only about 70 percent of the causes of wage-rate inequality. In this analysis 30 percent cannot be accounted for by these characteristics.[13] By comparing rural areas, towns, and cities, an inverse U-shaped pattern can be observed in the proportion of the explained inequality [$\hat{G}_w/G_w$]. That proportion rises from 57 percent to 82 percent and then declines to 69 percent. Such a pattern suggests that other, unidentified causes of the inequality of wage rates are more pronounced in rural areas and large cities than in towns. In towns, however, sex, education, age, and family influence together constitute a set of causal factors which can adequately explain the inequality of wage rates. The following analysis concentrates on this explained portion of wage-rate inequality—that is, it concentrates on $\hat{G}_w$, not on G_w.

The percentage contributions of sex, education, age, and family income to explained wage-rate inequality [$\hat{G}_w$] are shown in figure 4.3. The education characteristic, with a simple average of 39 percent for the three locations, makes the largest contribution. The age characteristic contributes 28 percent, the sex characteristic 17 percent, and the family-influence characteristic 16 percent. Thus education and age characteristics together account for about two-thirds of the explained inequality of the wage rate.

Because the productivity of workers with varying educational qualifications and experience (proxied by age) is different, the contribution of these two characteristics to wage-rate inequality can be viewed as rational or warranted. In contrast, the productivity differences of workers of different sex and family background are not as apparent. The contribution of these two factors to inequality, unrelated as they are to productivity, can thus be viewed as irrational or unwarranted. The substantial volume of unwarranted causes, which accounted for about one-third of the explained inequality, suggests that institutional discrimination against women

13. The unexplained portion of G_w could be further reduced by considering an additional dimension of the quality of labor, the job or occupational characteristic.

Figure 4.3. *Percentage Composition of Factor Contributions, by Location, 1966*

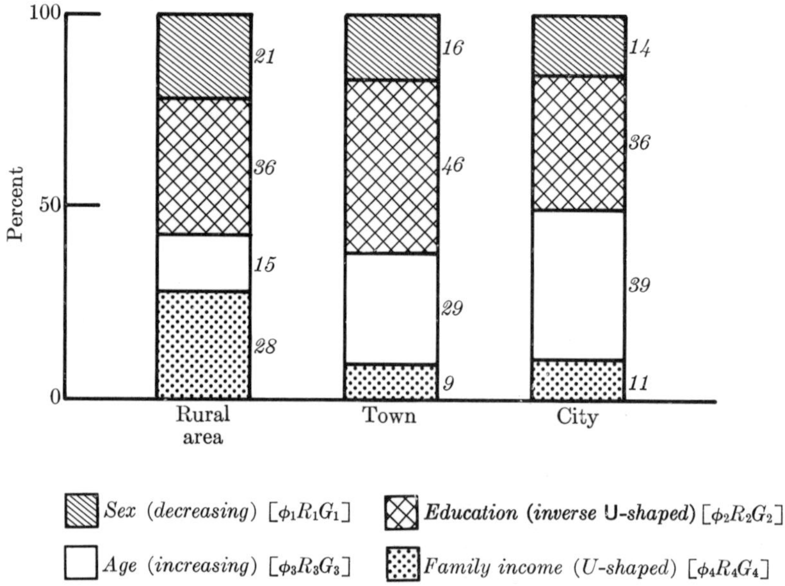

Source: Table 4.12.

and in favor of members of wealthy families was important in labor markets. Institutional discrimination declined from 49 percent for rural areas to 26 percent for cities. In other words, institutional discrimination was about twice as strong in rural areas as it was in cities. This evidence thus supports the assumption that modernization tends to reduce the discrimination against females and members of poorer families. Notice moreover that family influence was relatively more important than sex discrimination in rural areas, but that this ranking was reversed in cities. It seems that modernization removes the bias of family influence faster than that of sex discrimination.

The contribution of the education characteristic to wage-rate inequality [$\hat{G}_w$] was 36 percent for rural areas, 46 percent for towns, and 36 percent for cities. It thus exhibited something of an inverse U-shaped pattern. The age characteristic, with values of 15 percent for rural areas, 29 percent for towns, and 39 percent for cities, never-

Figure 4.4. *Composition of the Contribution of Education to Explained Inequality, by Location, 1966*

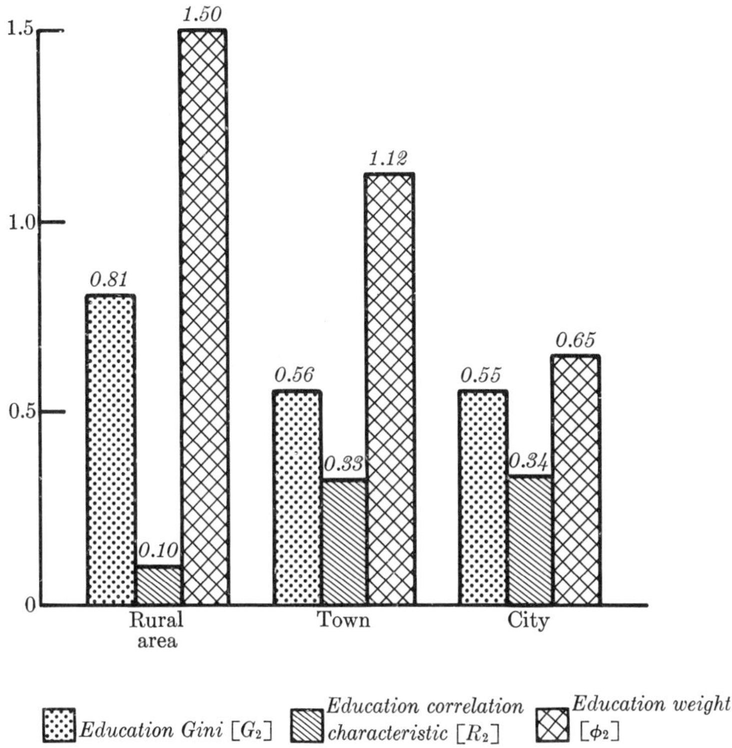

Source: Table 4.12.

theless presented an unmistakable increasing pattern. Age and experience together accounted for more wage-rate inequality in cities than in rural communities. In the following discussion an attempt will be made to explain why these two warranted characteristics of age and education exhibited such a pattern. Then the other two characteristics will be discussed.

THE CONTRIBUTION OF EDUCATION TO INEQUALITY. The data underlying the analysis of the contribution of education $[\phi_2 R_2 G_2]$ to wage-rate inequality $[\hat{G}_w]$ is graphically summarized in figure 4.4.

Based on the survey results for 1966, the education Gini [G_2] was 0.81 for rural areas, 0.56 for towns, and 0.55 for cities. The education weight [ϕ_2] was 1.50 for rural areas, 1.12 for towns, and 0.65 for cities. These declining values associated with increased urbanity reflect the high number of educated workers in cities. Both ϕ_2 and G_2 contributed to the reduction of $\phi_2 R_2 G_2$ for semiurban and urban areas. Education's contribution to overall wage-rate inequality exhibited an inverse U-shaped pattern for the three locations primarily because R_2 increased as both ϕ_2 and G_2 declined. The correlation characteristics [R_2] were 0.10 for rural areas, 0.33 for towns, and 0.34 for cities. In other words, the wage rate was correlated with educational qualifications to a much higher degree in cities than in rural areas. The economic interpretation of this evidence is that the wage rate in cities reflects formal educational qualifications of workers with a higher degree of sensitivity than it does age, sex, and other unspecified characteristics. This pattern is precisely what would be expected in a commercialized urban environment in which labor markets tend to be somewhat more perfect.

THE CONTRIBUTION OF AGE TO INEQUALITY. As was seen in figure 4.3, the contribution of age [$\phi_3 R_3 G_3$] to inequality [$\hat{G}_w$] was least in rural areas and greatest in cities. Although the age Gini was about 0.57 for the three sectors, the weighted correlation characteristic [$\phi_3 R_3$] was larger in cities than in rural areas, mainly because the correlation of age with wage income [R_3] was much higher in towns (figure 4.5). This evidence indicates that older workers, who assumedly were more experienced than their younger counterparts, participated much more in the urban work force than in the rural. The value of $\phi_3 R_3$ was about 0.22 for both towns and cities. But the contribution of age to inequality was greater in cities than in towns—0.39 compared with 0.29—primarily at the expense of the contribution of education, which was greater in towns than in cities—0.46 compared with 0.36. Thus age and experience began to overtake education as the most important factor contributing to the inequality of the wage rate in the cities. The reason probably is that work experience counted for relatively more in the industrial complexes of large cities.

By comparing rural areas and urban areas, three tendencies can be detected in the two warranted characteristics of education and age. First, the education Gini was lowest in cities and highest in rural areas, but the age Gini was highest in cities and lowest in rural

Figure 4.5. *Composition of the Contribution of Age to Explained Inequality, by Location, 1966*

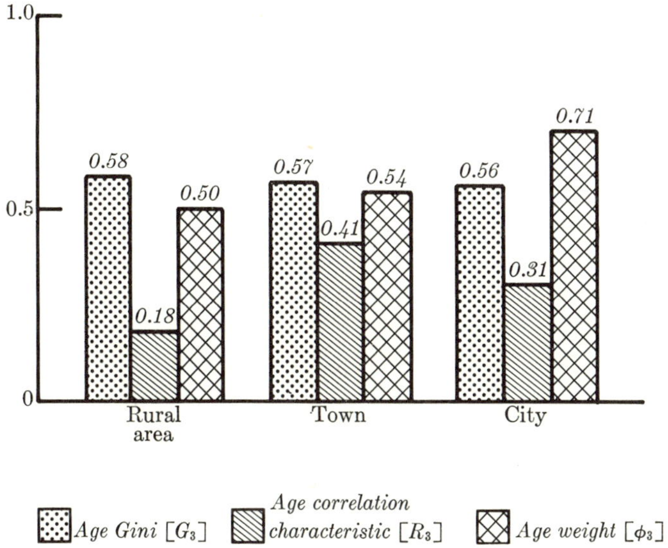

Source: Table 4.12.

areas. This pattern means that, when workers with higher formal education become more abundant, the experienced worker begins to gain in importance. In figure 4.1 the rural, town, and city situations for the education Gini are represented by the points R', T', and C' on the increasing portion of the inverse U-shaped curve (remember that the formation of a privileged group is indicated by movement from the point Θ_1 to the left toward the origin). Thus, when the labor force is modernizing, the development of education attributes precedes that of experience attributes. Although the age characteristic still contributes to inequality, the education characteristic begins to contribute to equality. Second, the education weight [ϕ_2] was lowest in cities and highest in rural areas, but the age weight [ϕ_3] was highest in cities and lowest in rural areas. Consequently, during modernization, age begins to count more heavily than education in production. Third, the correlation characteristic

[R_3] was higher in semiurban and urban areas than in rural areas. This evidence suggests that the better developed labor market is more sensitive in rewarding both education and experience in the commercialized milieu of large cities.

THE CONTRIBUTION OF SEX TO INEQUALITY. As already seen, institutional discrimination, particularly that against women, was weaker in cities than in rural areas. The sex contribution term [$\phi_1 R_1 G_1$] was 0.074 for rural areas and 0.047 for cities (see table 4.12). Of the factors of this term, the sex Gini [G_1] really is equivalent to the female participation rate. The sex correlation characteristic [R_1] represents the correlation between the wage rate and the maleness of workers. For example, if the pattern of the wage rates for five workers is given by ($10, $20, $35, $50, $100) and the sex of these workers is given by (0, 0, 0, 1, 1), the highly positive correlation [R_1] means that male workers get the better paid jobs. Conversely, if the sex pattern of these workers is given by (1, 1, 0, 0, 0), the negative correlation reveals that females get the better paid jobs. A high value of R_1 therefore is equivalent to job-availability discrimination: that is, the more a job pays, the less it will be available to females. The sex weight [ϕ_1] reflects the male premium in the wage structure: the higher the value of ϕ_1, the higher the degree of discrimination against women.

The contribution of sex to inequality was about the same for towns and rural areas. The reason for this pattern is that the higher urban R_1 canceled the lower urban G_1. More concretely, the female participation rate in towns, proxied by a G_1 of 0.23, was lower than that in rural areas, proxied by a G_1 of 0.33 (figure 4.6). At the same time, men were getting more of the better paid jobs in towns, proxied by an R_1 of 0.88, than in rural areas, proxied by an R_1 of 0.63. In cities, all three factors work in the relative favor of female workers. Compared with their counterparts in towns, female workers in cities had a slightly lower participation rate, obtained more of the better paid jobs, and benefited from a lower male premium.

THE CONTRIBUTION OF TOTAL FAMILY INCOME TO INEQUALITY. As with sex discrimination, the wage-rate favoritism for members of wealthier families was lower in urban areas than in rural areas. The family-influence contribution term [$\phi_4 R_4 G_4$] was 0.096 for rural areas, 0.037 for towns, and 0.041 for cities. The family-influence

Figure 4.6. *Composition of the Contribution of Sex to Explained Inequality, by Location, 1966*

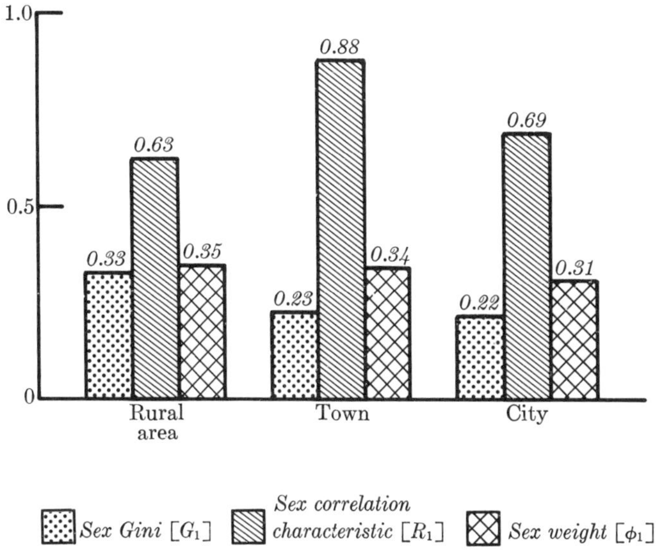

Source: Table 4.12.

Gini [G_4] simply is the Gini coefficient measuring the degree of inequality of total family income. The family-influence weight [ϕ_4] measures the wage advantage of members of relatively wealthy families: the higher the value of ϕ_4, the greater the wage-rate discrimination. The family-influence correlation characteristic [R_4] measures the extent to which wealthy families can secure better paid jobs for their members through nepotism. In effect it is a measure of job-availability discrimination. In 1966 total family income was distributed most equally in cities and least equally in rural areas. The family-influence Gini [G_4] was 0.44 for cities, 0.48 for towns, and 0.50 for rural areas (figure 4.7). It would also appear that the market mechanisms associated with increasing urbanity gradually weaken the role of special influence in the award of high-salary jobs to workers. The correlation characteristic associated with

Figure 4.7. *Composition of the Contribution of Family Influence to Explained Inequality, by Location, 1966*

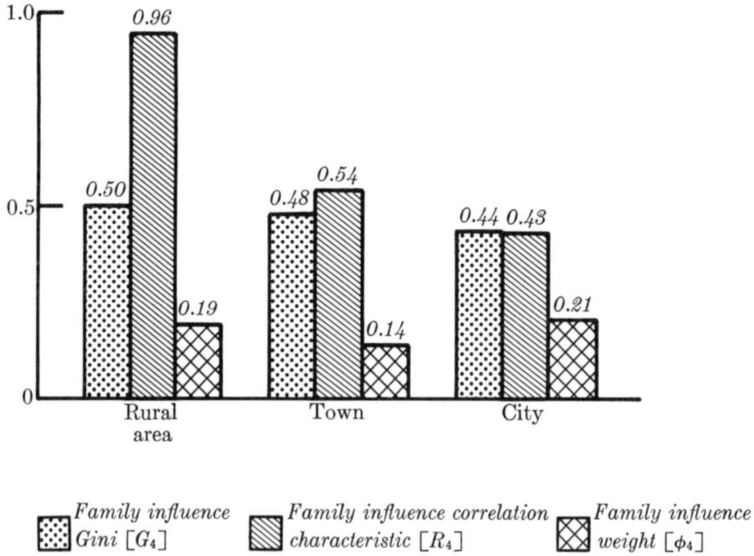

Source: Table 4.12.

family influence [R_4] was 0.96 for rural areas, 0.54 for towns, and 0.40 for cities. These factors help explain the decline of nepotism as a form of institutional discrimination in the commercialized milieu of urban areas.

Inequality of Family Wage Income: Third-level Analysis

If a family has more workers or family members with higher wage-earning power, it will clearly tend to have a higher total wage income. Assume that there are r types of worker with a pattern of wage rates given by $(w_1, w_2, \ldots, w_r)$. Suppose further that there are n families. Then let the pattern of total family wage income of these families be denoted by $W = \text{col}(W_1, W_2, \ldots, W_n)$. Suppose that the ith family has x_{ij} workers of the jth type. Then:

(4.14a) $$W = w_1X_1 + w_2X_2 + \ldots + w_rX_r, \quad \text{where}$$

(4.14b) $$X_i = \text{col}(x_{1i}, x_{2i}, \ldots, x_{ni}) \quad \text{and} \qquad (i = 1, 2, \ldots, r)$$

(4.14c) $$W_1 < W_2 < \ldots < W_n.$$

The column vector X_i stands for the pattern according to which the workers of the ith type are distributed among the n families. Notice in expression (4.14c) that the n families are arranged in a monotonically increasing order: in total wage income, the first family is the poorest, the last family wealthiest. Let G_w denote the Gini coefficient of the distribution of wage income [W] and measure the degree of inequality of family wage income. Make use of a decomposition equation of the following form:

(4.15) $$G_w = \phi_1R_1G_1 + \phi_2R_2G_2 + \ldots + \phi_rR_rG_r.$$

In equation (4.15) G_w measures the degree of inequality of total family wage income. The term $\phi_iR_iG_i$ will be referred to as the contribution of workers of the ith type to inequality.

The Gini coefficient [G_i] of the labor characteristic vector [X_i] measures the inequality of distribution of workers of the ith type among families. It will be referred to as the family membership Gini of the ith type. The term ϕ_i is defined as follows:

(4.16a) $$\bar{W} = w_1\bar{x}_1 + w_2\bar{x}_2 + \ldots + w_r\bar{x}_r, \quad \text{where}$$

(4.16b) $$\bar{W} = (W_1 + W_2 + \ldots + W_n)/n \quad \text{and}$$

$$\bar{x}_i = (x_{1i} + x_{2i} + \ldots + x_{ni})/n, \quad \text{and}$$

(4.16c) $$1 = \phi_1 + \phi_2 + \ldots + \phi_r, \quad \text{where}$$

(4.16d) $$\phi_i = w_i\bar{x}_i/\bar{W}. \qquad (i = 1, 2, \ldots, r)$$

In equation (4.16b) $\bar{W}$ is the average wage income of families, and $\bar{x}_i$ is the number of workers of the ith type per family. Thus ϕ_i is the fraction of wage income per family earned by workers of the ith type. Call this fraction the wage income weight.

The degree of family wage-income inequality [G_w] can also be affected by the correlation characteristic between W and X_i. Suppose there are five workers with a pattern of Ph.D. membership given by (0, 0, 1, 2, 1). As would be expected, these highly paid workers are concentrated among the wealthy families: that is, the correlation between W and X_i is high and positive. If the pattern of Ph.D.

membership were instead given by (1, 1, 2, 0, 0), the family membership Gini would be the same, but the negative correlation between W and X_i would obviously contribute to the equality of family wage income, not to its inequality. When the wage rates of r types of worker are arranged in a monotonically increasing order given by $(w_1 \leq w_2 \leq \ldots \leq w_r)$, the first type of worker is the lowest paid and the last type of worker is the highest paid. With such a pattern, the low-paid workers would be expected to be concentrated among the poor families, leading to a negative correlation between W and X_i; the high-paid workers would be expected to be concentrated among the wealthy families, thus leading to a positive correlation between W and X_i.

Empirical analysis

For purposes of empirical analysis at the third level, forty types of workers can be identified for the regression equation (4.2). The number 40 is the product of the number of values assumed by the sex, education, and age characteristics. Sex has two values: M for male, and F for female. Education has five values: L for primary school; I for junior high school; H for senior high school; T for technical school; and U for university or over. Age has four values: 1 for under 25; 2 for 25–45; 3 for 45–60; and 4 for over 60. Thus the combination of attributes embodied by a homogeneous group of workers can, for example, be denoted by $ML1$, which would indicate male workers under 25 having primary school education, or $FT3$, which would indicate female workers aged 45–60 and having technical school education. To simplify the analysis, the family influence variable is not used here.

Wage rates for the various types of workers in 1966 were computed from the following equation:

(4.17a) $w = a_o + a_1x_1 + a_2x_2 + a_3x_3,$ where

(4.17b) $a_o = 13.61, \quad a_1 = 5.277, \quad a_2 = 1.512, \quad a_3 = 3.486$ and

(4.17c) $x_1 = (0, 1), \quad x_2 = (6, 9, 12, 14, 16), \quad x_3 = (1, 2, 3, 3).$

[*sex*] [*education*] [*age*]

The values of the regression coefficients $[a_i]$ in equation (4.17b) were computed as the average of the rural, town, and city coefficients of table 4.6, weighted by the sample sizes indicated there.

When the values of x_i in equation (4.17c) are substituted into equation (4.17a), the wage rates [w_i] can be computed (table 4.13). Notice that the wage rate for females under 25 with primary education ($FL1$) becomes negative. The reason is that the term representing the influence of total family income [a_4x_4] in equation (4.2) has been omitted from equation (4.17a). Notice also that the wage rates in table 4.13 are arranged in a monotonically increasing order. And because three categories contain no workers ($FI4$, $FH4$, and $FT4$), there are thirty-seven wage rates, not forty. The lowest paid workers were females with primary education under 25 ($FL1$); their wage rate [w_1] was -3.212. The highest paid workers were males with university education aged 45–60 ($MU3$); their wage rate [w_{37}] was 20.557.

For each category the family membership Gini [G_i] reveals the degree of inequality of family ownership of the workers of the ith type. For example, suppose that there are five families and the ownership pattern of female workers with university education aged 25–45 ($FU2$) is given by (0, 0, 1, 2, 2). The two poorest families own no workers in this category; such workers are concentrated among wealthy families. The family membership Gini shows the degree of inequality of the ownership pattern of workers. For each category, R_i is the correlation characteristic between the ownership pattern and total family wage income. A high and positive R_i indicates that the ownership of workers of this type is concentrated in families with higher total wage income; a negative R_i, in families with lower total wage income.

To compute the wage income weight [ϕ_i] for every category, the following procedure was used. An estimated pattern of total family wage income pattern [$\hat{W} = \text{col}(\hat{W}_1, \hat{W}_2, \ldots, \hat{W}_n)$] was computed from equation (4.14a) to yield:

$$\text{(4.18a)} \qquad \hat{W} = \hat{w}_1X_1 + \hat{w}_2X_2 + \ldots + \hat{w}_{37}X_{37},$$

$$\text{(4.18b)} \qquad \bar{\hat{W}} = \bar{\hat{w}}_1\bar{x}_1 + \bar{\hat{w}}_2\bar{x}_2 + \ldots + \bar{\hat{w}}_{37}\bar{x}_{37}, \quad \text{and}$$

$$\text{(4.18c)} \qquad 1 = \phi_1 + \phi_2 + \ldots + \phi_{37}, \quad \text{where}$$

$$\text{(4.18d)} \qquad \phi_i = w_i\bar{x}_i/\bar{\hat{W}}.$$

In this estimation the wage rates given by ($\hat{w}_1, \hat{w}_2, \ldots, \hat{w}_{37}$) are first estimated from the regression coefficients in table 4.6. Thus the estimated wage income pattern [$\hat{W}$] differs from the actual pattern. The term ϕ_i represents the wage income per family earned

Table 4.13. *Wages Rates, Family Membership Ginis, and Other Variables for Thirty-seven Categories of Workers, 1966*

Level of education and variable	*Notation*	*Male* Under 25 years	25–45 years	45–60 years	Over 60 years
Primary school		(ML1)	(ML2)	(ML3)	(ML4)
Wage rate[a]	w_i	$w_4 =$ 2.065	$w_{10} =$ 5.551	$w_{18} =$ 9.037	$w_{17} =$ 9.037
Family membership Gini	G	0.125	0.110	0.030	0.340
Correlation characteristic	R	−0.080	−0.636	0.667	−0.674
Mean of x	$\bar{x}$	0.164	0.426	0.154	0.016
Wage income weight	ϕ	0.039	0.272	0.160	0.017
Contribution term	ϕRG	−0.0039	−0.019	0.0032	−0.0009
Junior high school		(MI1)	(MI2)	(MI3)	(MI4)
Wage rate	w_i	$w_9 =$ 5.521	$w_{16} =$ 9.007	$w_{25} =$ 12.493	$w_{24} =$ 12.493
Family membership Gini	G	0.372	0.380	0.350	0.730
Correlation characteristic	R	0.194	0.655	0.886	0.425
Mean of x	$\bar{x}$	0.021	0.078	0.023	0.001
Wage income weight	ϕ	0.013	0.081	0.033	0.001
Contribution term	ϕRG	0.0009	0.0202	0.0102	0.0003
Senior high school		(MH1)	(MH2)	(MH3)	(MH4)
Wage rate	w_i	$w_{15} =$ 8.977	$w_{23} =$ 12.463	$w_{32} =$ 15.949	$w_{31} =$ 15.949
Family membership Gini	G	0.350	0.380	0.543	0.880
Correlation characteristic	R	−0.266	0.942	0.996	0.318
Mean of x	$\bar{x}$	0.027	0.108	0.039	0.0004
Wage income weight	ϕ	0.028	0.155	0.072	0.001
Contribution term	ϕRG	−0.0026	0.0555	0.0389	0.0003
Technical school		(MT1)	(MT2)	(MT3)	(MT4)
Wage rate	w_i	$w_{21} =$ 11.281	$w_{28} =$ 14.767	$w_{35} =$ 18.253	$w_{34} =$ 18.253

Female					
Under 25 years	*25–45 years*	*45–60 years*	*Over 60 years*	*Notation*	*Level of education and variable*
(FL1)	(FL2)	(FL3)	(FL4)		*Primary school*
w_1 = −3.212	w_3 = 0.274	w_8 = 3.760	w_7 = 3.760	w_i	Wage rate[a]
0.130	0.190	0.280	0.660	G	Family membership Gini
−0.769	−0.842	−0.9253	−0.764	R	Correlation characteristic
0.196	0.147	0.0361	0.005	$\bar{x}$	Mean of x
0.073	0.005	0.016	0.002	ϕ	Wage income weight
0.0073	−0.0008	−0.0042	−0.0010	ϕRG	Contribution term
(FI1)	(FI2)	(FI3)	(FI4)		*Junior high school*
w_2 = 0.244	w_6 = 3.730	w_{13} = 7.216	—	w_i	Wage rate
0.240	0.670	0.770	—	G	Family membership Gini
0.838	0.910	−0.088	—	R	Correlation characteristic
0.018	0.012	0.001	—	$\bar{x}$	Mean of x
0.0005	0.005	0.001	—	ϕ	Wage income weight
0.0001	0.003	−0.0001	—	ϕRG	Contribution term
(FH1)	(FH2)	(FH3)	(FH4)		*Senior high school*
w_5 = 3.700	w_{12} = 7.186	w_{20} = 10.672	—	w_i	Wage rate
0.400	0.680	0.680	—	G	Family membership Gini
0.645	0.985	0.206	—	R	Correlation characteristic
0.017	0.012	0.003	—	$\bar{x}$	Mean of x
0.007	0.010	0.004	—	ϕ	Wage income weight
0.0018	0.0067	0.0006	—	ϕRG	Contribution term
(FT1)	(FT2)	(FT3)	(FT4)		*Technical school*
w_{11} = 6.004	w_{19} = 9.490	w_{26} = 12.948	—	w_i	Wage rate

(Table continues on the following pages)

Table 4.13 (*Continued*)

Level of education and variable	Notation	Male: Under 25 years	Male: 25–45 years	Male: 45–60 years	Male: Over 60 years
Family membership Gini	G	0.780	0.702	0.850	0.970
Correlation characteristic	R	0.218	0.944	0.953	1.000
Mean of x	$\bar{x}$	0.002	0.009	0.004	0.0004
Wage income weight	ϕ	0.003	0.015	0.008	0.001
Contribution term	ϕRG	0.0005	0.0099	0.0065	0.001
University or over		(MU1)	(MU2)	(MU3)	(MU4)
Wage rate	w_i	w_{27} = 13.585	w_{33} = 17.071	w_{37} = 20.557	w_{36} = 20.557
Family membership Gini	G	0.846	0.630	0.569	0.870
Correlation characteristic	R	0.366	0.968	0.967	0.840
Mean of x	$\bar{x}$	0.002	0.030	0.018	0.002
Wage income weight	ϕ	0.003	0.059	0.043	0.005
Contribution term	ϕRG	0.0009	0.0360	0.0237	0.0037

— Not applicable.
Sources: Calculated from tables 4.20–4.27 appended to this chapter.
a. In thousands of N.T. dollars; i is the wage rank.

by workers of the ith type expressed as a fraction of the estimated average family income $[\bar{\hat{W}}]$. The values of ϕ_i add up to one. For all thirty-seven categories, the contribution of workers of the ith type to inequality was 0.2060 (see table 4.13). This value is the Gini coefficient of total family wage income $[\hat{G}_w]$ for the estimated wage pattern $[\hat{W}]$ of equation (4.18a).[14] The values of ϕ_i, R_i, and $\phi_i R_i G_i$ are plotted against the wage rate in figures 4.8–4.11.

In figure 4.8 the contribution of the thirty-seven grades of labor $[\phi_i R_i G_i]$ to the inequality of total family wage income $[\hat{G}_w]$ is

14. We are not concerned in this section with the difference between the true G_w and $\hat{G}_w$—that is, with the unexplained portion of G_w measured by $G_w - \hat{G}_w$.

Female					
Under 25 years	*25–45 years*	*45–60 years*	*Over 60 years*	*Notation*	*Level of education and variable*
					Family membership
0.780	0.890	0.930	—	G	Gini
					Correlation
−0.474	0.787	0.752	—	R	characteristic
0.001	0.002	0.0004	—	$\bar{x}$	Mean of x
0.001	0.002	0.001	—	ϕ	Wage income weight
−0.0004	0.0014	0.0007	—	ϕRG	Contribution term
(FU1)	(FU2)	(FU3)	(FU4)		*University or over*
w_{14} =	w_{22} =	w_{30} =	w_{29} =	w_i	Wage rate
8.758	12.244	15.730	15.730		
					Family membership
0.850	0.820	0.920	0.960	G	Gini
					Correlation
0.804	0.915	1.000	0.903	R	characteristic
0.002	0.004	0.0013	0.0004	$\bar{x}$	Mean of x
0.002	0.006	0.002	0.001	ϕ	Wage income weight
0.0014	0.0045	0.0018	0.001	ϕRG	Contribution term

measured on the vertical axis. The grade of a particular type of labor corresponds to its rank in the wage-rate structure and is measured on the horizontal axis. The nine types of labor below the horizontal axis—that is, those having a negative $\phi_i R_i G_i$—contribute to equality, not to inequality. They constitute the so-called marginal labor force: the poorly educated male and female workers who are either very young and have little work experience or are very old and near retirement. The exception to this characterization is the category of poorly educated male workers aged 25–45 ($ML2$) who constitute the bulk of the unskilled labor force.

The dotted horizontal line aa' divides the types of workers who contribute to inequality into two groups. Those above the line essentially are male workers in their prime age—that is, 25–60. The exceptions are highly educated females in their prime age ($FU2$ and $FH2$)—that is, 25–45. This group, which can be referred to as

Figure 4.8. *Contribution to Family Wage Income Inequality, by Labor Grade, 1966*

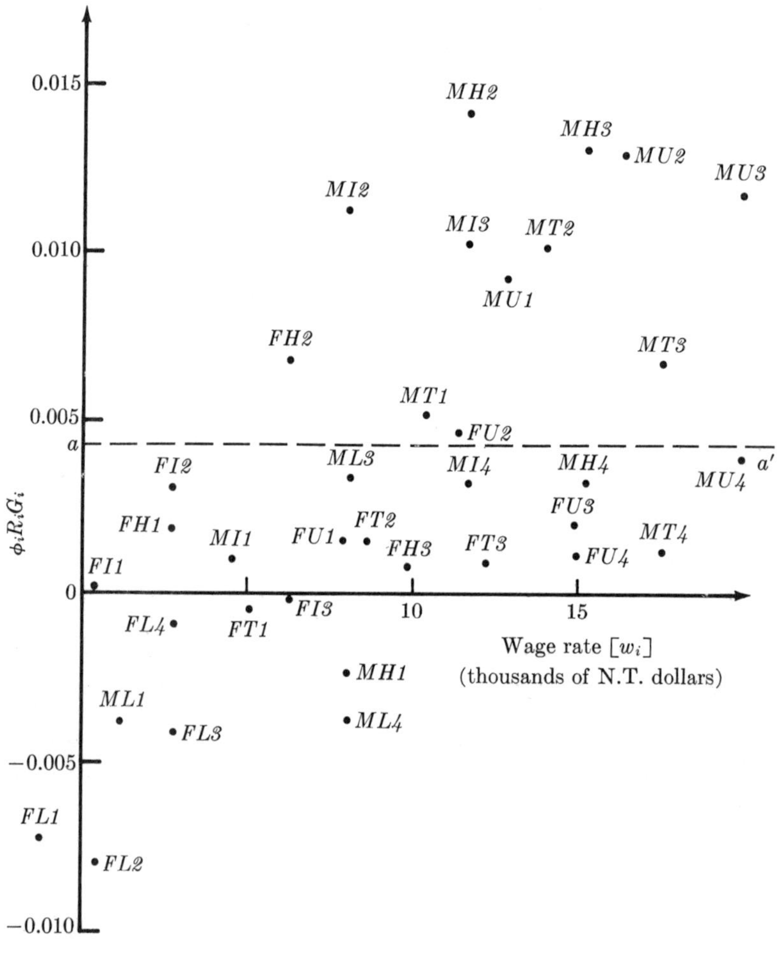

Source: Table 4.13.

the prime age group, makes a heavy contribution to inequality. It accounts for more than 100 percent of the inequality of family wage income (0.2135/0.2060 = 1.036). Its contribution adds up to more than 100 percent because the marginal labor force contributes to equality.

Given the foregoing conclusion, a sharp distinction can be drawn between two issues which are sometimes confused: the degree of inequality of family wage income; the welfare of the marginal labor force. Government relief or welfare measures—for example, minimum wage legislation—may represent attempts to help the marginal labor force, but they do little to resolve the basic inequality of family wage income. In other words, even if the welfare problem were solved, the degree of inequality of total family wage income would remain essentially unchanged. The reason for this outcome is that the inequality of family wage income is a condition that centers mainly around workers in the prime age group.

The correlation between the wage rate, or labor grade, and its contribution to inequality is significant and positive (see figure 4.8). It can be imagined that the labor force in a traditional society is homogeneous and that the wage rate is low. Industrialization then brings about wage increases as the labor force begins to be differentiated. The impact of such modernization is mainly directed at the prime labor group. The emergence of high-grade laborers and the increase in their number represent the major causes of family wage-income inequality.

The positive correlations in figures 4.9 and 4.10 explain the positive correlation between W_i and $\phi_i R_i G_i$. First, the positive correlation between the wage rate [W_i] and the degree of inequality of family ownership of workers of various grades [G_i] in figure 4.9 means that low-grade laborers are more evenly distributed among families than are laborers of higher grades. Put differently, as the higher grade laborers come into being, they are acquired by a minority of families. Second, the positive correlation in figure 4.10 between the wage rate [W_i] and the degree of correlation between total family wage income and family ownership of labor [R_i] suggests that the laborers of higher grades are acquired by wealthy families that have a higher total wage income. The inequality of family ownership of high-grade laborers thus must be regarded as the most important cause of family wage-income inequality.

Economic development can affect the inequality of family wage income through another set of factors which are purely economic. Consider this example. The mean values of the number of workers of various grades per family are denoted by $\bar{x}_i$ (see table 4.13). If N is the total number of families—N is equal to 2,379 in table 4.13

Figure 4.9. *Inequality of Family Ownership of Labor of Different Grades, 1966*

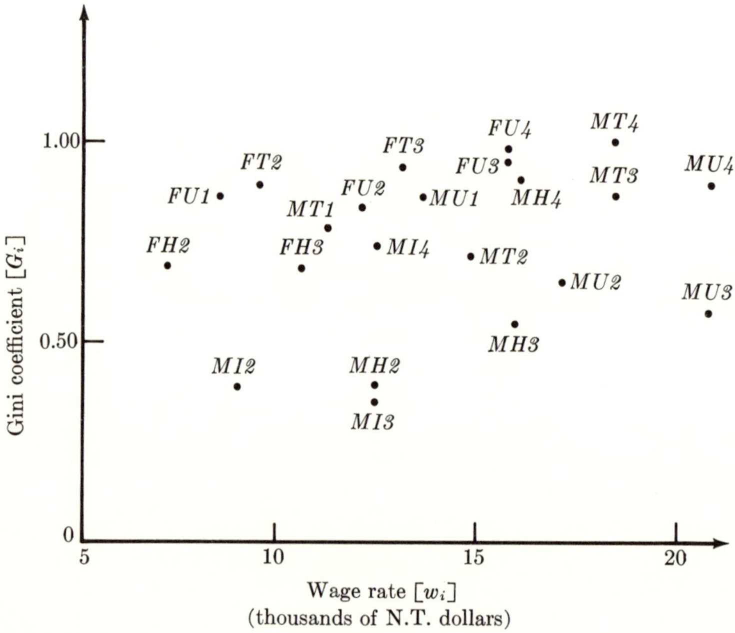

Source: Table 4.13.

—then the number of workers of various grades supplied by families to industry is denoted by Nx_i, where $i = 1, 2, \ldots, 37$. Industrial demand, labor supply, and discrimination determine the structure of the wage rates [W] which in turn determines the structure of wage income weights [ϕ_i]:

$$(4.19)\quad (\phi_1, \phi_2, \ldots, \phi_{37}) = (w_1x_1/\bar{W}, w_2x_2/\bar{W}, \ldots, w_{37}x_{37}/\bar{W}).$$

[see equation (4.16d)]

The structure of wage income weights thus reflects demand and supply for various grades of labor for the whole country.

The values of ϕ_i are plotted against the wage rate in figure 4.11. These wage income weights measure the contribution of the various grades of labor to the inequality of family wage income, as traced

Figure 4.10. *Correlation Characteristics between Total Family Income and Family Ownership of Labor, 1966*

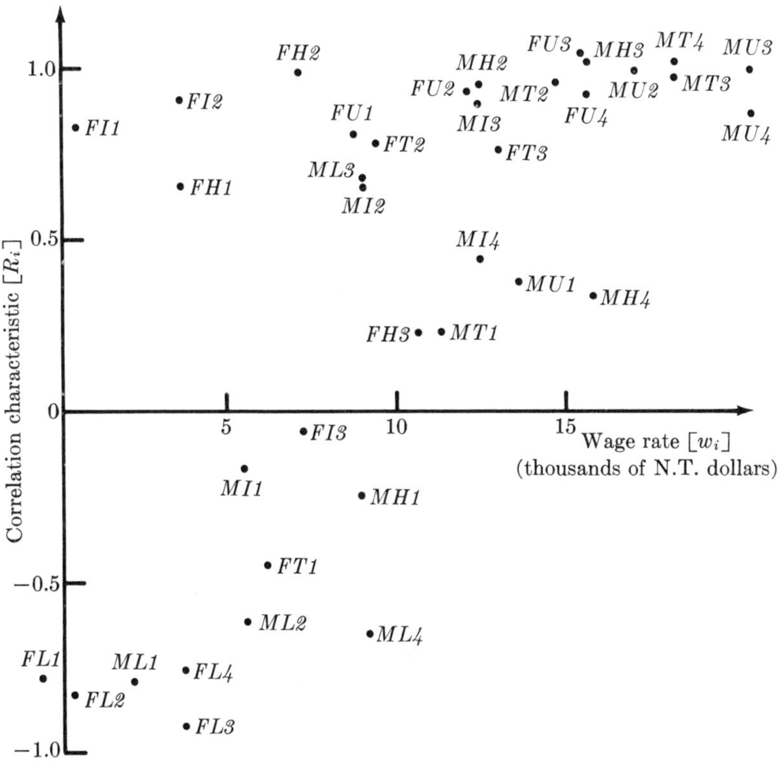

Source: Table 4.13.

to their respective economic importance arising from their large size, high wage, or both. In this sense, workers in the prime age are all economically important, as is seen from the fact that the values of ϕ_i are relatively high for them. As a general rule, these workers contribute heavily to inequality. There nevertheless are two exceptions: low-educated males in their prime age (*ML*2 and *ML*3). They are economically important because of their large numbers, but they do not contribute heavily to inequality because they are

Figure 4.11. *The Economic Weight of Different Grades of Labor, 1966*

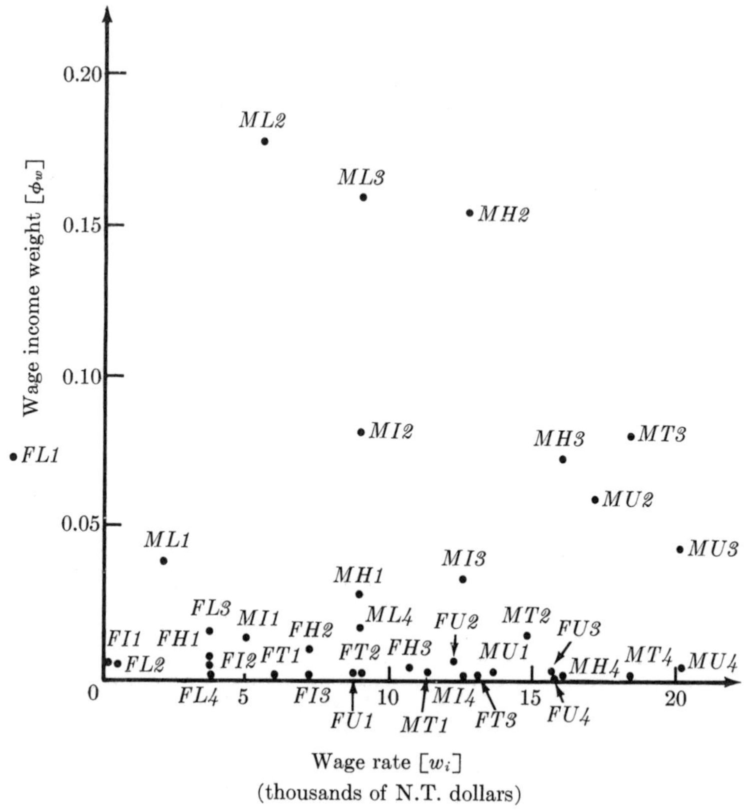

Source: Table 4.13.

more evenly distributed among families. As a result, family ownership of highly educated, prime-age workers contributes most to the inequality of family wage income.

Family size and composition

The inequality of family wage income is related in part to such economic causes as the demand for, and the supply of, labor having different characteristics, in part to such demographic causes as the rules governing the formation of families having different membership compositions. Thus the foregoing empirical analysis of the causes of inequality of family wage income merely scratches the surface of complex economic and demographic phenomena. Consider some aspects of demographic phenomena. The sex composition of a family is influenced by institutions of monogamous and polygamous marriage and by biological laws of reproduction. The age composition of a family is influenced by rules governing the formation of nuclear families, the age at first marriage for males and females, the age at which couples start a new family, and the support of aged parents and grandparents.[15] The educational composition of a family is influenced by that family's investment in the education of its members. What is needed, then, is a positive theory of family formation that can more satisfactorily explain the inequality of wage income. By positive is meant a theory based on tested and systematized experience, not on speculation.

To illustrate the kind of theory required, this discussion concentrates on the educational dimension of the labor force. Note that education is the most important labor characteristic influencing the inequality of family wage income.

For each educational attribute the weighted averages of ϕ_i, R_i, and G_i (weighted, that is, by sample size) from table 4.13 are plotted against the weighted average of the wage rates $[w_i]$ in figures 4.12, 4.13, and 4.14.[16] When the educational qualifications of labor increase from primary education, for which the wage rate $[w_i]$ was 3.32, to university education, for which the wage rate was 17.5, the distribution of the family ownership of labor becomes more unequal —that is, G_i increases with education in figure 4.12. At the same time, the ownership of high-quality labor is more concentrated in the high wage-income families—that is, R_i increases with education

15. The rules governing the formation of families with respect to sex and age are obviously linked. For example, if a female marries at an earlier age than a male, both the age and sex structure of the family would be affected. Moreover different societies have different rules governing the extent to which the young and old establish their own households or stay on as members of the nuclear household. These differences introduce the possibility of bias in all Gini measures.

16. For each variable in table 4.13 the weights are x_1/s_x, x_2/s_x, . . . , x_r/s_x, where $s_x = x_1 + x_2 + \ldots + x_r$. In words, the weights represent the percentage of the labor force for the various types of labor in each educational category.

Figure 4.12. *Weighted Average of the Education Gini plotted against the Average Wage Rate, by Level of Education, 1966*

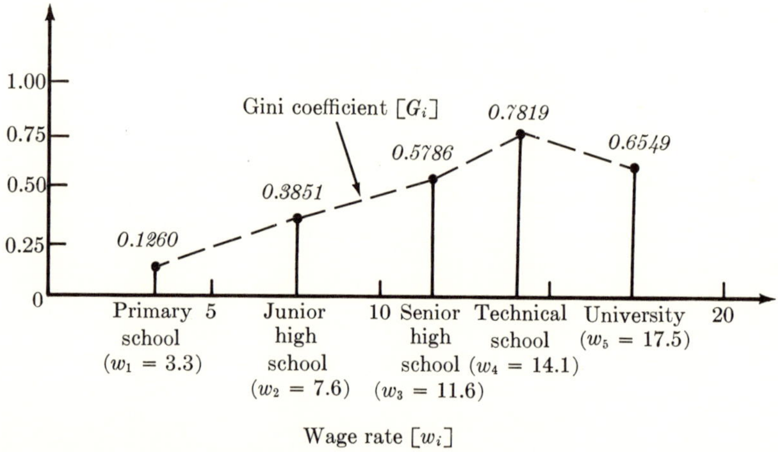

Source: Table 4.13.

Figure 4.13. *Weighted Average of the Education Correlation Characteristic Plotted against the Average Wage Rate, by Level of Education, 1966*

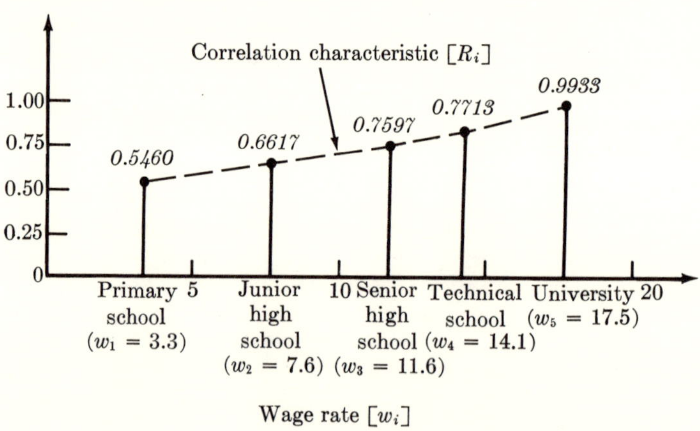

Source: Table 4.13.

Figure 4.14. *Weighted Average of the Education Weight Plotted against the Average Wage Rate, by Level of Education, 1966*

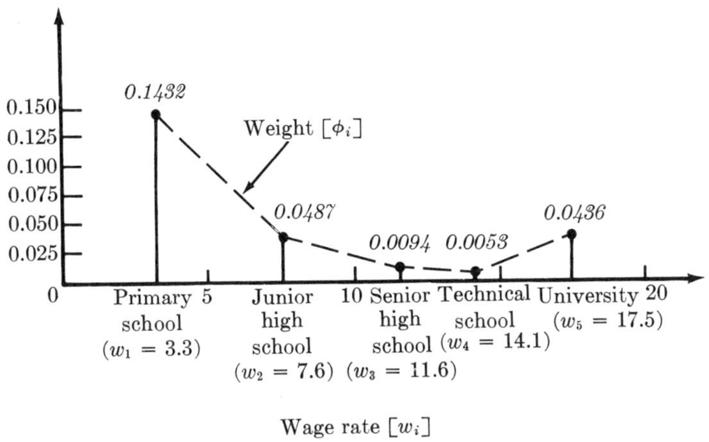

Source: Table 4.13.

in figure 4.13. The pattern of the wage weight [ϕ_i] is U-shaped—that is, ϕ_i decreases and then increases with education in figure 4.14.

In addition to the issue of how much every term $\phi_i R_i G_i$ contributes to inequality when the patterns above are empirically given, the theoretical issue is how these patterns are determined in the first place. Families may or may not have different numbers of wage earners. When all families have the same number of workers, the size characteristic is uniform; otherwise it is nonuniform. Similarly the educational qualifications of workers in individual families may or may not be the same. When all workers in individual families have the same educational qualifications, the composition characteristic is homogeneous; otherwise it is nonhomogeneous. Four cases will be examined here: uniform size and homogeneous composition; uniform size and semihomogeneous composition; nonuniform size and homogeneous composition; descending size and homogeneous composition. These four cases indicate the analytical issues in a theory which explains the patterns of ϕ_i, R_i, and G_i in relation to w_i for various labor characteristics.

THE UNIFORM-HOMOGENEOUS CASE. It is assumed for the uniform-homogeneous case, the simplest of the four cases, that there are ten families and that every family owns three workers (table 4.14). The first five families own only low-education workers; three families own only medium-education workers; two families own only high-education workers. Thus, of the thirty workers,

Table 4.14. *The Inequality of Wage Income: Numerical Example of Uniform Family Size and Homogeneous Family Composition*

	Family composition (number of members)			
Family number and variable	*Low education*	*Medium education*	*High education*	*Total wage income*
Family 1	3	0	0	60
Family 2	3	0	0	60
Family 3	3	0	0	60
Family 4	3	0	0	60
Family 5	3	0	0	60
Family 6	0	3	0	90
Family 7	0	3	0	90
Family 8	0	3	0	90
Family 9	0	0	3	165
Family 10	0	0	3	165
All families	15	9	6	900
Workers per family [$\bar{x}_i$]	1.5	0.9	0.6	—
Wage rate [$\bar{W}_i$]	20	30	55	—
Wage share [ϕ_i]	0.333	0.300	0.367	—
Gini [G_i]	0.500	0.700	0.800	—
Pseudo Gini [$\bar{G}_i$]	−0.500	0.300	0.800	—
Correlation characteristic [R_i]	−1.000	0.429	1.000	—
Wage Gini [G_w]	—	—	—	0.217[a]

— Not applicable.

Source: Constructed by the authors.

a. $G_w = \phi_l R_l G_l + \phi_m R_m G_m + \phi_h R_h G_h$
$= 0.333 \times -1.000 \times 0.500 + 0.300 \times 0.429 \times 0.700 + 0.367 \times 1.000 \times 0.800.$

fifteen have low education, nine have medium education, and six have high education. The average number of workers $[\bar{x}_i]$ of the first type per family is 1.5; that of the second type 0.9; that of the third type 0.6. The proportionality of these numbers reflects industrial demand. For example, the fifteen workers of the first type might be skilled or unskilled workers; the nine workers of the second type might be white-collar workers; the six workers of the third type might be engineers. The pyramiding pattern of the supply of workers having certain educational attributes, given by $(\bar{x}_1 > \bar{x}_2 > \bar{x}_3)$, shows that industry generally absorbs fewer highly educated workers than it absorbs lowly educated workers. The pattern of the wage rate for the three types of workers is ascending: the hypothetical wage rate is $20 for workers with low education, $30 for those with medium education, and $55 for those with high education, that is, $(w_1 < w_2 < w_3)$. The pattern of the values of the wage share is U-shaped: ϕ_1 is 0.33; ϕ_2 is 0.30; ϕ_3 is 0.37 (see figure 4.17 below).

The empirically observed U-shaped pattern of ϕ_i in figure 4.14 reflects the pyramiding pattern of worker numbers and the ascending pattern of the wage rate for higher educational qualifications. After the grade of technical education, the curve turns up because the effect of increasing wages overwhelms the effect of diminishing numbers. This U-shaped pattern of the wage share $[\phi_i]$ over the wage rate for increasing educational qualifications clearly is the result of the economics of industrial demand and supply. The pattern of family ownership of labor essentially is irrelevant. A positive theory of industrial supply and demand therefore underlies the explanation of the pattern of ϕ_i in the sense that they constitute the economic forces determining the diversity of wage rates as well as the numbers of workers receiving different levels of wage income.

For the uniform-homogeneous case the values of the Gini coefficient $[G_i]$ reveal an increasing pattern when plotted against the wage rate for workers having increasing educational qualifications: the hypothetical Gini coefficient is 0.50 for low education, 0.70 for medium education, and 0.80 for high education. This increasing pattern is the result of the pyramiding pattern of the mean number of workers of a particular educational grade per family $[\bar{x}_i]$ and the labor force's uniform size characteristic and homogeneous composition characteristic. Under the assumptions implicit for the uniform-homogeneous case, workers with low education are more equally distributed among families than are workers with high education, simply because more workers are in the low-education category.

The empirically observed pattern of the Gini coefficient [G_i] in figure 4.12 bears this relation out, except for the dip for university education, which will be explained later.

To determine the rank correlation characteristic [R_i] for the uniform-homogeneous case, the total wage income of families is used. The hypothetical values of R_i in table 4.14 show an increasing pattern: R_1 is -1; R_2 is 0.43; R_3 is 1. This increasing pattern directly results from the ascending pattern of the wage rate for higher educational qualifications and the labor force's uniform size characteristic and homogeneous composition characteristic. Under the assumptions for this case, high-income families own highly educated workers, a situation which leads to a high correlation between total wage income and the pattern of family ownership of labor; low-income families own lowly educated workers, a situation which leads to a low correlation between total wage income and the pattern of family ownership of labor. This conclusion is borne out by the empirically observed pattern of R_i in figure 4.13.

The uniform-homogeneous case thus can adequately explain all the observable patterns of the causes of the inequality of total wage income, which causes are summarized in figures 4.12, 4.13, and 4.14. Its real meaning is that the family is insignificant as a unit of labor ownership, as it will always be when the assumptions of the uniform-homogeneous case are satisfied. If family affiliation is completely disregarded and the Gini coefficient is computed for the thirty workers as individuals, the value of G_i becomes 0.217. Such a Gini coefficient measures the inequality of the wage rate and corresponds to the second level of analysis in the earlier sections of this chapter. Observe that this inequality of the wage rate is exactly the same as the inequality of family wage income. This equivalence indicates that a theory of the inequality of the wage rate is tantamount to a theory of the inequality of family wage income. Thus, for the education characteristic, the theory of the inequality of family wage income is almost completely economic and only slightly demographic: that is, the impact of education on family wage income is determined by the forces of labor supply, industrial demand, and institutional discrimination, not by the forces of family formation.

THE UNIFORM-SEMIHOMOGENEOUS CASE. For the uniform-semihomogeneous case it is assumed that all families have the same number of workers. With respect to the composition characteristic, however, the behavioristic hypothesis is that the family unit exerts

Table 4.15. *The Inequality of Wage Income: Numerical Example of Uniform Family Size and Semihomogeneous Family Composition*

Family number and variable	*Family composition (number of members)*			
	Low education	*Medium education*	*High education*	*Total wage income*
Family 1	3	0	0	60
Family 2	3	0	0	60
Family 3	3	0	0	60
Family 4	2	1	0	70
Family 5	2	1	0	70
Family 6	1	2	0	80
Family 7	1	2	0	80
Family 8	0	2	1	115
Family 9	0	1	2	140
Family 10	0	0	3	165
All families	15	9	6	900
Workers per family [$\bar{x}_i$]	1.5	0.9	0.6	—
Wage rate [$\bar{W}_i$]	20	30	55	—
Wage share [ϕ_i]	0.333	0.300	0.367	—
Gini [G_i]	0.447	0.500	0.767	—
Pseudo Gini [$\bar{G}_i$]	−0.447	0.233	0.767	—
Correlation characteristic [R_i]	−1.000	0.466	1.000	—
Wage Gini [G_w]	—	—	—	0.202[a]

— Not applicable.

Source: Constructed by the authors.

a. $G_w = \phi_l R_l G_l + \phi_m R_m G_m + \phi_h R_h G_h$
$= 0.333 \times -1.000 \times 0.447 + 0.300 \times 0.466 \times 0.500 + 0.367 \times 1.000 \times 0.767$.

pressure on all its members to acquire about the same level of education (table 4.15). The homogeneous case manifests the extreme form of such pressure. Here that pressure is more mild, and the education of family members is restricted to adjacent levels of attainment. Because the total number of workers for each level of attainment is the same as in the previous case, the values of the

Figure 4.15. *Gini Coefficients in Four Cases Plotted against the Wage Rate, by Level of Education*

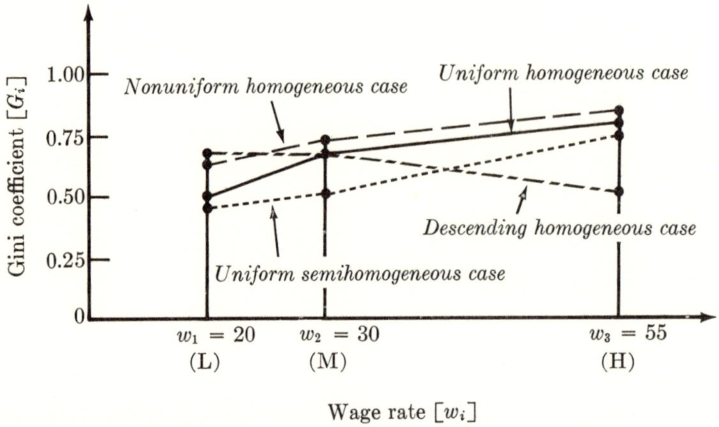

Sources: Tables 4.14–4.17.

wage share [ϕ_i] are unchanged. The economic aspect for the determination of ϕ_i therefore is the same in both cases.

The Gini coefficient and the correlation characteristic maintain the same increasing pattern in the uniform-semihomogeneous case as in the uniform-homogeneous case. The values for these variables are plotted against the wage rate in figures 4.15 and 4.16. Note in these figures that the only apparent impact of the semihomogeneous case is to make the distribution of workers more equal for each educational category—that is, for every category G_i is lower in this case than in the homogeneous case. Thus the uniform-semihomogeneous case probably provides a better explanation of the empirical reality observable in the patterns of figures 4.12, 4.13, and 4.14.

What then produces that decline in the Gini coefficient for workers with university education in figure 4.12? The Taiwanese greatly value a university education. Moreover, the policy of government for higher education enables persons from all classes of society to obtain a university degree. As a result, workers with a university education tend to be more equally distributed among families than workers with technical education.

Figure 4.16. *Correlation Characteristics in Four Cases Plotted against the Wage Rate, by Level of Education*

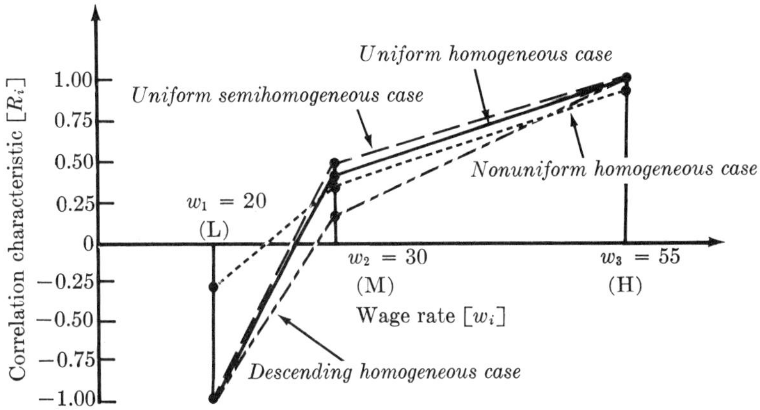

Sources: Tables 4.14–4.17.

Figure 4.17. *Weights in Four Cases Plotted against the Wage Rate, by Level of Education*

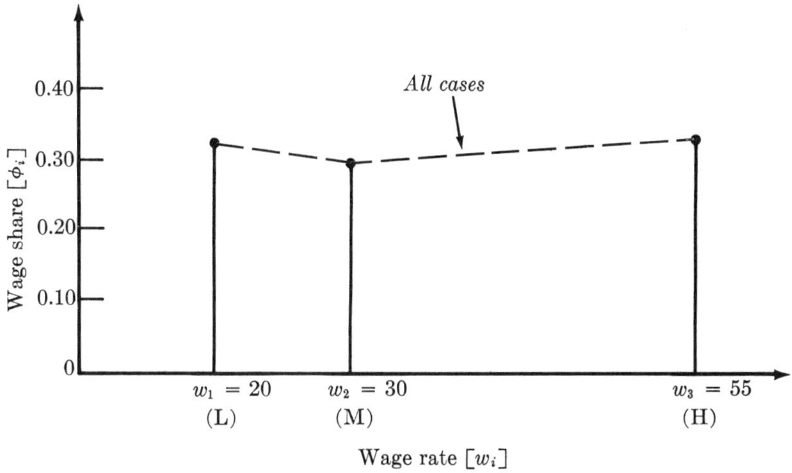

Sources: Tables 4.14–4.17.

THE NONUNIFORM-HOMOGENEOUS CASE. For the nonuniform-homogeneous case it is assumed that the number of workers is different for families, but that the educational qualifications of all workers in a family are the same. Once again, the values of ϕ_i are unchanged so that the other aspects of differences between this case and the uniform-homogeneous case can be concentrated on. What differs is that total family wage income no longer is in a monotonically increasing order (table 4.16). The reason for this change is that large families with low-grade workers can earn more wage income than small families with high-grade workers. For each educational category the distribution of workers among families is more unequal than in the two preceding cases (see figure 4.15). What also differs is that the pattern of the correlation characteristic [R_i] significantly changes: for the low-education category R_i is higher than in the preceding cases; for the high-education category it is lower (see figure 4.16). As with the uniform-semihomogeneous case, the nonuniform-homogeneous case is a more realistic explanation of the observed patterns in figures 4.12–4.14 than is the uniform-homogeneous case.

THE DESCENDING-HOMOGENEOUS CASE. For the descending-homogeneous case it is assumed that the educational qualifications for all workers in a family are the same, but that the number of workers differs in accord with the impact of a new behavioristic hypothesis: families with low-grade workers tend to be larger than those with high-grade workers. Under this assumption the ranking of families by total wage income is completely reversed (table 4.17). Both the Gini coefficient [G_i] and the correlation characteristic [R_i] decline as the educational level of workers increases. The observed empirical reality of figures 4.12 and 4.13 contradicts these patterns. Yet, in figure 4.13, R_i is positive for even the lowest level of education—a fact that is inconsistent with the assumptions of the first three cases. This evidence suggests that the behavioristic hypothesis of this case must, at best, be operating mildly. It may thus be concluded that the economic model of the uniform-homogeneous case provides the main explanatory framework for empirical reality and that the demographic forces of family formation of the other cases can only serve to moderate this basic pattern.

The similarity of patterns in the numerical examples and the

Table 4.16. *The Inequality of Wage Income: Two Numerical Examples of Nonuniform Family Size and Homogeneous Family Composition*

Family number and variable	Family composition (number of members): Low education, Example 1	Low education, Example 2	Medium education, Example 1	Medium education, Example 2	High education, Example 1	High education, Example 2	Total wage income, Example 1	Total wage income, Example 2
Family 1	1	1	0	0	0	0	20	20
Family 2	2	2	0	0	0	0	40	40
Family 3	3	3	0	0	0	0	60	60
Family 4	4	0	0	2	0	0	80	60
Family 5	5	4	0	0	0	0	100	80
Family 6	0	0	2	3	0	0	60	90
Family 7	0	5	3	0	0	0	90	100
Family 8	0	0	4	0	0	2	120	110
Family 9	0	0	0	4	2	0	110	120
Family 10	0	0	0	0	4	4	120	220
All families	15	15	9	9	6	6	900	900
Workers per family [$\bar{x}_i$]	1.5		0.9		0.6		—	
Wage rate [W_i]	20		30		55		—	
Wage share [ϕ_i]	0.333		0.300		0.367		—	
Gini [G_i]	0.633		0.744		0.833		—	
Pseudo Gini [$\bar{G}_i$]	−0.180		0.278		0.767		—	
Correlation characteristic [R_i]	−0.284		0.374		0.921		—	
Wage Gini [G_w]	—		—		—		0.304[a]	

— Not applicable.
Source: Constructed by the authors.
a. $G_w = \phi_l R_l G_l + \phi_m R_m G_m + \phi_h R_h G_h$
$= 0.333 \times -0.284 \times 0.633 + 0.300 \times 0.374 \times 0.744 + 0.367 \times 0.921 \times 0.833.$

observed evidence does not imply that the examples explain the evidence. A more rigorous explanation requires an abstract formulation of the ideas embedded in the numerical examples. The effort here has been restricted to pointing out the kind of behav-

Table 4.17. *The Inequality of Wage Income: Two Numerical Examples of Descending Family Size and Homogeneous Family Composition*

	Family composition (number of members)							
	Low education		*Medium education*		*High education*		*Total wage income*	
Family number and variable	*Example 1*	*Example 2*	*Example 1*	*Example 2*	*Example 1*	*Example 2*	*Example 1*	*Example 2*
Family 1	5	0	0	0	0	1.5	100.0	82.5
Family 2	5	0	0	0	0	1.5	100.0	82.5
Family 3	5	0	0	0	0	1.5	100.0	82.5
Family 4	0	0	3	0	0	1.5	90.0	82.5
Family 5	0	0	3	3	0	0	90.0	90.0
Family 6	0	0	3	3	0	0	90.0	90.0
Family 7	0	0	0	3	1.5	0	82.5	90.0
Family 8	0	5	0	0	1.5	0	82.5	100.0
Family 9	0	5	0	0	1.5	0	82.5	100.0
Family 10	0	5	0	0	1.5	0	82.5	100.0
All families	15	15	9	9	6.0	6.0		
Workers per family [$\bar{x}_i$]	1.5		0.9		0.6		—	
Wage rate [$\bar{W}_i$]	20		30		55			
Wage share [ϕ_i]	0.333		0.300		0.367		—	
Gini [G_i]	0.700		0.600		0.600		—	
Pseudo Gini [$\bar{G}_i$]	0.700		0.100		−0.600		—	
Correlation characteristic [R_i]	1.000		0.143		−1.000		—	
Wage Gini [G_w]	—		—		—		0.043[a]	

— Not applicable.
Source: Constructed by the authors.
a. $G_w = \phi_l R_l G_l + \phi_m R_m G_m + \phi_h R_h G_h$
$= 0.333 \times 1.000 \times 0.700 + 0.300 \times 0.143 \times 0.700 + 0.367 \times -1.000 \times 0.600.$

ioristic hypotheses that need to be made and tested about the rules of family formation if future analysis of the inequality of family wage income is to be improved.

Conclusion

In this chapter an attempt has been made to demonstrate that the analysis of the inequality of wage income can be traced to the nonhomogeneity of the labor force and the membership composition of families. The complexity of the problem required a multidimensional cross-listing of data. It also required the conceptual separation of inequality into several levels: the inequality of wage rates, individual wage income, and family wage income. It further required the design of a special analytical framework that combined the regression technique with the additive factor-components technique to process the data at each level. Finally, it required the formulation of new behavioristic hypotheses in areas tangential to traditional economic analysis, such as demography and sociology. At the pretheoretical stage which characterizes this work to date, much effort has gone into the measurement of inequality as an inductive device to examine empirical evidence, rather than into deductive reasoning. This effort should, in turn, help to identify pertinent behavioristic hypotheses which will be needed to determine the inequality of income distribution in the theoretical context of a formal model. Here, only a modest beginning has been made in the formulation of an analytical framework that incorporates the techniques of data generation and processing and the rudiments of theoretical ideas and hypotheses. Clearly, much work remains to be done.

Appendix 4.1. Data on the Distribution of Family Income in Taiwan

By standards of developing countries, statistical data on the distribution of family income in Taiwan is quite satisfactory. Since 1964 there has been a major effort to collect such data on a large scale. This effort has led to the annual publication of reports on the survey of family income and expenditure—reports which constitute the main source of published data.[17] This data, collected by the

17. DGBAS, *Report on the Survey of Family Income and Expenditure.*

Directorate-General of Budget, Accounting, and Statistics since 1964, will be collectively referred to as DGBAS data. In 1970 the collection of data for the municipality of Taipei became the responsibility of the Bureau of Budget and Statistics of the municipal government of Taipei.

Primary data

The DGBAS data is based on information contained in the primary questionnaires (schedules 4.1–4.4). These elaborate questionnaires consist of some 750 questions set up in 750 cells and are to be filled in for every family interviewed. The questions cover such topics as composition of household population, general status of family equipment, current family income, current family expenditure, family capital income and expenditure, agricultural capital income and expenditure, and a detailed breakdown of family consumption expenditure. The sample size—that is, the number of families interviewed—and the sample size as a fraction of the population appear for various years in table 4.18. The number of families interviewed was 3,000 in 1964; it increased to about 6,000 by 1973.

Based on the processing of the primary questionnaires, a typical DGBAS annual report contains about 700 pages of tables. The information in these tables provides a much broader coverage than is necessary for most studies of the distribution of family income.

Table 4.18. *Size of Sample for DGBAS Surveys, 1964–73*

Year	*Families*	*Percentage of population*
1964	3,000	0.146
1966	3,000	0.132
1968	3,000	0.126
1970	3,600	0.160
1972	5,730	0.204
1973	5,790	0.202

Sources: DGBAS, *Report on the Survey of Family Income and Expenditure*, various years.

Schedule 4.1 *Record of Family Interview on Income and Expenditure, Page One, 1966*

Stratum no.	Cluster no.	Household no.	Income	Age of the head of household	Occupation of the head of household	Sex of the head of household	Household population	Number of persons employed	Consumption expenditure	Savings

Name of household head______ Address______ Hsien______ Hsiang ______ Village______ Lin______ Household______

Town ______ Li ______

City ______ Road ______ Section______ Alley______ Lane______ No.______

District______ Street ______

	Item	Designation no.	Relationship to household's head	Name	Sex		Date of birth (year, month)	Place of original registration	Educational level	Name of school attended	Occupation essential second				Amount of personal income for family expenses		The ratio of personal living cost afforded by family	Age	Corresponding adult men
					Male	Female					Name of establishment	The position he holds	Name of establishment	The position he holds	The ratio to family expenditure	The ratio to total income			
Composition of household population	Registered in households register roster	1																	
		2																	
		7																	
		8																	
	Registered in other register roster	1																	
		2																	
		3																	
		4																	
	Living out but registered in same roster	1																	
		2																	
		3																	

	Relationship to the household	Lodger		Day boarder		Boarder		Number of corresponding adult men	Monthly charge amount	Annual total charge amount	Monthly cost of free meals and substance for relatives, workers, and servants	Remarks
		Sex	Age	Sex	Age	Sex	Age					
Lodgers, day boarders, and boarders	Domestic servants											
	Business employees											
	Farm employees											
	Relatives											

Source: DGBAS, *Report on the Survey of Family Income and Expenditure, 1966.*

Schedule 4.2. *Record of Family Interview on Income and Expenditure, Page Two, 1966*

General status of family equipment

Electrical equipment	Television sets:	Electric fans:	Radio:	Air conditioners:
	Household refrigerators:	Pick-up:	Electric cooker:	Washing machines:
Household appliance	Ice box:	Sewing machines:	Camera:	Telephones:
				Gas stove:
Transport equipment	Motor bicycle:	Bicycles:	Pedicab:	Sedan:
Cultural usage	Newspaper:	Magazine:		

Family current income

Individual income of population constituting the family

Name of income maker	Kinds and sources of income	Income amount				Amount retained for personal use	Amount for family consumption
		Total	Periodical income		Other (including temporary income)		
			Monthly or quarterly	Annual			

Consolidated income of the family

Item	Income kind	Yearly times	Amount of each time	Yearly income total	Item	Income kind	Yearly times	Amount of each time	Yearly income total
Net operating income					Interest				
					Investment				
					Transfers from household				
Net professional income					Transfers from government				
Net agricultural income					Transfers from enterprise				
					Transfers from abroad				
Rent					Others				

Family current expenditure

Charges	Item		Illustrations of various items	Expenditure amount		Remarks
				Monthly or quarterly	Yearly total	
Food charges	Total					
	Food staple	Rice	(omitted)			
		Flour				
		Sweet potato				
		Other cereals				
	Subsidiary food					
	Milk					
	Condiment					
	Eating out					
	Dinners for festivals					
	Marriages, births, birthdays, funerals, and feasts					
Beverage	Total					
	Nonalcoholic					
	Alcoholic					
Tobacco	Tobacco					

Source: Same as for schedule 4.1.

Schedule 4.3. *Record of Family Interview on Income and Expenditure, Page Three, 1966*

	Flour	Item	Illustrations of various items	Expenditure amount: Monthly or quarterly	Expenditure amount: Yearly total	Remarks
Family current expenditure	Miscellaneous consumption	Total				
		Monetary service	(omitted)			
		Education and research				
		Marriages, births, birthdays, and funerals				
		Other				
	Interest	Interest				
	Taxes	Taxes				
	Gifts and other transfers	Total				
		To households				
		To government				
		To enterprises				
		To abroad				
		Agricultural productive expenditure				

	Flour	Item	Illustrations of various items	Total	Remarks	Capital
Family capital income and expenditure	Capital Income	Total				
		Drawing from deposits	(omitted)			
		Mutual savings and capital				
		Loan repayment				
		Borrowing				
		Sales of land				
		Sales of houses				
		Purchases on credit				
		Other capital income				
	Capital Expenditure	Total				
		Deposits				
		Payment to mutual savings and insurance				
		Investment				
		Loan				
		Repayment of loan				
		Purchases of land				
		Purchases of houses				
		Repayment for purchases on credit				
		Other capital expenditure				
Agricultural capital income and expenditure		Agricultural income				
		Agricultural expenditure				

Record

Name of the respondent____________ The survey takes______minutes

The abode belongs to____________ The cooperation of this household______

Conductor: Enumerator: Survey date:

Source: Same as for schedule 4.1.

Schedule 4.4. *Record of Family Interview on Income and Expenditure, Page Four, 1966*

Stratum no.	Cluster no.	Household no.	Income	Age of the head of household	Occupation of the head of household	Sex of the head of household	Household population	Number of persons employed	Consumption expenditure	Savings

			Item	Illustrations of various items	Expenditure amount		Remark
	Flour				Monthly or quarterly	Yearly total	
Family current expenditure	Clothing and other personal effects	Total					
		Man's clothing		(omitted)			
		Woman's clothing					
		Child's clothing					
		Jewelry, ornaments, and miscellaneous					
	Rent and water charges	Total					
		Rent	Actual				
			Imputed				
		House repairing and installation					
		Water charges					
	Fuel and light	Total					
		Electricity bill					
		Charcoal					
		Coal					
		Liquid fuel					
		Gas fuel					
		Wood					
		Plant wastes					
		Other					
	Furniture, furnishings, and household equipment	Total					
		Furniture and equipment					
		Textiles					
		Appliances for kitchen and bath					
		Other					
	Household operation	Total					
		Domestic servants					
		Other household operation expenses					
	Personal and medical care	Total					
		Personal care					
		Hair dressing and bath					
		Medical and health expenses					
	Transport, communication, and correspondence	Total					
		Purchases of personal transport equipment					
		Operation of personal transport equipment					
		Purchased transportation					
		Others					
	Recreation and amusement	Total					
		Recreation					
		Books, newspapers, magazines, and stationery					
		Other recreation					

Source: Same as for schedule 4.1.

Nevertheless the framework underlying the design of these tables is not specifically suited to the analytical study, such as that in this chapter, of causes of the inequality of family income. Consequently we had to return to the primary questionnaires to obtain the cross-listing of information needed for this chapter.

Analytical cross-listing of data

For the joint project of Yale's Economic Growth Center and Taiwan's Economic Planning Council, the cross-listing of data is given by the coded family-income data form—to be referred to as the *coded form* (schedule 4.5). There are fifty-one cells in this form. From the information contained in the primary questionnaires of the DGBAS data, all cells are filled in for every family; every family has one card. These coded forms are preserved in cards (for 1966 in computer cards) for almost all 24,120 families covered in table 4.18.

The coded form contains two basic types of information: wage and nonwage income. There are three kinds of nonwage income: property income from interest, rent, and investment; mixed income from agricultural, business, and professional activities; and transfer income. Mixed income is a mixture of wage and property income. It occurs primarily because the family and the production unit coincide—for example, a family-operated farm, a family business, or a dentist's office—making it impossible to separate the wage and property components of income paid by the production unit to the family. Transfer income consists of government transfer or welfare payments; it accounts for less than 1 percent of total family income.

The coded form contains the following information on wage income for every wage earner: sex, age, education, occupation, job location, number of wage earners, and total income earned by each wage earner. Total family income (for example, NT$53,647 in schedule 4.5) is the sum of total wage income (NT$23,800), total property income (NT$3,600), total mixed income (NT$26,247), and transfer income (0). The coded form also contains information on family location, family type, and the year surveyed.

For this chapter, use was not made of the information on nonwage income, but all information relevant to the analysis of wage income was coded (table 4.19). Five characteristics are indicated in that table for individual wage earners and two characteristics for every wage-earning family. Each characteristic may be thought of as a

Table 4.19. *Coding for Characteristics of Individual Wage Earners and Income-earning Families*

Characteristic	*Value of characteristic* 1	2	3
Individual wage earners			
Sex	Female	Male	—
Age	Under 25	25–45	45–60
Education	Primary school (six years)	Junior high school (nine years)	Senior high school (twelve years)
Occupation	Public employee or serviceman	Specialist or professional	Service employee
Job location	Rural village	Township	City
Income-earning families			
Family type	Farm	Nonfarm	—
Family location	*Value of characteristic*: 1 2 3 4 5 6 7 8 9 10 11 12 13 14 15 16 (County)		

— Not applicable.
Source: Constructed by the authors.

variable that takes on one of a finite number of values. The sex variable can be coded either as female (1) or male (2). The age variable assumes one of four possible values: under 25 (1), 25–45 (2), 45–60 (3), or over 60 (4). The education variable takes on one of five values corresponding to the gradation of the formal education system: primary school (1), junior high school (2), senior high school (3), technical school (4), or university (5). Intuitively the characteristics just mentioned are most significant among the various factors relevant to the analysis of wage income inequality.

Value of characteristic			
4	*5*	*6*	*Characteristic*
			Individual wage earners
—	—	—	Sex
Over 60	—	—	Age
[T]echnical school (fourteen years)	University (sixteen years)	—	Education
[C]ommercial self-employee	Manual laborer	Agricultural employee	Occupation
—	—	—	Job location
			Income-earning families
—	—	—	Family type
	Value of characteristic 17 18 19 20 21 Municipality		Family location

The occupation variable has six values: government employee and serviceman (1), specialist or professional (2), service employee of business establishments (3), commercial self-employee (4), manual laborer (5), and agricultural employee (6). The classification of labor according to this criterion corresponds to the homogeneous groups within a "working class." The variable for job location has three values: rural village (1), township (2), and city (3). The variable for "family type" classifies a family as a farm (1) or non-farm (2) family. The definition of farm family adopted by the DGBAS is based on one of five possible criteria of agricultural activi-

Schedule 4.5. *Coded Form for Data on Family Income, with Sample Entries*

Year	Family location	Family type		Total wage income	Total property income	Total mixed income	Transfer income	Total family income
1973	01	2		23,800	3,600	26,247	0	53,647

Wage income

Wage earner	1	2	3	4	5	6
Wage income	9,600	1,000	7,200	6,000		
Sex	1	1	1	1		
Age	1	1	3	1		
Education	2	1	1	1		
Occupation	3	6	6	6		
Job location	1	1	1	1		

Nonwage income

Property income			Mixed income			
Interest income	Rent income	Investment income	Agricultural income	Business income	Professional income	Transfer income
0	3,600	0	26,247	0	0	0

Note: See table 4.19 for values assigned to characteristics.
Source: Constructed by the authors.

ties.[18] The "family location variable" has twenty-one values corresponding to the administrative districts of Taiwan.[19]

Thus, in the coded forms (schedule 4.5), individual wage income earners are coded according to the five "individual wage earner's characteristics" of table 4.19. At the same time, families are coded according to the two "family characteristics" of that table. The cross-listing of the data in this way constitutes the primary input of our analysis of wage income inequality (tables 4.20–4.27). It should be apparent that the identification of these characteristics is essentially guided by an intuitive notion of what is relevant to the analysis of wage income inequality.

Appendix 4.2. Linear Regression and the Model of Additive Factor Components

The method we have designed for the analysis of wage income inequality is built on a combination of the technique of linear regression and the technique of additive factor components. For expository convenience the analytical design has been presented in chapter four with the aid of numerical examples. The two techniques can also be stated abstractly—that is, independent of their empirical applications. The linear regression technique can be stated as follows:

$$y = a_o + a_1x_1 + a_2x_2 + \dots + a_rx_r \,, \tag{4.20}$$

where y is regressed on r explanatory variables $[x_i]$. If there are n empirical observations, this gives:

$$(y_i, x_{i1}, x_{i2}, \dots, x_{ir}) . \qquad (i = 1, 2, \dots, n) \tag{4.21}$$

With the aid of expression (4.21) the regression coefficients a_j $(j = 0, 1, 2, \dots, r)$ can be estimated. The data input required for

18. These criteria are cultivating an area of 0.2 hectares, raising more than three pigs of not less than sixty kilograms each, raising more than one buffalo, raising more than one hundred poultry, and yearly sales of agricultural products of more than NT$6,000. A "fishing family" is similarly defined by the number of fish-catching and fish-growing activities.

19. The twenty-one districts comprise sixteen counties—Taipei, Ilan, Taoyuan, Hsinchu, Miaoli, Taichung, Changhwa, Nantou, Yunlin, Chiayi, Tainan, Kaohsiung, Pingtung, Taitung, Hwalien, and Penghu—and five municipalities—Keelung, Taichung, Tainan, Kaohsiung, and Taipei.

Table 4.20. *Annual Wage Rates of Female Workers, by Age, Occupation, Job Location, and Level of Education, 1966*
(N.T. dollars)

Level of education and occupation	Under 25 years			25–45 years		
	Rural area	Town	City	Rural area	Town	City
Primary school						
Public employee	—	6,160	9,533	4,950	60,300	7,500
Specialist[a]	—	—	2,568	—	—	—
Service employee[b]	4,050	6,363	4,746	7,008	7,180	6,186
Commercial self-employee	—	—	8,200	16,640	4,400	18,400
Manual laborer	5,015	5,859	6,265	4,035	5,796	8,180
Agricultural employee	2,502	1,630	9,600	2,602	3,035	11,400
Junior high school						
Public employee	—	13,060	10,620	12,540	20,500	12,100
Specialist	4,800	7,000	—	—	—	—
Service employee	—	5,850	7,800	—	8,400	—
Commercial self-employee	—	3,500	—	0	11,650	—
Manual laborer	5,820	7,115	8,150	—	5,676	—
Agricultural employee	6,000	—	—	3,200	7,800	—
Senior high school						
Public employee	12,922	10,196	11,010	8,566	16,076	20,413
Specialist	—	—	—	—	—	—
Service employee	—	—	—	—	—	—
Commercial self-employee	—	7,470	16,710	—	—	23,375
Manual laborer	—	—	—	—	5,300	—
Agricultural employee	—	—	—	—	—	—
Technical school						
Public employee	—	—	20,500	—	—	20,866
Specialist	—	—	—	—	—	—
Service employee	—	—	12,000	—	—	—
Commercial self-employee	—	—	—	—	—	21,400
Manual laborer	—	—	—	—	—	—
Agricultural employee	—	—	—	—	—	—
University or over						
Public employee	17,908	—	—	—	10,050	—
Specialist	—	—	—	—	—	—
Service employee	—	—	—	—	—	—
Commercial self-employee	—	—	—	—	—	43,200
Manual laborer	—	—	—	—	—	—
Agricultural employee	—	—	—	—	—	—

— No entry.
Source: DGBAS, *Report on the Survey of Family Income and Expenditure*, 1966.

45–60 years			Over 60 years			
Rural area	*Town*	*City*	*Rural area*	*Town*	*City*	*Level of education and occupation*
						Primary school
—	12,222	3,900	—	—	—	Public employee
—	—	—	—	—	—	Specialist[a]
—	5,100	6,685	2,700	4,332	—	Service employee[b]
—	—	—	—	—	—	Commercial self-employee
8,550	5,783	5,600	—	—	7,800	Manual laborer
2,894	3,580	—	2,800	—	—	Agricultural employee
						Junior high school
13,661	—	—	—	—	—	Public employee
—	—	—	—	—	—	Specialist
—	9,900	—	—	—	—	Service employee
—	—	—	—	—	—	Commercial self-employee
—	—	—	—	—	—	Manual laborer
—	—	—	—	—	—	Agricultural employee
						Senior high school
—	29,703	24,080	—	—	—	Public employee
—	—	—	—	—	—	Specialist
—	—	—	—	—	—	Service employee
—	26,695	33,000	—	—	—	Commercial self-employee
—	—	—	—	—	—	Manual laborer
—	—	—	—	—	—	Agricultural employee
						Technical school
—	—	—	—	—	—	Public employee
—	—	—	—	—	—	Specialist
—	—	—	—	—	—	Service employee
—	—	—	—	—	—	Commercial self-employee
—	—	—	—	—	—	Manual laborer
—	—	—	—	—	—	Agricultural employee
						University or over
—	18,600	—	—	—	—	Public employee
—	—	30,000	—	—	—	Specialist
—	—	—	—	—	—	Service employee
—	—	—	—	—	—	Commercial self-employee
—	—	—	—	—	—	Manual laborer
—	—	—	—	—	—	Agricultural employee

a. Includes professionals.
b. Includes servicemen.

Table 4.21. *Annual Wage Rates of Male Workers, by Age, Occupation, Job Location, and Level of Education, 1966*
(N.T. dollars)

Level of education and occupation	Under 25 years			25–45 years		
	Rural area	Town	City	Rural area	Town	City
Primary school						
Public employee	10,590	8,104	15,900	20,721	18,017	17,256
Specialist[a]	—	—	—	—	—	—
Service employee[b]	3,103	5,852	8,871	12,300	14,175	15,627
Commercial self-employee	—	7,540	15,000	8,325	3,186	21,287
Manual laborer	9,015	7,573	7,082	12,470	14,365	19,034
Agricultural employee	3,248	3,107	2,250	5,239	5,292	22,900
Junior high school						
Public employee	—	11,736	12,750	19,319	18,487	21,901
Specialist	—	—	—	—	—	—
Service employee	41,000	7,600	7,600	—	8,840	16,985
Commercial self-employee	6,000	7,750	14,000	—	11,000	28,000
Manual laborer	1,070	9,710	12,033	14,750	1,475	9,540
Agricultural employee	4,500	1,500	4,800	5,200	11,875	—
Senior high school						
Public employee	11,635	10,881	11,160	19,177	22,404	22,404
Specialist	—	—	—	—	32,760	—
Service employee	1,600	19,200	11,280	9,600	17,935	32,230
Commercial self-employee	—	12,000	13,166	19,814	14,711	25,500
Manual laborer	—	11,200	12,900	—	12,961	23,133
Agricultural employee	—	—	—	4,200	7,300	—
Technical school						
Public employee	—	—	—	21,264	21,230	32,546
Specialist	—	4,095	—	46,800	—	—
Service employee	—	—	—	—	—	—
Commercial self-employee	—	8,100	21,500	—	24,260	—
Manual laborer	—	—	—	—	—	—
Agricultural employee	—	—	—	—	—	—
University or over						
Public employee	—	—	17,400	25,500	27,479	25,584
Specialist	—	—	—	—	12,600	—
Service employee	—	—	—	—	—	90,600
Commercial self-employee	—	—	—	12,600	41,500	56,671
Manual laborer	—	—	—	—	—	—
Agricultural employee	—	—	—	—	—	—

— No entry.
Source: Same as for table 4.20.

45–60 years			*Over 60 years*			
Rural area	*Town*	*City*	*Rural area*	*Town*	*City*	*Level of education and occupation*
						Primary school
16,616	21,803	22,803	11,942	7,959	8,070	Public employee
—	7,200	—	—	—	—	Specialist[a]
1,800	8,614	17,722	—	—	10,400	Service employee[b]
24,045	22,966	30,554	25,184	8,190	16,800	Commercial self-employee
10,161	13,606	19,367	2,600	8,757	12,440	Manual laborer
5,593	5,239	5,931	3,800	5,142	—	Agricultural employee
						Junior high school
23,982	20,585	28,492	—	—	—	Public employee
—	—	—	—	—	—	Specialist
—	12,550	18,650	—	—	—	Service employee
4,000	24,345	36,675	—	29,200	—	Commercial self-employee
—	16,000	30,300	—	—	57,360	Manual laborer
3,000	5,925	—	—	—	—	Agricultural employee
						Senior high school
26,960	22,783	32,054	—	17,975	26,100	Public employee
—	—	—	—	—	—	Specialist
—	3,000	—	—	—	—	Service employee
—	29,566	16,382	—	—	42,200	Commercial self-employee
—	14,200	28,953	—	—	—	Manual laborer
—	—	—	—	—	—	Agricultural employee
						Technical school
—	44,853	32,600	—	—	—	Public employee
—	—	7,200	19,100	—	—	Specialist
—	—	—	—	—	—	Service employee
—	—	—	—	—	—	Commercial self-employee
—	—	—	—	—	—	Manual laborer
—	—	—	—	—	—	Agricultural employee
						University or over
—	33,475	52,226	—	—	56,418	Public employee
—	16,800	56,610	—	—	—	Specialist
—	—	37,400	—	—	—	Service employee
—	34,150	34,600	—	—	—	Commercial self-employee
—	—	33,300	—	—	—	Manual laborer
—	—	—	—	—	—	Agricultural employee

a. Includes professionals.
b. Includes servicemen.

Table 4.22. *Number of Female Workers, by Age, Occupation, Job Location, and Level of Education, 1966*

Level of education and occupation	*Under 25 years*			*25–45 years*		
	Rural area	*Town*	*City*	*Rural area*	*Town*	*City*
Primary school						
Public employee	—	2	3	1	1	2
Specialist[a]	—	—	1	—	—	—
Service employee[b]	4	8	15	6	13	20
Commercial self-employee	—	—	1	1	1	1
Manual laborer	18	45	41	9	30	20
Agricultural employee	82	40	1	100	58	4
Junior high school						
Public employee	—	5	4	2	3	2
Specialist	1	1	—	—	—	—
Service employee	—	2	3	—	1	—
Commercial self-employee	—	1	—	—	3	—
Manual laborer	2	8	4	—	4	—
Agricultural employee	1	—	—	1	1	—
Senior high school						
Public employee	32	10	3	31	11	8
Specialist	—	—	—	—	—	—
Service employee	—	—	—	—	—	—
Commercial self-employee	—	5	4	—	—	4
Manual laborer	—	—	—	—	3	—
Agricultural employee	—	—	—	—	—	—
Technical school						
Public employee	—	—	1	—	—	3
Specialist	—	—	—	—	—	—
Service employee	—	—	1	—	—	—
Commercial self-employee	—	—	—	—	—	2
Manual laborer	—	—	—	—	—	—
Agricultural employee	—	—	—	—	—	—

45–60 years			*Over 60 years*			
Rural area	*Town*	*City*	*Rural area*	*Town*	*City*	*Level of education and occupation*
						Primary school
—	2	1	—	—	—	Public employee
—	—	—	—	—	—	Specialist[a]
—	1	7	1	2	—	Service employee[b]
—	—	—	—	—	—	Commercial self-employee
4	11	3	—	—	1	Manual laborer
20	10	—	2	—	—	Agricultural employee
						Junior high school
1	—	—	—	—	—	Public employee
—	—	—	—	—	—	Specialist
—	1	—	—	—	—	Service employee
—	—	—	—	—	—	Commercial self-employee
—	—	—	—	—	—	Manual laborer
—	—	—	—	—	—	Agricultural employee
						Senior high school
—	2	2	—	—	—	Public employee
—	—	—	—	—	—	Specialist
—	—	—	—	—	—	Service employee
—	1	2	—	—	—	Commercial self-employee
—	—	—	—	—	—	Manual laborer
—	—	—	—	—	—	Agricultural employee
						Technical school
—	—	—	—	—	—	Public employee
—	—	—	—	—	—	Specialist
—	—	—	—	—	—	Service employee
—	—	—	—	—	—	Commercial self-employee
—	—	—	—	—	—	Manual laborer
—	—	—	—	—	—	Agricultural employee

(*Table continues on the following pages*)

Table 4.22 (*Continued*)

Level of education and occupation	*Under 25 years*			*25–45 years*		
	Rural area	*Town*	*City*	*Rural area*	*Town*	*City*
University or over						
Public employee	1	—	—	—	2	—
Specialist	—	—	—	—	—	—
Service employee	—	—	—	—	—	1
Commercial self-employee	—	—	—	—	—	—
Manual laborer	—	—	—	—	—	—
Agricultural employee	—	—	—	—	—	—

— No entry.
Source: Same as for table 4.20.
a. Includes professionals.
b. Includes servicemen.

expression (4.21) can be written as column vectors:

(4.22a) $$Y = \text{col}(y_1, y_2, \ldots, y_n)$$

(4.22b) $$X_i = \text{col}(X_{1i}, X_{2i}, \ldots, X_{ni}) \qquad (i = 1, 2, \ldots, n)$$

With the aid of the estimated regression equation, this gives:

(4.23a) $$Y = A_o + a_1X_1 + a_2X_2 + \ldots + a_rX_r + \theta, \quad \text{where}$$

(4.23b) $$A_o = \text{col}(a_o, a_o, \ldots, a_o) \quad \text{and}$$

(4.23c) $$\theta = \text{col}(\theta_1, \theta_2, \ldots, \theta_n),$$

and where θ_i is the difference between y_i and $\hat{y}_i$, as estimated from regression equation (4.20) for the *i*th observation.

It can now be clearly seen how equation (4.23a) may be viewed as an abstract problem of additive factor components. An application of the general decomposition technique for such a problem immediately leads to:

(4.24) $$G_y = \phi_1R_1G(X_1) + \phi_2R_2G(X_2) + \ldots + \phi_rR_rG(X_r) + \phi_\theta R_\theta G(\theta),$$

where ϕ_i is the share, R_i the correlation characteristic, and $G(X_i)$ the

45–60 years			*Over 60 years*			
Rural area	*Town*	*City*	*Rural area*	*Town*	*City*	*Level of education and occupation*
						University or over
—	1	—	—	—	—	Public employee
—	—	1	—	—	—	Specialist
—	—	—	—	—	—	Service employee
—	—	—	—	—	—	Commercial self-employee
—	—	—	—	—	—	Manual laborer
—	—	—	—	—	—	Agricultural employee

Gini coefficient of X_i. The causation of G_y can thus be traced to the various quality dimensions emphasized in the regression equation.[20] The methodological innovation of this chapter thus resides in the *combination* of the linear regression technique with the additive factor-components technique. For this combination to work, the additive property of the Gini coefficient is essential—that is, it underlies equation (4.24). Moreover the additive property of the linear regression equation (4.20) is equally essential. For example, in the earnings equation in chapter four, the wage rate is assumed to be additively determined and traced to various dimensions of the quality of the labor force. The linearity of the regression is not essential for the combination of the two techniques. The combination still is possible when the regression equation is nonlinear, and this possibility indicates a direction in which the method can be generalized.

20. Because of the technical complexities, full treatment of the decomposition analysis for the problem of additive factor components is postponed to part two. Notice, however, that the term associated with $\phi_\theta R_\theta G(\theta)$ in equation (4.24) arises from the error term [θ] in equation (4.23a). To the extent that the error term is small—that is, to the extent that the multiple linear correlation in the regression analysis of equation (4.21) is high—the influence of this term in equation (4.24) similarly is small. One proviso is intuitively obvious: to the extent that the regression analysis is imperfect, we cannot hope to explain inequality fully.

Table 4.23. *Number of Male Workers, by Age, Occupation, Job Location, and Level of Education, 1966*

Level of education and occupation	Under 25 years			25–45 years		
	Rural area	Town	City	Rural area	Town	City
Primary school						
Public employee	3	9	2	13	60	32
Specialist[a]	1	—	—	—	—	—
Service employee[b]	4	9	7	5	17	20
Commercial self-employee	—	1	2	2	9	18
Manual laborer	19	50	72	46	121	112
Agricultural employee	74	43	4	202	154	3
Junior high school						
Public employee	—	5	2	7	28	19
Specialist	—	—	—	—	—	—
Service employee	2	2	1	—	3	7
Commercial self-employee	1	2	1	—	2	4
Manual laborer	1	13	3	4	10	10
Agricultural employee	3	2	1	7	4	—
Senior high school						
Public employee	4	4	1	13	66	34
Specialist	—	—	—	—	1	—
Service employee	1	1	1	1	7	3
Commercial self-employee	—	1	6	8	17	16
Manual laborer	—	2	2	—	6	9
Agricultural employee	—	—	—	2	2	—
Technical school						
Public employee	—	—	—	2	7	10
Specialist	—	1	—	1	—	—
Service employee	—	—	—	—	—	—
Commercial self-employee	—	1	1	—	1	—
Manual laborer	—	—	—	—	—	—
Agricultural employee	—	—	—	—	—	—

45–60 years			Over 60 years			
Rural area	*Town*	*City*	*Rural area*	*Town*	*City*	*Level of education and occupation*
						Primary school
10	23	23	2	4	3	Public employee
—	—	—	—	—	—	Specialist[a]
1	7	9	—	—	1	Service employee[b]
2	3	7	1	1	2	Commercial self-employee
10	51	43	2	8	5	Manual laborer
63	54	6	3	12	—	Agricultural employee
						Junior high school
2	12	9	—	—	—	Public employee
—	—	—	—	—	—	Specialist
—	2	2	—	—	—	Service employee
1	1	3	—	1	—	Commercial self-employee
—	1	2	—	—	—	Manual laborer
1	2	—	—	—	—	Agricultural employee
						Senior high school
6	35	20	—	2	1	Public employee
—	—	—	—	—	—	Specialist
—	1	—	—	—	—	Service employee
—	3	4	—	—	1	Commercial self-employee
—	1	3	—	—	—	Manual laborer
—	—	—	—	—	—	Agricultural employee
						Technical school
—	3	1	—	—	—	Public employee
—	—	1	1	—	—	Specialist
—	—	—	—	—	—	Service employee
—	—	—	—	—	—	Commercial self-employee
—	—	—	—	—	—	Manual laborer
—	—	—	—	—	—	Agricultural employee

(Table continues on the following pages)

Table 4.23 (*Continued*)

Level of education and occupation	Under 25 years			25–45 years		
	Rural area	Town	City	Rural area	Town	City
University or over						
Public employee	—	—	1	2	23	19
Specialist	—	—	—	—	1	—
Service employee	—	—	—	—	—	2
Commercial self-employee	—	—	—	1	4	7
Manual laborer	—	—	—	—	—	—
Agricultural employee	—	—	—	—	—	—

— No entry.
Source: Same as for table 4.20.
a. Includes professionals.
b. Includes servicemen.

When abstractly stated, the method can be applied to other problems as well—for example, to the analysis of the inequality of the distribution of family property income [G_π]. The total family property income [y] can, as in equation (4.20), first be regressed on a number of explanatory variables [x_i] representing particular types of assets, such as urban land, physical capital, and bonds, or the "class" affiliation of the family, such as that of the entrepreneurial class, the professional class, or the class of skilled workers. The regression results can then be combined with the model of additive factor components to trace the inequality of family property income to the unequal distribution of the ownership of assets, to the class affiliation of families, or to both.

The crude earnings function used in chapter four obviously does injustice to an approach which has received a good deal of professional attention of late.[21] In this chapter we have somewhat downgraded the

21. Among the shortcomings of the earnings function used in chapter four, the following may be mentioned: the ambiguity of age as a proxy for experience; the inadequacy of total family income as a proxy for family influence; the interpretation of G_x when x is an ordinal—for example, when education is measured by low, medium, and high, not by years of education; the lack of effort to compare our conclusions, such as those on returns to education, with other, independent studies.

45–60 years			*Over 60 years*			
Rural area	*Town*	*City*	*Rural area*	*Town*	*City*	*Level of education and occupation*
						University or over
—	14	16	—	—	3	Public employee
—	1	1	—	—	—	Specialist
—	—	1	—	—	—	Service employee
—	2	1	—	—	—	Commercial self-employee
—	—	1	—	—	—	Manual laborer
—	—	—	—	—	—	Agricultural employee

earnings-function approach. This approach by itself, used for the first level of analysis in our design, really is insufficient for the analysis of income inequality. It becomes significant for such analysis only after it is combined with the model of additive factor components. The argument in this appendix thus suggests that the regression approach can play a significant role in the analysis of income inequality when it is imbedded in a framework involving the model of additive factor components.

Table 4.24. *Number of Rural Workers and Average Annual Wage Rate, by Education, Sex, and Age, 1966*

	Number of workers					
Sex and age	*Primary school*	*Junior high school*	*Senior high school*	*Techni-cal school*	*Univer-sity or over*	*Total*
Female	248	8	6	—	1	263
Under 25 years	104	4	3	—	1	112
25–45 years	117	3	3	—	—	123
45–60 years	24	1	—	—	—	25
Over 60 years	3	—	—	—	—	3
Male	462	29	35	4	3	533
Under 25 years	100	7	5	—	—	112
25–45 years	268	18	24	3	3	316
45–60 years	86	4	6	—	—	96
Over 60 years	8	—	—	1	—	9
Both sexes	710	37	41	4	4	796
Under 25 years	204	11	8	—	1	224
25–45 years	385	21	27	3	3	439
45–60 years	110	5	6	—	—	121
Over 60 years	11	—	—	1	—	12

— No entry.
Source: Same as for table 4.20.

Annual wage rate						
Primary school	*Junior high school*	*Senior high school*	*Technical school*	*University or over*	*Total*	*Sex and age*
3,114	8,048	10,745	—	17,908	3,495	Female
2,997	5,610	12,923	—	17,908	3,489	Under 25 years
3,079	9,427	8,567	—	—	3,368	25–45 years
3,837	13,661	—	—	—	4,230	45–60 years
2,767	—	—	—	—	2,767	Over 60 years
6,864	13,385	18,164	27,107	26,367	8,222	Male
4,559	14,653	9,628	—	—	5,416	Under 25 years
7,387	12,813	17,742	29,776	26,367	8,875	25–45 years
7,791	13,741	26,961	—	—	9,237	45–60 years
8,209	—	—	19,100	—	9,419	Over 60 years
5,554	12,731	17,078	27,107	24,252	6,660	Both sexes
3,762	11,365	10,864	—	17,908	4,453	Under 25 years
6,077	12,330	16,723	29,766	26,367	7,332	25–45 years
6,928	13,725	26,961	—	—	8,203	45–60 years
6,724	—	—	19,100	—	7,756	Over 60 years

Table 4.25. *Number of Town Workers and Their Annual Wage Rate, by Education, Sex, and Age, 1966*

	Number of workers					
Sex and age	*Primary school*	*Junior high school*	*Senior high school*	*Technical school*	*University or over*	*Total*
Female	224	30	32	—	3	289
Under 25 years	95	17	15	—	—	127
25–45 years	103	12	14	—	2	131
45–60 years	24	1	3	—	1	29
Over 60 years	2	—	—	—	—	2
Male	637	90	149	13	45	934
Under 25 years	112	24	8	2	—	146
25–45 years	361	47	99	8	28	543
45–60 years	139	18	40	3	17	217
Over 60 years	25	1	2	—	—	28
Both sexes	861	120	181	13	48	1,223
Under 25 years	207	41	23	2	—	273
25–45 years	464	59	113	8	30	674
45–60 years	163	19	43	3	18	226
Over 60 years	27	1	2	—	—	30

— No entry.
Source: Same as for table 4.20.

Annual wage rate						
Primary school	*Junior high school*	*Senior high school*	*Technical school*	*University or over*	*Total*	*Sex and age*
4,633	9,636	12,422	—	2,900	6,103	Female
4,127	8,495	9,288	—	—	5,322	Under 25 years
4,932	11,230	13,767	—	10,050	6,531	25–45 years
5,374	9,900	22,034	—	18,600	7,709	45–60 years
4,333	—	—	—	—	4,333	Over 60 years
9,946	13,339	19,771	24,587	30,320	13,026	Male
5,763	9,109	12,141	6,098	—	6,667	Under 25 years
10,814	13,370	19,288	21,609	28,951	13,675	25–45 years
11,617	18,018	22,583	44,853	32,574	16,270	45–60 years
6,872	29,200	17,975	—	—	8,462	Over 60 years
8,564	12,414	18,475	24,857	29,231	11,390	Both sexes
5,012	8,855	10,280	6,098	—	6,041	Under 25 years
9,508	12,935	18,604	21,609	27,691	12,286	25–45 years
10,698	17,591	22,544	44,853	31,797	16,612	45–60 years
6,684	29,200	17,975	—	—	8,187	Over 60 years

Table 4.26. *Number of City Workers and Their Annual Wage Rate, by Education, Sex, and Age, 1966*

	Number of workers					
Sex and age	*Primary school*	*Junior high school*	*Senior high school*	*Techni-cal school*	*Univer-sity or over*	*Total*
Female	121	13	23	7	2	166
Under 25 years	62	11	7	2	—	82
25–45 years	47	2	12	5	1	67
45–60 years	11	—	4	—	1	16
Over 60 years	1	—	—	—	—	1
Male	361	65	101	13	52	592
Under 25 years	87	8	10	1	1	107
25–45 years	175	40	62	10	28	315
45–60 years	88	16	27	2	20	153
Over 60 years	11	1	2	—	3	17
Both sexes	482	78	124	20	54	758
Under 25 years	149	19	17	3	1	189
25–45 years	222	42	74	15	29	382
54–60 years	99	16	31	2	21	169
Over 60 years	12	1	2	—	3	18

— No entry.
Source: Same as for table 4.20.

Annual wage rate						
Primary school	*Junior high school*	*Senior high school*	*Techni-cal school*	*Univer-sity or over*	*Total*	*Sex and age*
6,766	12,772	20,471	19,700	36,600	10,040	Female
6,081	8,953	14,267	16,250	—	7,413	Under 25 years
7,794	33,780	21,401	21,080	43,200	12,527	25–45 years
6,136	—	28,540	—	30,000	13,229	45–60 years
7,800	—	—	—	—	7,800	Over 60 years
15,998	37,725	24,393	29,751	43,998	22,577	Male
7,389	11,000	12,724	21,500	17,400	8,383	Under 25 years
18,489	46,061	23,784	32,547	38,000	25,213	25–45 years
20,071	29,022	29,388	19,900	51,862	26,805	45–60 years
11,856	57,360	34,150	—	56,419	25,019	Over 60 years
13,680	33,566	23,665	26,233	43,724	19,831	Both sexes
6,845	9,815	13,360	18,000	17,400	7,962	Under 25 years
16,225	45,476	23,398	28,724	38,180	22,988	25–45 years
18,523	29,022	29,279	19,900	50,821	25,519	45–60 years
11,518	57,360	34,150	—	56,419	24,063	Over 60 years

Table 4.27. *Number of Workers and Average Annual Wage Rate, by Education, Sex, and Age, 1966*

	Number of workers					
Sex and age	*Primary school*	*Junior high school*	*Senior high school*	*Techni-cal school*	*Univer-sity or over*	*Total*
Female	593	51	61	7	6	718
Under 25 years	261	32	25	2	1	321
25–45 years	267	17	29	5	3	321
45–60 years	59	2	7	—	2	70
Over 60 years	6	—	—	—	—	6
Male	1,460	184	285	30	100	2,059
Under 25 years	299	39	23	3	1	365
25–45 years	804	105	185	21	59	1,174
45–60 years	313	38	73	5	37	466
Over 60 years	44	2	4	1	3	54
Both sexes	2,053	235	346	37	106	2,777
Under 25 years	560	71	48	5	2	686
25–45 years	1,071	122	214	26	62	1,495
45–60 years	372	40	80	5	39	536
Over 60 years	50	2	4	1	3	60

— No entry.
Source: Same as for table 4.20.

Annual wage rate						
Primary school	*Junior high school*	*Senior high school*	*Technical school*	*University or over*	*Total*	*Sex and age*
4,433	10,186	15,303	19,700	21,635	6,058	Female
4,141	8,292	11,118	16,250	17,908	5,217	Under 25 years
4,624	13,564	16,388	21,080	21,100	6,570	25–45 years
4,891	11,781	25,752	—	24,300	7,728	45–60 years
4,128	—	—	—	—	4,128	Over 60 years
10,647	21,961	21,211	27,161	37,314	14,529	Male
5,833	10,492	11,848	11,232	17,400	6,786	Under 25 years
11,342	25,728	20,594	27,984	33,114	15,479	25–45 years
12,943	22,201	25,460	34,872	43,000	18,280	45–60 years
8,361	43,280	26,063	19,100	56,419	13,834	Over 60 years
8,724	19,406	20,201	25,749	36,426	12,388	Both sexes
5,045	9,500	11,468	13,239	17,654	6,052	Under 25 years
9,667	24,033	20,024	26,656	32,533	13,566	25–45 years
11,666	21,680	25,485	34,872	19,100	25,749	45–60 years
7,853	43,280	26,063	19,100	56,419	12,863	Over 60 years

CHAPTER 5

Income Distribution and Economic Structure

THE CAUSES OF THE INEQUALITY of family income were explicitly traced in earlier chapters to additive factor-income components. In this chapter a more aggregate view is taken by deemphasizing additive factor components and concentrating on the structure of total family income. This aggregate view facilitates tracing the inequality of family income to various homogeneous categories of income recipients. Such analysis is hardly revolutionary. Kuznets's classical study, inquiring whether inequality in the distribution of family income increases in the course of industrialization and urbanization, emphasized sectoral and locational dimensions.[1] Subsequent studies by other investigators have done the same. In this chapter, too, sectoral and locational dimensions constitute the two focal points of an analysis that will be formulated as an abstract model of homogeneous groups. As part of this analysis, the inequality of family income will be examined in relation to family attributes.

The income gaps between families in different sectors and locations are an important and dynamic economic force that causes the urbanization of the population and the shift of farm workers to nonfarm activities. If labor were completely mobile, the income gaps would tend to be small. But the mobility of labor is often impeded by such factors as traditional ideologies and social systems, particularly during the early stages of economic development. Consequently it

1. Simon Kuznets, "Economic Growth and Income Inequality," *American Economic Review*, vol. 45, no. 1 (March 1955), pp. 1–28.

never is perfect. Because it is imperfect, part of the labor force remains in the lower productivity sectors and causes the gaps in income to widen between sectors.

In Taiwan the income gap between farm and nonfarm families widened during 1964–72 because farm income was growing at a slower rate than nonfarm income. The income gap between rural and urban sectors also widened. But despite these widening gaps between sectors, the inequality of income significantly declined at the national level. How could this have happened? How could the inequality of income decline for the entire country as the inequality of income increased between farm and nonfarm families? This chapter probes the reasons for that reduction in the inequality of family income by using a sectoral decomposition formula that measures two main effects: the inequality within sectors, and that among sectors. The root causes of the inequality of family income will thus be explained by analyzing an intersectoral effect and an intrasectoral effect.

The intersectoral effect, constituted by a family-weight effect and an income-disparity effect, is caused by changes in the shares of different sectors in the total number of families and in total family income. The family-weight effect is caused by changes in the weights of sectors as measured by the percentages of families in each sector. When an economy develops and labor is reallocated, the modern sectors expand while the more traditional sectors shrink. This shift of family weights among sectors has an effect on the distribution of income. In contrast, the income-disparity effect is caused by changes in the income parities among sectors. The gap of average family income between two sectors principally arises from productivity differences. Because of the differences in the technology used in agricultural and nonagricultural production, labor productivity usually is higher and growing more rapidly in the modern sector than in the traditional sector. That, too, has an effect on the distribution of income.

The intrasectoral effect is caused by changes in the inequality of income within each sector and is explained by numerous causative elements. Its principal cause, however, is the heterogeneity of families arising from differences in the ownership of assets and differences in the ownership of labor embodying particular characteristics. Thus, within each sector, it is possible to identify a number of social groups or classes of families based on the various types and quantities of physical and human assets owned by families. A group will be referred to as a homogeneous group. The heterogeneity of families in a sector can then be described by the coexistence of homogeneous groups.

This chapter is principally devoted to a study of the proximate causes of the reduction in the inequality of income in Taiwan. First, an equation for decomposition will be presented. Second, an attempt will be made to decompose national income according to classifications of income recipients by sector and homogeneous group. The sectoral classifications are based on farm and nonfarm activity and on the degree of urbanization, proxied by rural, semiurban, and urban residence. The group classifications are based on the number of persons employed per family and on the age, sex, and educational background of the head of family. Third, changes in the inequality of income over time will be analyzed in relation to industrialization and urbanization through the divergence in the income-relative, which is the ratio of the sectoral share in total income to the sectoral share in total households, and through the decomposition of income recipients into homogeneous groups. Fourth, demographic factors will be examined, and the causes of inequality identified in relation to the size and composition of families. The reduction in the inequality of income over time will be linked to changes in the size of families, the number of employed members per family, and the age, sex, and educational background of the head of family. Here, again, changes will be analyzed through the divergence in the income-relative for various sectors and the decomposition of income recipients into homogeneous groups.

The analysis of the intrasectoral and intersectoral effects will show that the reduction in the inequality of income within the nonfarm sector was the essential cause of the nationwide reduction in the inequality of income. That is, the favorable intrasectoral effect for the nonfarm sector more than compensated for the adverse intersectoral effect and made it possible for the inequality of income to be reduced across the entire country. The findings, based on the analysis of intragroup and intergroup effects, indicate the importance of demographic and economic forces in reducing the inequality of income among families in Taiwan.

The Decomposition Equation

Kuznets used agricultural and nonagricultural family weights, as well as intersectoral and intrasectoral inequalities, to analyze the interrelations between changes in the economic structure and the distribution of income.[2] Swamy decomposed the coefficient of variation in the two-sector model.[3] The decomposition in this chapter follows this general line of reasoning, but is generalized to n sectors.

The decomposition formula should separately identify the intrasectoral and intersectoral effects that contribute to overall income inequality. For this purpose, it helps if the inequality indicator of the whole economy can be explained in relation to such measures as the proportions of farm and nonfarm families, the mean incomes of the two sectors, and the indicators of income inequality of the two sectors. As an inequality indicator, the coefficient of variation is convenient for this purpose.[4]

Now consider the whole economy [w] to comprise a farm sector [a] and a nonfarm sector [n]. In the example of figure 5.1, the three sectors [w, a, and n] are represented by the three frequency distributions corresponding to the data in table 5.1. This example illustrates the type of data needed in this chapter.

When there are two groups of income recipients (agriculture and nonagriculture) and k income classes, the variances for agriculture [V_a], nonagriculture [V_n], and the whole economy [V_w] are defined as follows:

$$\text{(5.1a)} \quad V_a = \sum_{i=1}^{k} P_i^a (Y_i - y_a)^2, \qquad V_n = \sum_{i=1}^{k} P_i^n (Y_i - y_n)^2,$$

$$V_w = \sum_{i=1}^{k} P_i (Y_i - y_w)^2, \quad \text{where:}$$

$$\text{(5.1b)} \qquad f_i = f_i^a + f_i^n; \qquad (i = 1, 2, \ldots, k)$$

$$\left[\begin{array}{c} \textit{class frequency for whole economy} \\ \textit{as sum of group frequencies} \end{array}\right]$$

$$\text{(5.1c)} \quad f^a = \sum_{i=1}^{k} f_i^a, \quad f^n = \sum_{i=1}^{k} f_i^n, \quad f = f^a + f^n;$$

2. Kuznets, "Economic Growth and Income Inequality."

3. Subramanian Swamy, "Structural Changes and the Distribution of Income by Size: The Case of India," *Review of Income and Wealth*, vol. 12, no. 2 (June 1967), pp. 155–74.

4. It will be shown in chapter twelve that if the Gini coefficient were used for homogeneous group decomposition, a third term—for a crossover effect—would appear in addition to the intersectoral and intrasectoral effects. Consequently the coefficient of variation is used in this chapter to simplify the analysis.

Figure 5.1. *Income Distribution for Agricultural, Nonagricultural, and All Sectors*

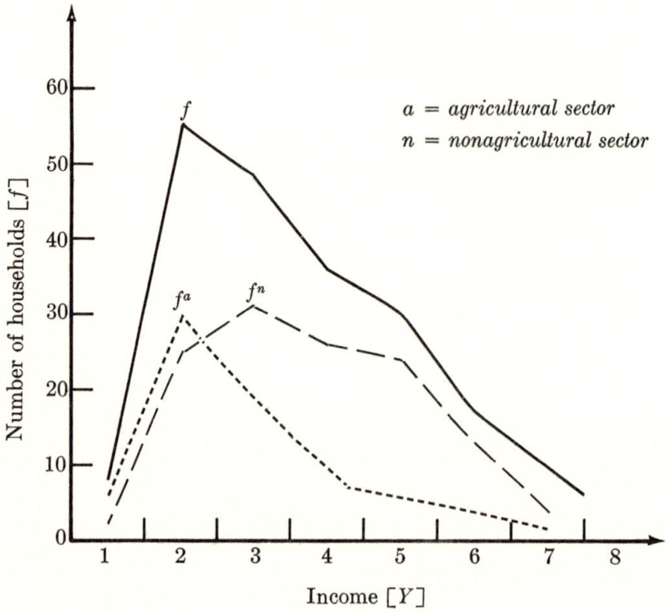

Source: Table 5.1.

(5.1d) $$h_a = f^a/f, \qquad h_n = f^n/f; \qquad (h_a + h_n = 1)$$

[*group family shares*]

(5.1e) $$P_i^a = f_i^a/f^a, \qquad P_i^n = f_i^n/f^n, \qquad P_i = h_a P_i^a + h_n P_i^n;$$

$$(i = 1, 2, \ldots, k)$$

$$\left(\sum_{i=1}^{k} P_i^a = 1\right) \qquad \left(\sum_{i=1}^{k} P_i^n = 1\right) \qquad \left(\sum_{i=1}^{k} P_i = 1\right)$$

[*relative class frequencies*]

(5.1f) $$y_a = \sum_{i=1}^{k} P_i^a Y_i, \qquad y_n = \sum_{i=1}^{k} P_i^n Y_i, \qquad y_w = \sum_{i=1}^{k} P_i Y_i$$

[*income means*] $$= h_a y_a + h_n y_n$$

by equation (5.1e).

Table 5.1. *Numerical Example of Income Distribution for Agricultural, Nonagricultural, and All Sectors*

Income group [i]	*Income range*	*Midpoint income* [Y_i]	*Number of households in agricultural sector* [f^a_i]	*Number of households in nonagricultural sector* [f^n_i]	*Number of households in all sectors* [$f_i = f^a_i + f^n_i$]
1	0.5–1.5	1	6	2	8
2	1.5–2.5	2	30	25	55
3	2.5–3.5	3	17	31	48
4	3.5–4.5	4	10	26	36
5	4.5–5.5	5	6	24	30
6	5.5–6.5	6	4	13	17
7	6.5–7.5	7	2	4	6
All groups	—	—	75	125	200

— Not applicable.
Source: Constructed by the authors.

It can be readily shown that:

(5.2a) $$V_w = A + B, \quad \text{where}$$

(5.2b) $$A = h_a V_a + h_n V_n \quad \text{and}$$

(5.2c) $$B = h_a(y_w - y_a)^2 + h_n(y_w - y_n)^2.$$

In equation (5.2b) A is the weighted average of the group variances [V_a and V_n]; the group family shares [h_a and h_n] are the weights. In equation (5.2c) B is the variance of all households when, for each group, total income is redistributed such that every household receives the mean income of the group [y_a and y_n]. The coefficients of variation for the two groups [I_a and I_n] and for the whole economy [I_w] are defined as follows:

(5.3) $$I_w = \sqrt{V_w}/y_w, \quad I_a = \sqrt{V_a}/y_a, \quad \text{and} \quad I_n = \sqrt{V_n}/y_n.$$

Substituting these definitions in equation (5.2) gives:

(5.4a) $$I_w^2 = h_a U_a^2 I_a^2 + h_n U_n^2 I_n^2 + h_a(1 - U_a)^2 + h_n(1 - U_n)^2,$$

where:

(5.4b) $$U_a = y_a/y_w \quad \text{and} \quad U_n = y_n/y_w.$$

In equation (5.4b) U_a and U_n express the mean income of each group as a fraction of the mean income of the whole economy. Because the object of this analysis is to assess the separate effects on I_w of the variation of the group family shares [h_a and h_n], the group coefficients of variation [I_a and I_n], and the group income parities [U_a and U_n], it is not convenient to use U_a and U_n. The reason is that the family shares [h_a and h_n] enter into the definition of y_w in equations (5.1e) and (5.1f). The group income parities are defined as follows:

(5.5a) $$Z_a = y_a/y \quad \text{and} \quad Z_n = y_n/y, \quad \text{where}$$

(5.5b) $$y = (y_a + y_n)/2.$$

These equations express the individual group means as a parity of the simple arithmetic average of the group means. Then:

(5.6a) $$U_a = F^a(Z_a, Z_n, h_a, h_n) = Z_a(Z_a + Z_n)/2(h_aZ_a + h_nZ_n)$$

and

(5.6b) $$U_n = F^n(Z_a, Z_n, h_a, h_n) = Z_n(Z_a + Z_n)/2(h_aZ_a + h_nZ_n)$$

by equations (5.4b), (5.5a), and (5.1f).

These equations show that U_a and U_n are functions of Z_a, Z_n, h_a, and h_n. When U_a and U_n in equation (5.5) are substituted in equation (5.4a):

(5.7) $$I_w = f(I_a, I_n, h_a, h_n, Z_a, Z_n).$$

That is, I_w is a function of I_a, I_n, h_a, h_n, Z_a, and Z_n. If there are m groups of income recipients, equation (5.7) can be readily generalized as:

(5.8) $$I_w = f(I_1, I_2, \ldots, I_j, \ldots, I_m; h_1, h_2, \ldots, h_j, \ldots, h_m; Z_1, Z_2, \ldots, Z_j, \ldots, Z_m).$$

I_j is the coefficient of variation; h_j is the family share; Z_j is the income parity of the jth group. Treating these variables as functions of time, I_w can be differentiated with respect to time to give:

(5.9a) $$\frac{dI_w}{dt} = R + D, \quad \text{where}$$

(5.9b) $$R = \sum_{j=1}^{m} \frac{\partial I_w}{\partial I_j}\frac{dI_j}{dt} \quad \text{and}$$

[*intrasectoral effect*]

(5.9c) $$D = W + P, \quad \text{where}$$

[*intersectoral effect*]

(5.9d) $$W = \sum_{j=1}^{m} \frac{\partial I_w}{\partial h_j} \frac{dh_j}{dt} \left(\sum_{j=1}^{m} \frac{dh_j}{dt} = 0 \right) \quad \text{and}$$

[*family-weight effect*]

(5.9e) $$P = \sum_{j=1}^{m} \frac{\partial I_w}{\partial Z_j} \frac{dZ_j}{dt} .$$

[*income-disparity effect*]

Empirical Decomposition by Sectors and Homogeneous Groups

The decomposition equation (5.4a) can be applied to decompose the nationwide coefficient I_w for various kinds of sectoral classification. This application is part of the strategy in this chapter of seeking additional causal relations by way of an essentially inductive methodology. Because the Taiwanese economy is dualistic, the nationwide coefficient of variation will first be decomposed into coefficients for the farm and nonfarm sectors. This nationwide coefficient will also be decomposed into sectors classified by varying degrees of urbanization. Because the age, sex, and educational level of the family head are attributes that affect family income, the same decomposition equation will then be applied to the classification of these families according to each of these factors. It will also be applied to groups based on the number of persons employed per family. In summary, the decomposition equation will be applied to the following sectoral and group classifications:

- Farm and nonfarm economic activity (two sectors)
- Degree of urbanization (six sectors and three sectors)
- Age of family head (six groups)
- Sex of family head (two groups)
- Educational level of family head (six groups)
- Persons employed per family (seven groups)

For each decomposition the information needed is the coefficient of variation for the *j*th sector or group [I_j], the proportion of families in the *j*th sector or group [h_j], and the ratio of the income per family

Table 5.2. *Decomposition Analysis, by Farm and Nonfarm Sectors, 1964–72*

Variable and sector	*Notation*	*1964*	*1966*	*1968*
Total Gini	G	0.3282	0.3301	0.3348
Sectoral Gini				
Farm sector	G_1	0.3153	0.3264	0.2916
Nonfarm sector	G_2	0.3363	0.3315	0.3383
Total coefficient	I	0.7493	0.7073	0.7939
Sectoral coefficient				
Farm sector	I_1	0.6524	0.6658	0.5952
Nonfarm sector	I_2	0.8035	0.7244	0.8109
Sectoral family fraction				
Farm sector	h_1	0.3959	0.3093	0.3154
Nonfarm sector	h_2	0.6041	0.6907	0.6846
Sectoral family income parity				
Farm sector	$Z_1 = y_1/y$	0.9888	0.9735	0.8350
Nonfarm sector	$Z_2 = y_2/y$	1.0112	1.0265	1.1650
Estimated coefficient	$\hat{I}$	0.7490	0.7087	0.7956
Error	$\epsilon = \hat{I} - I$	−0.0003	0.0014	0.0017
Percentage error (percent)	$D = \epsilon/I \times 100$	−0.04	0.20	0.21

Sources: Calculated from DGBAS data (Taiwan Province and Taipei City combined) for various years.

of sector or group j to the average income per family of all sectors or groups $[Z_j = (y_j/y)]$.

The results of each decomposition are shown in tables 5.2 through 5.8. The maximum error of estimation of equation (5.4a), expressed as a percentage of the original coefficient, is 1.69 percent among the seventeen estimates; the average error of estimation is 0.24 percent.

1970	*1971*	*1972*	*Notation*	*Variable and sector*
0.2991	0.3006	0.2953	G	Total Gini
				Sectoral Gini
0.2828	0.2974	0.2907	G_1	Farm sector
0.2852	0.2916	0.2876	G_2	Nonfarm sector
0.6120	0.6194	0.6021	I	Total coefficient
				Sectoral coefficient
0.5734	0.6218	0.6061	I_1	Farm sector
0.5822	0.6007	0.5857	I_2	Nonfarm sector
				Sectoral family fraction
0.3091	0.2363	0.2588	h_1	Farm sector
0.6909	0.7637	0.7412	h_2	Nonfarm sector
				Sectoral family income parity
0.8075	0.8464	0.8644	$Z_1 = y_1/y$	Farm sector
1.1925	1.1536	1.1356	$Z_2 = y_2/y$	Nonfarm sector
0.6115	0.6199	0.6032	$\hat{I}$	Estimated coefficient
−0.0005	0.0005	0.0011	$\epsilon = \hat{I} - I$	Error
−0.08	0.08	0.18	$D = \epsilon/I \times 100$	Percentage error (percent)

In all these tables the values of the sectoral and group Gini coefficients $[G_i]$ and the Gini coefficient for all families $[G]$ are shown for purposes of comparison.

Farm and nonfarm sectors

It is interesting to compare the results shown in table 5.2 with the income inequalities, family fractions, and family income parities of the DGBAS farm and nonfarm sectors used in chapter three. According to table 5.2 the situation in Taiwan over the 1964–72 period shows the following:

- The inequality of the distribution of income was less within the farm sector than within the nonfarm sector before 1971 and slightly greater in 1971 and 1972.
- The weight of the farm sector in the total declined.
- The per family income of the nonfarm sector was higher than that of the farm sector.
- The income distribution of the farm and nonfarm sectors improved, but the speed of improvement was less for the farm sector than for the nonfarm sector. The farm sector, which earlier showed less inequality than the nonfarm sector, showed more in 1972.

These results, using segmentation rather than additive-components decomposition, are comparable to those obtained in chapter three.

Degree of urbanization

Because of the importance of industrialization and urbanization in economic growth, the effect of urbanization on the distribution of income should be explored. This effect can be brought out more clearly with the help of the sectoral decomposition equation. The necessary data were compiled from the original questionnaires of the DGBAS surveys for 1966 and 1972. This compilation is divided into two parts. One model of six sectors is based on a county classification; another model of three sectors is based on a city-town-village classification. The six-sector classification is based on the degree of urbanization defined by a cluster of ratios: population to area, nonagricultural employment to area, nonagricultural wage to area, nonagricultural value added to area, government expenditure to area, nonagricultural capital to labor, nonagricultural wage to labor, nonagricultural value added to labor, nonagricultural employment to population, and agricultural products to total products. The three-sector classification is based on the definitions for urban, semiurban, and rural areas given by the DGBAS and used in chapter four.

The two classifications have their respective merits and demerits. The six-sector classification has the merit that many economic indicators are available at this level, so that the characteristics of urbanization can be identified and analyzed in relation to these indicators. That six-sector classification nevertheless deemphasizes the geographic or locational dimension; for this reason a town may well be included in a rural area. The three-sector classification is separated by smaller units and brings out more clearly the underlying characteristics of urbanization. But its usefulness for economic analysis is limited because not even the information on value added is available by this classification.

To identify the relations between urbanization and income distribution, the income data based on the city-town-village classification were compiled from the original questionnaires for 1966 and 1972. Tables 5.3 and 5.4 give the results of the six-sector and three-sector classifications and show the following for those two years:

- The inequality of the distribution of income within the more urban sectors was not necessarily worse than that within the less urban sectors.
- The proportion of families in the most urban sector in the total increased, while that of the least urban sector declined over time.
- The per family incomes of the more urban sectors generally were higher than those of the less urban sectors.
- Income inequality within a sector improved for every sector over time.

Age of family head

Table 5.5 indicates that the inequality of income distribution for each age category declined between 1964 and 1972. Moreover there seems to have been a tendency toward somewhat greater inequality for the higher age groups. As would be expected, earning power increased with age until age 60 and then declined.

Sex of family head

The percentage distribution of female and male family heads in each income bracket shows that females make up a majority of family heads in the two lowest income groups; there are none in the highest income group. Thus the presence of female heads of households is associated with poverty. In Taiwan, as elsewhere, job opportunities for females have generally been far from equal to those for males. The jobs offered to women are also relatively less important, and thus provide lower incomes. Although a female's earning power

Table 5.3. *Decomposition Analysis, by Degree of Urbanization in the Six-sector Classification, 1966 and 1972*

Variable and sector	*Notation*	*1966*	*1972*
Total Gini	G·	0.3237	0.3018
Sectoral Gini			
Most urban sector	G_1	0.3146	0.3052
Second urban sector	G_2	0.3066	0.2776
Third urban sector	G_3	0.2928	0.2566
Fourth urban sector	G_4	0.3325	0.2730
Fifth urban sector	G_5	0.3183	0.2876
Most rural sector	G_6	0.3321	0.2924
Total coefficient	I	0.6610	0.6290
Sectoral coefficient			
Most urban sector	I_1	0.6405	0.6406
Second urban sector	I_2	0.6380	0.5499
Third urban sector	I_3	0.5745	0.5016
Fourth urban sector	I_4	0.6869	0.5455
Fifth urban sector	I_5	0.6665	0.5848
Sixth urban sector	I_6	0.6593	0.6202
Sectoral family fraction			
Most urban sector	h_1	0.2122	0.2195
Second urban sector	h_2	0.0952	0.1431
Third urban sector	h_3	0.1469	0.1917
Fourth urban sector	h_4	0.3111	0.2259
Fifth urban sector	h_5	0.1150	0.1496
Sixth urban sector	h_6	0.1196	0.0702
Sectoral family income parity			
Most urban sector	$Z_1 = y_1/y$	1.1481	1.3740
Second urban sector	$Z_2 = y_2/y$	1.1073	1.1374
Third urban sector	$Z_3 = y_3/y$	0.9095	0.9893
Fourth urban sector	$Z_4 = y_4/y$	0.8993	0.8424
Fifth urban sector	$Z_5 = y_5/y$	1.0219	0.8677
Sixth urban sector	$Z_6 = y_6/y$	0.9138	0.7890
Estimated coefficient	$\hat{I}$	0.6620	0.6297
Error	$\epsilon = \hat{I} - I$	0.0010	0.0007
Percentage error (percent)	$D = \epsilon/I \times 100$	0.15	0.11

Note: The total Gini coefficient and the coefficient of variation differ from those in tables 5.2 and 5.5–5.8 because the ones used here are directly calculated from the original questionnaires.

Sources: Calculated from the original questionnaires of the DGBAS surveys.

Table 5.4. *Decomposition Analysis, by Degree of Urbanization in the Three-sector Classification, 1966 and 1972*

Variable and sector	*Notation*	*1966*	*1972*
Total Gini	G	0.3237	0.3018
Sectoral Gini			
Urban sector	G_1	0.3134	0.2974
Semiurban sector	G_2	0.3182	0.2719
Rural sector	G_3	0.3316	0.2800
Total coefficient	I	0.6610	0.6290
Sectoral coefficient			
Urban sector	I_1	0.6505	0.6182
Semiurban sector	I_2	0.6432	0.5433
Rural sector	I_3	0.6684	0.5628
Sectoral family fraction			
Urban sector	h_1	0.2826	0.3798
Semiurban sector	h_2	0.4137	0.3434
Rural sector	h_3	0.3037	0.2768
Sectoral family income parity			
Urban sector	$Z_1 = y_1/y$	1.1278	1.2632
Semiurban sector	$Z_2 = y_2/y$	0.9245	0.9223
Rural sector	$Z_3 = y_3/y$	0.9477	0.8145
Estimated coefficient	$\hat{I}$	0.6615	0.6291
Error	$\epsilon = \hat{I} - I$	0.0005	0.0001
Percentage error (percent)	$D = \epsilon/I \times 100$	0.08	0.02

Note: Same as to table 5.3.
Sources: Same as for table 5.3.

on average is less than that of a male, the data compiled by sex of head of household distort the real earning power of a female (table 5.6). In the ordinary family, the husband's name is registered as the head of his family, which results in the large proportion of male heads in the total. For the distribution of income, a family headed by a female has broader implications than its literal meaning. Such a family is most likely to be headed by a single woman or a widow;

Table 5.5. *Decomposition Analysis, by Age of Head of Family, 1964 and 1972*

Variable and age	*Notation*	*1964*	*1972*
Total Gini	G	0.3282	0.2953
Sectoral Gini			
Under 20 years	G_1	0.3289	0.2645
20–30 years	G_2	0.3131	0.2875
30–40 years	G_3	0.2995	0.2672
40–50 years	G_4	0.3227	0.2817
50–60 years	G_5	0.3401	0.3150
Over 60 years	G_6	0.4107	0.4038
Total coefficient	I	0.7493	0.6021
Sectoral coefficient			
Under 20 years	I_1	0.6280	0.5122
20–30 years	I_2	0.7867	0.5840
30–40 years	I_3	0.6364	0.5434
40–50 years	I_4	0.8244	0.5798
50–60 years	I_5	0.6933	0.6287
Over 60 years	I_6	0.8407	0.7971
Sectoral family fraction			
Under 20 years	h_1	0.0083	0.0090
20–30 years	h_2	0.1136	0.0956
30–40 years	h_3	0.3274	0.2916
40–50 years	h_4	0.3181	0.3582
50–60 years	h_5	0.1721	0.1839
Over 60 years	h_6	0.0605	0.0617
Sectoral family income parity			
Under 20 years	$Z_1 = y_1/y$	0.6388	0.7758
20–30 years	$Z_2 = y_2/y$	0.9437	0.9577
30–40 years	$Z_3 = y_3/y$	0.9893	0.9862
40–50 years	$Z_4 = y_4/y$	1.0833	1.0876
50–60 years	$Z_5 = y_5/y$	1.2130	1.1681
Over 60 years	$Z_6 = y_6/y$	1.1318	1.0245
Estimated coefficient	$\hat{I}$	0.7519	0.6029
Error	$\epsilon = \hat{I} - I$	0.0026	0.0008
Percentage error (percent)	$D = \epsilon/I \times 100$	0.35	0.13

Sources: Same as for table 5.2.

Table 5.6. *Decomposition Analysis, by Sex of Head of Family, 1964 and 1972*

Variable and sex	*Notation*	*1964*	*1972*
Total Gini	G	0.3282	0.2953
Sectoral Gini			
Male	G_1	0.3245	0.2899
Female	G_2	0.3575	0.3617
Total coefficient	I	0.7493	0.6021
Sectoral Coefficient			
Male	I_1	0.7591	0.5953
Female	I_2	0.7511	0.7239
Sectoral family fraction			
Male	h_1	0.9235	0.9327
Female	h_2	0.0765	0.0673
Sectoral family income parity			
Male	$Z_1 = y_1/y$	1.1173	1.0722
Female	$Z_2 = y_2/y$	0.8827	0.9278
Estimated coefficient	$\hat{I}$	0.7620	0.6039
Error	$\epsilon = \hat{I} - I$	0.0127	0.0018
Percentage error (percent)	$D = \epsilon/I \times 100$	1.69	0.30

Sources: Same as for table 5.2.

in the absence of a male spouse, the number of working persons in the family may be less than that in a family with a male head. These factors, when added to the lower earning power of the female, make the income parity of female-headed households lower than that of male-headed households.

Number of persons employed per family

The number of persons employed per family is considered to be an important factor affecting family income and its distribution. The

Table 5.7. *Decomposition Analysis, by Number of Persons Employed in Family, 1964 and 1972*

Variable and number employed	*Notation*	*1964*	*1972*
Total Gini	G	0.3282	0.2953
Sectoral Gini			
None	G_1	0.4889	0.4297
1	G_2	0.3213	0.2877
2	G_3	0.3232	0.2805
3	G_4	0.2968	0.2949
4	G_5	0.3158	0.2740
5	G_6	0.2655	0.2415
6 or more	G_7	0.2785	0.2682
Total coefficient	I	0.7493	0.6021
Sectoral coefficient			
None	I_1	1.0472	0.8999
1	I_2	0.7316	0.6102
2	I_3	0.7018	0.5645
3	I_4	0.5962	0.5892
4	I_5	1.0119	0.5719
5	I_6	0.5497	0.4777
6 or more	I_7	0.5348	0.4942

conclusions from the decomposition effort are summarized in table 5.7.

- Income generally increased as the number of persons employed increased, which can be observed by comparing the income parity of each category.
- Income inequality seems to have had a slight tendency to decline as the number of employed rose; the category, zero persons employed, had the widest income inequality.

Educational level of family head

As already seen with respect to the explanation of the distribution of the wage share in chapter four, the effect of education on the level and distribution of income is crucial. The data reveal that illiterates

Table 5.7 (*Continued*)

Variable and number employed	*Notation*	*1964*	*1972*
Sectoral family fraction			
None	h_1	0.0140	0.0185
1	h_2	0.3929	0.4218
2	h_3	0.2760	0.3220
3	h_4	0.1464	0.1206
4	h_5	0.0895	0.0686
5	h_6	0.0434	0.0295
6 or more	h_7	0.0378	0.0190
Sectoral family income parity			
None	$Z_1 = y_1/y$	0.5818	0.6121
1	$Z_2 = y_2/y$	0.8129	0.8228
2	$Z_3 = y_3/y$	0.8816	0.9104
3	$Z_4 = y_4/y$	0.9167	1.0947
4	$Z_5 = y_5/y$	1.0964	1.0606
5	$Z_6 = y_6/y$	1.1460	1.1121
6 or more	$Z_7 = y_7/y$	1.5646	1.3873
Estimated coefficient	$\hat{I}$	0.7552	0.6037
Error	$\epsilon = \hat{I} - I$	0.0059	0.0016
Percentage error (percent)	$D = \epsilon/I \times 100$	0.79	0.27

Source: Same as for table 5.2.

had the least earning power (table 5.8). They were followed in ascending order by graduates of primary school, junior high school, and senior high and vocational school. The highest income could generally be earned by college graduates, not by graduate school graduates. The relation between wealth and higher levels of education is known not to be close.[5] Although educational attainments up to a point are required for obtaining higher incomes, a person's income-earning ability does not seem to be monotonically related to

5. Shirley W. Y. Kuo, "Income Distribution by Size in Taiwan Area—Changes and Causes," in *Income Distribution, Employment and Economic Development in Southeast and East Asia*, 2 vols. (Tokyo: Japan Economic Research Center, 1975), vol. 1, pp. 80–146.

Table 5.8. *Decomposition Analysis, by Educational Level of Head of Family, 1972*

Variable and educational level	*Notation*	*1972*
Total Gini	G	0.2820
Sectoral Gini		
Graduate school graduate	G_1	0.1852
College graduate	G_2	0.2438
Senior high school graduate	G_3	0.2547
Junior high school graduate	G_4	0.2521
Primary school graduate	G_5	0.2769
Illiterate	G_6	0.3059
Total coefficient	I	0.5651
Sectoral coefficient		
Graduate school graduate	I_1	0.3450
College graduate	I_2	0.4725
Senior high school graduate	I_3	0.5132
Junior high school graduate	I_4	0.5062
Primary school graduate	I_5	0.5627
Illiterate	I_6	0.5895
Sectoral family fraction		
Graduate school graduate	h_1	0.0011
College graduate	h_2	0.0706
Senior high school graduate	h_3	0.1607
Junior high school graduate	h_4	0.1301
Primary school graduate	h_5	0.5141
Illiterate	h_6	0.1234
Sectoral family income parity		
Graduate school graduate	$Z_1 = y_1/y$	1.1247
College graduate	$Z_2 = y_2/y$	1.1840
Senior high school graduate	$Z_3 = y_3/y$	1.1458
Junior high school graduate	$Z_4 = y_4/y$	0.9626
Primary school graduate	$Z_5 = y_5/y$	0.8505
Illiterate	$Z_6 = y_6/y$	0.7324
Estimated coefficient	$\hat{I}$	0.5635
Error	$\epsilon = \hat{I} - I$	−0.0016
Percentage error (percent)	$D = \epsilon/I \times 100$	−0.28

Source: Calculated from DGBAS data. Only 1972 data for Taiwan Province is available.

education beyond a certain income level. What is more interesting, the equity of income distribution tends to be higher for the more educated groups.

Changes in Income Inequality Associated with Industrialization and Urbanization

During the 1964–72 period, as already seen, overall income inequality significantly declined. But with farm-family income growing less rapidly than nonfarm-family income, the income gap between the two kinds of family widened. In addition, the income gaps among family groups in different locations, classified by the degree of urbanization, widened during the same period. The widening gap caused by industrialization and urbanization can be observed through changes in income disparities, an indicator suggested by Kuznets, in sectors classified by farm and nonfarm families and by different degrees of urbanization.[6]

Disparities in the shares of farm and nonfarm families increased from 1964 to 1972, indicating increasing inequality between the two sectors (table 5.9). The respective divergence of the income-relative from unity in each sector also shows increasing inequality. Income disparities by degree of urbanization show that the widening was mainly caused by the most urban and rural sectors (tables 5.10 and 5.11). Levels and trends in income differences among the sectors reveal that per family income was rising at a higher-than-average rate in the nonfarm sector and the most urban sector. In contrast, per family income was rising at a lower-than-average rate in the farm sector and the most rural sector.

How, then, was more equity generated for the whole economy? In an attempt to answer this question, equation (5.9) was used to determine intrasectoral and intersectoral effects for the 1964–72 period.[7] The intersectoral effect will be further divided into a family-

6. Simon Kuznets, "Demographic Components in Size Distribution of Income," in *Income Distribution, Employment and Economic Development in Southeast and East Asia*, vol. 2, pp. 389–472.

7. In earlier chapters 1968 was identified as the turning point for growth and distribution. In this regard separate causal analyses should be made for the 1964–68 and 1968–72 subperiods. We nevertheless restrict ourselves to the entire 1964–72 period because the data required for the separate analysis of causal subperiods are lacking. For example, data on urbanization can be used only for 1966 and 1972.

Table 5.9. *Income Disparities, by Farm and Nonfarm Families, 1964 and 1972*

Type of family	Share of income (percent) 1964	1972	Share of families (percent) 1964	1972	Disparity in shares (percentage points) 1964	1972	Income relative[a] 1964	1972
Farm families	39.1	21.0	39.6	25.9	−0.5	−4.9	0.99	0.81
Nonfarm families	60.9	79.0	60.4	74.1	0.5	4.9	1.01	1.07
All families	100.0	100.0	100.0	100.0	1.0[b]	9.8[b]	1.00	1.00

Sources: Same as for table 5.2.
a. The ratio of the share of income to the share of families.
b. The sum of the absolute values.

Table 5.10. *Income Disparities, by Degree of Urbanization in the Six-sector Classification, 1966 and 1972*

Degree of urbanization	Share of income (percent) 1966	1972	Share of families (percent) 1966	1972	Disparity in shares (percentage points) 1966	1972	Income relative[a] 1966	1972
Most urban	24.6	29.3	21.2	21.9	3.4	7.4	1.16	1.34
Second urban	10.7	15.8	9.5	14.3	1.2	1.5	1.13	1.10
Third urban	13.5	18.4	14.7	19.2	−1.2	−0.8	0.92	0.96
Fourth urban	28.3	18.5	31.1	22.6	−2.8	−4.1	0.91	0.82
Fifth urban	11.9	12.6	11.5	15.0	0.4	−2.4	1.03	0.84
Most rural	11.0	5.4	12.0	7.0	−1.0	−1.6	0.92	0.77
All sectors	100.0	100.0	100.0	100.0	10.0[b]	17.8[b]	1.00	1.00

Sources: Same as for table 5.3.
a. The ratio of the share of income to the share of families.
b. The sum of the absolute values.

Table 5.11. *Income Disparities, by Degree of Urbanization in the Three-sector Classification, 1966 and 1972*

Degree of urbanization	Share of income (percent)		Share of families (percent)		Disparity in shares (percentage points)		Income relative[a]	
	1966	1972	1966	1972	1966	1972	1966	1972
Urban	32.2	46.9	28.2	38.0	4.0	8.9	1.14	1.23
Semiurban	38.7	31.0	41.4	34.3	−2.7	−3.3	0.93	0.90
Rural	29.1	22.1	30.4	27.7	−1.3	−5.6	0.96	0.80
All sectors	100.0	100.0	100.0	100.0	8.0[b]	17.8[b]	1.00	1.00

Sources: Same as for table 5.3.
a. The ratio of the share of income to the share of families.
b. The sum of the absolute values.

weight effect and an income-disparity effect. The change in the nationwide inequality depends on the sum of these effects and cannot be explained by any single one.

Causes traced to the farm-nonfarm decomposition

The intrasectoral and intersectoral effects calculated for the farm and nonfarm sectors are shown in table 5.12.

- Because of the reduction in internal inequality within both the farm and nonfarm sectors, the favorable intrasectoral effect contributed to the reduction in income inequality. The farm sector contributed 7 percent to the intrasectoral effect; the nonfarm sector 93 percent.
- The intersectoral effect, constituted by the adverse family-weight effect and the adverse income-disparity effect, was adverse to the distribution of income. The family-weight effect contributed 26 percent to the intersectoral effect; the income disparity effect 74 percent. That is, the change in the weights of farm and nonfarm family numbers and the widening of the income gap between the two sectors adversely affected the distribution of income. The magnitude of adverse effects, expressed as a percentage of the absolute value of the total change, was 18.1 percent.

Table 5.12. *Causes of the Reduction in Income Inequality, by Farm and Nonfarm Sectors, 1964–72*

Sector	*Total effect* $\left[\sum_i\right]$	*Intra-sectoral effect*[a] $\left[\sum_i \frac{\partial I_w}{\partial I_i}\cdot\frac{dI_i}{dt}\right]$	*Inter-sectoral effect*	=	*Family weight effect* $\left[\sum_i \frac{\partial I_w}{\partial h_i}\cdot\frac{dh_i}{dt}\right]$	+	*Income disparity effect* $\left[\sum_i \frac{\partial I_w}{\partial Z_i}\cdot\frac{dZ_i}{dt}\right]$
Both sectors	−0.1457	−0.1727	0.0270		0.0057		0.0213
Percentage of total effect	−100.0	−118.5	18.5		3.9		14.6
Farm sector	—	−0.0117 (−6.8)	—		0.0512		0.0115
Nonfarm sector	—	−0.1610 (−93.2)	—		−0.0455		0.0098

— Not applicable.

Note: Positive coefficients represent effects which act to increase income inequality; negative coefficients, those which act to reduce income inequality.

Source: Calculated from table 5.2.

a. The figures in parentheses indicate the percentage composition of the intrasectoral effect.

- The decomposition of the intrasectoral and intersectoral effects shows that the essential cause of the reduction in income inequality in Taiwan was the reduction in income inequality within the nonfarm sector. That is, the reduction in intrasectoral inequality within the nonfarm sector more than compensated for the adverse intersectoral effect and made possible the reduction in income inequality for the total economy.

Causes traced to the urbanization decomposition

The causes of the overall reduction in income inequality related to the degree of urbanization are examined next (table 5.13). The following intrasectoral and intersectoral effects were observed:

- The reduction in internal inequality within each of the six sectors contributed most to the reduction in income inequality. The rate of contribution to the reduction in income inequality of the total economy was 183.7 percent. The reduction in intra-

Table 5.13. *Causes of the Reduction in Income Inequality, by Degree of Urbanization in the Six-sector Classification, 1966–72*

Sector	*Total effect* $\left[\sum_i\right]$	*Intra-sectoral effect*[a] $\left[\sum_i \frac{\partial I_w}{\partial I_i}\cdot\frac{dI_i}{dt}\right]$	*Inter-sectoral effect*	=	*Family weight effect* $\left[\sum_i \frac{\partial I_w}{\partial h_i}\cdot\frac{dh_i}{dt}\right]$	+	*Income disparity effect* $\left[\sum_i \frac{\partial I_w}{\partial Z_i}\cdot\frac{dZ_i}{dt}\right]$
All sectors	−0.0332	−0.0610	0.0278		−0.0066		0.0344
Percentage of total effect	−100.0	−183.7	83.7		−19.9		103.6
Most urban	—	−0.00003 (0.0)	—		−0.0018		0.0259
Second urban	—	−0.0118 (−19.4)	—		−0.0175		0.0004
Third urban	—	−0.0091 (−14.9)	—		−0.0181		−0.0042
Fourth urban	—	−0.0282 (−46.2)	—		0.0267		0.0047
Fifth urban	—	−0.0091 (−14.9)	—		−0.0110		0.0040
Most rural	—	−0.0028 (−4.6)	—		0.0151		0.0036

— Not applicable.

Note: Positive coefficients represent effects which act to increase income inequality; negative coefficients, those which act to reduce income inequality.

Source: Calculated from table 5.3.

a. The figures in parentheses indicate the percentage composition of the intrasectoral effect.

sectoral inequality compensated for the adverse intersectoral effect and thus significantly contributed to the reduction of income inequality for the whole economy.

- The fourth urban sector made the highest contribution to the intrasectoral effect, recording 46.2 percent of the total. Other important contributions came from the second, third, and fifth urban sectors; their contribution rates ranged from 14.9 percent to 19.4 percent. The most rural sector contributed 4.6 percent; the most urban sector contributed nothing. This seems to indicate that the income inequality was reduced much more within a semiurban area than within either the most urban or the most rural area.
- The intersectoral effect was unfavorable to the reduction of income inequality. Combining the family-weight effect and the income-disparity effect, the total adverse contribution was 83.7 percent.

Table 5.14. *Causes of the Reduction in Income Inequality, by Degree of Urbanization in the Three-sector Classification, 1966–72*

Sector	Total effect $\left[\sum_i\right]$	Intra-sectoral effect[a] $\left[\sum_i \frac{\partial I_w}{\partial I_i}\cdot\frac{dI_i}{dt}\right]$	Inter-sectoral effect	= Family weight effect $\left[\sum_i \frac{\partial I_w}{\partial h_i}\cdot\frac{dh_i}{dt}\right]$	+ Income disparity effect $\left[\sum_i \frac{\partial I_w}{\partial Z_i}\cdot\frac{dZ_i}{dt}\right]$
All sectors	−0.0334	−0.0679	0.0345	0.0049	0.0296
Percentage of total effect	−100.0	−203.3	103.3	14.7	88.6
Urban	—	−0.0151 (−22.2)	—	−0.0279	0.0179
Semiurban	—	−0.0296 (−43.6)	—	0.0245	0.0002
Rural	—	−0.0232 (−34.2)	—	0.0083	0.0115

— Not applicable.

Note: Positive coefficients represent effects which act to increase income inequality; negative coefficients, those which act to reduce income inequality.

Source: Calculated from table 5.4.

a. The figures in parentheses indicate the percentage composition of the intrasectoral effect.

- The change in the weights of family numbers had a moderately favorable effect on the reduction of income inequality for the total economy.
- The widening income gaps among the six sectors adversely affected the distribution of income. The magnitude of the adverse income-disparity effect, expressed as a percentage of the absolute value of the total change, was 103.6 percent.

Another observation for the effects of urbanization on the distribution of family income is based on the three-sector classification of cities, towns, and villages. Causes of reduction in income inequality observed by this three-sector classification are presented in table 5.14. Essentially the results are the same as those observed with the six-sector classification.

- The favorable intrasectoral effect more than compensated for the adverse intersectoral effect.
- The contribution by the semiurban sector to the intrasectoral effect was largest; that by the urban sector, smallest.

- The intersectoral effect was adverse to the reduction of income inequality. Based on this city-town-village classification, the change in the family weight had a slightly adverse effect on the change in income equality.

In summary, the intersectoral income gap widened during the course of industrialization and urbanization in Taiwan, but intrasectoral inequality was reduced more than enough to compensate for the adverse intersectoral effect. This performance confirms that decentralization of economic development may contribute substantially to the reduction of income inequality.

Additional Reflections

Rapid economic growth in Taiwan during the 1964–72 period raised the average income of households in every bracket and led to absolute increases in the welfare of all income groups. What are the policies that seem to have contributed to Taiwan's success in reducing income inequality during a period of rapid growth? Many, to be sure. But some of the more important and obvious policies are the following: the pursuit of a labor-intensive and outward-looking growth path; early land reform; the reduction in the collection of a hidden tax on rice; and reductions in the relative tax burden of farmers and the poor. Moreover, the size and composition of families moved in a direction favorable to a reduction of income inequality. The causal interrelations among these and other factors still are far from clear and require further analysis.

The importance of rural by-employment

As noted in chapter three, a distinguishing characteristic of Taiwan's farm-family income is that it has a substantial component of nonagricultural income. The proportion of nonagricultural income in farm income was 34.1 percent in 1964 and 53.7 percent in 1975. How did the composition of nonagricultural income relate to different levels of farm income? The lower the income level, the bigger the proportion of nonagricultural income (table 5.15). In 1975 the lowest 80 percent of families received more than half their income from nonagricultural sources. About 98 percent of nonfarm income

Table 5.15. *Sources of Income of Farm and Nonfarm Families, by Decile, 1966 and 1975*
(percent)

	Composition of total family income							
	1966				1975			
	Farm families		Nonfarm families		Farm families		Nonfarm families	
Decile[a]	Agricultural income	Nonagricultural income	Agricultural income	Nonagricultural income	Agricultural income	Nonagricultural income	Agricultural income	Nonagricultural income
1	54.7	45.3	2.9	97.1	33.9	66.1	2.1	97.9
2	55.3	44.7	2.8	97.2	37.3	62.7	2.0	98.0
3	57.3	42.7	3.0	97.0	39.0	61.0	2.1	97.9
4	61.0	39.0	2.4	97.6	40.6	59.4	1.9	98.1
5	64.3	35.7	1.8	98.2	43.1	56.9	1.6	98.4
6	65.5	34.5	2.4	97.6	44.4	55.6	1.9	98.1
7	68.5	31.5	1.7	98.3	46.0	54.0	1.8	98.2
8	70.1	29.9	2.2	97.8	48.4	51.6	2.7	97.3
9	70.2	29.8	2.3	97.7	50.8	49.2	1.9	98.1
10	67.6	32.4	1.8	98.2	52.4	47.6	2.4	97.6
All deciles	65.9	34.1	2.2	97.8	46.3	53.7	2.1	97.9

Sources: Calculated from DGBAS, *Report on the Survey of Family Income and Expenditure,* 1966 and 1975.
a. Arranged from lowest to highest income.

was from nonagricultural activities. Thus the role of agricultural income in nonfarm household income was negligible.

During the 1964–75 period the real income of both farm and nonfarm families considerably increased in every income bracket. The increase was much higher in the lower income groups than in the higher income groups (table 5.16). For the nonfarm sector, the lowest decile had a 368 percent increase in income; the highest decile a 199 percent increase. For the farm sector, the lowest decile had a 235 percent increase in income; the highest decile had only a 17 percent increase. Furthermore, the increase of nonagricultural income brought about the increase in total farm-family income.

The higher growth rates of income from nonagricultural activities

Table 5.16. *Growth of Income of Farm and Nonfarm Families, by Decile, 1966–75*
(percent)

Decile[a]	Farm families: Total income	Farm families: Agricultural income	Farm families: Nonagricultural income	Total income of nonfarm families
1	235	107	388	368
2	251	137	392	335
3	238	130	382	315
4	232	121	406	303
5	228	120	423	298
6	213	112	405	290
7	202	103	417	278
8	185	97	392	262
9	182	104	367	240
10	170	110	297	199
All deciles	199	110	372	261

Sources: Same as for table 5.15.
a. Arranged from highest to lowest income.

among the lower-income family groups give additional support to the notion that two main factors were responsible for the good overall performance: the relatively rapid rate of employment generation for members of the lower income groups initially; the change in their wages subsequently. During the period under observation, rapid labor absorption finally eliminated rural unemployment or underemployment. Newcomers and unemployed individuals were mainly absorbed by the nonagricultural sector, particularly by light manufacturing industries. Thus unskilled labor was efficiently used. As the economy grew, such labor became relatively more scarce, until wage rates of unskilled labor finally were rising more rapidly than those of skilled labor. Undoubtedly the early and rapid absorption of unskilled labor substantially contributed to the rise in relative incomes of the lower income families, both urban and rural. Industrial decentralization clearly contributed to this labor absorption and was an essential factor contributing to the reduction of overall income inequality.

Table 5.17. *Gini Index of Land Concentration in Selected Countries, Comparisons for Various Years*

Country	*Year*	*Gini index*	*Year*	*Gini index*	*Decline in Gini index (percent)*
Colombia	1960	0.864	1969	0.818	5.32
India	1953–54	0.628	1960–61	0.589	6.14
Mexico	1930	0.959	1960	0.694	27.64
Philippines	1948	0.576	1960	0.534	7.26
Taiwan	1952	0.618	1960	0.457	26.08
United Arab Republic	1952	0.810	1964	0.674	16.74

Source: Hung-Chao Tai, *Land Reform and Politics* (Berkeley: University of California Press, 1974), p. 310, reproduced in Yung Wei, "Modernization Process in Taiwan: An Allocative Analysis," *Asian Survey*, vol. 16, no. 3, (March 1976), pp. 249–69.

Effects of land reform

Income inequality is naturally related to initial conditions. That is, it is related to the original distribution of such assets as land, capital, and educational training, which provide rents, dividends, interest, and salaries. The inequality usually is much more severe in asset holdings than in income. For these reasons, measures to distribute assets more equally may be important for a more equal distribution of income.

Table 5.17 shows the Gini index of land concentration in selected countries. The Gini index for Taiwan was 0.618 in 1952, before land reform had its full effect, and 0.457 by 1960.[8] Taiwan's land reform, already discussed in chapter two, resulted in smaller scale farming. Landholdings of more than three hectares constituted 42 percent of the total cultivated area before land reform, but only 23 percent after its implementation. Landholdings of one hectare or less, which originally constituted 25 percent of the total area, increased to 35 percent. The smaller average size farms in turn brought about a more intensive use of labor and of multiple-cropping practices.

8. Yung Wei, "Modernization Process in Taiwan: An Allocative Analysis," *Asian Survey*, vol. 16, no. 3 (University of California Press, March 1976), pp. 249–69.

Table 5.18. *Indexes of the Productivity of Land and Labor in Agriculture, Taiwan, 1950 and 1955*

Year	*Land area*	*Land productivity*	*Labor inputs*	*Labor productivity*
1950	100.0	100.0	100.0	100.0
1955	100.7	121.5	107.6	113.2

Source: T. H. Lee, "Impact of Land Reform on the Farm Economy Structure," (n.p., n.d.).

After the land reform, farmers had a freer choice of crops. As owner-cultivators, they were under no obligation to produce rice for rental payments. Thus the land reform tended to reduce the share of rice and to increase the share of other such crops of higher value as livestock and poultry. Moreover labor productivity increased more slowly than land productivity during 1950–55, indicating the labor-using bias of technological change in agriculture (table 5.18).

Reduction in the collection of the hidden tax on rice

For market control, all commercial activities of farmers' associations and private rice dealers in Taiwan were subject to government supervision. Control of rice not only stabilized the supply and price of rice, but also generated considerable revenue for government. A hidden tax on rice was imposed through land taxes, compulsory rice purchases, a rice-fertilizer barter system, and the payment for land in kind. All these taxes were levied by government purchases at lower-than-market prices. The revenue from these hidden taxes was important: it exceeded total income tax collections every year before 1963, but declined gradually after 1964 and rapidly after 1969, especially in comparison with the income tax. This rapid reduction in the collection of the hidden tax on rice undoubtedly contributed to the more even distribution of income over time.

Relative reduction in the tax burden of farm families

The ratio of the tax burden of farm families to that of nonfarm families was 1.73 to 1 in 1966; it declined to 0.35 to 1 by 1975 (table 5.19). Even more noteworthy is that the reversal from farm families having a heavier to a lighter tax burden than nonfarm families was more pronounced for the lower income brackets. A cross-sectional

Table 5.19. *Relative Tax Burden of Farm and Nonfarm Families, by Income Range, 1966 and 1975*

Income range (thousands of N.T. dollars)	*Ratio of tax burden of farm families to that of nonfarm families*	
	1966	*1975*
Less than 10	3.92	—
10–20	3.60	0.85
20–30	3.22	1.16
30–40	2.59	1.39
40–50	1.67	1.34
50–60	2.07	1.12
60–70	2.02	0.95
70–80	1.42	0.83
80–90	1.31	0.82
90–100	0.68	0.60
100–150	0.68	0.49
150–200	1.17	0.56
More than 200	—	0.19
All income ranges	1.73	0.35

— Not applicable.
Sources: Calculated from DGBAS, *Report on the Survey of Family Income and Expenditure*, 1966 and 1975.

analysis of the relation of taxes to distribution is discussed in the next chapter.

Changing size and composition of families

In chapter four on the inequality of family wage income, the causes of inequality were related to the size and composition of families. Some additional inductive evidence is cited here to support that analysis. These observations are based, however, on total family income, not on family wage income.

How can the reduction in income inequality during the 1964–72 period be traced to changes in the size of families, the number of employed per family, the age of the family head, and the sex of the family head? Because the income gap widened between the farm and nonfarm sectors, it is desirable to keep the two sectors separate, lest the positive and negative demographic effects of each sector act to compensate each other. But because of the lack of sectorally separated data for demographic effects on the distribution of income, these effects are observed in a combined framework that takes into account the whole economy. The income disparities by the number of employed, by age, and by sex are calculated. The causes of the reduction in the income inequality are also identified, based on the decomposition equation for each classification. All statistical results are shown in tables 5.20–5.29 appended to this chapter.

During 1966–72 the average family sizes for the total economy, farm families, and nonfarm families all declined.[9] The variance of family size also declined for each kind of family. The reduction of family size and its variance thus increased the homogeneity of family composition, a pattern that may have contributed to the reduction of income inequality. When the income disparity by size of family is calculated for the total economy, the results show that income disparities between various sizes of families considerably narrowed during the period. The disparities were mostly reduced by changes in the incomes of one-person families and of the family group of ten persons or more.

The income disparities by number employed per family also declined. The greatest reduction of disparities occurred in family groups with the larger numbers of employed. Using the same decomposition formula to calculate the three effects, it is found that all of them contributed to the reduction of overall income inequality. The family-weight effect contributed 1.3 percent; the income-disparity effect 5.9 percent; the intrasectoral effect 92.8 percent.

The income disparities by age of family head slightly declined. The reduction mainly resulted from the groups of under 20, 50–60, and over 60. The income disparities classified by sex of family head also declined. The per family income share of female-headed families rose during the period. The decomposition analysis shows that, whereas all effects contributed to the reduction in income inequality, the intrasectoral effect was dominant.

In brief, when families are classified by size or composition, a reduction in income disparities is observed between groups in every case. The intrasectoral effect was dominant in each of the three cases. A favorable intersectoral effect is also observed in every case,

9. The year 1966 is observed because of the inadequacy of the relevant DGBAS data for 1964. We are grateful to Professor Kuznets for pointing this out.

but its magnitude was not large. This suggests that changes in the size and composition of families must have contributed to the reduction of income inequality. The picture is not clear, however, because many of these changes were in turn the result of economic growth and by no means exogenous. Because interrelations between demographic change and economic growth are close, the intrasectoral reduction in income inequality observed in the demographic classification must have been caused by a large number of economic factors that are still too complicated to be unraveled here. More theoretical work, departing from the preliminary inductive evidence gathered in this chapter, is required.

Table 5.20. *Average Size of Families, by Income Bracket, 1966 and 1972*

	1966[a]		*1972*[b]	
Income bracket (thousands of N.T. dollars)	*Average number of persons in family*	*Deviation from the mean*	*Average number of persons in family*	*Deviation from the mean*
Less than 10	2.0	−3.9	1.2	−4.5
10–20	4.4	−1.5	2.7	−3.0
20–30	5.5	−0.4	4.4	−1.3
30–40	6.5	0.6	5.2	−0.5
40–50	7.9	2.0	5.5	−0.2
50–60	8.4	2.5	5.9	0.2
60–70	7.2	1.3	6.1	0.4
70–80	8.8	2.9	6.4	0.7
80–90	8.2	2.3	6.9	1.2
90–100	8.2	2.3	6.5	0.8
100–200	9.3	3.4	7.5	1.8
More than 200	4.2	−1.7	7.0	1.3
All brackets	5.9	—	5.7	—

— Not applicable.

Note: The average sizes of family in the same income brackets may not be directly comparable for the two years because of a possible escalation in the income level in each bracket during the period.

Sources: Calculated from DGBAS, *Report on the Survey of Family Income and Expenditure,* 1966 and 1972.

a. For 1966 the variance divided by the square of the mean is 0.0747.

b. For 1972 the variance divided by the square of the mean is 0.0330.

Table 5.21. *Average Size of Farm Families, by Income Bracket, 1966 and 1972*

	1966[a]		*1972*[b]	
Income bracket (thousands of N.T. dollars)	*Average number of persons in family*	*Deviation from the mean*	*Average number of persons in family*	*Deviation from the mean*
Less than 10	3.2	−4.0	2.0	−4.5
10–20	5.5	−1.7	3.2	−3.3
20–30	6.7	−0.5	5.0	−1.5
30–40	7.8	0.6	6.1	−0.4
40–50	8.8	1.6	6.7	0.2
50–60	9.7	2.5	7.0	0.5
60–70	9.1	1.9	7.6	1.1
70–80	11.6	4.4	8.2	1.7
80–90	9.5	2.3	8.8	2.3
90–100	11.8	4.6	9.1	2.6
100–200	13.9	6.7	10.1	3.6
More than 200	—	—	9.9	3.4
All brackets	7.2	—	6.5	—

— Not applicable.

Note: The average sizes of family in the same income brackets may not be directly comparable for the two years because of a possible escalation in the income level in each bracket during the period.

Sources: Same as for table 5.20.

a. For 1966 the variance divided by the square of the mean is 0.0709.

b. For 1972 the variance divided by the square of the mean is 0.0583.

Table 5.22. *Average Size of Nonfarm Families, by Income Bracket, 1966 and 1972*

	1966[a]		*1972*[b]	
Income bracket (thousands of N.T. dollars)	*Average number of persons in family*	*Deviation from the mean*	*Average number of persons in family*	*Deviation from the mean*
Less than 10	1.6	−3.7	1.1	−4.2
10–20	3.8	−1.5	2.0	−3.3
20–30	5.0	−0.3	3.7	−1.6
30–40	6.0	0.7	4.7	−0.6
40–50	7.4	2.1	5.1	−0.2
50–60	7.8	2.5	5.5	0.2
60–70	6.5	1.2	5.7	0.4
70–80	7.5	2.2	5.8	0.5
80–90	7.4	2.1	6.5	1.2
90–100	7.3	2.0	6.1	0.8
100–200	7.1	1.8	6.9	1.6
More than 200	4.2	−1.1	6.1	0.8
All brackets	5.3	—	5.3	—

— Not applicable.

Note: The average sizes of family in the same income brackets may not be directly comparable for the two years because of a possible escalation in the income level in each bracket during the period.

Sources: Same as for table 5.20.

a. For 1966 the variance divided by the square of the mean is 0.0828.

b. For 1972 the variance divided by the square of the mean is 0.0357.

Table 5.23. *Income Disparities, by Size of Household, 1966 and 1972*

Number of persons in household	Share of income (percent)		Share of households (percent)		Disparity in shares (percentage points)		Income relative[a]	
	1966	1972	1966	1972	1966	1972	1966	1972
1	2.6	1.4	6.6	3.3	−4.0	−1.9	0.39	0.42
2	4.3	2.8	5.4	4.2	−1.1	−1.4	0.80	0.67
3	5.8	7.8	7.7	9.3	−1.9	−1.5	0.75	0.84
4	9.7	12.5	11.5	13.7	−1.8	−1.2	0.84	0.91
5	14.0	20.9	15.3	21.2	−1.3	−0.3	0.92	0.99
6	14.5	19.5	14.8	19.3	−0.3	0.2	0.98	1.01
7	16.2	13.7	14.9	12.6	1.3	1.1	1.09	1.09
8	10.3	9.0	9.4	7.6	0.9	1.4	1.10	1.18
9	6.8	4.8	5.6	3.9	1.2	0.9	1.21	1.23
10 or more	15.8	7.6	8.8	4.9	7.0	2.7	1.80	1.55
All households	100.0	100.0	100.0	100.0	20.8[b]	12.6[b]	1.00	1.00

Sources: Same as for table 5.20.

a. The ratio of the share of income to the share of households.

b. The sum of the absolute values.

Table 5.24. *Income Disparities, by Number of Persons Employed in Family, 1964 and 1972*

Number of persons employed in family	Share of income (percent)		Share of families (percent)		Disparity in shares (percentage points)		Income relative[a]	
	1964	1972	1964	1972	1964	1972	1964	1972
None	1.2	1.2	1.8	1.8	−0.6	−0.6	0.67	0.67
1	37.3	37.9	42.2	42.2	−4.9	−4.3	0.88	0.90
2	27.9	32.0	29.1	32.2	−1.2	−0.2	0.96	0.99
3	11.8	14.4	11.1	12.1	0.7	2.3	1.06	1.19
4	11.5	8.0	8.9	6.9	2.6	1.1	1.29	1.16
5	5.2	3.6	4.0	2.9	1.2	0.7	1.30	1.24
6 or more	5.1	2.9	2.9	1.9	2.2	1.0	1.76	1.53
All families	100.0	100.0	100.0	100.0	13.4[b]	10.2[b]	1.00	1.00

Sources: Same as for table 5.2.

a. The ratio of the share of income to the share of families.

b. The sum of the absolute values.

Table 5.25. *Causes of the Reduction in Income Inequality, by Number of Persons Employed in Family, 1964–72*

Number of persons employed in family	*Total effect* $\left[\sum_i\right]$	*Intra-sectoral effect*[a] $\left[\sum_i \frac{\partial I_w}{\partial I_i}\cdot\frac{dI_i}{dt}\right]$	*Inter-sectoral effect*	=	*Family weight effect* $\left[\sum_i \frac{\partial I_w}{\partial h_i}\cdot\frac{dh_i}{dt}\right]$	+	*Income disparity effect* $\left[\sum_i \frac{\partial I_w}{\partial Z_i}\cdot\frac{dZ_i}{dt}\right]$
All categories	−0.1532	−0.1422	−0.0110		−0.0020		−0.0090
Percentage of total effect	−100.0	−92.8	−7.2		−1.3		−5.9
None	—	0.0015 (−1.0)	—		−0.0002		−0.0002
1	—	−0.0395 (−27.8)	—		−0.0096		−0.0011
2	—	−0.0371 (−26.1)	—		−0.0175		−0.0012
3	—	−0.0010 (−0.7)	—		0.0103		0.0008
4	—	−0.0577 (−40.6)	—		0.0022		−0.0024
5	—	−0.0031 (−2.2)	—		0.0070		−0.0002
6 or more	—	−0.0023 (−1.6)	—		0.0058		−0.0047

— Not applicable.

Note: Positive coefficients represent effects which act to increase income inequality; negative coefficients, those which act to reduce income inequality.

Source: Calculated from table 5.7.

a. The figures in parentheses indicate the percentage composition of the intrasectoral effect.

Table 5.26. *Income Disparities, by Age of Head of Family, 1964 and 1972*

Age of head of family	Share of income (percent)		Share of families (percent)		Disparity in shares (percentage points)		Income relative[a]	
	1964	1972	1964	1972	1964	1972	1964	1972
Under 20	0.5	0.7	0.8	0.9	−0.3	−0.2	−.63	0.78
20–30	10.1	8.7	11.4	9.6	−1.3	−0.9	0.89	0.91
30–40	30.6	27.3	32.7	29.2	−1.1	−1.9	0.94	0.93
40–50	32.6	36.9	31.9	35.8	0.7	1.1	1.02	1.03
50–60	19.7	20.4	17.2	18.4	2.5	2.0	1.15	1.11
Over 60	6.5	6.0	6.0	6.1	0.5	−0.1	1.08	0.98
All families	100.0	100.0	100.0	100.0	6.4[b]	6.2[b]	1.00	1.00

Sources: Same as for table 5.2.
a. The ratio of the share of income to the share of families.
b. The sum of the absolute values.

Table 5.27. *Causes of the Reduction in Income Inequality, by Age of Head of Family, 1964–72*

Age of head of family	Total effect $\left[\sum_i\right]$	Intra-sectoral effect[a] $\left[\sum_i \frac{\partial I_w}{\partial I_i}\cdot\frac{dI_i}{dt}\right]$	Inter-sectoral effect	= Family weight effect $\left[\sum_i \frac{\partial I_w}{\partial h_i}\cdot\frac{dh_i}{dt}\right]$	+ Income disparity effect $\left[\sum_i \frac{\partial I_w}{\partial Z_i}\cdot\frac{dZ_i}{dt}\right]$
All families	−0.1487	−0.1474	−0.0013	0.0034	−0.0047
Percentage of total effect	−100.0	−99.1	−0.9	−2.3	−3.2
Under 20	—	−0.0004 (−0.3)	—	−0.0002	−0.0009
20–30	—	−0.0174 (−11.8)	—	0.0057	−0.0003
30–40	—	−0.0220 (−14.9)	—	0.0144	0.0003
40–50	—	−0.0898 (−60.9)	—	−0.0123	0.0002
50–60	—	−0.0144 (−9.8)	—	−0.0040	−0.0018
Over 60	—	−0.0034 (−2.3)	—	−0.0002	−0.0022

— Not applicable.

Note: Positive coefficients represent effects which act to increase income inequality; negative coefficients, those which act to reduce income inequality.

Source: Calculated from table 5.5.

a. The figures in parentheses indicate the percentage composition of the intrasectoral effect.

Table 5.28. *Income Disparities, by Sex of Head of Family, 1964 and 1972*

Sex of head of family	Share of income (percent) 1964	1972	Share of families (percent) 1964	1972	Disparity in shares (percentage points) 1964	1972	Income relative[a] 1964	1972
Male	93.9	94.1	92.3	93.3	1.6	0.8	1.02	1.01
Female	6.1	5.9	7.7	6.7	−1.6	−0.8	0.79	0.88
All families	100.0	100.0	100.0	100.0	3.2[b]	1.6[b]	1.00	1.00

Sources: Same as for table 5.2.
a. The ratio of the share of income to the share of families.
b. The sum of the absolute values.

Table 5.29. *Causes of the Reduction in Income Inequality, by Sex of Head of Family, 1964–72*

Sex of head of family	Total effect $\left[\sum_i\right]$	Intra-sectoral effect[a] $\left[\sum_i \frac{\partial I_w}{\partial I_i}\cdot\frac{dI_i}{dt}\right]$	Inter-sectoral effect =	Family weight effect $\left[\sum_i \frac{\partial I_w}{\partial h_i}\cdot\frac{dh_i}{dt}\right]$ +	Income disparity effect $\left[\sum_i \frac{\partial I_w}{\partial Z_i}\cdot\frac{dZ_i}{dt}\right]$
All families	−0.1597	−0.1576	−0.0021	−0.0007	−0.0014
Percentage of total effect	−100.0	−98.7	−1.3	−0.4	−0.9
Male	—	−0.1561 (−99.0)	—	−0.0032	−0.0006
Female	—	−0.0015 (−1.0)	—	−0.0025	−0.0008

— Not applicable.
Note: Positive coefficients represent effects which act to increase income inequality; negative coefficients, those which act to reduce income inequality.
Source: Calculated from table 5.6.
a. The figures in parentheses indicate the percentage composition of the intrasectoral effect.

CHAPTER 6

Taxation and the Inequality of Income and Expenditure

A TYPICAL FAMILY'S TOTAL INCOME $[y]$ is the sum of several income components, such as wage income $[w]$, property income $[\pi]$, and transfer income $[n]$. It also is the sum of various additive expenditure components, such as spending for food and clothing $[c_1]$, housing $[c_2]$, and education $[c_3]$, payments of direct tax $[t_1]$ and indirect tax $[t_2]$, and savings $[s]$. Thus:

(6.1a) $$y = w + \pi + n;$$

(6.1b) $$y = c_1 + c_2 + c_3 + t_1 + t_2 + s.$$

According to equation (6.1b), y is total family income before tax. If there are n income-receiving families, column vectors can be used to describe the structures of family income and expenditure:

(6.2a) $$Y = C_1 + C_2 + C_3 + T_1 + T_2 + S, \quad \text{where}$$

(6.2b) $$Y = \text{col}\ (y_1, y_2, \ldots, y_n),$$

(6.2c) $$C_i = \text{col}\ (c_{i1}, c_{i2}, \ldots, c_{in}), \qquad (i = 1, 2, 3)$$

(6.2d) $$T_i = \text{col}\ (t_{i1}, t_{i2}, \ldots, t_{in}), \quad \text{and} \qquad (i = 1, 2)$$

(6.2e) $$S = \text{col}\ (s_1, s_2, \ldots, s_n).$$

Thus Y is the structure of family income, C_i is the structure of consumption of the ith commodity, T_i is the structure of tax payments, and S is the structure of savings.

When the family income structure $[Y]$ is given, economists can apply the familiar theory for determining the various consumption structures $[C_i]$ and tax structures $[T_i]$. For example, the various consumption structures $[C_i]$ are determined by consumption functions measuring the propensities to consume the commodity c_i when y is given; family savings $[S]$ are a residual. The structure of direct tax payments $[T_1]$ is related to the structure of total family income $[Y]$ through rates of income tax. The structure of indirect tax payments $[T_2]$ is related to the various consumption structures through the rates of sales tax and commodity tax imposed upon various commodities. This chapter is not concerned, however, with the theory for the determination of C_i and T_i. They are assumed to be given and are the points of departure for the analysis here.[1]

Total family income $[y]$ clearly is the means by which to obtain family welfare; the various consumption categories $[c_i]$ and family savings $[s]$ are the ends. The inequality of family income, measured for example by the Gini coefficient $[G(Y)]$, thus is tantamount to the inequality of the means to obtain family welfare. The inequality of family income $[G(Y)]$ is important, then, only because it ultimately leads to the inequality of consumption $[G(C_i)]$ and savings $[G(S)]$—the two measures focused upon in this analysis.

The structures of family savings $[S]$ and family expenditure on education $[C_3]$ respectively represent family investment in physical and human resources. The inequality of these investment patterns in one year, measured by $G(S)$ and $G(C_3)$, leads to the inequality of total family income in subsequent years. Thus the inequality of family income persists mainly because the inequality of family investment persists.

The inequality of the various family consumption patterns, measured by $G(C_1)$ and $G(C_2)$, can indicate the economic welfare of families in the narrow sense. In a poor, underdeveloped economy with a consumption standard not far above the subsistence level, the inequality of the consumption of a basic food item corresponds to the inequality of family welfare. In wealthier countries, however, some items are consumed because they are conspicuous. For such items of conspicuous consumption as clothing and housing, a large $G(C_i)$ indicates a sharp distinction in status or among classes. For this reason a large $G(C_i)$ is expected to be positively correlated with $G(Y)$, suggesting that the inequality of total family income

1. The outline of how such deterministic theories might be formulated is discussed at the end of this chapter.

leads to the inequality of conspicuous consumption. In the present state of knowledge, it is not known whether the designation of a particular commodity as "conspicuous" bears any relation to cultural traits. For purposes of analysis the expenditure on housing [C_3] has been separated as a special category of consumption. This separation is based on the intuition that housing expenditure in Taiwan is conspicuous insofar as it is more unequal among income-receiving families than expenditure for food and clothing—a hypothesis that can be refuted by the empirical finding that $G(C_2)$ does not significantly differ from $G(C_1)$.

The inequality of the tax structure, measured by $G(T_1)$ and $G(T_2)$, indicates the primary impact of taxation on the inequality of family income. Equation (6.2a) can be rewritten as:

$$V = C_1 + C_2 + C_3 + S, \quad \text{where} \tag{6.3a}$$

$$\begin{bmatrix} \textit{family} \\ \textit{income} \\ \textit{after} \\ \textit{tax} \end{bmatrix} = \begin{bmatrix} \textit{family spending} \\ \textit{on consumer} \\ \textit{goods} \end{bmatrix} + \begin{bmatrix} \textit{family spending} \\ \textit{on housing} \end{bmatrix} + \begin{bmatrix} \textit{family spending} \\ \textit{on education} \end{bmatrix} + \begin{bmatrix} \textit{family} \\ \textit{savings} \end{bmatrix}$$

$$V = Y - T_1 - T_2 \quad \text{and} \tag{6.3b}$$

$$\begin{bmatrix} \textit{family} \\ \textit{income} \\ \textit{after} \\ \textit{tax} \end{bmatrix} = \begin{bmatrix} \textit{family} \\ \textit{income} \\ \textit{before} \\ \textit{tax} \end{bmatrix} - \begin{bmatrix} \textit{payments of} \\ \textit{direct tax} \end{bmatrix} - \begin{bmatrix} \textit{payments of} \\ \textit{indirect tax} \end{bmatrix}$$

$$Y = V + T_1 + T_2 . \tag{6.3c}$$

$$\begin{bmatrix} \textit{family} \\ \textit{income} \\ \textit{before} \\ \textit{tax} \end{bmatrix} = \begin{bmatrix} \textit{family} \\ \textit{income} \\ \textit{after} \\ \textit{tax} \end{bmatrix} + \begin{bmatrix} \textit{payments of} \\ \textit{direct tax} \end{bmatrix} + \begin{bmatrix} \textit{payments of} \\ \textit{indirect tax} \end{bmatrix}$$

In the foregoing equations the column vector $V = \text{col}\ (V_1, V_2, \ldots, V_n)$ stands for the structure of family income after tax—that is, for the structure of net income. When the structure and inequality of family income before tax are given, the inequality of the tax structure [$G(T_1)$ and $G(T_2)$] determines the inequality of income after tax [$G(V)$]. The relations among $G(Y)$, $G(V)$, and $G(T_i)$ will be indicated more clearly as the analysis unfolds.

In summary, the analysis of the inequality of family expenditure has three purposes: to study the inequality of investment, to study the patterns of consumption, and to study the inequality of taxation —all in relation to their separate impact on the inequality of family income. Having explained the economic significance of this analysis, the discussion now proceeds to introduce the statistical data and the analytical framework. The empirical analysis using this framework will be undertaken in the final two sections.

Statistical Data

The statistical data used in the empirical analysis are for 1964, 1966, 1968, 1970, 1972 and 1973 (see tables 6.5–6.10 in appendix 6.1 at the end of this chapter). Each table presents the following data: the income classes for total family income; the number of families and the total family income for each income class; the expenditure on housing [c_2] and education [c_3], the expenditure on all other consumption [c_1], the direct tax [t_1] and indirect tax [t_2]; and the family savings [s]. When the families are grouped into classes, the underlying assumption is that all families within the same class receive the same family income and spend the same amount for each category of consumption.[2]

The main source for these tables is the DGBAS data, which give a fairly detailed classification of family expenditure.[3] For 1966 the classification contained sixteen major categories as well as detailed subcategories (table 6.1). In all, it had sixty-four items.[4]

As applied to appendix tables 6.5–6.10, housing expenditure [c_2] includes the categories for rent and water charges and for furniture, furnishings, and household equipment; these items are indicated by an asterisk in table 6.1. Educational expenditure [c_3] includes

2. The tendency with such a procedure is to underestimate the inequality of all expenditure components that do not have a high positive correlation with the structure of total family income. This difficulty can be avoided only when use is made of the original data—that is, when families are not grouped—rather than published data, which groups families into classes. The original data is in the original DGBAS questionnaires (see the tables appended to chapter four).

3. See appendix 4.1 to chapter four for the sample sizes and other details of the DGBAS data.

4. For different years the DGBAS classifications differ slightly.

the categories for personal and medical care and for recreation and amusement, as well as the subcategory of miscellaneous consumption expenditure for education and research; these items are indicated by a double asterisk in table 6.1. Therefore c_3 is a proxy for investment in human resources; c_2 for conspicuous consumption. Obviously the judgments involved in such definitions of these variables

Table 6.1. *Categories of Household Expenditure and Their Indirect Tax Burden, 1966*

Category	*Indirect tax burden (percent)*
Food	4.10
Beverages and tobacco	42.85
Clothing and other personal effects	5.60
Rent and water charges*	0.54
Rent	0.50
House repairs and installation	0.50
Water charges	1.78
Fuel and light	11.39
Furniture, furnishings, and household equipment*	5.93
Furniture and furnishings	2.41
Textile furnishings	5.60
Appliances for kitchen and bathroom	10.68
Other	10.68
Household operation	3.84
Personal and medical care**	6.59
Personal care	n.a.
Barber and bath shop services	n.a.
Medical and health expenses	n.a.
Transport and communication	7.00
Recreation and amusement**	1.73
Recreation	n.a.
Books, newspapers, magazines, and stationery	n.a.
Other	n.a.

Table 6.1 (*Continued*)

Category	*Indirect tax burden (percent)*
Miscellaneous consumption expenditure	18.59
Financial services	n.a.
Education and research**	n.a.
Marriages, birthdays, and funerals	n.a.
Other	n.a.
Interest	—
Taxes	—
Household tax	—
House tax	—
Land value tax	—
Land tax	—
Land value improvement tax	—
Land value added tax	—
Inheritance tax	—
Bicycle license tax	—
Income tax	—
Other	—
Gifts and other transfer expenditure	—
Savings	—

* Indicates items of housing expenditure [c_2].
** Indicates items of educational expenditure [c_3].
— Not applicable.
n.a. Not available.
Source: DGBAS, *Report on the Survey of Family Income and Expenditure,* 1966.

are a priori. For example, the expenditure for fuel and light is excluded from conspicuous consumption [c_2] because it is for cooking.

The direct tax [t_1] in the appendix tables includes all ten items in the category for taxes in table 6.1. In addition to these direct tax payments, families pay indirect tax when consumption expenditures are made. Because the DGBAS data are based on household surveys, the consumption expenditures listed under the various categories in table 6.1 include indirect taxes. A separate procedure was used to estimate the indirect tax payments [t_2], which have been subtracted from the DGBAS data to give family consumption expenditures exclusive of indirect tax payments [c_1, c_2, and c_3]. The procedure for this computation is explained in appendix 6.1.

Analytical Framework

It can be seen from equations (6.3a) and (6.3c) that both V and Y are vector sums of a number of components. Thus the inequality of total family income [$G(Y)$] and of family income after tax [$G(V)$] can be decomposed into factor components according to the following equations[5]:

$$G(V) = \phi_1^c R_1^c G_1^c + \phi_2^c R_2^c G_2^c + \phi_3^c R_3^c G_3^c + \phi_s R_s G_s; \tag{6.4a}$$

$$\begin{bmatrix} \textit{inequality} \\ \textit{of family} \\ \textit{income} \\ \textit{after} \\ \textit{tax} \end{bmatrix} = \begin{bmatrix} \textit{effect on} \\ \textit{consumption} \\ \textit{expenditure} \end{bmatrix} + \begin{bmatrix} \textit{effect on} \\ \textit{housing} \\ \textit{expenditure} \end{bmatrix} + \begin{bmatrix} \textit{effect on} \\ \textit{educational} \\ \textit{expenditure} \end{bmatrix} + \begin{bmatrix} \textit{effect on} \\ \textit{saving} \end{bmatrix}$$

$$G(Y) = \phi_v R_v G_v + \phi_1^t R_1^t G_1^t + \phi_2^t R_2^t G_2^t. \tag{6.4b}$$

$$\begin{bmatrix} \textit{inequality} \\ \textit{of family} \\ \textit{income} \\ \textit{before} \\ \textit{tax} \end{bmatrix} = \begin{bmatrix} \textit{effect on} \\ \textit{after-tax} \\ \textit{income} \end{bmatrix} + \begin{bmatrix} \textit{effect on} \\ \textit{direct tax} \end{bmatrix} + \begin{bmatrix} \textit{effect on} \\ \textit{indirect tax} \end{bmatrix}$$

Each effect is the product of a weight term [ϕ_i], a correlation term [R_i], and a Gini term [G_i].

The terms G_1^c, G_2^c, G_3^c, and G_s are the Gini coefficients of the structures of consumption [C_i] and savings [S] in equation (6.3a)—that is, $G_i^c = G(C_i)$ and $G_s = G(S)$. Therefore G_3^c and G_s respectively measure the inequality of family investment in human and physical resources. Similarly G_1^c and G_2^c respectively measure the inequality of family expenditure on other consumption and housing consump-

5. The equations are directly obtained by applying equation (10.5) in chapter ten to equations (6.3a) and (6.3c). Notice in equation (6.4) that $G(V) = G_v$.

tion. The terms G_1^t and G_2^t respectively measure the inequality of payments by families for direct and indirect tax.

The terms R_1^c, R_2^c, R_3^c, and R_s measure the correlation of the vectors C_1, C_2, C_3, and S with the vector of V. High and positive values of R_3^c and R_s indicate that human and physical investments are heavily concentrated among wealthy families. A high and positive value of R_2^c means that expenditure on housing is very sensitive to the level of total family income and suggests that housing is an item of conspicuous consumption.

The terms R_v, R_1^t, and R_2^t express the correlations of the vectors V, T_1, and T_2 with the vector Y. R_v would be expected to be close to 1 because any rationally designed tax system should not overtly disturb the rankings of families in the structure of income [Y]—that is, families should have the same rank before and after their tax payments. For a progressive direct tax, R_1^t would be expected to be high and positive, indicating that tax payments become progressively higher as total family income increases. For a regressive indirect tax, R_2^t would be expected to be negative and close to -1, indicating that the heavier tax burden falls upon low-income families. Equation (6.4b) can be rewritten as:

$$G(V) = (1/\phi_v R_v)G(Y) - (\phi_1^t R_1^t/\phi_v R_v)G_1^t - (\phi_2^t R_2^t/\phi_v R_v)G_2^t. \tag{6.5}$$

When the inequality of family income [$G(Y)$] is given, equation (6.5) shows the impact of taxes on family income after tax. A high and positive R_1^t, which would be associated with a progressive tax, contributes to the equality of family income after tax. A negative R_i, which would be associated with a regressive tax, contributes to the inequality of family income after tax.

The weight terms [ϕ_i] in equations (6.4a) and (6.4b) are defined as follows. Let $\bar{X}$ be the mean value of any vector X. Then equations (6.3a) and (6.3c) imply that:

$$\bar{V} = \bar{C}_1 + \bar{C}_2 + \bar{C}_3 + \bar{S} = \bar{Y} - \bar{T}_1 - \bar{T}_2; \tag{6.6a}$$

$$\phi_1^c = \bar{C}_1/\bar{V},\ \phi_2^c = \bar{C}_2/\bar{V},\ \phi_3^c = \bar{C}_3/\bar{V},\ \phi_s = \bar{S}/\bar{V};\quad \text{and} \tag{6.6b}$$

$$\phi_v = \bar{V}/\bar{Y},\ \phi_1^t = \bar{T}_1/\bar{Y},\ \phi_2^t = \bar{T}_2/\bar{Y};\quad \text{where} \tag{6.6c}$$

$$\phi_1^c + \phi_2^c + \phi_3^c + \phi_s = 1 \quad \text{and} \tag{6.6d}$$

$$\phi_v + \phi_1^t + \phi_2^t = 1. \tag{6.6e}$$

In equation (6.6b) ϕ_1^c is the consumption expenditure of the ith type expressed as a fraction of total family income excluding taxes;

ϕ_s is the fraction of average savings in average family income after tax, or the average propensity to save. In equation (6.6c) ϕ_v is the ratio of income after tax to income before, or including, tax; ϕ_i^t is the total tax payment of the ith type expressed as a fraction of income including tax.

Decomposition of Family Income after Tax

The results of the decomposition according to equation (6.4a) of the Gini coefficient of family income after tax [$G(V)$] are presented in table 6.2. The time series in this table are graphically represented in figures 6.1–6.4. Figure 6.1 shows the time series of $G(V)$ and that of the four contribution terms [$\phi_i R_i G_i$]. The once-for-all decline of $G(V)$ indicates that the distribution of family income after tax was generally becoming more equal in this ten-year period. The

Figure 6.1. *Contributions to the Inequality of Family Income after Tax, by Category of Expenditure, 1964–73*

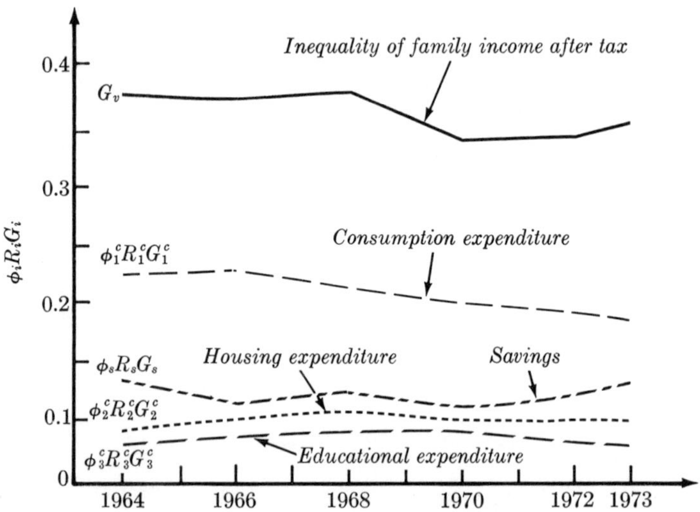

Source: Table 6.2.

Figure 6.2. *Correlation Terms for the Decomposition of Family Income after Tax, by Category of Expenditure, 1964–73*

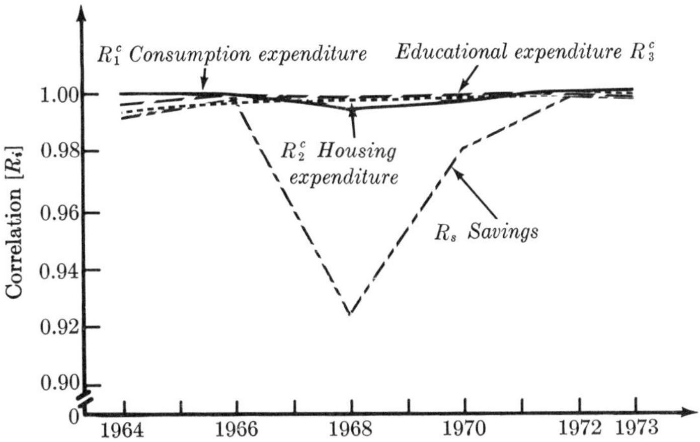

Source: Table 6.2.

expenditure on food, clothing, and other consumer goods accounted for about 50 percent of the inequality of family income after tax [$G(V)$]; educational expenditure accounted for about 10 percent. Savings and expenditure on housing respectively accounted for 16 percent and 23 percent. The contrast is sharp between the two consumption components. The term for housing expenditure shows an increasing trend; that for other expenditure a decreasing trend. No increasing or decreasing trend could be detected for the two investment components. The difference between them is that the curve for the savings term is mildly U-shaped and that for the education term is inverse U-shaped. In the following discussion the behavior patterns for consumption and investment are separately explained.

Consumption

The values of the correlation terms for consumption expenditure [R_1^c] and housing expenditure [R_2^c] are very close to the unit value (figure 6.2). The higher the family income is after tax, the higher

Table 6.2. *Decomposition of the Inequality of Family Income after Tax, 1964–73*

Item	*Notation*	*1964*	*1966*	*1968*
Shares				
Other expenditure	ϕ_1^c	0.6744	0.6559	0.6478
Housing expenditure	ϕ_2^c	0.1211	0.1425	0.1567
Educational expenditure	ϕ_3^c	0.0897	0.0924	0.1039
Savings	ϕ_s	0.1149	0.1092	0.0916
Gini coefficients				
Other expenditure	G_1^c	0.2598	0.2736	0.2550
Housing expenditure	G_2^c	0.3462	0.3481	0.3582
Educational expenditure	G_3^c	0.3587	0.3804	0.3751
Savings	G_s	0.7363	0.5908	0.8843
Correlation terms				
Other expenditure	R_1^c	1.0000	1.0000	0.9945
Housing expenditure	R_2^c	0.9948	0.9977	0.9983
Educational expenditure	R_3^c	0.9967	0.9979	0.9979
Savings	R_s	0.9921	0.9983	0.9240
Effects				
Other expenditure	$\phi_1^c R_1^c G_1^c$	0.1752	0.1795	0.1643
Housing expenditure	$\phi_2^c R_2^c G_2^c$	0.0417	0.0495	0.0560
Educational expenditure	$\phi_3^c R_3^c G_3^c$	0.0321	0.0350	0.0389
Savings	$\phi_s R_s G_s$	0.0839	0.0644	0.0748
Composition of effects (percent)				
Other expenditure		52.6	54.7	49.2
Housing expenditure		12.5	15.1	16.8
Educational expenditure		9.6	10.7	11.6
Savings		25.3	19.5	22.4
Gini coefficient of income after tax	G_v	0.3329	0.3284	0.3340

Sources: Calculated from tables 6.5–6.10 appended to this chapter.

the family expenditure is for both types of consumption. Thus the effect of the variation of the correlation characteristic can be neglected—that is, it can be assumed that R_1^c and R_2^c are equal to 1— and the analysis can concentrate on ϕ_i and G_i.

The share of consumption expenditure [ϕ_1^c] exhibits a decreasing trend; the share of housing expenditure [ϕ_2^c] an increasing trend

1970	*1972*	*1973*	*Notation*	*Item*
				Shares
0.6521	0.6150	0.6000	ϕ_1^c	Other expenditure
0.1407	0.1619	0.1620	ϕ_2^c	Housing expenditure
0.1185	0.0870	0.0812	ϕ_3^c	Educational expenditure
0.0887	0.1361	0.1568	ϕ_s	Savings
				Gini coefficients
0.2304	0.2343	0.2319	G_1^c	Other expenditure
0.3220	0.3256	0.3534	G_2^c	Housing expenditure
0.3300	0.3299	0.3478	G_3^c	Educational expenditure
0.6915	0.5134	0.5335	G_s	Savings
				Correlation terms
0.9974	1.0000	1.0000	R_1^c	Other expenditure
1.0000	1.0000	1.0000	R_2^c	Housing expenditure
0.9988	0.9994	0.9994	R_3^c	Educational expenditure
0.9806	1.0000	0.9989	R_s	Savings
				Effects
0.1498	0.1441	0.1391	$\phi_1^c R_1^c G_1^c$	Other expenditure
0.0453	0.0527	0.0573	$\phi_2^c R_2^c G_2^c$	Housing expenditure
0.0391	0.0287	0.0282	$\phi_3^c R_3^c G_3^c$	Educational expenditure
0.0601	0.0699	0.0836	$\phi_s R_s G_s$	Savings
				Composition of effects (percent)
50.9	48.8	45.1		Other expenditure
15.4	17.8	18.6		Housing expenditure
13.3	9.7	9.2		Educational expenditure
20.4	23.7	22.1		Savings
0.2943	0.2954	0.3082	G_y	Gini coefficient of income after tax

(figure 6.3). Because the increase of family income was rapid during this ten-year period, the foregoing trends reveal that the family housing expenditure is income-elastic and other family expenditure is income-inelastic. This pattern is consistent with expectations based on the conventional theory of consumer behavior.

The inequality of the distribution of family expenditure on hous-

Figure 6.3. *Shares for the Decomposition of Family Income after Tax, by Category of Expenditure, 1964–73*

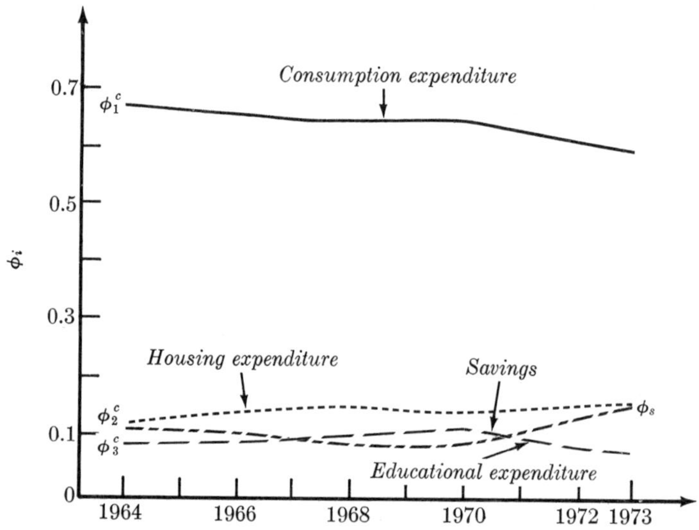

Source: Table 6.2.

ing [G_2^c] was much greater than that of family expenditure on other consumption [G_1^c] (figure 6.4). Thus the expenditure on housing, more than that on other consumer goods, distinguished the class of wealthy families and therefore took on the character of conspicuous consumption. This was true despite the rapid growth of family income over the period. It may be concluded that the difference in the income elasticity of demand for housing and for other consumption expenditure mainly explained the long-run declining trend of $\phi_1^c R_1^c G_1^c$ and the long-run increasing trend of $\phi_2^c R_2^c G_2^c$ seen in figure 6.1.

Investment

It can be seen from the correlation characteristics in figure 6.2 that educational expenditure and savings were highly correlated with family income after tax. Even the lowest value of R_s, registered

Figure 6.4. *Gini Coefficients for the Decomposition of Family Income after Tax, by Category of Expenditure, 1964–73*

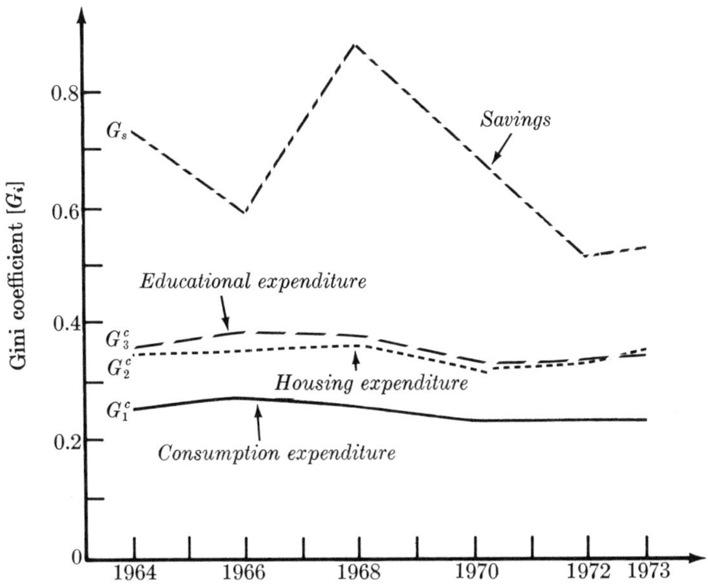

Source: Table 6.2.

in 1968, is 0.9024. Thus the correlation characteristic can again be neglected, enabling concentration upon ϕ_i and G_i.[6]

The shares of expenditure on education [ϕ_3^c] and savings [ϕ_s] both present a constant time trend, fluctuating around 10 percent over the ten-year period (see figure 6.3). Families therefore spent about the same percentage of their income on investment in human resources and on physical resources. Notice that the movements of ϕ_s and ϕ_3^c always are in the opposite direction. When ϕ_s moves up-

6. That all values of R_i in figure 6.2 are close to 1 should come as no surprise. It simply means that wealthier families spent more on each of the items.

ward, ϕ_3^c moves downward, and vice versa. The reason is that when families decide to spend more on education—as they did, for example, before 1970—they saved relatively less. Conversely, when they spent less on education—as they did, for example, after 1970—they saved more. Together the two curves seem to indicate a constant propensity to "save" of about 20 percent up to 1972. In 1973 the sum of ϕ_3^c and ϕ_s increased to 24 percent. It remains to be seen whether this was indicative of a new, increasing trend.

Finally the inequality of savings [G_s] and the inequality of educational expenditure [G_3^c] were consistently greater than the inequality of housing expenditure [G_2^c] and the inequality of consumption expenditure [G_1^c]. Consequently the inequality of family income after tax led more to the inequality of investment (in education or savings) than to the inequality of consumption. The fact that the inequality of investment in one year leads to the inequality of income in subsequent years in part explains the persistence of the inequality of family income over time.

It should be observed that the inequality of family saving was much greater than the inequality of family expenditure on education. As pointed out earlier, the percentages of income applied to education and savings were approximately the same at around 10 percent for earlier years (see figure 6.3). Thus the inequality of investment in physical resources is more responsible than the inequality of investment in human resources for the persistent inequality of family income. In arriving at this conclusion, it should be borne in mind that government spends heavily on public education—both on education up to the nine-year level, which became compulsory in 1968, and on higher education. This expenditure is, in principle, very equally distributed among the families benefiting from this policy. The education policy thus has greatly reduced the role of private expenditure on education as a causal factor in contributing to the inequality of family income over time.

It should also be noticed that there is a long-run declining trend of G_s over time. This means that as family income increases, the low-income families begin to save proportionately more of their income than high-income families. The persistence of such a time trend implies that the inequality of investment in physical resources in the future will contribute less to the inequality of family income than it has in the past. For this reason the distribution of family income in Taiwan can be expected to continue improving.

The Impact of Taxation on Income Inequality

The results of the decomposition of the inequality of family income $[G(Y)]$ according to equation (6.4b) appear in table 6.3. The primary purpose of the decomposition is to show whether payments of direct and indirect tax contributed to the equality of family income after tax. The ratio of the Gini coefficient after tax $[G_v]$ to the Gini coefficient before tax $[G_y]$ shows that there was no significant difference between G_v and G_y in all the years examined—that is:

$$G_v \cong G_y \,. \tag{6.6}$$

It can thus be concluded for this ten-year period that the direct impact of taxation on the distribution of family income was neutral and that it brought about neither greater equality nor greater inequality. It follows that the cause of the near-equivalence of G_v and G_y in the past should be investigated and that future measures should be introduced so that tax policy can contribute more to the equality of family income. As a first step in this investigation, it should be determined whether the taxation system in Taiwan satisfies certain minimum requirements for being "reasonable."

Is Taiwan's system of taxation reasonable?

The impact of taxation is graphically represented by the flow chart in figure 6.5. The income before tax $[Y = (y_1, y_2, y_3)]$ is received by the families $[(f_1, f_2, f_3)]$; from this income, families make tax payments $[T = (t_1, t_2, t_3)]$ which constitute the structure of the tax burden. That tax burden $[T]$ is the sum of the direct tax burden $[T_1 = (t_1^1, t_2^1, t_3^1)]$ and the indirect tax burden $[T_2 = (t_1^2, t_2^2, t_3^2)]$. What remains is family income after tax $[V = (v_1, v_2, v_3)]$. The near-equivalence of G_v and G_y in expression (6.6) implies that the tax burden $[T]$ causes no difference between the degree of inequality in before-tax income $[Y]$ and after-tax income $[V]$. Thus:

$$Y = V + T, \quad \text{where} \tag{6.7a}$$

$$T = T_1 + T_2 \,. \tag{6.7b}$$

Table 6.3. *Decomposition of the Inequality of Family Income before Tax, 1964–73*

Item	*Notation*	*1964*	*1966*	*1968*
Shares				
Income after tax	ϕ_v	0.9341	0.9277	0.9189
Direct tax	ϕ_1^t	0.0268	0.0122	0.0139
Indirect tax	ϕ_2^t	0.0591	0.0601	0.0672
Gini coefficients				
Income after tax	G_v	0.3329	0.3284	0.3340
Direct tax	G_1^t	0.4381	0.5208	0.5902
Indirect tax	G_2^t	0.2605	0.3229	0.2945
Correlation terms				
Income after tax	R_v	0.9988	1.0000	0.9997
Direct tax	R_1^t	0.9781	0.9965	0.9949
Indirect tax	R_2^t	0.9724	0.9913	0.9891
Effects				
Income after tax	$\phi_v R_v G_v$	0.3106	0.3047	0.3068
Direct tax	$\phi_1^t R_1^t G_1^t$	0.0029	0.0064	0.0082
Indirect tax	$\phi_2^t R_2^t G_2^t$	0.0150	0.0192	0.0196
Inequality of income before tax	G_v	0.3285	0.3303	0.3346
Ratio of inequality of income before tax to that of income after tax	G_v/G_y	1.0133	0.9942	0.9982

Sources: Calculated from tables 6.5–6.10 appended to this chapter.

When total family incomes are arranged in a monotonically non-decreasing order, any rationally designed tax system should satisfy the following conditions:

(6.8a) $$y_1 \leq y_2 \leq \ldots \leq y_n ,$$

which implies that:

(6.8b) $$v_1 \leq v_2 \leq \ldots \leq v_n ,$$

[*no reversal of rank*]

1970	*1972*	*1973*	*Notation*	*Item*
				Shares
0.9234	0.9154	0.9176	ϕ_v	Income after tax
0.0112	0.0150	0.0146	ϕ_1^t	Direct tax
0.0654	0.0695	0.0678	ϕ_2^t	Indirect tax
				Gini coefficients
0.2943	0.2954	0.3082	G_v	Income after tax
0.5450	0.5758	0.5830	G_1^t	Direct tax
0.2559	0.2423	0.2485	G_2^t	Indirect tax
				Correlation terms
1.0000	0.9983	1.0000	R_v	Income after tax
0.9989	1.0000	1.0000	R_1^t	Direct tax
0.9984	0.9992	1.0000	R_2^t	Indirect tax
				Effects
0.2718	0.2699	0.2828	$\phi_v R_v G_v$	Income after tax
0.0061	0.0086	0.0085	$\phi_1^t R_1^t G_1^t$	Direct tax
0.0167	0.0168	0.0168	$\phi_2^t R_2^t G_2^t$	Indirect tax
0.2946	0.2953	0.3081	G_v	Inequality of income before tax
0.9983	1.0003	1.0003	G_v/G_y	Ratio of inequality of income before tax to that of income after tax

$$t_1^1 \leq t_2^1 \leq \ldots \leq t_n^1, \tag{6.8c}$$

$$\begin{bmatrix} \textit{minimum progressiveness} \\ \textit{of direct tax} \end{bmatrix}$$

$$t_1^2 \leq t_2^2 \leq \ldots \leq t_n^2, \quad \text{and} \tag{6.8d}$$

$$\begin{bmatrix} \textit{minimum progressiveness} \\ \textit{of indirect tax} \end{bmatrix}$$

$$t_1 \leq t_2 \leq \ldots \leq t_n. \tag{6.8e}$$

$$\begin{bmatrix} \textit{minimum progressiveness} \\ \textit{of total tax} \end{bmatrix}$$

Figure 6.5. *Flows of Income before Tax to Taxes and Income after Tax, by Family*

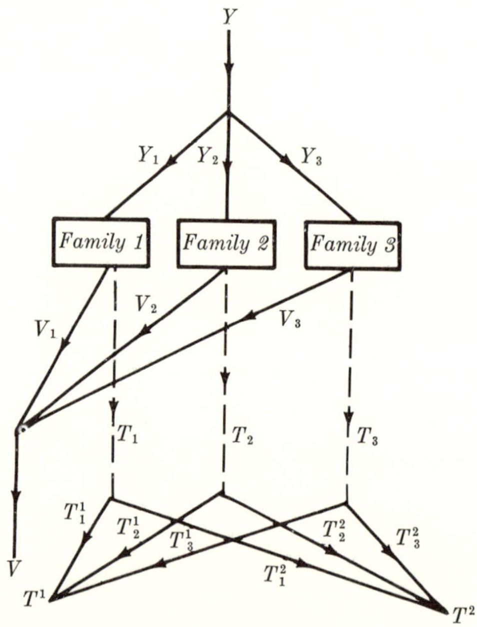

Income before tax = (Y_1, Y_2, Y_3)
Income after tax = (V_1, V_2, V_3)
Total tax = (T_1, T_2, T_3)
Direct tax = (T_1^1, T_2^1, T_3^1)
Indirect tax = (T_1^2, T_2^2, T_3^2)

Source: Constructed by the authors.

The no-reversal-of-rank condition in expression (6.8b) means that the family income rank before tax in expression (6.8a) should not be overtly disturbed by tax payments. In other words, to minimize the disincentive effect of taxes, a high-income family should not be taxed so heavily that its after-tax income is lower than the after-tax income of a low-income family. The no-reversal-of-rank condition then means that the tax system should not be too progressive. The conditions of minimum progressiveness in expressions (6.8c) and (6.8d) mean that the tax system should not be too regressive—that is, the higher a family's income, the more it should pay in direct and indirect taxes. Notice that the condition of minimum progressiveness in expression (6.8e) follows from expressions (6.8c) and (6.8d) by equation (6.7b).

When the conditions in expressions (6.8b), (6.8c), and (6.8d) are satisfied, the rank correlation is perfect between the vector Y and the vectors V, T_1, and T_2. Because it follows that the correlation characteristics R_v, R_1^t, and R_2^t then take on unit value, equation (6.4b) assumes the special form[7]:

(6.9a) $R_v = R_1^t = R_2^t = 1$ by expression (6.8);

(6.9b) $G_y = \phi_v G_v + \phi_1^t G_1^t + \phi_2^t G_2^t$ by equations (6.4b) and (6.9a).

The applicability of equation (6.9a) to Taiwan is verified by the values for the correlation terms [R_i] in table 6.3. With the exception of the value of 97 percent observed for 1964, the values of R_i for all other years are very close to the unit value. It can thus be concluded that the taxation system in Taiwan does meet the minimum requirements for being reasonable, at least as defined in equation (6.9a) which gives the conditions for no reversal of rank and minimum progressiveness.

The burden of taxation

The system of taxation in Taiwan, although reasonable, was not very progressive during the period under observation because of its neutrality with respect to the distribution of income (see expression [6.6]). To discover the reasons for this to have been so requires analysis of the structure of the tax burden. The decomposition of the index of inequality of the distribution of income [G_y] according to equation (6.7a) leads to:

(6.10a) $G_y = \phi_v R_v G_v + \phi_T R_T G_T$, where

(6.10b) $\phi_T = \phi_1^t + \phi_2^t$ and

(6.10c) $\phi_1^t + \phi_2^t = 1.$

In equation (6.10a) ϕ_T is the share of taxes in total income and the sum of the shares of direct and indirect taxes; G_T is the Gini coeffi-

7. See the section on correlation characteristics at the end of chapter nine.

Figure 6.6. *Contributions to the Inequality of the Tax Burden, 1964–73*

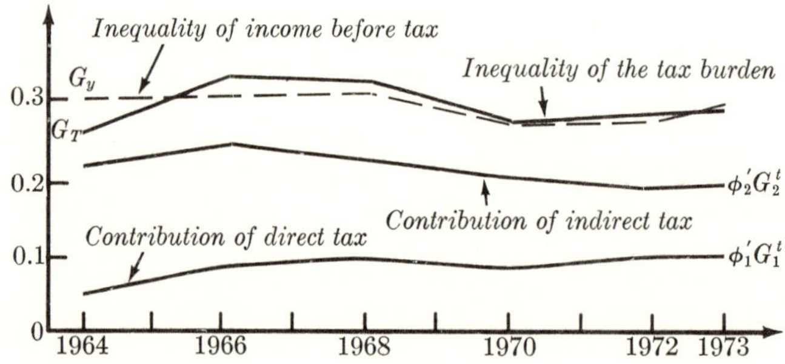

Source: Table 6.4.

cient of the tax burden. The reasonable properties of the taxation system specified in equation (6.9a) immediately imply that:

(6.11a) $G_y = \phi_v G_v + \phi_T G_T$ by $R_v = R_T = 1$ from (6.9a) and

(6.11b) $G_v = (G_y - \phi_T G_T)/\phi_v$.

According to equation (6.11b) the total tax burden should, if taxation is to be used as a policy instrument to bring about the equality of the distribution of family income, be unequally distributed and reflected by high values of G_T. Because G_y is a weighted average of G_v and G_T, income after tax can be more equally distributed than income before tax if and only if the inequality of taxation is greater than the inequality of income. That is:

(6.12) $$G_v < G_y \text{ if and only if } G_T > G_y .$$

The neutrality of taxation observed in expression (6.6) implies that the conditions of expression (6.12) were not satisfied. The conditions associated with expression (6.6) and equation (6.11a) immediately show that:

(6.13) $$G_y = G_v = G_T.$$

In other words, the taxation system in Taiwan did not bring about a more equitable distribution of income because the total tax burden was distributed with the same degree of inequality as income before tax. The time paths of G_T and G_y are shown in figure 6.6. The curve for G_y is very close to the curve for G_T, and they become closer over time. This verifies the conditions stated in equation (6.13).

The equivalence of G_y and G_T can be analyzed from another angle. Assume a hypothetical marginal tax rate of m:

$$\mathrm{d}T/\mathrm{d}Y = m, \quad \text{where} \quad m < 1. \tag{6.14}$$

Whenever the total family income increases by one dollar, the additional total tax payment is m dollars. The average tax rate for all families is given by:

$$\phi_T = (t_1 + t_2 + \ldots + t_n)/(y_1 + y_2 + \ldots + y_n). \tag{6.15}$$

Under the assumptions of equation (6.14) G_T and G_y satisfy the following equation[8]:

$$G_T = (m/\phi_T)G_y\,. \tag{6.16}$$

The equivalence of G_T and G_y shown in equation (6.13) immediately implies that:

$$m = \phi_T. \tag{6.17}$$

Equation (6.17) indicates the equivalence of the average and marginal tax rates. This equivalence means that the total tax burden is such that the same percentage of family income is collected as taxes from all families, regardless of their income. Thus, despite the reasonable properties of Taiwan's system of taxation, the overall tax burden was highly regressive according to a modern standard.

Analysis of the burden of taxation

The total tax burden is the sum of the direct and indirect tax burdens (see equation [6.7b]). The inequality of the tax burden [G_T] is traced in turn to the direct and indirect tax burdens. Applying the decomposition formula to equation (6.7b) gives:

$$G_T = \phi_1' R_1^t G_1^t + \phi' R_2^t G_2^t\,, \quad \text{where} \tag{6.18a}$$

$$\phi_1' = \phi_1^t/\phi_T, \quad \phi_2' = \phi_2^t/\phi_T, \quad \text{and} \tag{6.18b}$$

$$\phi_1' + \phi_2' = 1. \tag{6.18c}$$

8. See theorem 12.2 in chapter twelve. Notice that if the taxation system is reasonable, the value of m must lie between zero and 1—that is, $0 < m < 1$. Thus, according to theorem 12.2, the tax payment T corresponds to a type one or type two income when m is a positive fraction.

Table 6.4. *Decomposition of the Inequality of the Tax Burden, 1964–73*

Item	*Notation*	*1964*	*1966*	*1968*
Shares				
Direct tax	ϕ_1'	0.1031	0.1687	0.1713
Indirect tax	ϕ_2'	0.8968	0.8312	0.8286
Effects				
Direct tax	$\phi_1'G_1^t$	0.0451	0.0878	0.1011
Indirect tax	$\phi_2'G_2^t$	0.2336	0.2683	0.2440
Composition of effects (percent)				
Direct tax		16.2	24.7	29.3
Indirect tax		83.8	75.3	70.7
Gini coefficient of tax burden	G_T	0.2787	0.3561	0.3451
Error term	$(G_T - G_y)/G_y$	0.1515	0.0781	0.0313

Sources: Calculated from tables 6.5–6.10 appended to this chapter.

In equation (6.18b) ϕ_1' and ϕ_2' are the percentages of direct and indirect taxes in total taxes. In equation (6.18a) R_1^t and R_2^t are the correlation characteristics of T_1 and T_2 with T. The reasonable property associated with the expressions of (6.8) implies that[9]:

(6.19a) $$R_1^t = R_2^t = 1.$$

Hence:

(6.19b) $$G_T = \phi' G_1^t + \phi' G_2^t.$$

9. The condition of minimum progressiveness of total tax in expression (6.8e) implies that Y and T have a perfect rank correlation; the conditions of minimum progressiveness of direct and indirect tax in expressions (6.8c) and (6.8d) imply that T_1 and T_2 also have a perfect rank correlation with Y. Therefore T_1 and T_2 have a perfect rank correlation with T. The economic interpretation is that as a higher income family pays more in total taxes, it also pays more in direct and indirect taxes.

1970	*1972*	*1973*	*Notation*	*Item*
				Shares
0.1462	0.1775	0.1771	ϕ_1'	Direct tax
0.8537	0.8224	0.8228	ϕ_2'	Indirect tax
				Effects
0.0796	0.1022	0.1032	$\phi_1'G_1^t$	Direct tax
0.2184	0.1992	0.2044	$\phi_2'G_2^t$	Indirect tax
				Composition of effects (percent)
26.7	33.9	33.6		Direct tax
73.3	66.1	66.4		Indirect tax
0.2980	0.3014	0.3076	G_T	Gini coefficient of tax burden
0.0115	0.0206	0.0016	$(G_T - G_y)/G_y$	Error term

The results of the decomposition of G_T according to equation (6.19b) are given in table 6.4. According to equation (6.19b) the values of G_T in this table are the sums of the values of $\phi' G_1^t$ and $\phi' G_2^t$. The shares of direct and indirect taxes in the share of total taxes are defined as in equation (6.18b); the values of G_1^t and G_2^t were taken from table 6.3. The time patterns of these variables are graphically represented in figures 6.6–6.8.

Indirect taxes contributed much more than direct taxes to the inequality of taxation [G_T] (see figure 6.6). Direct taxes on average accounted for 27 percent of G_T; indirect taxes for 73 percent. There nevertheless was a long-run declining trend for the indirect tax contribution and an increasing trend for the direct tax contribution. Thus, although the indirect tax contribution was quantitatively important, that importance relative to the direct tax contribution declined.

The two relative tax shares [ϕ_1' and ϕ_2'] maintained a constant time trend over the ten-year period (figure 6.7). The indirect tax share [ϕ_2'] was much greater than the direct tax share [ϕ_1']. The

Figure 6.7. *Shares for the Decomposition of the Tax Burden, 1964–73*

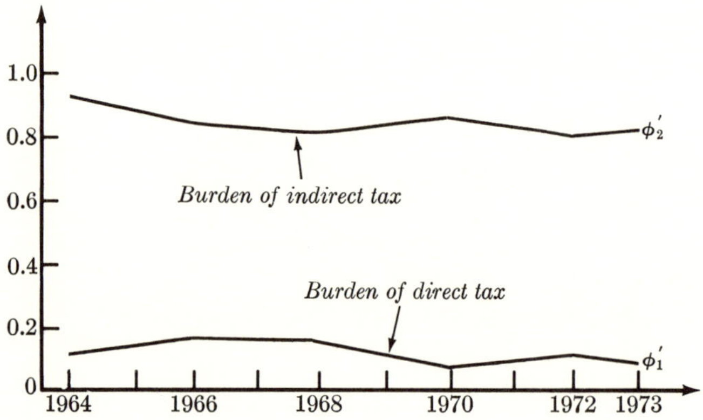

Source: Table 6.4.

average value of the indirect tax share was 84 percent; that of the direct tax share 16 percent. Thus the quantitative importance of the indirect tax contribution indicated in figure 6.6 was entirely the result of the importance of indirect tax as a source of government revenue.

The burden of indirect tax payments was much more evenly distributed than the burden of the progressive direct tax payments (figure 6.8). Over the ten-year period, the average value of G_1^t was 0.54; that of G_2^t 0.27. Moreover the inequality of the burden of direct taxes exhibited a long-run increasing trend; that of indirect taxes a long-run declining trend. These patterns conform to those observed in figure 6.6.

It can be seen from the foregoing analysis that the canceling of the quantitatively less important and more progressive direct tax payments by the quantitatively more important and regressive indirect tax payments brought about the neutrality of the total tax burden. For tax policy to be an instrument for improving the distribution of income after tax, one practical method is to shift the reliance of government from indirect taxes to direct taxes. The reason is that the progressive features of taxation are built into direct taxes. The curve for the inequality of the indirect tax burden

Figure 6.8. *Gini Coefficients of Direct and Indirect Tax, 1964–73*

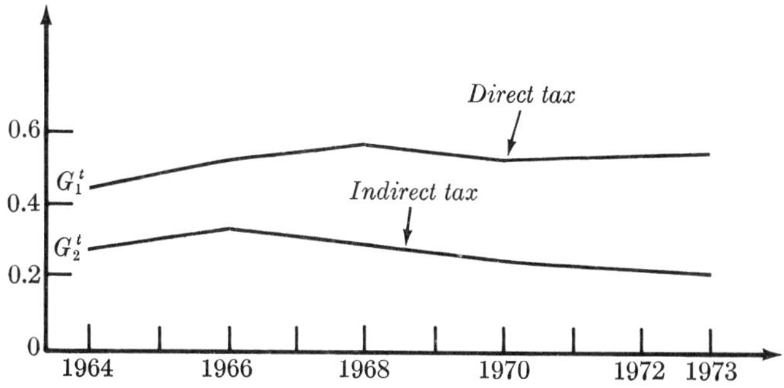

Source: Table 6.4.

$[G_2^t]$ in figure 6.8 shows a long-run decline—a decline which is not favorable to the equality of income distribution. To reverse this trend the tax rates should be increased for commodities likely to be consumed by families in higher income brackets. In addition to promoting the equality of family income, such a policy would encourage higher saving rates which, in turn, would contribute to economic development.

Future Research

This study of the inequality of family expenditure provides only a partial picture of the inequality of family welfare. There are four reasons for this. First, by concentrating only on the expenditure by families, this study neglects the impact of government expenditure on family welfare. Second, it relies on household surveys for tax data, not on agencies collecting taxes. Third, it does not take full advantage of the household data that is available. Fourth, the method adopted for this study lacks the basis of a positive, deterministic theory.

The failure to take government expenditure into account is the major deficiency of this chapter. Family expenditure constitutes only part of the aggregate demand for gross national product. For example, the taxes paid by families are spent by government on various programs. Because many families benefit from such public expenditure, the analysis of the inequality of family welfare is incomplete without considering its impact.[10] But assigning this expenditure to households, or classes of households, is not easy. The reason is that unemployment compensation or welfare payments to needy families, which could be calculated with relative ease, are not that important in developing countries. In contrast, public expenditure on health and education is very important. Generally, however, the benefits that families derive from public expenditure must be imputed. Because this expenditure both substitutes and supplements private expenditure in similar categories, it can and should, to the extent possible, be imputed in future studies. Primary data on the administration of government programs for health and education will be needed for this purpose.

Because of this study's exclusive reliance on data based upon household surveys, certain issues arose which should be resolved in future research. For one thing, the payments of direct and indirect tax reported by families obviously differ in magnitude from those collected. Moreover the calculation of the indirect tax burden, outlined earlier in this chapter, is only a crude approximation. Satisfactory analysis of the burden of indirect tax, which is quantitatively more important than the burden of direct tax, requires a more adequate framework for the analysis of the shifting incidence of the indirect tax burden in the context of general equilibrium. In addition to data from household surveys, other primary data for the fiscal operations of government will be needed.

Despite these requirements for additional data, not even existing data were used to the fullest extent. The wealth of data on family expenditure, such as that detailed in the classification for consumption expenditure in table 6.1, has not been adequately explored. If these data were used more fully, the inequality of family expenditure on consumption could be calculated at a more disaggregated level to provide a firmer grasp of the meaning of the inequality of welfare associated with family consumption.

How have these deficiencies affected the results? The failure to incorporate government expenditure probably resulted in an over-

10. There is, moreover, no consideration of hidden taxes, such as those imposed through the rice and fertilizer exchanges.

estimation of the inequality of family welfare. The failure to incorporate the undistributed profits of corporations and other similar items probably led to an underestimation of the inequality of savings and income. The failure to examine household data at a more disaggregated level of detail probably obscured some underlying trends. Nevertheless a start has been made. The intent here was to show how the basic theory of decomposition presented in this volume might be applied to the inequality of additive expenditure components, just as it was applied to the inequality of additive income components.

Finally a word on theory. The method of decomposition used in this chapter basically is empirical. It lacks the foundation of a positive deterministic theory. Therefore one direction for future research into the inequality of expenditure and savings would be to construct a positive deterministic theory based on assumptions about consumer behavior. A theory of this type would not be as difficult to construct, at least conceptually, as that which would apply to some other areas of the analysis of income inequality—for example, to the determination of the inequality of wage income, as posited in chapter four. One possible approach to such a formulation is now discussed.

Deterministic theories of the inequality of consumption and taxation are relatively easy to formulate because conventional economic theory has already provided some of the foundations. Abstractly a functional relation is postulated:

$$y = f(x). \tag{6.20}$$

For example, $f(x)$ represents a consumption function when x stands for income and y stands for consumption. Alternatively $f(x)$ represents a tax function when x stands for income and y stands for tax payments. A special case of equation (6.20) is represented by a linear function:

$$y = b + ax, \tag{6.21}$$

which represents a linear consumption or other function. To see how equation (6.20) is related to inequality analysis involving patterns in vectors $Y = (y_1, y_2, \ldots, y_n)$ and $X = (x_1, x_2, \ldots, x_n)$ for n families, use the following definition:

DEFINITION 6.1. *The vector Y is an f-transformation of X if $y_i = f(x_i)$ $(i = 1, 2, \ldots, n)$.*

A *linear transformation* gives the following theorem[11]:

THEOREM 6.1. $G_y = (a/\phi)G_x$, *where* $\phi = \bar{y}/\bar{x}$.

The same language can be used to describe equation (6.21) as a type one, two, or three transformation, depending upon the signs of b and a [see equation (3.7) in chapter three]. When equation (6.21) is interpreted as a consumption function for a particular commodity, a type three commodity (with $a < 0$) is an "inferior" good. Similarly a type one commodity is a "superior" good, such that the percentage of income spent on this commodity increases with income [see equation (3.13) in chapter three]. In all cases, theorem 6.1 provides information on the inequality of consumption [G_y] as related to the inequality of income [G_x] [see equation (3.12) in chapter three]. Precisely the same classification and interpretation can be given when equation (6.21) is interpreted as a tax function: For example, a type three tax is in fact a subsidy which declines with the level of income.

When the transformation function (6.20) is nonlinear, theorems similar to 6.1 cannot be readily deduced. For example, for a progressive system of income tax, the transformation function becomes:

$$y = b + tx^2/2, \quad \text{with} \tag{6.22a}$$

$$\frac{dy}{dx} = tx \quad \text{for} \quad t > 0, \tag{6.22b}$$

when the marginal tax rate [dy/dx] is a linear function of income [x]. When the tax payment pattern [$Y = (y_1, y_2, \ldots, y_n)$] is a transformation of the income pattern [$X = (x_1, x_2, \ldots, x_n)$] by equation (6.22a), it is not easy to relate the inequality of the tax burden [G_y] to the inequality of income distribution [G_x]. The primary reason for this is that the nonlinearity of equation (6.22a) is not amenable to the linearity property of the Gini coefficient. The difficulty, however, is technical rather than conceptual. What needs to be done is to search for another inequality index—one other than the Gini coefficient—that satisfies certain "multiplicative" properties. This points the direction future research efforts should probably take to deal with deterministic theories on the problems encountered in this chapter.

11. This theorem was proved as equation (3.12) in chapter three, where a/ϕ is the elasticity of the linear regression line at the mean point.

Appendix 6.1. Estimation of Indirect Tax

The procedure for computing the indirect tax payments of households uses information contained in input-output flow matrices. Let the prices of the n commodities be denoted by the row vector $P' = (p_1, p_2, \ldots, p_n)$. Let $A = (a_{ij})$ be the $n \times n$ coefficient matrix, and let $W' = (w_1, w_2, \ldots, w_n)$ and $T' = (t_1, t_2, \ldots, t_n)$ be the values added and indirect tax payments per unit of output for the industries. Then:

$$(6.23) \qquad P' = P'A + W' + T',$$

where, for $C' = P'A = (c_1, c_2, \ldots, c_n)$, the element c_i stands for the intermediary factor cost per unit output of the ith industry. It follows that:

$$(6.24a) \qquad P' = W'E + T'B, \quad \text{where}$$

$$(6.24b) \qquad B = (I - A)^{-1}$$

is the Leontief inverse matrix. By using the two-industry case as an illustration, the input-output flow table becomes:

Item	*Intermediary inputs*		*Final demand*	*Total output*
	Industry 1	*Industry 2*		
Industry 1	p_1X_{11}	p_1X_{12}	p_1Y_1	p_1X_1
Industry 2	p_2X_{21}	p_2X_{22}	p_2Y_2	p_2X_2
Value added	w_1X_1	w_2X_2	—	—
Indirect tax	$T_1 = t_1X_1$	$T_2 = t_2X_2$	—	—

— Not applicable.

In the table X_{ij}, Y_i, and X_i respectively are interindustry flows, final demand, and total output in physical units. For any base year a monetary input-output flow table contains all the numbers in such cells. Thus the indirect tax rates $[t_i]$ are estimated by:

$$(6.25) \qquad t_i = T_i/X_i = (T_i/X_ip_i)p_i, \qquad (i = 1, 2, \ldots, n)$$

where T_i and X_ip_i are the marginal entries in the table. If the unit of measurement for output is normalized so that $p_i = 1$, then equation

(6.25) reduces to:

$$t_i = T_i/X_ip_i, \qquad (i = 1, 2, \ldots, n) \tag{6.26}$$

which can be estimated from the marginal entries. The rates of tax burden, given by $(b_1, b_2, \ldots, b_n)$, are defined by having b_i be the amount of indirect tax payment for every dollar spent on the ith commodity or, equivalently, for every normalized unit of commodity purchased. Thus:

$$b_i = t_i. \qquad (i = 1, 2, \ldots, n) \tag{6.27}$$

This procedure of estimation is based on the assumption that all purchasers of a commodity pay the indirect taxes—that is, all indirect tax burdens are shifted to the consuming public.

By using input-output tables for 1966, the average values of the indirect tax burden $[(b_1, b_2, \ldots, b_n)]$ were calculated for the various consumption categories.[12] The rates of tax burden were revised whenever input-output tables were available for years other than 1966. These rates were then applied to the DGBAS data for the various categories of family consumption to obtain the structure of indirect tax payments given in tables 6.5–6.10, beginning on page 296.

12. Economic Planning Council, *Interregional Input-Output Tables, Taiwan Area Republic of China, 1966*. (Taipei, n.d.).

Table 6.5. *Family Income and Expenditure, by Category and Income Class, 1964*

(thousands of N.T. dollars)

Income class (N.T. dollars)	*Number of families* [N]	*Total family income* [Y_i]	*All other expenditure* [C_1]	*Housing expenditure* [C_2]
Less than 6,000	22,288	97,612	74,206	12,938
6,000–8,000	45,294	318,829	247,062	39,524
8,000–10,000	51,046	458,795	365,144	54,750
10,000–12,000	86,994	955,018	794,188	107,260
12,000–14,000	113,596	1,471,883	1,117,165	160,293
14,000–16,000	130,132	1,960,103	1,492,311	200,924
16,000–18,000	132,289	2,244,952	1,556,775	241,157
18,000–20,000	140,916	2,664,356	1,937,333	237,670
20,000–22,000	153,857	3,226,015	2,343,125	346,986
22,000–24,000	144,511	3,325,103	2,243,790	372,368
24,000–26,000	127,975	3,194,728	2,206,247	341,771
26,000–28,000	140,916	3,793,958	2,511,383	451,987
28,000–30,000	105,687	3,061,453	2,084,927	354,635
30,000–32,000	79,805	2,469,080	1,614,334	280,026
32,000–34,000	78,367	2,586,469	1,699,524	320,036
34,000–36,000	76,210	2,664,522	1,681,692	285,621
36,000–38,000	63,268	2,335,582	1,473,956	242,951
38,000–40,000	43,138	1,684,054	1,032,257	223,682
40,000–45,000	100,654	4,248,315	2,625,497	504,021
45,000–50,000	73,334	3,467,577	1,976,334	400,296
50,000–55,000	50,327	2,631,650	1,510,906	365,021
55,000–60,000	44,576	2,558,480	1,470,207	295,625
60,000–65,000	30,915	1,930,572	1,027,877	233,646
65,000–70,000	21,569	1,447,266	763,400	201,672
70,000–75,000	17,255	1,242,817	658,269	189,453
75,000–80,000	13,660	1,054,572	604,423	127,617
80,000–90,000	20,131	1,687,238	902,263	191,357
90,000–100,000	13,660	1,293,438	646,044	79,978
100,000–150,000	23,006	2,819,096	1,319,552	316,022
150,000–200,000	4,314	722,397	359,226	77,929
200,000–300,000	1,438	345,660	123,723	11,186
More than 300,000	719	394,943	77,529	9,256
Total income	2,151,847	64,356,533	40,540,669	7,277,658

Source: DGBAS, *Report on the Survey of Family Income and Expenditure*, 1964.

Educational expenditure $[C_3]$	*Direct tax* $[T_1]$	*Indirect tax* $[T_2]$	*Savings* $[S]$	*Income class* (*N.T. dollars*)
7,340	522	8,489	−5,883	Less than 6,000
24,954	1,033	24,921	−18,665	6,000–8,000
31,370	1,745	45,146	−39,360	8,000–10,000
66,647	3,860	67,929	−84,866	10,000–12,000
102,587	6,640	92,862	−7,664	12,000–14,000
137,658	11,277	121,694	−3,761	14,000–16,000
156,026	15,033	227,912	48,049	16,000–18,000
203,476	12,824	168,031	105,022	18,000–20,000
245,260	25,023	208,803	56,818	20,000–22,000
231,470	19,681	200,723	257,071	22,000–24,000
297,754	15,394	196,947	136,615	24,000–26,000
353,339	15,990	232,621	228,638	26,000–28,000
276,981	19,153	188,234	137,523	28,000–30,000
253,947	13,564	147,725	159,484	30,000–32,000
228,298	16,115	156,895	165,601	32,000–34,000
217,505	15,376	157,477	306,851	34,000–36,000
203,499	13,169	144,727	257,280	36,000–38,000
139,284	10,824	92,619	185,388	38,000–40,000
320,786	24,945	243,601	529,465	40,000–45,000
320,217	28,094	182,970	559,666	45,000–50,000
240,236	29,174	139,923	346,390	50,000–55,000
243,711	22,161	138,547	388,229	55,000–60,000
192,855	9,316	100,311	366,567	60,000–65,000
149,340	8,538	79,668	244,648	65,000–70,000
122,918	15,420	63,072	193,685	70,000–75,000
83,144	4,550	59,945	174,893	75,000–80,000
137,731	18,447	82,962	354,478	80,000–90,000
126,150	13,805	61,651	365,810	90,000–100,000
179,539	38,199	113,025	852,759	100,000–150,000
66,048	4,529	33,494	181,171	150,000–200,000
15,329	936	14,192	180,294	200,000–300,000
15,088	91	6,456	286,523	More than 300,000
5,390,487	435,428	3,803,572	6,908,719	Total income

Table 6.6. *Family Income and Expenditure, by Category and Income Class, 1966*

(thousands of N.T. dollars)

Income class (*N.T. dollars*)	*Number of families* [N]	*Total family income* [Y_i]	*All other expenditure* [C_1]	*Housing expenditure* [C_2]
Less than 6,000	13,044	62,367	45,999	7,924
6,000–8,000	36,228	273,539	197,469	34,811
8,000–10,000	54,624	533,261	377,014	68,484
10,000–12,000	61,417	710,762	516,788	84,344
12,000–14,000	109,990	1,505,136	1,058,954	175,794
14,000–16,000	112,595	1,761,244	1,222,373	212,237
16,000–18,000	131,632	2,321,090	1,607,048	274,464
18,000–20,000	141,767	2,799,545	1,964,355	340,322
20,000–22,000	165,090	3,570,040	2,421,485	434,864
22,000–24,000	137,202	3,254,517	2,153,717	459,149
24,000–26,000	138,421	3,511,997	2,349,874	466,070
26,000–28,000	122,909	3,407,384	2,212,159	467,090
28,000–30,000	125,897	3,693,025	2,432,312	449,887
30,000–32,000	101,761	3,228,045	2,081,560	428,139
32,000–34,000	81,221	2,732,158	1,712,836	358,813
34,000–36,000	75,132	2,671,424	1,726,170	344,376
36,000–38,000	73,454	2,770,170	1,707,057	401,896
38,000–40,000	55,910	2,194,434	1,330,121	302,788
40,000–45,000	118,578	5,214,635	3,145,169	710,392
45,000–50,000	84,411	4,135,582	2,432,101	556,068
50,000–55,000	73,255	3,958,065	2,326,276	549,979
55,000–60,000	56,536	3,328,065	1,904,726	523,617
60,000–65,000	49,381	3,145,084	1,792,069	455,654
65,000–70,000	27,181	1,861,423	939,498	258,880
70,000–75,000	23,948	1,774,913	1,021,464	191,537
75,000–80,000	18,563	1,464,804	763,174	195,764
80,000–90,000	26,928	2,358,611	1,167,754	311,798
90,000–100,000	16,646	1,640,462	805,344	266,784
100,000–150,000	33,140	3,943,986	1,908,467	474,443
150,000–200,000	9,833	1,711,977	750,419	189,974
More than 200,000	4,341	957,819	457,922	116,412
Total income	2,281,035	76,495,564	46,549,674	10,112,754

Source: DGBAS, *Report on the Survey of Family Income and Expenditure,* 1966.

Educational expenditure $[C_3]$	*Direct tax* $[T_1]$	*Indirect tax* $[T_2]$	*Savings* $[S]$	*Income class* (*N.T. dollars*)
3,849	817	3,536	242	Less than 6,000
20,401	669	14,122	6,067	6,000–8,000
34,570	2,861	35,335	14,997	8,000–10,000
50,756	5,482	46,193	7,199	10,000–12,000
104,107	11,253	93,755	61,273	12,000–14,000
121,609	13,860	106,626	84,539	14,000–16,000
163,236	16,630	137,731	121,981	16,000–18,000
204,125	20,184	165,739	104,820	18,000–20,000
268,183	27,898	218,141	199,469	20,000–22,000
244,487	27,596	185,825	183,743	22,000–24,000
264,690	25,475	205,756	200,132	24,000–26,000
260,988	27,035	201,686	238,426	26,000–28,000
303,707	36,810	221,112	249,197	28,000–30,000
284,319	25,316	196,888	211,823	30,000–32,000
224,592	21,328	223,391	191,198	32,000–34,000
242,185	28,019	162,461	168,213	34,000–36,000
269,747	27,251	170,517	193,702	36,000–38,000
179,888	30,077	133,288	218,272	38,000–40,000
514,604	64,918	317,467	462,085	40,000–45,000
432,182	59,208	258,465	394,558	45,000–50,000
369,419	54,757	230,930	426,704	50,000–55,000
312,544	33,614	206,249	347,315	55,000–60,000
325,390	36,066	197,792	338,113	60,000–65,000
169,672	24,776	107,799	360,798	65,000–70,000
200,324	25,797	112,163	223,628	70,000–75,000
109,913	18,154	85,716	292,083	75,000–80,000
227,136	49,345	131,922	470,656	80,000–90,000
140,639	36,321	92,269	299,105	90,000–100,000
313,797	87,404	207,176	952,699	100,000–150,000
100,353	45,234	78,058	547,939	150,000–200,000
94,423	49,033	46,328	175,701	More than 200,000
6,558,835	933,188	4,594,436	7,746,677	Total income

Table 6.7. *Family Income and Expenditure, by Category and Income Class, 1968*

(thousands of N.T. dollars)

Income class (N.T. dollars)	*Number of families* [*N*]	*Total family income* [Y_i]	*All other expenditure* [C_1]	*Housing expenditure* [C_2]
Less than 6,000	8,717	35,623	54,197	9,683
6,000–8,000	11,883	84,843	59,334	11,651
8,000–10,000	24,464	216,705	145,623	42,804
10,000–12,000	48,397	543,308	366,065	83,187
12,000–14,000	40,271	528,317	370,345	74,419
14,000–16,000	72,769	1,103,666	789,980	152,426
16,000–18,000	103,715	1,806,929	1,275,112	242,767
18,000–20,000	119,195	2,290,129	1,733,917	299,601
20,000–22,000	123,418	2,605,688	1,853,384	319,900
22,000–24,000	112,758	2,603,833	1,792,427	296,260
24,000–26,000	134,010	3,386,270	2,364,914	445,470
26,000–28,000	106,404	2,875,279	1,904,022	354,415
28,000–30,000	128,242	3,751,380	2,510,261	538,790
30,000–32,000	133,719	4,192,962	3,284,440	542,595
32,000–34,000	87,112	2,881,135	1,820,324	469,365
34,000–36,000	89,516	3,148,092	2,022,361	454,944
36,000–38,000	79,764	2,966,426	1,851,886	397,883
38,000–40,000	79,784	3,126,891	1,937,608	435,450
40,000–45,000	168,012	7,243,895	4,677,913	1,055,272
45,000–50,000	152,750	7,244,441	4,491,360	1,067,183
50,000–55,000	125,936	6,651,426	3,798,543	995,421
55,000–60,000	81,178	4,692,924	2,675,855	768,522
60,000–65,000	69,395	4,367,069	2,404,218	695,035
65,000–70,000	53,806	3,636,707	1,987,697	613,914
70,000–75,000	42,780	3,096,804	1,798,128	517,994
75,000–80,000	27,902	2,164,001	1,150,017	344,747
80,000–90,000	42,728	3,760,734	1,880,158	585,319
90,000–100,000	32,712	3,078,102	1,673,003	430,228
100,000–150,000	41,821	5,318,524	2,264,500	803,367
150,000–200,000	14,725	2,549,714	1,078,425	375,230
200,000–300,000	10,902	2,835,251	1,051,300	376,549
More than 300,000	3,831	1,581,337	296,235	79,433
Total income	2,372,616	96,368,405	57,363,552	13,879,824

Source: DGBAS, *Report on the Survey of Family Income and Expenditure,* 1968.

Educational expenditure $[C_3]$	*Direct tax* $[T_1]$	*Indirect tax* $[T_2]$	*Savings* $[S]$	*Income class* (*N.T. dollars*)
3,783	248	4,682	−36,971	Less than 6,000
7,360	584	6,529	−615	6,000–8,000
12,643	505	15,628	−498	8,000–10,000
42,658	3,119	43,213	5,066	10,000–12,000
41,352	3,873	38,978	−650	12,000–14,000
86,052	5,022	82,809	−12,623	14,000–16,000
135,314	12,142	134,300	7,294	16,000–18,000
175,764	14,610	135,355	−69,188	18,000–20,000
233,165	14,958	191,661	−7,380	20,000–22,000
234,553	16,316	196,667	67,610	22,000–24,000
313,122	26,028	237,262	−526	24,000–26,000
219,181	18,214	197,124	182,323	26,000–28,000
326,565	25,314	263,808	86,642	28,000–30,000
356,717	29,728	389,915	−410,433	30,000–32,000
259,031	26,435	196,544	109,436	32,000–34,000
274,268	28,058	212,945	155,516	34,000–36,000
251,795	15,843	198,418	250,601	36,000–38,000
322,405	32,569	217,924	180,935	38,000–40,000
720,730	77,721	550,087	162,172	40,000–45,000
812,897	91,705	500,460	280,836	45,000–50,000
669,678	100,345	433,001	654,438	50,000–55,000
454,778	81,903	309,853	402,013	55,000–60,000
447,287	55,957	277,947	486,625	60,000–65,000
316,821	45,940	232,206	440,129	65,000–70,000
345,589	47,558	203,802	183,733	70,000–75,000
257,627	21,915	140,840	248,855	75,000–80,000
381,971	90,996	212,303	609,987	80,000–90,000
326,565	76,994	195,231	376,081	90,000–100,000
458,436	117,656	368,717	1,305,848	100,000–150,000
287,372	73,831	117,593	617,263	150,000–200,000
239,649	67,047	114,502	986,204	200,000–300,000
185,709	119,976	53,458	846,527	More than 300,000
9,200,837	1,343,110	6,473,762	8,107,320	Total income

Table 6.8. *Family Income and Expenditure, by Category and Income Class, 1970*

(thousands of N.T. dollars)

Income class (*N.T. dollars*)	*Number of families* [N]	*Total family income* [Y_i]	*All other expenditure* [C_1]	*Housing expenditure* [C_2]
Less than 6,000	5,072	−12,852	49,797	8,163
6,000–8,000	13,354	95,173	76,922	15,128
8,000–10,000	11,012	96,943	83,258	14,865
10,000–12,000	14,763	163,810	105,736	22,203
12,000–14,000	26,796	351,231	259,537	45,215
14,000–16,000	41,593	622,151	427,667	79,408
16,000–18,000	50,611	857,590	630,763	92,926
18,000–20,000	64,726	1,225,430	896,503	131,563
20,000–22,000	76,780	1,619,145	1,252,162	194,703
22,000–24,000	67,784	1,560,938	1,380,001	189,467
24,000–26,000	106,759	2,666,382	1,819,552	324,928
26,000–28,000	110,679	2,986,573	1,996,355	341,263
28,000–30,000	96,886	2,798,284	1,859,128	328,274
30,000–32,000	106,133	3,290,549	2,147,211	377,167
32,000–34,000	105,405	3,479,122	2,252,726	415,203
34,000–36,000	105,273	3,686,013	2,417,061	417,609
36,000–38,000	124,543	4,592,604	2,911,929	588,941
38,000–40,000	91,980	3,579,819	2,309,551	462,964
40,000–45,000	205,860	8,707,838	5,442,467	1,128,665
45,000–50,000	181,317	8,564,914	5,264,774	1,117,375
50,000–55,000	118,746	6,221,924	3,728,342	846,048
55,000–60,000	106,340	6,096,172	3,500,004	833,203
60,000–65,000	89,350	5,559,718	3,144,018	811,549
65,000–70,000	69,658	4,688,358	2,566,119	678,630
70,000–75,000	48,114	3,486,654	1,933,123	517,292
75,000–80,000	33,838	2,620,015	1,410,393	356,708
80,000–90,000	44,887	3,794,328	2,088,656	535,956
90,000–100,000	42,926	4,050,229	2,165,341	566,552
100,000–150,000	56,607	6,670,916	3,348,734	814,693
150,000–200,000	18,849	3,132,936	1,470,198	444,447
200,000–300,000	7,032	1,636,277	655,435	143,279
More than 300,000	731	256,802	112,018	35,818
Total income	2,244,404	99,145,986	59,705,481	12,880,205

Source: DGBAS, *Report on the Survey of Family Income and Expenditure,* 1970.

Educational expenditure $[C_3]$	*Direct tax* $[T_1]$	*Indirect tax* $[T_2]$	*Savings* $[S]$	*Income class (N.T. dollars)*
10,286	630	4,581	−86,309	Less than 6,000
13,793	484	6,415	−17,569	6,000–8,000
10,007	518	7,598	−19,303	8,000–10,000
14,176	578	13,254	7,863	10,000–12,000
29,495	1,432	32,809	−17,257	12,000–14,000
84,065	3,656	46,702	−19,347	14,000–16,000
70,077	3,555	68,627	−8,358	16,000–18,000
108,784	7,046	67,150	14,384	18,000–20,000
134,379	8,717	115,912	−86,728	20,000–22,000
142,500	10,633	108,313	−269,976	22,000–24,000
254,516	10,143	191,926	65,317	24,000–26,000
284,275	17,310	210,269	137,101	26,000–28,000
290,619	15,191	197,540	107,532	28,000–30,000
296,876	17,255	223,875	228,165	30,000–32,000
367,080	22,297	242,746	179,070	32,000–34,000
392,666	23,438	261,728	173,511	34,000–36,000
455,356	24,614	308,055	303,709	36,000–38,000
405,405	30,559	237,839	133,501	38,000–40,000
933,292	70,214	609,660	523,540	40,000–45,000
958,163	75,199	582,127	567,276	45,000–50,000
729,562	50,299	411,696	455,977	50,000–55,000
716,513	60,621	400,311	585,520	55,000–60,000
681,695	74,324	360,647	487,485	60,000–65,000
569,761	73,659	297,041	503,148	65,000–70,000
409,049	42,954	221,380	362,856	70,000–75,000
325,179	44,690	173,506	309,539	75,000–80,000
464,104	53,525	243,317	408,770	80,000–90,000
475,541	71,795	258,012	512,983	90,000–100,000
701,009	174,798	282,320	1,349,362	100,000–150,000
307,215	72,385	187,506	651,185	150,000–200,000
176,982	34,843	94,094	531,644	200,000–300,000
37,841	12,424	15,007	43,694	More than 300,000
10,850,261	1,109,786	6,481,963	8,118,290	Total income

Table 6.9. *Family Income and Expenditure, by Category and Income Class, 1972*

(thousands of N.T. dollars)

Income class (N.T. dollars)	*Number of families* [N]	*Total family income* [Y_i]	*All other expenditure* [C_1]	*Housing expenditure* [C_2]
Less than 10,000	11,418	93,232	58,129	16,820
10,000–15,000	24,575	314,301	207,526	46,255
15,000–20,000	63,724	1,128,238	778,304	142,963
20,000–25,000	106,913	2,443,578	1,615,347	313,822
25,000–30,000	157,288	4,312,587	2,886,558	562,800
30,000–35,000	216,839	7,044,936	4,653,777	924,673
35,000–40,000	248,665	9,371,680	5,990,899	1,256,042
40,000–45,000	252,387	10,720,908	6,735,904	1,509,213
45,000–50,000	248,324	11,790,427	7,246,380	1,689,363
50,000–55,000	200,652	10,555,480	6,360,216	1,523,170
55,000–60,000	186,462	10,721,843	6,359,583	1,515,719
60,000–65,000	148,420	9,271,515	5,415,123	1,412,963
65,000–70,000	136,792	9,215,939	5,291,237	1,374,419
70,000–75,000	122,339	8,838,724	5,008,457	1,397,870
75,000–80,000	94,762	7,332,131	4,104,498	1,117,977
80,000–85,000	76,330	6,303,236	3,381,900	966,197
85,000–90,000	68,550	6,003,608	3,262,912	883,129
90,000–95,000	55,417	5,109,051	2,645,938	841,060
95,000–100,000	36,458	3,554,360	1,821,546	554,000
100,000–150,000	236,255	27,872,800	14,163,585	4,552,994
150,000–200,000	52,057	8,879,408	3,843,180	1,400,525
200,000–300,000	21,966	5,076,387	1,902,820	635,211
More than 300,000	4,864	1,746,755	674,682	220,433
Total income	2,771,457	167,701,124	94,408,501	24,857,618

Source: DGBAS, *Report on the Survey of Family Income and Expenditure,* 1972.

Educational expenditure [C_3]	*Direct tax* [T_1]	*Indirect tax* [T_2]	*Savings* [S]	*Income class* (*N.T. dollars*)
7,026	173	5,906	5,178	Less than 10,000
21,176	1,142	27,758	10,444	10,000–15,000
81,909	3,487	93,935	27,640	15,000–20,000
162,080	9,157	196,920	146,252	20,000–25,000
305,916	20,589	340,636	196,088	25,000–30,000
466,922	35,873	543,905	419,786	30,000–35,000
677,383	48,909	717,500	680,947	35,000–40,000
745,254	77,828	812,416	840,293	40,000–45,000
894,649	91,681	879,792	988,562	45,000–50,000
864,473	103,121	834,234	870,266	50,000–55,000
888,558	123,214	773,020	1,061,749	55,000–60,000
701,356	118,086	661,359	962,628	60,000–65,000
753,610	118,826	658,866	1,018,981	65,000–70,000
721,286	112,321	619,651	979,139	70,000–75,000
621,313	92,842	529,684	865,817	75,000–80,000
561,288	96,570	420,132	877,149	80,000–85,000
554,572	94,819	412,853	795,323	85,000–90,000
448,308	98,609	338,819	736,317	90,000–95,000
326,160	66,582	245,080	540,992	95,000–100,000
2,393,664	655,079	1,748,797	4,358,681	100,000–150,000
685,128	285,057	495,164	2,170,354	150,000–200,000
357,276	158,975	225,048	1,797,057	200,000–300,000
123,588	110,673	74,946	542,433	More than 300,000
13,362,895	2,523,613	11,656,421	20,892,076	Total income

Table 6.10. *Family Income and Expenditure, by Category and Income Class, 1973*

(thousands of N.T. dollars)

Income class (N.T. dollars)	*Number of families* [N]	*Total family income* $[Y_i]$	*All other expenditure* $[C_1]$	*Housing expenditure* $[C_2]$
Less than 10,000	4,706	32,729	43,155	7,396
10,000–15,000	13,142	173,702	177,907	33,372
15,000–20,000	33,413	601,385	453,219	93,377
20,000–25,000	63,584	1,447,121	981,868	181,356
25,000–30,000	93,436	2,579,618	1,713,159	310,933
30,000–35,000	147,877	4,789,163	3,262,488	579,117
35,000–40,000	187,831	7,061,009	4,485,162	872,249
40,000–45,000	178,633	7,591,085	4,904,235	978,339
45,000–50,000	228,614	10,845,636	6,885,053	1,410,873
50,000–55,000	202,529	10,634,583	6,796,902	1,420,303
55,000–60,000	185,412	10,645,307	6,578,248	1,467,923
60,000–65,000	185,849	11,572,819	7,158,236	1,587,324
65,000–70,000	157,879	10,606,557	6,284,235	1,537,840
70,000–75,000	142,171	10,291,020	5,992,513	1,536,800
75,000–80,000	125,281	9,703,135	5,604,665	1,432,037
80,000–85,000	109,654	9,039,353	5,171,099	1,485,437
85,000–90,000	104,333	9,110,737	5,134,329	1,385,537
90,000–95,000	77,403	7,141,273	3,975,464	1,075,972
95,000–100,000	68,908	6,701,063	3,619,996	1,039,971
100,000–150,000	383,675	45,830,233	23,269,023	7,566,972
150,000–200,000	98,356	16,631,725	7,470,937	2,763,891
200,000–300,000	45,401	11,113,270	4,350,321	1,746,133
More than 300,000	20,425	8,997,359	3,024,034	1,162,432
Totai income	2,858,512	213,140,882	117,336,248	31,675,584

Source: DGBAS, *Report on the Survey of Family Income and Expenditure*, 1973.

Educational expenditure [C_3]	*Direct tax* [T_1]	*Indirect tax* [T_2]	*Savings* [S]	*Income class* (*N.T. dollars*)
1,881	251	7,368	−27,322	Less than 10,000
24,357	1,119	19,208	−82,261	10,000–15,000
55,311	2,445	53,914	56,881	15,000–20,000
94,660	6,286	118,565	64,386	20,000–25,000
144,763	12,082	214,482	184,199	25,000–30,000
300,236	20,666	376,728	249,928	30,000–35,000
431,468	39,025	557,565	675,540	35,000–40,000
514,269	39,233	573,203	581,806	40,000–45,000
696,253	65,314	794,873	993,270	45,000–50,000
679,973	77,628	784,418	875,359	50,000–55,000
716,455	79,408	773,263	1,030,010	55,000–60,000
813,520	87,733	861,387	1,064,619	60,000–65,000
822,757	100,674	783,415	1,077,636	65,000–70,000
772,428	120,361	728,338	1,140,580	70,000–75,000
766,824	106,504	707,480	1,086,625	75,000–80,000
646,411	123,319	627,028	986,059	80,000–85,000
735,645	125,243	634,321	1,095,662	85,000–90,000
553,968	99,321	494,723	828,825	90,000–95,000
616,227	99,808	475,210	849,851	95,000–100,000
3,835,007	811,851	2,982,699	7,364,681	100,000–150,000
1,382,955	427,850	995,448	3,590,643	150,000–200,000
807,556	285,697	549,114	3,374,448	200,000–300,000
475,088	390,255	337,190	3,608,360	More than 300,000
15,880,012	3,122,073	14,449,940	30,669,025	Total income

CHAPTER 7

Relevance of Findings for Policy

THE ULTIMATE PURPOSE of the examination of Taiwan's development experience, indeed any country's development experience, should be more than simply attempting to understand what happened during a specified period. It should be to distill conclusions that may be relevant to other developing societies and to determine special features that are likely to be irrelevant elsewhere. We consequently have tried to illuminate the possibilities, at various levels of aggregation and analysis, for minimizing the conflict between growth and equity. Readers may nevertheless expect a listing of policy recommendations that stem from such an analysis. Thus, even where our work is preliminary and tentative, which it generally is, we will at least indicate the kinds of policy conclusions that seem to be supported by the empirical findings.

Before proceeding to such a listing, however, two general precautions are necessary. One has to do with the extent to which policy is based on sound theory or on a combination of vaguely conceived relations and good intentions. The other has to do with the extent to which analysis of the distribution of income is purely economic or intertwined with other disciplines.

Postwar growth has been associated with the observed general worsening of the distribution of income in most developing countries. This pattern has elicited strong protests: "Growth has failed. Governments must resort to direct, even radical actions to correct the situation." The actions proposed usually include land and fiscal reform, public works programs, and major packages of poverty relief and welfare. But what is the basis for the contention that the primary strategy of growth has failed and that direct intervention is required to fix up FID after the fact? All too frequently the evidence is little more than a crude correlation between high rates of growth and worsening indexes of income inequality.

It is easy to sympathize with the humanitarian instincts, and to honor the political instincts, that propel observers to the conclusion that radical change is required. But the general absence of underlying positive analysis is open to question. Consider medicine. After many years of basic research and the accumulation of substantial knowledge, a sure cure for cancer still has not been found. Yet few experts favor declaring a "war on cancer" if that means abandoning a step-by-step scientific approach to the problem. Similarly it would be unwise to reject the basic accumulated tool kit of economics, to claim that growth does not work without specifying alternative growth paths, or to raise false hopes by stating that a "quick fix" is possible and has been worked out analytically. To do any of these things would probably impede the cause, not advance it.

Accumulated economic theory must provide a framework that enables economists and planners to differentiate the relevant from the irrelevant and to rule out logical absurdities. Such a framework, to be achieved through the traditional mixture of deductive and inductive analysis, is a prerequisite for understanding the relations between distribution and growth—and thus for knowing what to do about them. True, such a framework is only now beginning to emerge. Although still inadequate, it is the best we have, and it can be improved in the future. The policy implications listed in this chapter should therefore be interpreted in this context. They have been developed within the limits of existing theory and method, and much additional work is required to corroborate or refute them.

A second general precaution is related to the realization that a society's modernization involves, in addition to economic elements, important noneconomic elements relevant to the problem at hand. For example, inductive evidence and deductive logic may indicate that institutional discrimination against women in the labor force is relevant to wage income inequality (see chapter four). Although this finding may decidedly be relevant to policy, we find it difficult, as economists, to go beyond the stylized prescription that such discrimination should be removed, and we leave to others the task of designing an appropriate action program. In fact, policies relevant to the family distribution of income seldom are purely economic. Many interdisciplinary complexities relate to such issues as nepotism, family formation, and imperfections in educational access. If some of the policy conclusions cited below seem terse and barren, the excuse is that we have followed a natural tendency to appeal to a division of labor among social scientists.

Here, as elsewhere, good policy should be based on good theory. The analysis of determinants of the family distribution of income still is at an early, largely inductive, and pretheoretical stage. In the introduction we tried to explain the overall framework of reasoning adopted to guide the work of this volume. Our findings and their relevance for policy are presented following the same pattern.

At the aggregate level, the most important, if general, policy conclusion which may be derived from our work is this:

- It is possible for economic growth to be compatible with an improved distribution of income during every phase of the transition from colonialism to modern growth.

Taiwan's experience demonstrates that if assets are not distributed too unequally, a growth path initially based on a flexible version of primary import substitution, followed by the timely reduction of the veil between a changing endowment and relative factor and commodity prices, can yield this result. True, few other developing countries have the same combination of a relatively favorable initial distribution of assets and a willingness to deploy the market mechanism effectively over time. But the experience in Taiwan does not support those who argue that because tinkering with relative prices did not work in the 1950s and 1960s, we must now reach for the radical medicine bottle. Nor does it support the argument that the market solution at every step of the way will, in the presence of powerful landed or industrial interests, yield the desired complementarity between the objectives of growth and equity. What it does support is the conclusion that, given initial conditions that are not too unfavorable, such complementarity can be achieved by affecting the basic growth path, not by following what may be called a secondary or mop-up strategy through direct interventions by government. That is, such complementarity can be achieved by following a different primary strategy of transition growth.

The basic thesis of this volume then is that an equitable level of FID can come about mainly through the *kind* of economic growth which is generated and hence that FID policy should center on growth-related policies. This thesis is in turn predicated on the idea that economic growth is typologically and historically sensitive. In other words, the transition to modern growth is an historical event characterized by meaningful subphases. Furthermore, because of inherited economic, geographic, and institutional characteristics, different LDCs will undergo this transformation by following different patterns or subphases. Thus the policy focus elaborated here would not necessarily be relevant for types of countries very different from Taiwan—for example, countries large in size, rich in oil, or having a surplus of land. Moreover any suggestions relevant to policy must be sensitive to the particular subphase that a country has reached in the transition to modern growth. In this volume we have concentrated on Taiwan as a successful example. The transferability of policy suggestions to other countries must be strictly based on the understanding that good FID policy, along with growth policy, must be sensitive to typological and historical considerations.

Much can be said about what is unique or not unique in any particular experience and the consequent applicability or inapplicability to other countries. As was pointed out at the outset, no country's experience can ever be fully transferred. Taiwan unquestionably had some unique advantages: its initial endowment of human resources, its cultural heritage, its early colonial experience, its strong support by the United States. But some popular notions about the large quantitative role played by U.S. foreign aid early, and private investment later, are factually incorrect.[1] Moreover Taiwan also had some substantial disadvantages not shared by many other contemporary LDCs: its initially unfavorable man-land ratio, its heavy population pressure over time, its felt need to spend a large part of its resources on national defense, its growing international diplomatic isolation. We recognize, when all is said and done, that readers will have to determine for themselves what is unique in, or transferable from, the Taiwan experience. We believe that many elements from the analysis in this volume, and the policy conclusions derived therefrom, have relevance in other contexts.

As was pointed out earlier, the postwar transition to modern growth in Taiwan moved from the initial subphase of primary import substitution into that of export substitution in the early 1960s. By means mainly of a labor-intensive export drive, a landmark of transition growth appeared in about 1968, when the economy's

1. Although aid may have been of strategic importance in encouraging the important policy changes of 1961, public and private foreign capital contributed less than 6 percent of cumulative investment during the 1953–72 period.

labor-surplus condition ended and real wages began to increase at an accelerated rate. Thus any respectable analysis of the essential growth phenomenon in such a labor-surplus, dualistic economy must explore the reallocation of labor from the agricultural sector to the nonagricultural sector and the changing pattern of the functional distribution of income. That changing pattern, measured by the relative size of the wage and property income shares, is brought about by changes in wage rates, factor endowment, and technology.

The impact of growth on FID can be examined from three viewpoints: that of all families, that of urban families (receiving wage and property income), and that of rural families (receiving agricultural income as well as wage and property income). We naturally are interested in the relations between growth and equity for the entire population. We nevertheless found it useful, for both analytical and policy reasons, to focus first on the underlying sectoral level.

The Inequality of Family Income

The first specific empirical findings emanating from our analysis were these:

- For all households and urban households, virtual constancy in FID before 1968—the turning point marking off labor surplus from labor scarcity—gave way to significant improvement thereafter.
- For rural households, significant improvement before 1968 gave way to virtual constancy thereafter.

These empirical findings support our basic thesis that FID equity indeed is a growth-sensitive phenomenon, as can be seen from the fact that, for urban and rural sectors separately and for the economy as a whole, this turning point demarcates markedly different phases of both growth and FID performance. Furthermore the transition involves the transformation of an agrarian economy into an industrial economy. Our findings indicate that the favorable impact of growth on FID in that context must occur in the relatively more dominant sector of the economy—that is, in agriculture before 1968 and in nonagriculture thereafter—if growth is to have a consistently favorable effect on FID over time. The unusually high priority Taiwan attached to the agricultural sector—to land reform, infrastructural investments, and relative prices before commercialization—represents an example of the selection of the correct policy focus from the points of view of both growth and distribution in this general historical perspective.

Analysis of the underlying causes of this aggregate performance can be conducted by identifying a reallocation effect which captures changes in the relative size of the agricultural and nonagricultural sectors, a functional distribution effect which captures changes in the relative shares of wage and property income, and a factor Gini effect which captures changes in inequality of distribution of a particular component of family income. What policy implications can be derived from this tripartite division of the causes of inequality? The main implication is that different types of policy are required to deal with the first two effects, which can be more directly related to analysis in the context of growth theory, than with the third. Thus it becomes important to know something about the relative quantitative significance of the three effects as causes of overall FID equity. The empirical findings, more specific than those related to the degree of income inequality, once again support the general thesis that the nature of economic growth determines much of FID in both sectors of the dualistic economy.

- For urban households the functional distribution effect, which was highly unfavorable before 1968 and favorable after 1968, was a dominant cause of FID performance.
- For rural households the reallocation effect, which was favorable both before and after 1968, was a dominant cause of FID performance.

The phenomena related to growth here are not only *relevant* but *dominant* as explanatory causes of changes in the family distribution of income. As summarized in the foregoing findings, the difference between urban households and rural households is an important growth-relevant phenomenon. For the urban sector the accumulation of capital and human assets is at the heart of the industrialization effort. For this reason the functional distribution effect is a dominant cause of FID. For the rural sector, in contrast, the reallocation of labor from agricultural to nonagricultural production represents a much more crucial development issue. Consequently the reallocation effect turns out to be a dominant cause of FID performance. The implications of these findings help in the identification of the proper policy focus. For the urban sector the wage rate, factor endowment, and technology choice—all elements affecting the functional distribution of income—are the dominant policy issues related to FID. For the rural sector the growth of rural-based industries and services alongside a productive agricultural sector, and the additional employment opportunities thus offered to rural households, are the dominant policy issues.

To see more precisely how these growth-relevant forces affect FID, we first concentrated on rural families, which receive both agricultural and nonagricultural income.

- For rural families agricultural income consistently was less equally distributed than nonagricultural income—that is, $G_a > G_x$.
- Over time, agricultural income became more equally distributed—that is, G_a declined.
- Rural families received a surprisingly large and increasing share of income from rural industries and services, which were increasingly labor-using—that is, ϕ_a declined and ϕ_w/ϕ_π increased.

As an economy modernizes, analysis of the equality of income distribution for rural families involves issues quite different from those affecting urban families. The main reason is the importance of agricultural production. Two central issues here are the equality of the distribution of agricultural income, which is the dominant income component for traditional rural societies, and the increase in the equality of the distribution of nonagricultural income associated with the growth of rural industries during the transition to modern growth. The foregoing empirical findings for rural areas show that the distribution of income from the traditional agricultural base is more unequal than that of the new income associated with rural-based industrialization.

Worldwide concern about inequality in the distribution of agricultural income in rural communities has led to the laudable advocacy of direct government interference with the market mechanism where productive assets in agriculture (mainly land) are highly unequally distributed. In Taiwan early land reform, followed by increases in multiple cropping and the cultivation of new crops by the poorer (smaller) farmers, caused agricultural income to become significantly more equally distributed over time. That experience seems to indicate that land reform is an important input. But if the distribution of agricultural income is to be improved when agricultural growth is rapid, a fairly equal distribution of landed assets is also required, and the "right" growth-oriented policies must follow such reform.

How did the favorable reallocation effect cited earlier work to bring about a more equitable distribution of income for rural families over time? Because nonagricultural income was more equally distributed than agricultural income, the growth of rural industries and services made a substantial contribution to FID equity. Furthermore, when compared with urban industries, rural industries were found to be much more "labor using" (increasingly so over time). Thus the steady increase of opportunities in rural by-employment available to members of rural families, especially the poorer ones, greatly contributed to the complementarity of growth and FID. All these factors lie behind the reallocation effect's being a dominant factor contributing favorably to FID equity.

The basic policy implication of the foregoing empirical findings for rural households is relevant to industrial location. As was pointed out in chapter three, nonagricultural income has always been an important component of rural family income in Taiwan. Given the spatially dispersed pattern of industrial location, the growth of rural-based industries and services offered new opportunities for employment and investment. These opportunities made it possible in later years for nonagricultural income to overwhelm agricultural income and become the most important source of rural family income. All the advantages of such a decentralized pattern of industrial location—for example, those related to agricultural modernization arising from direct contact with industrial activity to avoiding the costs associated with labor dislocation and transport, and to reducing urban congestion and social overhead expenditure—need not be elaborated here. But the development of rural industries and the abandonment of the all-too-frequent incentives for urban concentration and agglomeration must be emphasized as prime policy recommendations emerging from our work. It is interesting to note, moreover, that most of the workers migrating from agriculture to nonagriculture were part-time or commuting farmers who were readily available for agricultural tasks at peak harvest time.

Advocacy of a spatially dispersed pattern of industrial location provides a good example of the typological sensitivity required in policymaking. The pattern that emerged in Taiwan was largely the result of such demographic and geographic features as high population density, such topological features as the location of principal ports and mountain ranges, and such historical features as the transport and energy networks established during the Japanese period. That pattern was also the result of government policies to equalize the cost of industrial energy and fuel throughout the island and to provide additional rural infrastructure as needed —policies which did not succumb to the normal subsidization and artificial encouragement of industrial agglomeration in urban areas. Consequently, competitive market forces yielded a dispersed pattern of industrial location and a labor-intensive output mix. Relative to these forces, economies of scale played a minor role. When these basic demographic and geographic conditions are not met—as, for example, in the Philippines—and when, moreover, governments pursue policies intended to give special encouragement to large-scale, capital-intensive industry—as, for example, in Thailand and the Philippines—a centralized pattern of urban industrialization results. FID equity can be improved only in the context of a growth policy that is typologically sensitive.

How did the functional distribution effect work to affect FID equity among urban households? First, the operation of the observed funtional distribution effect further supports the thesis that equity is a growth-sensitive phenomenon. As the conditions of labor surplus gave way to those of labor scarcity after 1968, the impact of the functional distribution effect on FID changed from being unfavorable to favorable. The reason is this. Only when labor becomes a scarce commodity, as evidenced by the sharp increase in the real wage, does the functional distribution effect become favorable. Two empirical findings explain more precisely the essential behavior of the functional distribution effect on urban FID.

- For urban households property income was more unequally distributed than wage income.
- The share of wage income declined relative to the share of property income before 1968 and gained at the expense of property income after 1968.

Because property income was more unequally distributed than wage income, the functional distribution effect was unfavorable or favorable depending upon whether the labor share was falling—as it was before 1968—or rising—as it was after 1968. Before 1968 the real wage was relatively stable because of the continued surplus of labor. The urban family's share of wage income declined slightly, mainly because employment opportunities were not expanding at a pace significantly greater than the rate of capital accumulation. That was in turn caused by the relatively weak labor-using bias of technology in urban industries. When the surplus of labor was exhausted after 1968, the increase in the real wage and the rapid increase of capital per worker (capital deepening) led to the expected increase in the wage share relative to the property share. In this way the functional distribution effect became favorable to FID after the turning point for conventional reasons.

For the entire 1964–72 period, and disregarding additive factor components as in chapter five, it appears that overall income inequality declined mainly because of a reduction in inequality in the urban sector over time. This occurred despite the existence of a widening income gap between the urban and rural sectors. The declining trend in income inequality can be attributed to the rapid rate of labor absorption in light manufacturing industries, which were competitive in international trade before the turning point, and to the more conventional rise in wages thereafter.

It often is said that growth in the 1960s and 1970s has failed to produce a more equitable distribution of family income. This statement has led, directly or indirectly, to the conclusion that radical government intervention is required to transfer assets from rich to poor, or at least to effect redistribution after the fact. The findings here, based on the analysis of the relations between growth and FID in Taiwan, indicate that the frequent conclusion in favor of continuous direct government intervention is not necessarily warranted. A relatively favorable initial distribution of assets clearly helped in Taiwan. But the major accomplishment of substantially eliminating the conflict between growth and FID before the turning point was the result of three basic policies: the early attention to agriculture; the mild version of import substitution followed by thorough-going export-oriented industrialization; and the decentralization of industrial operations.

The Inequality of Family Wage Income

For the more disaggregate analysis of the inequality of family wage income, our conceptual framework recognized the formation of a heterogeneous labor force as crucial in industrialization. Differences in education, age, sex, and family income characterize that heterogeneity. Distinctions were drawn among three types of issues and reflected at three levels of analysis. At the first level we attempted to trace the differentiated structure of wage rates to principal characteristics of the labor force. At the second level we attempted to trace the inequality of individual wage income to the differentiated wage rate structure and the composition of the labor force. At the third level we attempted to trace the inequality of family wage income to the membership composition of families. The policy implications of the findings will be summarized separately for each of the three levels.

At the first level, the analysis of the differentiated wage structure, we accepted the convention that differences in wage rates arising from differences in education and age are justifiable or warranted, but those arising from differences in sex and family influence are not. We acknowledge that not everyone will necessarily agree with this convention. The analysis at the first level nevertheless confirms that:

- Overall differences in wage rates reflected a mixture of both warranted and unwarranted causes.

The policy implications of warranted causes clearly are neutral. Wage rates are supposed to differ for warranted reasons, and nothing should be done to influence them. The policy implications of unwarranted causes are stylized. Institutional discrimination against females and members of poorer families exists and should be removed.

More significant, of course, is the issue of how stylized policy conclusions are to be related to growth. Using rural, town, and city residence as proxies for the increasing degree of industrialization, it was found that the modern commercialized milieu of large cities tends to evaluate sex and family influences with more sensitivity than the more tradition-bound milieu of rural communities. Institutional discrimination thus appears to be a by-product, perhaps an inevitable by-product, of modernization in its early phases. But because policy measures clearly affect more than the economic sphere, caution is required when dealing with wage differences that can be traced to institutional discrimination.

For the education characteristic, it was found that there was no significant difference between large cities and rural communities in evaluating this warranted cause of differences in wage rates. In other words, the premium for education was about the same everywhere. Thus, in the more tradition-bound rural communities, market forces can more or less sensitively value this most important labor attribute. The policy implication again is negative or inactive. Government does not need, for example, to make a special effort in rural communities to render the labor market more perfect or to offer special inducement for labor migration to ensure a more efficient spatial pattern of educated manpower use.

At the second level, the analysis of wage income inequality, the crucial issue about the relative overall importance of warranted and unwarranted causes can be addressed.

- Discrimination by sex or family influence is not as quantitatively important as discrimination by education or experience (age).

Together sex and family influence accounted for only 33 percent of the explained inequality. This type of conclusion provides an indication of what a policy that is calculated to eliminate institutional discrimination might accomplish, presumably at some cost.

The findings at the first level of analysis show for differences in wage rates that labor markets in large cities tend to discriminate more against females and members of poor families than those in rural communities. But the composition of the labor force in the large cities apparently tends to compensate for this inequality. The findings at the second level of analysis indicate that institutional discrimination accounted for a smaller percentage of wage income inequality in large cities than in rural communities. In other words, females and members of poor families tend to get a larger share of better jobs in large cities. The implication of this finding for policy is that industrialization can be relied upon, despite the higher degree of institutional discrimination of wage rates, to bring about greater equality in the distribution of wage income. This conclusion tends to confirm the earlier assertion that policies to eliminate institutional discrimination should proceed cautiously. With an eye to future research, it can be added here that the analysis at the first level, which constitutes the focal point of what can be called traditional analysis, might give a misleading picture by concentrating only on institutional discrimination of wage rates. To assess the quantitative significance of institutional discrimination for wage income inequality, the changing composition of the labor force must also be known. The empirical findings presented here are a perfect illustration of this crucial point.

At the third level, the analysis of family wage-income inequality, it was recognized that labor is a very heterogeneous factor of production. Even the crude classification by sex, age, and education used in this analysis leads to thirty-seven grades of labor. Within our framework of reasoning, the unequal family ownership pattern—that is, the unequal composition of family membership by these grades—lies behind family wage-income inequality. Some "inferior" grades, such as the poorly educated old female, can be interpreted as being part of the marginal labor force; some "superior" grades, as part of the prime labor force.

- The pattern of unequal ownership of the marginal labor force is a minor problem as far as overall family wage-income inequality is concerned.

The policy implication is that government relief and welfare measures may help the marginal labor force, but have little impact on the basic problem of family wage-income inequality. Such a conclusion may at least force policymakers to think a little harder about the likely impact of policy options that seemingly are politically attractive. A related conclusion may do the same:

- The most important cause of overall family wage-income inequality is the pattern of unequal ownership of high-grade workers.

High grade, it will be recalled, can mean one or a combination of three attributes: prime age, male, and highly educated. If inequality is traced, for example, to differences in age and sex ownership—that is, to the contrast between families having a preponderance of prime-age males and families having a preponderance of old or very young females—there is no obvious government policy relevant to correcting this inequality. Any such policy would have to be very far-fetched, interfering with rules of family formation by preventing divorce or the formation of secondary nuclear families.[2]

The inequality of family ownership of the educated labor force is a different matter. The thesis of a tendency for the unequal distribution of the opportunity for higher education to perpetuate the inequality of family income has many adherents. According to this

2. The low causal effect attributable to age, by itself, gives us some confidence that the problem of life-time earning relative to observed earning may not be as serious as is sometimes believed. It was not possible, however, to examine this potentially important issue more rigorously in this volume.

thesis the wealthier families can provide better education, and better paying jobs, to their members—advantages that conceivably could be principal causes of family wage-income inequality. The findings here cast some doubt on this thesis, because as far as education is concerned the family turns out to be insignificant as the unit of labor ownership. This means that the degree of inequality of wage income of, say, 1,000 workers would remain the same, irrespective of whether the family affiliations of these workers are taken into consideration.

For Taiwan this finding is not particularly surprising. The imperial examination system, institutionalized long ago in traditional China, continues to hold sway. Rigorous and impartial entrance examinations are annually held at all levels of formal education. Because wealthy families do not have the marked special advantages frequently encountered elsewhere, access to educational opportunities is thus relatively equal for all. Whether such a policy is feasible for other countries not having a similar cultural bias would seem to be at the heart of policy discourse in this general area.

The Inequality of Taxation and Expenditure

The analysis in this volume suggests a number of more specific policy conclusions based on findings related to patterns of taxation, disposable income, and family consumption. Economists and noneconomists have traditionally thought of taxes as an easy after-the-fact method of improving FID if the primary or growth-related outcome proves unsatisfactory. In this context, there usually is a secondary strategy concerned with minimizing the so-called disincentive effects of a taxation system that is too progressive.

In Taiwan the system of taxation was found to be reasonable from the viewpoint of incentives—that is, it was not unduly progressive or regressive. In fact:

- The distribution of the total tax burden was neutral with respect to its impact on the equity of distribution of family income.

In other words, the degree of inequality of family income before and after taxes was about the same. The policy implication of this empirical finding lends further support to the overall conclusion of this volume: adequate FID performance is mainly the result of an appropriate primary—that is, growth-related—strategy. Other work relating to fiscal impact seems to support this position.[3] Thus, even when the fiscal capacity of an LDC is relatively strong, as it is in Taiwan, direct government intervention after the fact will probably do little to affect FID performance.[4] A second and related finding also has an obvious implication for policy:

- The total tax burden was neutral because the quantitatively more important and regressive indirect tax payments canceled the quantitatively less important and more progressive direct tax payments.

Thus if the tax system is to be an instrument for bringing about a more equitable distribution of income, the tax basis should be shifted to direct taxation from its present overwhelming reliance on indirect taxation. This conclusion nevertheless is weakened because considerations other than equity considerations often prevail. During most of the period after 1962, Taiwan has been in a growth subphase of primary export substitution. The dominant phenomenon in this subphase is the export of labor-intensive goods, such as textiles, in exchange for the import of mainly producer goods, such as raw materials and capital goods. With the exhaustion of surplus labor around 1968 and the rapid increase in real wages subsequently, there has been a growing consensus that Taiwan now faces the transition into a sequence of secondary import and export substitution. That sequence aims first at the production, and later at the export, of those capital-intensive and skill-intensive producer goods which now are largely being imported.

Given this change, it follows that Taiwan in the near future cannot hope to continue relying on cheap labor as the basis of its comparative advantage in foreign trade. The accumulation of skills, technology, and capital is likely to replace cheap labor and make unprecedented demands on Taiwan's private entrepreneurial resources. Consequently the primary emphasis in any future revisions of tax policy is likely to be on investment incentives, not on equity. For this reason, a shift

3. See for example Jacob Meerman, "Fiscal Incidence in Empirical Studies of Income Distribution in Poor Countries," AID Discussion Paper, no. 25 (Washington, D.C.: U.S. Agency for International Development, June 1972).

4. The possible redistributive effect of changes in the pattern of government expenditure, especially for such social services as health and education, is not dealt with here.

from the regressive system of indirect taxation to a more progressive system of direct taxation may be inappropriate for Taiwan. Instead, movement toward a more progressive consumption tax, which would be very heavy on items likely to be consumed by high-income families, may be more appropriate. Entrepreneurs could still be encouraged to earn income and required to pay little tax as long as they reinvest their profits. Another interesting finding relates to expenditure:

- For high- and low-income families the distribution of family expenditure on housing is significantly more unequal than that on other consumption.

This finding indicates that a progressive consumption tax on housing, such as that based on the space or construction cost of residential units, could be considered as a major component of any proposed tax reform. Unlike the luxury consumption associated with night clubs, golf courses, and imported cars, housing is a popular item of mass consumption. It accounts for a larger portion of household expenditure than either savings or expenditure on education. Housing, more than clothing and food, seems to symbolize class distinctions in the cultural milieu of contemporary Taiwan. If the experience in other countries is a guide, such class-differentiated consumption patterns will probably become socially and politically offensive in Taiwan as well. Consequently the introduction of progressive consumption taxation conforms well to the relatively egalitarian pattern of income and the goals set for the future.

Future Research

We believe that the work of this volume, including the effort to derive general and specific policy conclusions from it, has demonstrated the desirability of integrating income distribution with the general framework of development theory. It also has demonstrated the complexity attached to many dimensions of the problem—dimensions that still are inadequately understood. We have not, moreover, even attempted to tackle some other issues, even though we recognize them to be important subjects for future analysis. Further investigation of the causation underlying the inequality of property income is one example.

By making a highly selective and inductive effort, we have tried to contribute to a less ad hoc and more analytical treatment of the distribution of family income as a dimension of development. By pointing out that at least one developing economy could "have its cake and eat it, too," we hope at least to make the tradeoff pessimists sit up and take notice. We have examined the whys and wherefores of that experience from a number of directions. We have concluded that the *way* transition growth is generated largely determines the levels of transition equity. By so doing we have perhaps contributed to the integrated deterministic theory of income distribution—a theory which still eludes us—and shed some light on the direction of policy choices that must be made in the meantime.

What, then, are the implications for future research? Good policies for income distribution must be based on good theory. The prime focus of theoretical research must therefore be to attempt to explain empirically observed realities in order to understand the causal nexus between growth and equity. At this stage of understanding, much of that effort still is inductive. Much attention still is paid to gathering, organizing, and processing data in accord with certain pretheoretical frameworks. The additive factor-components model and its combination with the linear regression technique illustrate the nature of these frameworks. Motivated by theoretical notions, they require a mathematical design that is broad enough for application to different types of problems. With more refined analytical tools, we can hope to separate the quantitatively important causes of inequality, such as access to educational opportunities, from the less important causes, such as sex discrimination. The policy focus could then be aimed at the important causes, and additional efforts could be directed at a determination of the feasibility and practicality of various policy options. Moreover it may be necessary to depart from subject areas familiar to the economist to those more tangential to traditional analysis. In this volume we hope merely to have demonstrated that it is feasible to make progress along these lines.

PART TWO

The Methodology of Gini Coefficient Analysis

THE SECOND PART OF THIS VOLUME is devoted to a systematic discussion of decomposition procedures and the derivation of decomposition formulas that use the Gini coefficient $[G_y]$ to measure the degree of inequality of a pattern of income distribution $[Y = (Y_1, Y_2, \ldots, Y_n)]$.[1] All decomposition equations used in part one amount to special cases developed in this part. All the formulas deduced can be applied to empirical analyses of the inequality of income distribution, as will be emphasized through the use of numerical examples that show the computation procedures involved. This part has five

1. Many authors have worked out and published Gini decomposition formulas. They include, but perhaps are not limited to, the following. N. Bhattacharya and B. Mahalanobis, "Regional Disparities in Household Consumption in India," *Journal of the American Statistical Association*, vol. 62, no. 317 (March 1967), pp. 143–61. V. M. Rao, "Two Decompositions of Concentration Ratio," *Journal of the Royal Statistical Society*, series A, vol. 132, pt. 3 (1969), pp. 418–25. Mahar Mangahas, "Income Inequality in the Philippines: A Decomposition Analysis," World Employment Programme, *Population and Employment Working Papers*, no. 12 (Geneva: International Labour Organisation, 1975). Graham Pyatt, "On the Interpretation and Disaggregation of Gini Coefficients," *Economic Journal*, vol. 86 (June 1976), pp. 243–55. Two other authors have published alternative indexes of inequality: Henri Theil, *Economics and Information Theory* (Amsterdam: North-Holland, 1967); Anthony B. Atkinson, "On the Measurement of Inequality," *Journal of Economic Theory*, vol. 2 (1970), pp. 244–63. The relatedness of their contributions to the work of this volume will be indicated where appropriate.

chapters:

- Basic Concepts
- Testing Hypotheses
- The General and Special Models of Additive Factor Components
- Applications and Extensions of the Models of Decomposition
- Regression Analysis, Homogeneous Groups, and Aggregation Error

Chapter eight presents an investigation of the alternative definitions of the Gini coefficient, as well as of the pseudo Gini coefficient, when Y is given. In chapter nine we formulate a problem of testing hypotheses when an observable quality characteristic—such as education with high, medium, and low values—is associated with variations in the income levels in Y. The ideas developed in these two chapters are essential for the analysis in chapters ten, eleven, and twelve.

Chapter ten is concerned with the derivation of decomposition formulas when Y has a finite number of additive factor components given by $W^i = (W_1^i, W_2^i, \ldots, W_n^i)$, where $i = 1, 2, \ldots, p$. Its purpose is to trace G_y to $G(W^i)$, the factor Gini coefficients defined for W^i. In addition to a general model, decomposition formulas are deduced for a linear model and a monotonic model, which are special cases of the general model when additional restrictions are postulated for W^i. Methods of approximation are developed when these restrictions are only approximately fulfilled, as often is the case in empirical work. Two other special cases are developed in chapter eleven. In one special case the sum of all values of W_j^i in one component W^i is assumed to be zero, leading to a model of "income components with observation error." In the other special case several factor components are assumed to be negative.

In chapter twelve a linear regression equation, estimated by the method of least squares, is combined with the model of additive factor components. Also in that chapter the analysis is directed at a situation in which Y is segmented into a finite number of subvectors:

$$Y = (Y^1, Y^2, \ldots, Y^q),$$

$$Y^i = (Y_1^i, Y_2^i, \ldots, Y_{n_i}^i), \qquad (i = 1, 2, \ldots, q)$$

where Y^i is interpreted as a homogeneous group. The purpose of this analysis is to trace G_y to $G(Y^i)$, the intragroup inequality, as well as to other effects. Finally the question of grouping error is addressed.

In empirical research on the problem of additive factor components, such as that in chapter three, the "grouped data" that often is used leads to a "grouping error" in the Gini coefficient. The problem is investigated as an application of the decomposition equation for homogeneous groups, and the possibility of future research on this issue is explored.

CHAPTER 8

Basic Concepts

THE PURPOSE of this chapter is to define the basic concepts used in this volume and to illuminate them with numerical examples and figures. First, the Gini coefficient is defined in relation to the Lorenz curve, as is conventional. Second, two alternative definitions of the Gini coefficient are presented and proved: one in relation to weighted income fractions; the other to the average gap between income fractions. Third, the pseudo Gini coefficient is defined in relation to the pseudo Lorenz curve, which obtains when incomes are not necessarily ranked in a monotonically nondecreasing order. These concepts constitute the foundation for the discourse on methodology in subsequent chapters.

Definition of the Gini Coefficient

Suppose there are n families with income Y_i ($i = 1, 2, \ldots, n$) and compute the income fractions y_i:

(8.1a) $Y = (Y_1, Y_2, \ldots, Y_n) \geq 0,$

(8.1b) $s_y = Y_1 + Y_2 + \ldots + Y_n > 0,$ and

(8.1c) $y = (y_1, y_2, \ldots, y_n) = (Y_1/s_y, Y_2/s_y, \ldots, Y_n/s_y),$ where

(8.1d) $y_1 + y_2 + \ldots + y_n = 1$ and

(8.1e) $Y_1 \leq Y_2 \leq \ldots \leq Y_n.$

In equation (8.1b) s_y is the sum of incomes for all families; in equation (8.1c) the income fractions $[y_i]$ form a system of weights.

Figure 8.1. *The Lorenz Curve*

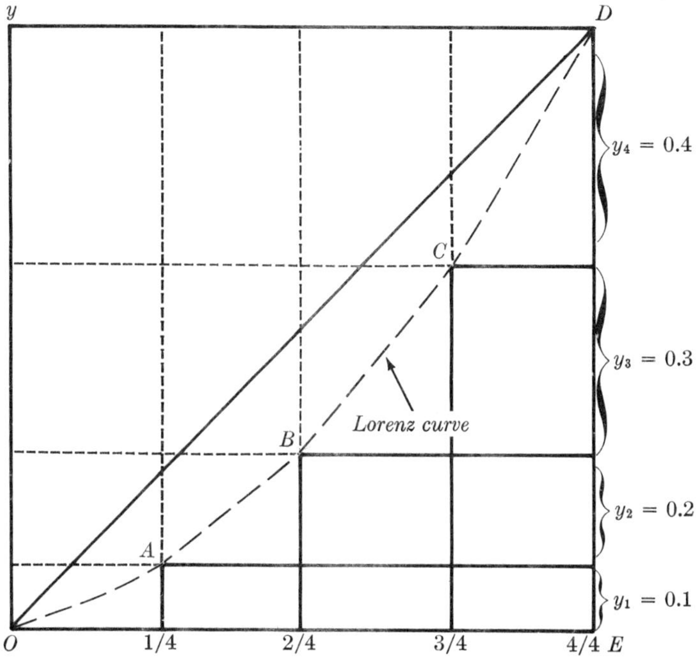

Source: Constructed by the authors.

Notice that family incomes are arranged in a monotonically non-decreasing order, such that the first family is poorest and the last family is wealthiest.

The Lorenz curve is a real-valued function defined on $(1/n, 2/n, \ldots, n/n)$:

$$L_Y(j/n) = y_1 + y_2 + \ldots + y_j. \quad (j = 1, 2, \ldots, n) \tag{8.2a}$$

For example, when n equals 4:

$$Y = (y_1, y_2, y_3, y_4) = (0.1, 0.2, 0.3, 0.4). \tag{8.2b}$$

If B denotes the area under the Lorenz curve of the unit square of figure 8.1, the Gini coefficient is defined as:

$$G_y = (1/2 - B)/(1/2) = 1 - 2B. \tag{8.3}$$

In words, G_y is the area above the Lorenz curve inside the triangle $0ED$, expressed as a fraction of that triangle's area, which is 1/2. For the numerical example in equation (8.2b) the Gini coefficient is 0.25. The Gini coefficient, according to its definition in equation (8.3), is a nonnegative fraction. It takes on extreme values of 1 to represent extreme inequality and zero to represent extreme equality. For these extremes:

(8.4a) $Y_1 = Y_2 = \ldots = Y_n$, which implies that $G_y = 0$, and

[*perfect equality*]

(8.4b) $Y_1 = Y_2 = \ldots = Y_{n-1} = 0$, which implies that $G_y = 1$.

[*perfect inequality*]

When equality is perfect, the Lorenz curve coincides with the diagonal $0D$ in figure 8.1. When inequality is perfect and n is large, the Lorenz curve coincides with the unit square's edge $0ED$.

Because the Gini coefficient of Y_i is defined in relation to income fractions $[y_i]$, the following result is elementary:

if:

(8.5a) $$Z = (kY_1, kY_2, \ldots, kY_n),$$

then:

(8.5b) $$G_z = G_y.$$

In words, if the incomes of all families change by a common multiple, the Gini coefficient will not change.

The Gini Coefficient as Related to the Rank Index of Y

The intuitive explanation of the geometrically defined Gini coefficient as a measure of income inequality can be seen from two alternative definitions, the first of which is presented in this section.

THEOREM 8.1. *The Gini coefficient of Y, as defined in equation (8.3), is:*

$$G_y = \alpha u_y - \beta, \quad \textit{where}$$

(*a*) $$\alpha = 2/n,$$

(*b*) $\beta = (n + 1)/n,$ *and*

(*c*) $u_y = \lambda_1 y_1 + \lambda_2 y_2 + \ldots + \lambda_n y_n,$ *where*

(*d*) $y_1 \leq y_2 \leq \ldots \leq y_n$ *and*

(*e*) $\lambda_1 = 1, \lambda_2 = 2, \ldots, \lambda_n = n.$

In this theorem λ_i is the income rank of the ith family. The term u_y is the weighted average of income ranks and will be referred to as the rank index of Y. Theorem 8.1 states that the Gini coefficient is a linear transformation of the rank index of Y. Using the figures from the numerical example in equation (8.2) gives:

(8.6a) $u_y = 1(0.1) + 2(0.2) + 3(0.3) + 4(0.4) = 3$ and

(8.6b) $G_y = (2/4)(3) - 5/4 = 0.25.$

To prove theorem 8.1 observe that the area above the Lorenz curve is:

$$1 - B = (1/n)(y_1/2 + y_2 + \ldots + y_n)$$
$$+ (1/n)(y_2/2 + y_3 + \ldots + y_n) + \ldots + (1/n)(y_n)$$
$$= (1/n)u_y - (1/n)(y_1 + y_2 + \ldots + y_n)/2$$

by theorem 8.1(c)

$$= (1/n)(u_y - 1/2) \quad \text{by equation (8.1d)}.$$

Thus:

$$G_y = 1 - 2B \quad \text{by equation (8.3)}$$
$$= 1 - 2[1 - (1/n)(u_y - 1/2)]$$
$$= 2u_y/n - (n + 1)/n.$$

This proves theorem 8.1 and provides the first alternative definition of the Gini coefficient.

The Gini Coefficient as the Average Fractional Gap

Consider the following numerical example of a pattern of monotonically ranked income fractions, as defined in equation (8.1c):

(8.7a) $y = (y_1, y_2, y_3, y_4, y_5) = (0.05, 0.10, 0.15, 0.30, 0.40),$

(8.7b) $0 \leq y_1 \leq y_2 \leq y_3 \leq y_4 \leq y_5,$ and

(8.7c) $1 = y_1 + y_2 + y_3 + y_4 + y_5.$

Now define the following fractional gaps:

$$(8.8)\quad \begin{bmatrix} y_1 - y_1 & y_2 - y_1 & y_3 - y_1 & y_4 - y_1 & y_5 - y_1 \\ 0 & y_2 - y_2 & y_3 - y_2 & y_4 - y_2 & y_5 - y_2 \\ 0 & 0 & y_3 - y_3 & y_4 - y_3 & y_5 - y_3 \\ 0 & 0 & 0 & y_4 - y_4 & y_5 - y_4 \\ 0 & 0 & 0 & 0 & y_5 - y_5 \end{bmatrix} = \begin{bmatrix} 0 & 0.05 & 0.10 & 0.25 & 0.35 \\ 0 & 0 & 0.05 & 0.20 & 0.30 \\ 0 & 0 & 0 & 0.15 & 0.25 \\ 0 & 0 & 0 & 0 & 0.10 \\ 0 & 0 & 0 & 0 & 0 \end{bmatrix}.$$

Because the values of y_i are monotonically ranked according to expression (8.7b), the elements of this matrix indicate all the non-negative income gaps between all possible pairs of families. Denote the sum of all these numbers by S_y, which in the general case of n families is defined as:

(8.9a) $S_y = \sum(y_i - y_j)$ for all $i \geq j.$

Using the figures from the numerical example in equation (8.8) gives:

$$(8.9b)\quad \begin{aligned} S_y &= 0.05 + 0.10 + 0.25 + 0.35 + 0.05 + 0.20 + 0.30 \\ &\quad + 0.15 + 0.25 + 0.10 \\ &= 1.8. \end{aligned}$$

A term such as $y_4 - y_2 = 0.20$ indicates the gap of income fractions between a wealthy family (the fourth) and a poor family (the second) and measures the extent or degree of inequality between them. In equation (8.9a) the sum of all fractional gaps is S_y. The average fractional gap for n families is S_y/n. When equality is perfect, as in equation (8.4a), the average fractional gap $[S_y/n]$ obviously is equal to zero. The following theorem states that the Gini coefficient is precisely the average fractional gap[1]:

THEOREM 8.2. *$G_y = S_y/n$, where S_y is defined as in equation (8.9a).*

Proof: Take the sum of positive and negative entries of the matrix on the left-hand side of equation (8.8) separately, which gives:

$$S_y = u_y - [ny_1 + (n-1)y_2 + \ldots + 1y_n] \quad \text{by theorem 8.1(c)}$$

$$= u_y - [ny_1 + ny_2 + \ldots + ny_n]$$
$$+ [0y_1 + 1y_2 + 2y_3 + \ldots + (n-1)y_n]$$

$$= u_y - n + [0y_1 + 1y_2 + 2y_3 + \ldots + (n-1)y_n \quad \text{by equation (8.1d)}$$

$$= u_y - n - 1 + (y_1 + y_2 + \ldots + y_n)$$
$$+ [0y_1 + 1y_2 + 2y_3 + \ldots + (n-1)y_n]$$

$$= u_y - n - 1 + u_y \quad \text{by theorem 8.1(c)}$$

$$= 2u_y - (n+1)$$

$$= n[(2/n)u_y - (n+1)/n] = nG_y \quad \text{by theorem 8.1.}$$

This completes the proof.

The numerical example in equation (8.7) can verify theorems 8.1 and 8.2, which posit that the Gini coefficient can be calculated as the average fractional gap:

$$G_y = S_y/n = 1.8/5 = 0.36,$$

1. Bhattacharya and Mahalanobis, in their analysis of regional disparity in household consumption, give the equivalence of the two definitions of the Gini coefficient. If, in their model, every region contains exactly one household, their special case becomes equivalent to the theorem stated here. N. Bhattacharya and B. Mahalanobis, "Regional Disparities in Household Consumption in India," *Journal of the American Statistical Association*, vol. 62, no. 317 (March 1967), p. 149.

or as a linear function of the rank index of Y:

$$u_y = 1(0.05) + 2(0.10) + 3(0.15) + 4(0.30) + 5(0.40) = 3.9;$$

$$G_y = (2/5)(3.9) - 6/5 = 0.36.$$

The Pseudo Gini Coefficient

Let $Y = (Y_1, Y_2, \ldots, Y_n)$ be an income distribution pattern which is not necessarily monotonically arranged—that is, which may not satisfy the conditions of expression (8.1e). Now define a pseudo Lorenz curve as:

$$L_y^s(j/n) = y_1 + y_2 + \ldots + y_j. \quad (j = 1, 2, \ldots, n) \tag{8.10}$$

For the following numerical example:

$$y = (y_1, y_2, y_3, y_4) = (0.2, 0.4, 0.1, 0.3), \tag{8.11}$$

the pseudo Lorenz curve is indicated by the curve $A'B'C'D'$ in figure 8.2. When $\bar{B}$ denotes the area under the pseudo Lorenz curve, a pseudo Gini coefficient can be defined in a way similar to equation (8.3):

$$\bar{G}_y = 1 - 2\bar{B}. \tag{8.12}$$

Notice that the only difference between the Gini coefficient defined in equation (8.3) and the pseudo Gini coefficient defined here is this: for G_y the terms of the expression $Y = (Y_1, Y_2, \ldots, Y_n)$ are arranged in a monotonically nondecreasing order, thus satisfying the conditions of expression (8.1e); for $\bar{G}_y$ they are not so arranged. Theorem 8.1 then rigorously implies:

THEOREM 8.3. *The pseudo Gini coefficient of Y is:*

$$\bar{G}_y = \alpha \bar{u}_y - \beta, \quad \textit{where}$$

$$\bar{u}_y = \lambda_1 y_1 + \lambda_2 y_2 + \ldots + \lambda_n y_n,$$

and where α, β, and λ_i are defined as in theorem 8.1.

The term $\bar{u}_y$ in theorem 8.3 will be referred to as the pseudo u index. To illustrate, the numerical example in equation (8.11) can be used to calculate the pseudo Gini coefficient:

$$\bar{u}_y = 1(0.2) + 2(0.4) + 3(0.1) + 4(0.3) = 2.5; \tag{8.13a}$$

$$\bar{G}_y = (2/4)(2.5) - 5/4 = 0. \tag{8.13b}$$

Figure 8.2. *The Pseudo Lorenz Curve*

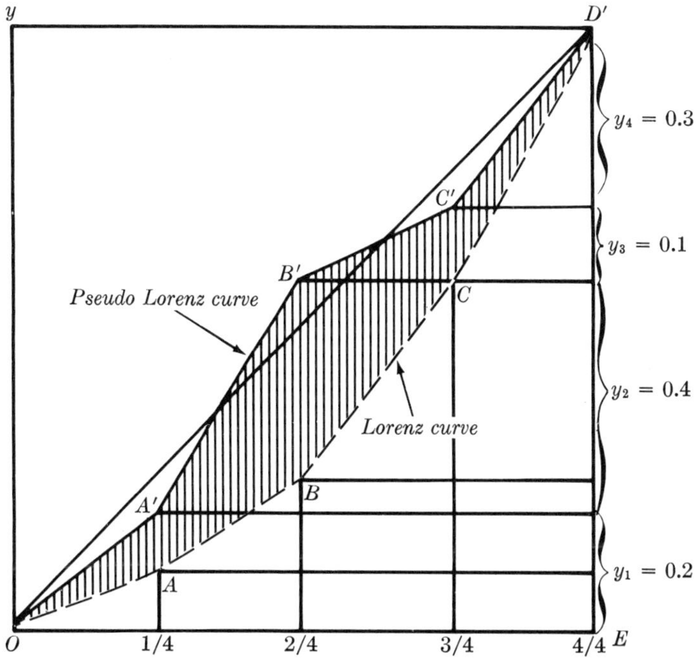

Source: Constructed by the authors.

The pseudo Gini coefficient, as defined, is an abstract, geometrical concept which will be applied in subsequent chapters.

When an income distribution pattern $[Y = (Y_1, Y_2, \ldots, Y_n)]$ is not necessarily monotonically arranged, there can be a permutation $[(i_1, i_2, \ldots, i_n)]$ of the n integers such that:

(8.14a) $$Y^* = (Y_{i_1}, Y_{i_2}, \ldots, Y_{i_n})$$

satisfies:

(8.14b) $$Y_{i_1} \geq Y_{i_2} \geq \ldots \geq Y_{i_n}.$$

In words, Y^* is a rearrangement of Y into a monotonically non-decreasing order. For example:

$$Y^* = (0.1, 0.2, 0.3, 0.4)$$

in the numerical example of equation (8.2b) is a rearrangement of:

$$Y = (0.2, 0.4, 0.1, 0.3)$$

in equation (8.11).

The difference between the Gini coefficient of Y [$G(Y^*)$] and the pseudo Gini coefficient [G_y] can be defined as a Gini error [E]:

$$E = G(Y^*) - \bar{G}_y \geq 0, \tag{8.15}$$

which always is nonnegative. From the numerical examples in equations (8.2b) and (8.11) it can be seen that:

$$E = G(Y^*) - \bar{G}_y = 0.25 - 0 = 0.25 \geq 0. \tag{8.16}$$

[see equations (8.6b) and (8.13b)]

Equation (8.16) shows that the Gini coefficient is at least as large as the pseudo Gini coefficient. The Gini error [E] will later be proved to be nonnegative.

A geometric interpretation of the Gini error is evident from:

$$\begin{aligned} E &= (1 - 2B) - (1 - 2\bar{B}) \quad \text{by equations (8.3) and (8.12)} \\ &= 2(\bar{B} - B). \end{aligned} \tag{8.17}$$

Thus the area between the pseudo Lorenz curve and the Lorenz curve is equal to one-half the value of the Gini error (see figure 8.2). In that figure the area corresponding to $\bar{B} - B$ is shaded. In figure 8.3 a pseudo Lorenz curve [$A''B''C''D''$] is shown for $y = (0.4, 0.3, 0.2, 0.1)$ which is in a reverse monotonic order, that is, a monotonically nonincreasing order. This curve is now rotationally symmetrical with the Lorenz curve $ABCD$ from figure 8.1 with respect to the 45-degree line OD''. Thus the shaded area in figure 8.3 is:

$$\bar{B} - B = 2A = 2(1/2 - B),$$

where A is the area between the Lorenz curve and the line OD'', and the Gini error becomes:

$$E = 2(\bar{B} - B) = 2(1 - 2B) = 2G(Y^*) \quad \text{by equation (8.3)}, \tag{8.18a}$$

which implies that:

$$\bar{G}(Y) = -G(Y^*) \quad \text{by equation (8.16)}. \tag{8.18b}$$

Figure 8.3. *The Pseudo Lorenz Curve for an Inverse Wage Pattern*

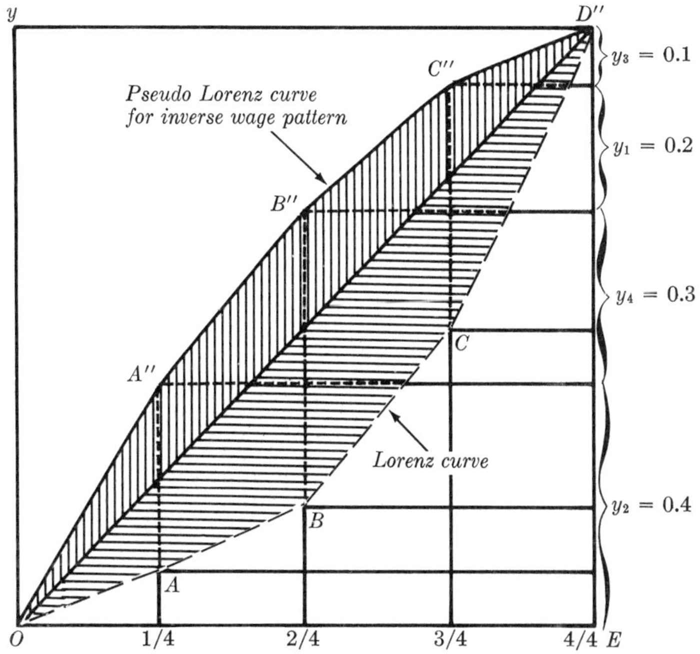

Source: Constructed by the authors.

For later reference, this equation can be summarized as:

THEOREM 8.4. *For a monotonically nonincreasing pattern of income distribution:*

$$\bar{G}(Y) = -G(Y^*),$$

that is, the pseudo Gini coefficient is the negative of the Gini coefficient.

CHAPTER 9

Testing Hypotheses

CERTAIN QUALITY CHARACTERISTICS, denoted by C, can be intuitively identified as relevant to the analysis of causes of income inequality:

$$(9.1) \qquad C = (c_1 \leq c_2 \leq \ldots \leq c_m).$$

$$\left[\begin{array}{c}\textit{ordinally ranked values}\\ \textit{of a quality characteristic}\\ \textit{affecting } G_y\end{array}\right]$$

For example, C can represent the sex characteristic and have values of c_1 for female and c_2 for male; it can represent the education characteristic and have values of c_1 for low education, c_2 for medium education, and c_3 for high education; or it can represent the age characteristic and have values of c_i, where i is the age of the head of household or income earner. Whenever C is given, the presumption —that is, the hypothesis—is that its values will affect the levels of family income. In such a situation the minimum information to be postulated is that the values $[c_i]$ are ordinally ranked attributes that contribute to the earning power of families. For the ranking in equation (9.1), c_1 is assumed to make the least contribution to the level of family income; c_m the greatest contribution. If C is education, the values of the education characteristic are assumed to contribute to higher income levels in an ascending order:

$$(9.2) \qquad c_1 \quad \leq \quad c_2 \quad \leq \quad c_3.$$

$$\left[\begin{array}{c}\textit{low}\\ \textit{education}\end{array}\right] \leq \left[\begin{array}{c}\textit{medium}\\ \textit{education}\end{array}\right] \leq \left[\begin{array}{c}\textit{high}\\ \textit{education}\end{array}\right]$$

Assume that such a quality characteristic as education is given

Table 9.1. *Numerical Example of Income Fractions, Income Ranks, and Education Ranks for Five Families*

Variable	*Family 1*	*Family 2*	*Family 3*	*Family 4*	*Family 5*
Income fraction[a]	$y_1 = 0.05$	$y_2 = 0.10$	$y_3 = 0.15$	$y_4 = 0.30$	$y_5 = 0.40$
Income rank	$\lambda_1 = 1$	$\lambda_2 = 2$	$\lambda_3 = 3$	$\lambda_4 = 4$	$\lambda_5 = 5$
Education rank	$r_1 = 5$	$r_2 = 4$	$r_3 = 1$	$r_4 = 2$	$r_5 = 3$
Value of education characteristic[b]	$c_3 = H$	$c_3 = H$	$c_1 = L$	$c_1 = L$	$c_2 = M$

Source: Constructed by the authors.
a. These values are from the numerical example in equation (8.6a) in chapter eight.
b. In accord with expression (9.2), c_1 and L stand for low education, c_2 and M for medium education, and c_3 and H for high education.

and that every family receives a value $[c_i]$ for that characteristic $[C]$. The n families can then be ranked with respect to C (table 9.1). In this table the first family receives the lowest income rank because it is the poorest; curiously it also receives the highest education rank because its income earner has the most education.

When the number of families $[n]$ is large and the number of characteristic values $[m]$ is small, the n families are classified in m education groups. Families belonging to the same group—that is, families with tied rank—are arbitrarily assigned a numerical ranking. In the numerical example, the first two families received the two highest education ranks: family one's education rank $[r_1]$ is 5; family two's $[r_2]$ is 4. The alternative way of assigning ranks to these two families is: $r_1 = 4$; $r_2 = 5$. In general the following permutations of the first n integers can stand for the characteristic ranking of the n families:

$$r = (r_1, r_2, \ldots, r_n), \tag{9.3}$$

and it can be hypothesized that a higher characteristic rank should lead to a higher income rank[1]:

HYPOTHESIS 9.1. *The relation $r_i > r_j$ implies that $y_i > y_j$ or $\lambda_i > \lambda_j$.*

1. Graham Pyatt of the World Bank has presented an ingenious interpretation of the Gini coefficient as the expected value of a game and demonstrated the usefulness of that interpretation to socioeconomic problems relevant to

If the characteristic is education, the hypothesis is that higher education should lead to higher income. Because the first two families in table 9.1 are the most educated, and yet the poorest, they clearly violate this hypothesis. The purpose of this chapter is to investigate how a hypothesis, such as hypothesis 9.1, can be systematically tested.

Testing Hypotheses by Supporting and Contradicting Gaps

Postulate the income fractions $[y_i]$, income ranks $[\lambda_i]$, and characteristic ranks $[r_i]$ as follows:

(9.4a) $y = (y_1, y_2, \ldots, y_n)$, where $y_1 \leq y_2 \leq \ldots \leq y_n$ and $\sum y_i = 1$;
[*income fractions*]

(9.4b) $\lambda = (\lambda_1, \lambda_2, \ldots, \lambda_n) = (1, 2, \ldots, n)$;
[*income ranks*]

(9.4c) $r = (r_1, r_2, \ldots, r_n)$, which is a permutation of $(1, 2, \ldots, n)$.
[*characteristic ranks*]

Notice that the pattern of income fractions $[y]$ is arranged in a monotonically nondecreasing order in accord with the conditions of expression (8.1e). Consequently the pattern of income ranks $[\lambda]$ is just the natural order of the first n integers. The pattern of characteristic ranks $[r]$ is a permutation of the first n integers, such that $r_i > r_j$ implies that the ith family should have a higher income than the jth family by null hypothesis 9.1.

When y is given as in equation (9.4a), the nonnegative income gaps $[y_i - y_j]$ between all pairs of families can be defined as in equation (8.8). When λ_i and r_i are given in addition, these income

income inequality, such as discrimination and migration. The approach adopted in this chapter is tantamount to an alternative interpretation of the decomposition of Gini coefficients in relation to testing a null hypothesis about the role of quality characteristics in the analysis of income distribution equality. This approach will be adhered to throughout this chapter. Graham Pyatt, "On the Interpretation and Disaggregation of Gini Coefficients," *Economic Journal*, vol. 86 (June 1976), pp. 243–55.

gaps can be classified into two types: a type that supports the hypothesis; a type that contradicts it. In the numerical example of table 9.1, the income gap between family one and family three clearly contradicts the hypothesis. On the other hand, the income gap between family four and family five clearly supports the hypothesis. Use that numerical example to see how the two types of gap can be systematically identified, and construct the following matrix from the characteristic ranks in equation (9.4c):

$$
(9.5)\qquad
\begin{array}{c}
 \\ r_1 \\ r_2 \\ r_3 \\ r_4 \\ r_5
\end{array}
\begin{array}{c}
\begin{array}{ccccc} r_1 & r_2 & r_3 & r_4 & r_5 \end{array} \\
\begin{bmatrix}
0 & r_2 - r_1 & r_3 - r_1 & r_4 - r_1 & r_5 - r_1 \\
 & 0 & r_3 - r_2 & r_4 - r_2 & r_5 - r_2 \\
 & & 0 & r_4 - r_3 & r_5 - r_3 \\
 & & & 0 & r_5 - r_4 \\
 & & & & 0
\end{bmatrix}
\end{array}
=
\begin{bmatrix}
0 & \mathit{-1} & \mathit{-4} & \mathit{-3} & \mathit{-2} \\
 & 0 & \mathit{-3} & \mathit{-2} & \mathit{-1} \\
 & & 0 & 1 & 2 \\
 & & & 0 & 1 \\
 & & & & 0
\end{bmatrix}.
$$

An element of this matrix indicates the difference, or gap, between the characteristic ranks of a pair of families. Because the income fractions $[y_i]$ are monotonically ranked in accord with equation (9.4b), a negative entry in this matrix indicates that the hypothesis is contradicted; a positive entry, that it is supported. In the right-hand matrix, all negative entries are in italics. They indicate all pairs of families which contradict the hypothesis. [In the matrix of equation (8.8) the corresponding family pairs are also in italics.] The other entries indicate the supporting gaps.

Let S^+ denote the sum of all supporting gaps and S^- the sum of all contradicting gaps. Formally the definitions of S^+ and S^- thus are:

(9.6a) $S_y = S^+ + S^-$, where

(9.6b) $S^- = \sum (y_i - y_j) \geq 0$ for $i > j$ and $r_i < r_j$, and

[*contradicting gaps*]

(9.6c) $S^+ = \sum (y_i - y_j) \geq 0$ for $i > j$ and $r_i > r_j$.

[*supporting gaps*]

Equation (9.6a) shows that S_y, which is defined in equation (8.9a) as the sum of all fractional gaps, is partitioned into two nonnegative components, S^+ and S^-. Figures from the numerical example of table 9.1 give:

(9.7a) $S_y = 1.3 + 0.5 = 1.8$, where

(9.7b) $S^- = 0.05 + 0.10 + 0.25 + 0.35 + 0.05 + 0.20 + 0.30 = 1.3$ and

(9.7c) $S^+ = 0.15 + 0.25 + 0.10 = 0.5$.

In the example, S^- is larger than S^+, a relation which indeed subjects to doubt the hypothesis that education contributes to income-earning.

Gini Decomposition for Hypothesis Testing

Theorem 8.2 showed the Gini coefficient to be the average fractional gap [S_y/n]. This definition, or interpretation, is quite independent of any quality characteristic [C], as postulated in equation (9.1). When a quality characteristic [C] and a corresponding characteristic rank [r] are given, the result in equation (9.6) immediately shows that the Gini coefficient can be decomposed into an average supporting gap [s^+] and an average contradicting gap [s^-]:

(9.8a) $G_y = s^+ + s^-$ by equation (9.6) and theorem 8.2, where

(9.8b) $s^+ = S^+/n \geq 0$ and

[*average supporting gap*]

(9.8c) $s^- = S^-/n \geq 0$.

[*average contradicting gap*]

The values in equation (9.7) give:

(9.9a) $G_y = S_y/n = 0.36 = s^+ + s^- = 0.10 + 0.26 = 0.36$, where

(9.9b) $s^+ = S^+/n = 0.5/5 = 0.10$ and

[*average supporting gap*]

(9.9c) $s^- = S^-/n = 1.3/5 = 0.26.$

[*average contradicting gap*]

G_y can now be interpreted as the "total variation" of y_i. Before a characteristic is introduced, all variations $[y_i - y_j]$ are unexplained. After such a characteristic as education or age is introduced, a part of the variation, corresponding to s^+, can be explained by that characteristic; the other part, corresponding to s^-, cannot be explained by that characteristic. In fact, s^- reduces the explanatory power of s^+.

Net Supporting Gap

For testing the hypothesis, it is natural to find out the comparative magnitudes of s^+ and s^-. If s^+ is much larger than s^-—that is, if the average supporting gap overwhelms the average contradicting gap—we would tend to accept such a null hypothesis as 9.1. Thus it is natural to define a net supporting gap as:

(9.10) $$N = s^+ - s^-,$$

[*net supporting gap*]

and to accept the null hypothesis when N is positive, reject it when N is negative, or regard it as irrelevant when N is close to zero. The purpose of this section is to show that N is precisely the pseudo Gini coefficient defined in theorem 8.3 of chapter eight. Recall that a pseudo Gini coefficient $[\bar{G}(Y)]$ can be defined for any pattern of income $[Y = (Y_1, Y_2, \ldots, Y_n)]$ which is not necessarily monotonically ranked.

When y, λ, and r of equation (9.4) are given, the following weighted ranks can be defined:

(9.11a) $$u_y = 1y_1 + 2y_2 + \ldots + ny_n;$$

[*weighted income rank*]

(9.11b) $$\bar{u}_y = r_1y_1 + r_2y_2 + \ldots + r_ny_n.$$

[*weighted characteristic rank*]

Respectively applying theorems 8.1 and 8.3 gives:

(9.12a) $$G_y = (2/n)u_y - (n+1)/n \quad \text{and}$$

[*Gini coefficient*]

(9.12b) $$\bar{G}_y = (2/n)\bar{u}_y - (n-1)/n.$$

[*pseudo Gini coefficient*]

To illustrate with figures from the numerical example:

(9.13a) $$u_y = 1(0.05) + 2(0.10) + 3(0.15) + 4(0.30) + 5(0.40) = 3.9;$$

(9.13b) $$\bar{u}_y = 5(0.05) + 4(0.10) + 1(0.15) + 2(0.30) + 3(0.40) = 2.6$$
$$= \mathit{1(0.15) + 2(0.30) + 3(0.40) + 4(0.10) + 5(0.05)} = 2.6.$$

Hence:

(9.14a) $$G_y = (2/5)(3.9) - 6/5 = 0.36;$$

(9.14b) $$\bar{G}_y = (2/5)(2.6) - 6/5 = -0.16.$$

Notice that the italicized expression in equation (9.13b) is merely a rearrangement of the terms of $\bar{u}_y$—the weighted characteristic rank of equation (9.11b)—into an ordering by the characteristic rank. Now the income fractions (y_i) are not monotonically arranged. Thus $\bar{G}_y$ in equations (9.12b) and (9.14b) indeed is the pseudo Gini coefficient as defined in theorem 8.3 of chapter eight.

By comparing equation (9.13) with equation (9.7b) it can be seen that the contradicting gap [$S^- = 1.3$] is the difference between the weighted income rank [$u_y = 3.9$] and the weighted characteristic rank [$\bar{u}_y = 2.6$]. This relation may be stated as:

LEMMA 9.1. $S^- = u_y - \bar{u}_y$.

Proof: $$S^- = \sum (y_i - y_j) \quad \text{for} \quad i > j \quad \text{and} \quad r_i < r_j$$
$$= d_1y_1 + d_2y_2 + \ldots + d_ny_n$$
$$= (u_1 - v_1)y_1 + (u_2 - v_2)y_2 + \ldots + (u_n - v_n)y_n.$$

It can be seen that the coefficient d_i of y_i is the difference between u_i and v_i, where u_i is the number of families with an income rank lower than the ith family and a characteristic rank higher than the ith family, and where v_i is the number of families with an income rank higher than the ith family and a characteristic rank lower than the ith family. It is obvious that:

$$r_i = \lambda_i + v_i - u_i ,$$

for in order to compute the characteristic rank $[r_i]$ of the ith family from its income rank $[\lambda_i]$, u_i must be subtracted from λ_i and v_i must be added to λ_i. Thus:

$$d_i = u_i - v_i = \lambda_i - r_i .$$

Hence:

$$\begin{aligned} S^- &= (\lambda_1 - r_1)y_1 + (\lambda_2 - r_2)y_2 + \ldots + (\lambda_n - r_n)y_n \\ &= u_y - \bar{u}_y . \end{aligned}$$

This completes the proof.

Lemma 9.1 will now be used to prove the following theorem, which states that the net supporting gap $[N = s^+ - s^-]$ defined in equation (9.10) is precisely the pseudo Gini coefficient.

THEOREM 9.1. $\bar{G}_y = s^+ - s^-$.

Proof:
$$\begin{aligned} s^- &= S_y^-/n \quad \text{by equation (9.8c)} \\ &= 1/n[u_y - \bar{u}_y] \quad \text{by lemma 9.1} \\ &= [(\langle 2/n \rangle u_y - \langle n+1 \rangle/n) - (\langle 2/n \rangle \bar{u}_y - \langle n+1 \rangle /n)]/2 \\ &= (G_y - \bar{G}_y)/2 \quad \text{by equation (9.12)} \\ &= (s^+ + s^- - \bar{G}_y)/2 \quad \text{by equation (9.8a)}; \end{aligned}$$

$$s^+ + s^- - \bar{G}_y = 2s^-.$$

Thus:

$$\bar{G}_y = s^+ - s^-.$$

This completes the proof.

Theorem 9.1 states that the pseudo Gini coefficient is the difference between the average supporting gap and the average contradicting gap and thus is the net supporting gap. The hypothesis is supported when $\bar{G}_y$ is positive—that is, when the supporting gaps $[S^+]$ overwhelm the contradicting gaps $[S^-]$. Similarly the hypothesis is rejected when $\bar{G}_y$ is negative.

In summary:

(9.15a) $G_y = s^+ + s^-;$

(9.15b) $\bar{G}_y = s^+ - s^-;$

(9.15c) $G_y = \bar{G}_y + 2s^-,$ or $E = G_y - \bar{G}_y = 2s^- \geq 0.$

Thus the Gini coefficient $[G_y]$ is the sum of the average supporting and contradicting gaps; the pseudo Gini coefficient $[\bar{G}_y]$ is their difference. In addition, the difference between G_y and $\bar{G}_y$ is $2s^-$, which always is nonnegative. This proves that the Gini error $[E]$ is nonnegative, as was stated in equation (8.16).

Graphic Summary of the Gini and Pseudo Gini Coefficients

It has been shown that the Gini coefficient and the pseudo Gini coefficient can be defined when the income fractions $[y]$, income ranks $[\lambda]$, and characteristic ranks $[r]$ of equation (9.4) are given. The relation between G_y and $\bar{G}_y$ is graphically summarized in this section.

Let s^+ be measured on the horizontal axis in figure 9.1 and s^- on the vertical axis. Because the value of G_y lies between zero and one, all possible combinations of the coordinates (s^+, s^-) can be represented by points in the equilateral triangle OAB $(OA = OB = 1)$. The parallel and negatively sloped 45-degree lines represent iso Gini coefficient contour lines. Thus all points on the line FF'', for example, have a Gini coefficient equal to OF. The line AB represents perfect inequality—that is, $G_y = 1$.

Also in figure 9.1 the 45-degree line OR_3 divides the triangle OAB into two regions: r^+ lies below OR_3; r^- lies above OR_3. A point such as P in the region r^+ indicates that the average supporting gap $[s^+]$ overwhelms the average contradicting gap $[s^-]$ and hence that empirical evidence supports a hypothesis such as 9.1. A point such as Q on or near OR_3 indicates that empirical evidence does not support the hypothesis. A point such as T in the region r^- indicates that empirical evidence contradicts the hypothesis.

The straight lines parallel to OR_3 are the equal pseudo Gini contour lines. On the line FF'', the value of the pseudo Gini is OF. The

Figure 9.1. *Iso Gini Coefficient Contour Lines*
($OA = OB = 1$)

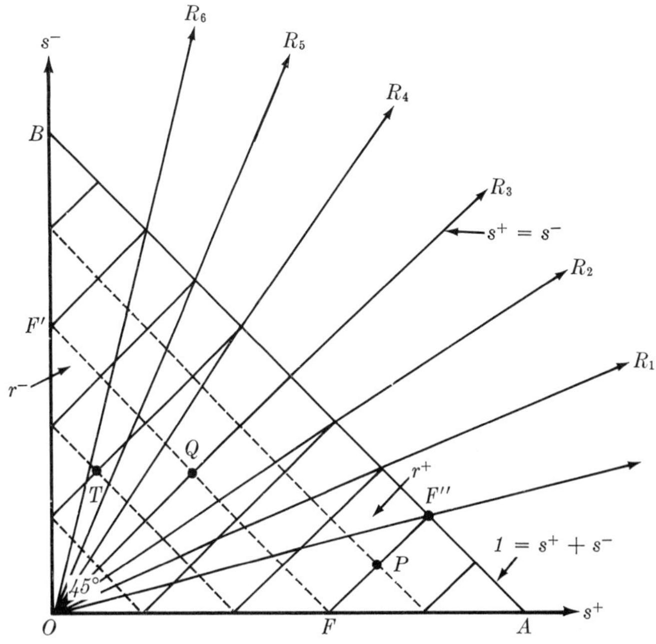

Source: Constructed by the authors.

pseudo Gini coefficient is positive in r^+ and negative in r^-. Furthermore it can be seen that:

$$-1 \leq \bar{G}_y \leq 1. \tag{9.16}$$

A higher positive value of $\bar{G}_y$ is represented by a contour line closer to point A; a higher negative value, by a contour line closer to point B. A positive value of $\bar{G}_y$ close to 1 would therefore indicate that the hypothesis is strongly supported; a negative value close to -1, that the hypothesis is strongly contradicted.

Two extreme cases are to be mentioned:

(9.17a) $r_i = \lambda_i$, which implies that $s^- = 0$ and $\bar{G}_y = G_y = s^+$;

(9.17b) $r_i = n - (i + 1)$, which implies that $s^+ = 0$ and $\bar{G}_y = - G_y = s^-$.

The economic interpretation of equation (9.17a) is that the correlation between the income rank [λ_i] and characteristic rank [r_i] is perfect and positive. In this case the contradicting gap vanishes and the Gini coefficient equals the pseudo Gini coefficient [see equations (9.11) and (9.17)]. Points on the horizontal axis $0A$ in figure 9.1 represent this special case. The economic interpretation of equation (9.17b) is that the correlation between the income rank [λ_i] and characteristic rank [r_i] is perfect and negative. The supporting gap vanishes, and the pseudo Gini coefficient equals the negative value of the Gini coefficient. Points on the vertical axis $0B$ represent this special case (see theorem 8.4).

Correlation Characteristics

Now express the pseudo Gini coefficient as a fraction of the Gini coefficient:

(9.18a) $$R = \bar{G}_y/G_y = \frac{s^+ - s^-}{s^+ + s^-} \quad \text{by equation (9.15);}$$

(9.18b) $$R = \frac{s^+ - s^-}{s^+ + s^-} = \frac{1 - s^-/s^+}{1 + s^-/s^+}.$$

In economic terms R is the net supporting gap expressed as a fraction of the "total gap"—that is, as a fraction of the sum of the average supporting and contradicting gaps. To arrive at another interpretation of R, the ordinary correlation coefficient $r(x,y)$ between two vectors, x and y, is introduced to define:

(9.19a) $$r(y,\lambda) = \operatorname{cov}(y,\lambda)/\sigma_y\sigma_r \quad \text{for} \quad y = (y_1, y_2, \ldots, y_n) \text{ and } \lambda = (1, 2, \ldots, n);$$

(9.19b) $$r(y,r) = \operatorname{cov}(y,r)/\sigma_y\sigma_r \quad \text{for} \quad r = (r_1, r_2, \ldots, r_n);$$

(9.19c) $$\sigma_r = \sigma_\lambda.$$

Therefore $r(y,\lambda)$ is the ordinary correlation coefficient between the family income fractions and the income rank [λ]; $r(y,r)$ is the ordinary correlation coefficient between those fractions and the characteristic rank [r]. Notice that equation (9.19c) is valid because both terms represent the standard deviation of the first n integers. In equations (9.19a) and (9.19b) the notation $\operatorname{cov}(x,y)$

stands for the covariance between x and y. This leads to the following theorem:

THEOREM 9.2. $R = r(y,r)/r(y,\lambda)$.

Proof: We know that:

$$\bar{y} = 1/n \quad \text{by equation (8.1d);}$$

$$\bar{r} = \bar{\lambda} = (1 + 2 + \ldots + n)/n = n(n + 1)/2n = (n + 1)/2;$$

$$\begin{aligned} \text{cov}(y,r) &= \sum (y_i - \bar{y})(r_i - \bar{r}) = \sum y_i r_i - n\bar{y}\bar{r} \\ &= \bar{u}_y - n\bar{y}\bar{r} \quad \text{by equation (9.11b)} \\ &= \bar{u}_y - n(n + 1)/2n \\ &= \bar{u}_y - (n + 1)/2 = (n/2)[(2/n)\bar{u}_y - (n + 1)/n] \\ &= (n/2)\bar{G}_y \quad \text{by equation (9.12b).} \end{aligned}$$

Similarly:

$$\text{cov}(y,\lambda) = (n/2)G_y.$$

Thus:

$$\begin{aligned} r(y,r)/r(y,\lambda) &= [(n/2)\bar{G}_y/\sigma_y\sigma_r]/[(n/2)G_y/\sigma_y\sigma_\lambda] \quad \text{by equation (9.19)} \\ &= \bar{G}_y/G_y \\ &= R \quad \text{by equation (9.18).} \end{aligned}$$

This completes the proof.

Therefore R can also be considered as a ratio of two ordinary correlation coefficients—that is, $r(y,r)$ expressed as a fraction of $r(y,\lambda)$.[2] From equation (9.18b) it can be seen that the value of R is completely determined by the ratio of s^- to s^+. In figure 9.1 the radial lines OR_1, OR_2, ... , OR_6 then represent iso R contour lines. In the region r^+, R is positive, and a radial line such as OR_1 takes on a value close to 1. In the region r^-, R is negative and a radial line such as OR_6 takes on a value close to -1.

It directly follows from expression (9.16) and equation (9.18)

2. There thus are two alternative interpretations of R as defined in equation (9.18) and theorem (9.2). Pyatt first suggested the second interpretation in a private discussion with the authors.

that R lies between 1 and -1. Two types of case—a positive R and a negative R—can be identified:

(9.20a) $-1 \leq R \leq 1;$

(9.20b) $R \geq 0$ if and only if $0 \leq \bar{G}_y$ or $s^+ \geq s^-;$

[*positive R*]

(9.20c) $R < 0$ if and only if $\bar{G}_y < 0$ or $s^+ \leq s^-.$

[*negative R*]

In words, R is positive if and only if the pseudo Gini coefficient is positive. When R is positive, the average supporting gap [s^+] overwhelms the average contradicting gap [s^-]. The ratio of $\bar{G}_y$ to G_y is R. Their sum is:

(9.21a) $$G_y + \bar{G}_y = G_y(1 + R) = 2s^+ \geq 0,$$

and their difference is:

(9.21b) $$G_y - \bar{G}_y = G_y(1 - R) = 2s^- \geq 0.$$

Thus their sum is twice the average supporting gap, or $2s^+$; their difference is twice the average contradicting gap, or $2s^-$. Both are nonnegative numbers.

So far certain basic ideas have been developed for testing hypotheses when the pattern of income of n families is associated with one ordinal characteristic [C]. This method can be applied to other related empirical problems of hypothesis testing. But our purpose is to apply these ideas to the derivation of the various decomposition formulas used in the earlier chapters of this volume.

CHAPTER 10

The General and Special Models of Additive Factor Components

AS NOTED EARLIER, a situation is frequently encountered in which family income is the sum of several types of income. Consider the example used in chapter three with five families and three income components (table 10.1). In this example the factor income components correspond to components of the functional distribution of income. In another example family income may come from such sources as industry and agriculture. In short, a components problem is formed once there is a classification of the sources of income. Generally, when there are n families and p income components, the components problem is summarized by:

$$Y_i = W_i^1 + W_i^2 + \dots + W_i^p; \quad (i = 1, 2, \dots, n) \tag{10.1a}$$

$$S_i = W_1^i + W_2^i + \dots + W_n^i; \quad (i = 1, 2, \dots, p) \tag{10.1b}$$

$$s_y = S_1 + S_2 + \dots + S_p; \tag{10.1c}$$

$$\phi_i = S_i/s_y; \tag{10.1d}$$

$$1 = \phi_1 + \phi_2 + \dots + \phi_p; \tag{10.1e}$$

$$Y_1 \leq Y_2 \leq \dots \leq Y_n. \tag{10.1f}$$

In equation (10.1a) the total income $[Y_i]$ of the ith family has p components. In equation (10.1d) the values of ϕ_i $(i = 1, 2, \dots, p)$ form a system of weights and correspond to the fraction of the ith type of income received by all families. It will be assumed that total family income $[Y_i]$ is arranged in a monotonically nondecreasing order as in equation (10.1f).

Table 10.1. *Numerical Example of the Problem of Additive Factor Components*

Item	*Family 1*	*Family 2*	*Family 3*	*Family 4*	*Family 5*	*Total*
Wage income	3	1	17	15	9	45
Wage income rank	2	1	5	4	3	—
Property income	0	0	2	8	25	35
Property income rank	1	2	3	4	5	—
Transfer income	8	12	0	0	0	20
Transfer income rank	4	5	3	2	1	—
Total income	11	13	19	23	34	100
Total income rank	1	2	3	4	5	—

— Not applicable.
Source: Constructed by the authors.

The components problem can be restated in vector notation:

(10.2a) $$Y = W^1 + W^2 + \ldots + W^p, \quad \text{where}$$

(10.2b) $$Y = (Y_1, Y_2, \ldots, Y_n) \quad \text{and}$$

[*pattern of total income*]

(10.2c) $$W^i = (W^i_1, W^i_2, \ldots, W^i_n). \qquad (i = 1, 2, \ldots, p)$$

[*pattern of the* ith *factor component*]

Denote the Gini coefficient of Y by $G(Y)$ or G_y, and the Gini coefficient of W^i by $G(W^i)$ or G_i. The basic purpose of the approach using factor income components is to investigate the relations between the total Gini [G_y] and the factor Ginis [G_i].

Decomposition of G_y into Pseudo Factor Ginis

When the total income pattern [Y] is monotonically arranged, a particular factor component [W^i] may not be monotonically arranged (see table 10.1). Thus, to see how the earlier analysis can contribute to the understanding of the factor components problem, it is natural to define for each factor component a pseudo factor Gini $[\bar{G}_i]$ in which the exogenously postulated characteristic $[C]$ is the total income rank $[\lambda]$:

(10.3a) $\bar{G}_i = (2/n)\bar{u}_i - (n+1)/n$ by theorem 8.3, where

(10.3b) $\bar{u}_i = \lambda_1 w_1^i + \lambda_2 w_2^i + \ldots + \lambda_n w_n^i$, where $(i = 1, 2, \ldots, n)$

(10.3c) $\lambda_i = i$,

(10.3d) $w_j^i = W_j^i/S_i$, and

(10.3e) $w_1^i + w_2^i + \ldots + w_n^i = 1$.

From the discussion in chapter nine and from theorem 9.1 in particular, it can be seen that the pseudo factor Gini $[\bar{G}_i]$ is the net supporting gap $[N]$ when the total income rank $[\lambda_i]$ is used as a quality characteristic to explain the variation of a factor income component.

This definition of the pseudo factor Gini leads to:

THEOREM 10.1. *The Gini coefficient is the weighted average of the pseudo factor Ginis, that is:*

$$G_y = \phi_1\bar{G}_1 + \phi_2\bar{G}_2 + \ldots + \phi_p\bar{G}_p,$$

where the distributive shares $[\phi_i]$ defined in equation (10.1d) are the weights.

Proof: By theorem 8.1(c) the u index of Y is:

$$\begin{aligned}
u_y &= \lambda_1 y_1 + \lambda_2 y_2 + \ldots + \lambda_n y_n \\
&= \lambda_1[\phi_1(W_1^1/S^1) + \phi_2(W_1^2/S^2) + \ldots + \phi_r(W_1^p/S^r)] \\
&\quad + \lambda_2[\phi_1(W_2^1/S^1) + \phi_2(W_2^2/S^2) + \ldots + \phi_r(W_2^p/S^r)] \\
&\quad + \ldots + \lambda_n[\phi_1(W_n^1/S^1) + \phi_2(W_n^2/S^2) + \ldots + \phi_r(W_n^p/S^r)] \\
&= \phi_1[\lambda_1(W_1^1/S^1) + \lambda_2(W_2^1/S^1) + \ldots + \lambda_n(W_n^1/S^1)] \\
&\quad + \phi_2[\lambda_1(W_1^2/S^2) + \lambda_2(W_2^2/S^2) + \ldots + \lambda_n(W_n^2/S^2)] \\
&\quad + \ldots + \phi_p[\lambda_1(W_1^p/S^p) + \lambda_2(W_2^p/S^p) + \ldots + \lambda_n(W_n^p/S^p)] \\
&= \phi_1\bar{u}_1 + \phi_2\bar{u}_2 + \ldots + \phi_p\bar{u}_p \quad \text{by equation (10.1b)},
\end{aligned}$$

where $\bar{u}_i$ is the pseudo u index of the ith factor component $[W^i]$.

Table 10.2. *Gini Decomposition by Pseudo Factor Ginis, 1964–72*

Model and variable	*Notation*	*1964*	*1966*	*1968*
All households				
Total Gini	G_y	0.321	0.323	0.326
Pseudo wage Gini	$\bar{G}_w$	0.237	0.270	0.293
Pseudo property Gini	$\bar{G}_\pi$	0.449	0.410	0.459
Pseudo agricultural Gini	$\bar{G}_a$	0.354	0.341	0.178
Pseudo miscellaneous Gini	$\bar{G}_m$	0.256	0.302	0.363
Wage share	ϕ_w	0.432	0.476	0.507
Property share	ϕ_π	0.240	0.256	0.278
Agricultural share	ϕ_a	0.275	0.212	0.152
Miscellaneous share	ϕ_m	0.052	0.057	0.063
Wage correlation	$R_w = \bar{G}_w/G_w$	1.000	1.000	1.000
Property correlation	$R_\pi = \bar{G}_\pi/G_\pi$	1.000	1.000	0.997
Agricultural correlation	$R_a = \bar{G}_a/G_a$	0.999	1.000	0.979
Urban households				
Total Gini	G_y	0.329	0.324	0.330
Pseudo wage Gini	$\bar{G}_w$	n.a.	0.280	0.273
Pseudo property Gini	$\bar{G}_\pi$	n.a.	0.419	0.425
Pseudo agricultural Gini	$\bar{G}_a$	n.a.	0.256	0.311
Pseudo miscellaneous Gini	$\bar{G}_m$	n.a.	0.273	0.337
Wage share	ϕ_w	0.573	0.593	0.567
Property share	ϕ_π	0.323	0.322	0.337
Agricultural share	ϕ_a	0.037	0.022	0.029
Miscellaneous share	ϕ_m	n.a.	0.064	0.067
Wage correlation	$R_w = \bar{G}_w/G_w$	n.a.	1.000	1.000
Property correlation	$R_\pi = \bar{G}_\pi/G_\pi$	n.a.	1.000	1.000
Agricultural correlation	$R_a = \bar{G}_a/G_a$	n.a.	0.959	0.990
Rural households				
Total Gini	G_y	0.308	0.320	0.284
Pseudo wage Gini	$\bar{G}_w$	n.a.	0.187	0.187
Pseudo property Gini	$\bar{G}_\pi$	n.a.	0.332	0.278
Pseudo agricultural Gini	$\bar{G}_a$	n.a.	0.353	0.337
Pseudo miscellaneous Gini	$\bar{G}_m$	n.a.	0.410	0.365

1970	*1971*	*1972*	*Notation*	*Model and variable*
				All households
0.293	0.295	0.290	G_y	Total Gini
0.278	0.273	0.260	$\bar{G}_w$	Pseudo wage Gini
0.428	0.427	0.424	$\bar{G}_\pi$	Pseudo property Gini
0.060	0.107	0.106	$\bar{G}_a$	Pseudo agricultural Gini
0.354	0.301	0.324	$\bar{G}_m$	Pseudo miscellaneous Gini
0.507	0.545	0.590	ϕ_w	Wage share
0.256	0.242	0.258	ϕ_π	Property share
0.131	0.102	0.103	ϕ_a	Agricultural share
0.068	0.060	0.050	ϕ_m	Miscellaneous share
1.000	1.000	1.000	$R_w = \bar{G}_w/G_w$	Wage correlation
1.000	1.000	1.000	$R_\pi = \bar{G}_\pi/G_\pi$	Property correlation
0.910	0.961	0.958	$R_a = \bar{G}_a/G_a$	Agricultural correlation
				Urban households
0.279	0.279	0.281	G_y	Total Gini
0.233	0.240	0.235	$\bar{G}_w$	Pseudo wage Gini
0.369	0.399	0.387	$\bar{G}_\pi$	Pseudo property Gini
0.154	0.247	0.168	$\bar{G}_a$	Pseudo agricultural Gini
0.329	0.271	0.280	$\bar{G}_m$	Pseudo miscellaneous Gini
0.602	0.650	0.634	ϕ_w	Wage share
0.302	0.268	0.298	ϕ_π	Property share
0.029	0.026	0.024	ϕ_a	Agricultural share
0.073	0.058	0.047	ϕ_m	Miscellaneous share
1.000	1.000	1.000	$R_w = \bar{G}_w/G_w$	Wage correlation
1.000	1.000	1.000	$R_\pi = \bar{G}_\pi/G_\pi$	Property correlation
0.885	0.906	0.879	$R_a = \bar{G}_a/G_a$	Agricultural correlation
				Rural households
0.277	0.291	0.284	G_y	Total Gini
0.204	0.220	0.238	$\bar{G}_w$	Pseudo wage Gini
0.359	0.337	0.348	$\bar{G}_\pi$	Pseudo property Gini
0.314	0.318	0.298	$\bar{G}_a$	Pseudo agricultural Gini
0.282	0.396	0.434	$\bar{G}_m$	Pseudo miscellaneous Gini

(Table continues on the following pages)

Table 10.2 (*Continued*)

Model and variable	*Notation*	*1964*	*1966*	*1968*
Wage share	ϕ_w	0.213	0.202	0.323
Property share	ϕ_π	0.112	0.100	0.099
Agricultural share	ϕ_a	0.647	0.660	0.526
Miscellaneous share	ϕ_m	n.a.	0.039	0.052
Wage correlation	$R_w = \bar{G}_w/G_w$	n.a.	0.968	0.995
Property correlation	$R_\pi = \bar{G}_\pi/G_\pi$	n.a.	0.994	1.000
Agricultural correlation	$R_a = \bar{G}_a/G_a$	n.a.	1.000	1.000

n.a. Not available.
Note: Compare this table with table 3.2 in chapter three.
Sources: Calculated from DGBAS, *Report on the Survey of Family Income and Expenditure,* 1964, 1966, 1968, 1970, 1971, and 1972.

Thus the Gini coefficient of total income $[Y]$ by theorem 8.1 is:

$$\begin{aligned} G_y &= (2/n)u_y - (n+1)/n \\ &= (2/n)[\phi_1\bar{u}_1 + \phi_2\bar{u}_2 + \ldots + \phi_p\bar{u}_p] - (n+1)/n \\ &= \phi_1[(2/n)\bar{u}_1 - (n+1)/n] + \phi_2[(2/n)\bar{u}_2 - (n+1)/n] \\ &\qquad + \ldots + \phi_p[(2/n)\bar{u}_p - (n+1)/n] + \phi_1(n+1)/n \\ &\qquad + \phi_2(n+1)/n + \ldots + \phi_p(n+1)/n - (n+1)/n \\ &= \phi_1\bar{G}_1 + \phi_2\bar{G}_2 + \ldots + \phi_r\bar{G}_r \quad \text{by equations (10.3a) and (10.1e).} \end{aligned}$$

This completes the proof.

In the model of additive factor components, there is a natural interpretation of the pseudo Gini coefficient $[\bar{G}_i]$ as the concentration ratio, which measures the extent to which the ith factor component is concentrated among wealthy families. Despite the attractiveness of its economic interpretation and the exactness of its decomposition, the pseudo Gini coefficient has not been used much in the empirical work of this volume. The reasons are these. The pseudo Gini coefficient $[\bar{G}_i]$ not only differs from G_i, but is in fact a more complicated concept. Although the factor Gini coefficient $[G_i]$ measures the degree of inequality of a factor component by itself, the pseudo Gini coefficient is definable only in terms of the relatedness of the pattern of factor income, given by $(W_1^i, W_2^i, \ldots, W_n^i)$,

1970	*1971*	*1972*	*Notation*	*Model and variable*
0.360	0.357	0.423	ϕ_w	Wage share
0.103	0.122	0.107	ϕ_π	Property share
0.487	0.452	0.423	ϕ_a	Agricultural share
0.050	0.068	0.047	ϕ_m	Miscellaneous share
0.997	0.998	1.000	$R_w = \bar{G}_w/G_w$	Wage correlation
0.995	1.000	1.000	$R_\pi = \bar{G}_\pi/G_\pi$	Property correlation
1.000	1.000	1.000	$R_a = \bar{G}_a/G_a$	Agricultural correlation

to the pattern of total family income, given by $(Y_1, Y_2, \ldots, Y_n)$. Thus, from the substantive economic point of view, the socioeconomic forces determining G_i are very different from those determining $\bar{G}_i$.

The decomposition equation in theorem 10.1 can nevertheless be applied in empirical work. Using the same set of data as in table 3.2 of chapter three, the empirical decomposition of the Gini coefficient of total family income [G_y] into the pseudo Gini coefficients of wage income [$\bar{G}_w$], property income [$\bar{G}_\pi$], and agricultural income [$\bar{G}_a$] is shown in table 10.2. The decomposition of the Gini coefficient is exact for all three models: all households, urban households, and rural households.

Exact Decomposition of G_y into Factor Ginis

For each factor component [W^i] a factor Gini [G_i] and a pseudo factor Gini [$\bar{G}_i$] can be computed. The correlation characteristic of the ith factor can then be calculated:

$$R_i = \bar{G}_i/G_i. \qquad (i = 1, 2, \ldots, p) \tag{10.4}$$

[*factor correlation characteristics*]

Theorem 10.1 immediately leads to:

$$G_y = \phi_1 R_1 G_1 + \phi_2 R_2 G_2 + \ldots + \phi_p R_p G_p. \tag{10.5}$$

Equation (10.5) will be referred to as the exact Gini decomposition

Table 10.3. *Numerical Example of Exact Decomposition of G_y into Factor Ginis*

Variable	*Notation*	*Wage income*	*Property income*	*Transfer income*	*Total income*
Factor share	ϕ_i	0.4500	0.3500	0.2000	1.0000
Factor Gini	G_i	0.3912	0.6628	0.6400	—
Weighted factor Gini	$\phi_i G_i$	0.1760	0.2320	0.1280	—
Total Gini	$\hat{\hat{G}}_y$	—	—	—	0.5360
Pseudo factor Gini	$\bar{G}_i$	0.2308	0.6628	−0.5600	—
Weighted pseudo factor Gini	$\phi_i \bar{G}_i$	0.1039	0.2320	−0.1120	—
Total Gini	G_y	—	—	—	0.2239
Average contradicting gap[a]	s_i^-	0.0802	0.0000	0.6000	—
Average supporting gap[b]	s_i^+	0.3110	0.6628	−0.0004	—
Factor correlation characteristic[c]	R_i	0.5900	1.0000	−0.8750	—
Gini error	E	—	—	—	0.3121
Gini decomposition	$\phi_i R_i G_i$; G_y	0.1039	0.2320	−0.1120	0.2239

— Not applicable.
Source: Constructed by the authors.
a. $s_i^- = (G_i - \bar{G}_i)/2$.
b. $s_i^+ = (G_i + \bar{G}_i)/2$.
c. $R_i = \bar{G}_i/G_i$.

formula. It shows that three types of factors affect G_y. If an income component is positively correlated with total family income ($R_i > 0$), then this component contributes heavily to total income inequality when the factor income is unequally distributed (indicated by a large G_i) and when the share of this factor is large (indicated by a large ϕ_i). Conversely, when an income component is negatively correlated with total family income ($R_i < 0$), a large G_i and a large ϕ_i indicate that the component contributes to total income equality.

Table 10.3 uses figures from table 10.1 to give the values for the factor shares [ϕ_i], the pseudo factor Ginis [$\bar{G}_i$], the factor Gini coefficients $[G_i]$, the factor correlation characteristics $[R_i]$, and the Gini coefficient of total income $[G_y]$. Table 10.3 also indicates the decomposition of G_y into pseudo factor Ginis according to theorem 10.1 and the decomposition of G_y according to equation (10.5). Notice for transfer income that R_i and $\bar{G}_i$ are negative. Hence a large share of transfer income $[\phi_i]$ and a more unequal distribution of transfer income $[G_i]$ contribute to total income equality.

Computation Procedure for Exact Decomposition

The following values can be computed for an exact decomposition according to equation (10.5):

(10.6a) $G_y = (2/n)u_y - (n+1)/n,$

[*total income Gini*]

(10.6b) $G_i = (2/n)u_i - (n+1)/n,$ and $(i = 1, 2, \ldots, p)$

[*factor Gini*]

(10.6c) $\bar{G}_i = (2/n)\bar{u}_i - (n+1)/n,$ where $(i = 1, 2, \ldots, p)$

[*pseudo factor Gini*]

(10.6d) $u_y = 1(y_1) + 2(y_2) + \ldots + n(y_n)$ for

$y_1 \leq y_2 \leq \ldots \leq y_n,$

(10.6e) $u_i = 1(w^i_{j1}) + 2(w^i_{j2}) + \ldots + n(w^i_{jn})$ for

$w^i_{j1} \leq w^i_{j2} \leq \ldots \leq w^i_{jn},$ and

(10.6f) $\bar{u}_i = 1(w^i_1) + 2(w^i_2) + \ldots + n(w^i_n),$ where

(10.6g) $(w^i_1, w^i_2, \ldots, w^i_n) = (W^i_1/S_i, W^i_2/S_i, \ldots, W^i_n/S_i).$

$(i = 1, 2, \ldots, p)$

Notice when the original data are given as in equation (10.1) or (10.2) that a factor component $[W^i]$ may not be monotonically arranged. For the computation of u_i and G_i, the elements in $(w^i_1, w^i_2, \ldots, w^i_n)$ defined in equation (10.6g), which are not necessarily in a monotonic order, must be rearranged into nondecreasing order. That rearrangement is shown in equation (10.6f) by the permutation $(j_1, j_2, \ldots, j_n)$ of the first n integers. For each factor component:

(10.7a) $\quad G_i = s_i^+ + s_i^-,$ and $\quad (i = 1, 2, \ldots, p)$

(10.7b) $\quad \bar{G}_i = s_i^+ - s_i^-$ by theorem 9.1. $\quad (i = 1, 2, \ldots, p)$

Consequently, when G_i and $\bar{G}_i$ are first computed, s_i^+ and s_i^- can be computed:

(10.8a) $\quad s_i^+ = (G_i + \bar{G}_i)/2; \quad (i = 1, 2, \ldots, p)$

(10.8b) $\quad s_i^- = (G_1 - \bar{G}_i)/2. \quad (i = 1, 2, \ldots, p)$

The values of s_i^+ and s_i^- are given in table 10.3.

For an empirical application, the correlation characteristics R_w, R_π, and R_a are indicated for the three models: all households, urban households, and rural households. Together with the factor Gini coefficients G_w, G_π, and G_a indicated in table 3.2 of chapter three, an exact decomposition of G_y can be attempted for all three models according to the basic decomposition equation (10.5).

Notice that the factor correlation characteristics $[R_i]$ can be defined by using equation (9.18) and written as:

(10.9) $\quad R_i = \bar{G}_i/G_i = r(w^i, \lambda)/r(w^i,r^i) = (s_i^+ - s_i^-)/(s_i^+ + s_i^-).$

$(i = 1, 2, \ldots, p)$

In this expression, $r(w^i,r^i)$ is the correlation coefficient between factor income fractions $[w^i]$ and factor income ranks $[r^i]$; $r(w^i,\lambda)$ is the correlation coefficient between factor income fractions $[w^i]$ and total income ranks $[\lambda]$. There thus are two interpretations for the term R_i in the basic decomposition equation: as the correlation characteristic according to theorem 9.2; as the fractional net supporting gap according to equations (9.18a) and (9.18b).

In the example in table 10.3, where the Gini coefficient of wage income $[G_w]$ is 0.3912, the average supporting gap $[s_w^+]$—that is, the variation of wage income that total family income can explain —is 0.3110; the average contradicting gap $[s_w^-]$ is 0.0802. These values lead to a pseudo wage Gini $[\bar{G}_w]$ of 0.2308. Notice that the property Gini $[G_\pi]$ of 0.6628 is entirely explained by the supporting gap $(\bar{G} = G = s^+)$, indicating that the correlation between total income rank and property income rank is perfect and positive. The opposite is true for transfer income.

The Gini Coefficient under Linear Transformation

Let the vectors $X = (X_1, X_2, \ldots, X_n)$ and $Y = (Y_1, Y_2, \ldots, Y_n)$ be nonnegative. X is a linear transformation of Y if there is a linear function:

$$x = b + ay, \tag{10.10}$$

where a and b are not both negative, such that:

$$X_i = b + aY_i. \qquad (i = 1, 2, \ldots, n) \tag{10.11}$$

It is obvious when $Y \geq 0$ that the coefficients a and b cannot both be negative if X is to be nonnegative ($X \geq 0$). The following means can be defined:

$$\bar{X} = (X_1 + X_2 + \ldots + X_n)/n; \tag{10.12a}$$

[*the mean of X*]

$$\bar{Y} = (Y_1 + Y_2 + \ldots + Y_n)/n; \tag{10.12b}$$

[*the mean of Y*]

$$\phi_{xy} = \bar{X}/\bar{Y} = (X_1 + X_2 + \ldots + X_n)/(Y_1 + Y_2 + \ldots + Y_n). \tag{10.12c}$$

In equation (10.12c) ϕ_{xy} is the ratio of the mean $\bar{X}$ to the mean $\bar{Y}$.

The theorem to be proved in this section is:

THEOREM 10.2. *If $X = (X_1, X_2, \ldots, X_n)$ is a linear transformation of $Y = (Y_1, Y_2, \ldots, Y_n)$—that is, if $X_i = b + aY_i$ for $i = 1, 2, \ldots, n$—then:*

(*a*) $G(X) = (a/\phi_{xy})G(Y)$ *if* $a \geq 0$, *and*

(*b*) $G(X) = -(a/\phi_{xy})G(Y)$ *if* $a < 0$,

where $\phi_{xy} = \bar{X}/\bar{Y}$ and where $G(X)$ and $G(Y)$ respectively are the Gini coefficients of X and Y.

For a geometric interpretation of this theorem, notice that:

$$\bar{X} = b + a\bar{Y}, \tag{10.13a}$$

which implies that:

$$(10.13b) \quad (b/\bar{X}) - 1 = -a/\phi_{xy} \quad \text{by equation (10.12c).}$$

Because the elasticity of the linear function in theorem 10.2 is:

$$(10.14) \qquad (dx/dy)(y/x) = a/(x/y),$$

it can be seen that $a/(\bar{X}/\bar{Y}) = a/\phi_{xy}$ is the elasticity of the linear function at the mean point $(\bar{X},\bar{Y})$. Thus theorem 10.2 states that $G(X)$ can be obtained from $G(Y)$ by multiplying $G(Y)$ by the elasticity at the mean point $(\bar{X},\bar{Y})$. Theorem 10.2 can be proved as follows:

Proof: Assume that $Y_1 \leq Y_2 \leq \ldots \leq Y_n$. If $a \geq 0$ and $X_1 \geq X_2 \geq \ldots \geq X_n$, then by theorem 8.1:

$$\begin{aligned} u_x &= (1X_1 + 2X_2 + \ldots + nX_n)/n\bar{X} \\ &= [(b + aY_1) + 2(b + aY_2) + \ldots + n(b + aY_n)]/n\bar{X} \\ &= b(1 + 2 + \ldots + n)/n\bar{X} + a(n\bar{Y}/n\bar{X})u_y \quad \text{by theorem 8.1} \\ &= (n + 1)b/2\bar{X} + au_y/\phi_{xy} \quad \text{by equation (10.12c).} \end{aligned}$$

Thus by theorem 8.1:

$$\begin{aligned} G(X) &= (2/n)[(n + 1)b/2\bar{X} + au_y/\phi_{xy})] - (n + 1)/n \\ &= (a/\phi_{xy})(2/n)u_y + b(n + 1)/n\bar{X} - (n + 1)/n \\ &= (a/\phi_{xy})(2/n)u_y + [(n + 1)/n](b/\bar{X} - 1) \\ &= (a/\phi_{xy})[(2/n)u_y - (n + 1)/n] \quad \text{by equation (10.13b)} \\ &= (a/\phi_{xy})G(Y). \end{aligned}$$

This proves the case for $a \geq 0$. If $a < 0$ and $Y_1 \leq Y_2 \leq \ldots \leq Y_n$, the values of X_i are in a reverse monotonic order $X_1 \geq X_2 \geq \ldots \geq X_n$. The above proof implies that $\bar{G}(X) = (a/\phi_{xy})G(Y)$ by theorem 8.3. Now, however:

$$\bar{G}(X) = -G(X) \quad \text{by theorem 8.4.}$$

This completes the proof.

A positive coefficient a in equation (10.10) gives:

THEOREM 10.3. *If* $X = (X_1, X_2, \ldots, X_n)$ *is a linear transformation of* $Y = (Y_1, Y_2, \ldots, Y_n)$ *with a positive coefficient* $a > 0$

in $x = b + ay$, *then*:

(*a*) $G(X) > G(Y)$ *if and only if* $a/\phi_{xy} > 1$ *or* $b < 0$, *and*

(*b*) $G(X) < G(Y)$ *if and only if* $a/\phi_{xy} < 1$ *or* $b > 0$.

Proof: From theorem 10.2 it can be seen that $G(X) \gtrless G(Y)$ if and only if:

$$a \gtrless \phi_{xy} = \bar{X}/\bar{Y} = (b + a\bar{Y})/\bar{Y} \quad \text{by equation (10.13a), or}$$

$$aY \gtrless b + a\bar{Y}.$$

This completes the proof.

The theorem essentially states that b is negative when the function defined in equation (10.10) is elastic at the mean point $(\bar{X},\bar{Y})$, and that b is positive when the function is inelastic at the mean point $(\bar{X},\bar{Y})$. The rest of the proof directly follows from theorem 10.2.

Linear Model of Additive Factor Components

Now consider a special case of the additive factor-components problem defined in equation (10.1). For this special case, postulate:

$$\text{(10.15a)} \qquad w_i = b_i + a_i y, \quad \text{where} \qquad (i = 1, 2, \ldots, p)$$

$$\text{(10.15b)} \qquad a_1 + a_2 + \ldots + a_p = 1 \quad \text{and}$$

$$\text{(10.15c)} \qquad b_1 + b_2 + \ldots + b_p = 0,$$

such that the ith factor component $[W^i = (W^i_1, W^i_2, \ldots, W^i_n)]$ is a linear transformation of the total income pattern $[Y = (Y_1, Y_2, \ldots, Y_n)]$ according to the ith linear function in equation (10.15a). In other words:

$$\text{(10.16)} \quad W^i = (W^i_1, W^i_2, \ldots, W^i_n)$$

$$= (b_i, b_i, \ldots, b_i) + a_i(Y_1, Y_2, \ldots, Y_n). \qquad (i = 1, 2, \ldots, p)$$

Notice when the restrictions of equations (10.15b) and (10.15c) are postulated for a_i and b_i that:

$$\text{(10.17)} \qquad Y = W^1 + W^2 + \ldots + W^n,$$

so that Y is the sum of all values of W^i, as in equation (10.2).

This model will be referred to as the linear model of additive factor components. It is a special case of the general model defined earlier.

Notice in equation (10.15a) that some values of a_i may be negative. But when a_i is negative, b_i must be positive (see equation [10.10]). Thus with no loss of generality the pairs (a_i,b_i) can be classified into three types of case.

For a type one component:

(10.18a) $$a_i > 0 \quad \text{and} \quad b_i < 0; \qquad (i = 1, 2, \ldots, q)$$

for a type two component:

(10.18b) $$a_i > 0 \quad \text{and} \quad b_i > 0; \quad (i = q + 1, q + 2, \ldots, t)$$

for a type three component:

(10.18c) $$a_i < 0 \quad \text{and} \quad b_i > 0. \quad (i = t + 1, t + 2, \ldots, n)$$

Let G_i be the Gini coefficient of W^i and G_y be the Gini coefficient of Y. Applying theorem 10.2 gives:

(10.19a) $$G_i = (a_i/\phi_i)G_y, \quad \text{or} \quad \mathrm{a_iG_y} = \phi_i\mathrm{G_i}, \quad \text{and} \qquad (i = 1, 2, \ldots, t)$$

(10.19b) $$G_i = -(a_i/\phi_i)G_y, \quad \text{or} \quad \mathrm{a_iG_y} = -\phi_i\mathrm{G_i}, \qquad (i = t + 1, t + 2, \ldots, n)$$

where $\phi_1, \phi_2, \ldots, \phi_p$ are the distributive shares defined in equation (10.1d). When all the romanized terms in equations (10.19a) and (10.19b) are added, equation (10.15b) implies that:

(10.20a) $$G_y = H_1 + H_2 - H_3, \quad \text{where}$$

(10.20b) $$H_1 = \phi_1G_1 + \phi_2G_2 + \ldots + \phi_qG_q,$$

[*type one components*]

(10.20c) $$H_2 = \phi_{q+1}G_{q+1} + \phi_{q+2}G_{q+2} + \ldots + \phi_tG_t, \quad \text{and}$$

[*type two components*]

(10.20d) $$H_3 = \phi_{t+1}G_{t+1} + \phi_{t+2}G_{t+2} + \ldots + \phi_nG_n.$$

[*type three components*]

Equation (10.20a) is an exact decomposition of G_y for the linear model of this section. Notice that this decomposition equation is a special case of the general decomposition equation (10.5). For this special case, theorem 10.3 further implies that:

for type one income:

(10.21a) $$G_i \geq G_y, \quad \text{and} \qquad (i = 1, 2, \ldots, q)$$

for type two income:

(10.21b) $$G_i \leq G_y. \qquad (i = q + 1, q + 2, \ldots, t)$$

Thus, in the linear model, a type one factor component is distributed more unequally than Y. A type two factor component is distributed more equally than Y. A type three factor component contributes more to income equality the more unequally it is distributed—that is, when G_i increases, G_y decreases.

Monotonic Model of Additive Factor Components

Postulate for the generally defined model of additive factor components in equation (10.1) that every factor component [$W^i = (W_1^i, W_2^i, \ldots, W_n^i)$] satisfies:

(10.22a) $$W_1^i \leq W_2^i \leq \ldots \leq W_p^i, \quad \text{or}$$

[*monotonically nondecreasing conditions*]

(10.22b) $$W_1^i \geq W_2^i \geq \ldots \geq W_p^i.$$

[*monotonically nonincreasing conditions*]

The linear model obviously is a special case of this monotonic model. When the total income pattern [Y] is monotonically nondecreasing, a type one or type two income obviously is monotonically nondecreasing; a type three income is monotonically nonincreasing.

Applying equations (9.17a) and (9.17b) to W^i in the monotonic model gives:

(10.23a) $$G_i = \bar{G}_i,$$

when W^i is in a monotonically nondecreasing order, and:

(10.23b) $$G_i = -\bar{G}_i,$$

when W^i is in a monotonically nonincreasing order. In the first case the factor Gini coefficient equals the pseudo factor Gini coefficient. In the second case it equals the negative value of the pseudo factor Gini coefficient. Substituting equations (10.23a) and (10.23b) in the equation of theorem 10.1 gives:

THEOREM 10.4. *In the monotonic model:*

$$G_y = U_1 - U_2, \quad \textit{where}$$

(a) $$U_1 = \phi_1 G_1 + \phi_2 G_2 + \ldots + \phi_t G_t \quad \textit{and}$$

[monotonically nondecreasing W^i]

(b) $$U_2 = \phi_{t+1} G_{t+1} + \phi_{t+2} G_{t+2} + \ldots + \phi_n G_n.$$

[monotonically nonincreasing W^i]

In comparison with the general decomposition equation (10.5) it can be seen in the monotonic model that all values of R_i, the correlation characteristic, equal 1 or -1. Furthermore the decomposition equation in the linear model (10.20) is a special case of theorem 10.4. In other words, the linear model is a sufficient, but not a necessary, condition for deducing R_i to be 1 or -1.

The monotonic model of this section is useful for empirical application because, when total income is monotonically arranged $[Y_1 \leq Y_2 \leq \ldots \leq Y_n]$, it can often be assumed, as a first approximation, that all factor components $[W^i]$ satisfy the monotonic conditions of expression (10.22). The primary advantage of the monotonic model is the simplicity that accrues to theoretical analysis when all correlation characteristics are assumed to be 1 or -1. Consider the following numerical example:

(10.24a) $$(Y_1, Y_2, Y_3) = (20, 30, 50), G_y = 0.2;$$

(10.24b) $$(W_1, W_2, W_3) = (10, 24, 46), G_w = 0.3,$$
$$\phi_w = 0.8, (W_1 \leq W_2 \leq W_3);$$

(10.24c) $$(\pi_1, \pi_2, \pi_3) = (10, 6, 4), G_\pi = 0.2,$$
$$\phi_\pi = 0.2, (\pi_1 \geq \pi_2 \geq \pi_3);$$

(10.24d) $$(Y_1, Y_2, Y_3) = (W_1, W_2, W_3) + (\pi_1, \pi_2, \pi_3);$$

(10.24e) $$G_y = \phi_w G_w - \phi_\pi G_\pi = (0.8)(0.3) - (0.2)(0.2) = 0.2.$$

Notice that the two factor components are not linear transformations of (Y_1, Y_2, Y_3). Yet theorem 10.4 can be applied because the monotonic conditions are satisfied. Notice also that a minus sign is attached to the component (π_1, π_2, π_3) because it is in a monotonically nonincreasing order.

Linear Approximation of Factor Components

Suppose that Y and W^i $(i = 1, 2, \ldots, p)$ are interpreted as original data and given as in equation (10.2) such that some W^i is not a linear transformation of Y. In this section the purpose is to investigate the construction of approximated factor components $[\hat{W}^i = (\hat{W}^i_1, \hat{W}^i_2, \ldots, \hat{W}^i_n)\ (i = 1, 2, \ldots, p)]$ which satisfy the following conditions:

(10.25a) $Y = \hat{W}^1 + \hat{W}^2 + \ldots + \hat{W}^p$, and

(10.25b) $\phi_i = (W^i_1 + W^i_2 + \ldots + W^i_n)/n\bar{Y}$

$= (\hat{W}^i_1 + \hat{W}^i_2 + \ldots + \hat{W}^i_n)/n\bar{Y}, \qquad (i = 1, 2, \ldots, n)$

where $\hat{W}^i$ is a linear transformation of Y according to:

(10.25c) $w_i = \hat{b}_i + a_i y, \qquad (i = 1, 2, \ldots, p)$

(10.25d) $\hat{a}_1 + \hat{a}_2 + \ldots + \hat{a}_p = 1,$

(10.25e) $\hat{b}_1 + \hat{b}_2 + \ldots + \hat{b}_p = 0,$ and

(10.25f) $\hat{W}^i_j = \hat{b}_i + \hat{a}_i Y_j. \quad (i = 1, 2, \ldots, p;\ j = 1, 2, \ldots, n)$

The vector $\hat{W}^i$ constructed in this way will be referred to as a linear approximation of W^i. Condition (10.25a) states that Y, interpreted as original data, is the additive sum of the linear approximations of the factor components $[\hat{W}^i]$. This condition is ensured by the fact that $\hat{W}^i$ is a linear transformation of Y with the conditions postulated in equations (10.25d) and (10.25e). Condition (10.25b) states that the factor share $[\phi_i]$, originally defined for W^i, remains unchanged when $\hat{W}^i$ replaces W^i. With such an approximation, the original additive factor-components problem, which in equation (10.2) is stated as:

(10.26) $Y = W^1 + W^2 + \ldots + W^p,$

is now replaced by a new additive factor-components problem through a linear approximation.

The primary advantage of the formulation of this new problem is the theoretical simplification the linear approximation brings about. If $G(W^i)$ is the Gini coefficient for the approximated factor components $(\hat{W}^i)$, equation (10.20a) immediately implies that:

(10.27a) $G_y = \hat{H}_1 + \hat{H}_2 - \hat{H}_3$, where

(10.27b) $\hat{H}_1 = \phi_1 G(\hat{W}^1) + \phi_2 G(\hat{W}^2) + \ldots + \phi_q G(\hat{W}^q)$

for type one incomes satisfying $\hat{a}_i > 0$ and $\hat{b}_i < 0$;

(10.27c) $\hat{H}_2 = \phi_{q+1} G(\hat{W}^{q+1}) + \phi_{q+2} G(\hat{W}^{q+2}) + \ldots + \phi_t G(\hat{W}^t)$

for type two incomes satisfying $\hat{a}_i > 0$ and $\hat{b}_i > 0$; and

(10.27d) $\hat{H}_3 = \phi_{t+1} G(\hat{W}^{t+1}) + \phi_{t+2} G(\hat{W}^{t+2}) + \ldots + \phi_p G(\hat{W}^p)$

for type three incomes satisfying $\hat{a}_i < 0$ and $\hat{b}_i > 0$.

Equation (10.27a) is comparable to the general decomposition equation (10.5) when the correlation characteristics $[R_i]$ are 1 or -1. Furthermore the classification of income into types one, two, and three, hitherto definable only in the context of the linear model, becomes applicable. The new decomposition problem thus becomes simpler and wealthier in economic content.

To proceed with the construction of $\hat{W}^i$, the linear function in equation (10.25c) is treated as a linear regression equation in which the parameters a_i and b_i are estimated from the original data for Y and W^i ($i = 1, 2, \ldots, p$) by the method of least squares. Condition (10.26), a property of the original data, ensures that equations (10.25d) and (10.25e) are satisfied when the method of least squares is used. When these regression functions are constructed, the estimated factor components $[\hat{W}^i = (\hat{W}^i_1, \hat{W}^i_2, \ldots, \hat{W}^i_n)$ $(i = 1, 2, \ldots, p)]$ are obtained by substituting Y^i in the regression equation (10.25f). To prove equation (10.25b) it can be seen for the ith regression equation that:

(10.28a) $\theta^i = (\theta^i_1, \theta^i_2, \ldots, \theta^i_n)$

$$= (W^i_1, W^i_2, \ldots, W^i_n) - (\hat{W}^i_1, \hat{W}^i_2, \ldots, \hat{W}^i_n);$$

(10.28b) $(\hat{W}^i_1, \hat{W}^i_2, \ldots, \hat{W}^i_n)$

$$= (b_i, b_i, \ldots, b_i) + a_i(Y_1, Y_2, \ldots, Y_n)$$

by equation (10.25f);

(10.28c) $\theta^i_1 + \theta^i_2 + \ldots + \theta^i_n = 0;$

(10.28d) $W^i_1 + W^i_2 + \ldots + W^i_n = \hat{W}^i_1 + \hat{W}^i_2 + \ldots + \hat{W}^i_n$

$$= a_i(Y_1 + Y_2 + \ldots + Y_n) + nb_i.$$

In equation (10.28a) θ^i contains all the deviations [θ^i_j ($j = 1, 2, \ldots, n$)] of W^i_j from the estimated $\hat{W}^i_j$. The least-squares method of estimation implies that the sum of all deviations is zero [equation (10.28c)]. Summing both sides of equation (10.28a) directly leads to equation (10.28d) which shows that the sum of all elements in W^i, the original data, is the same as the sum of all elements in the pattern of approximated factor incomes [$\hat{W}^i$]. Thus ϕ_i remains unchanged.

Linearity Error

When the original data are given for Y and W^i ($i = 1, 2, \ldots, p$), the method of linear approximation can be used only when every W^i approximately is a linear transformation of Y. In computing the regression coefficients [$\hat{a}_i$ and $\hat{b}_i$] in equation (10.25c), the correlation coefficients should also be calculated:

(10.29) $$r_i = r(Y, W^i). \qquad (i = 1, 2, \ldots, p)$$

[*correlation coefficients*]

The values of r_i give an indication of how close the linear approximation is. It is recommended that the method of the preceding section be used only when all absolute values of r_i are sufficiently close to 1—that is, only when all values of W^i are nearly perfectly correlated with Y, whether positively or negatively. When this condition is not met, the following approximation formula can be defined by replacing every $G(\hat{W}^i)$, the factor Gini of the approximated factor component, by $G(W^i)$, the true factor Gini:

(10.30a) $\hat{G}_y = \hat{H}_1 + \hat{H}_2 - \hat{H}_3$, where

(10.30b) $\hat{H}_1 = \phi_1 G(W^1) + \phi_2 G(W^2) + \ldots + \phi_q G(W^q)$,

(10.30c) $\hat{H}_2 = \phi_{q+1} G(W^{q+1}) + \phi_{q+2} G(W^{q+2}) + \ldots + \phi_t G(W^t)$, and

(10.30d) $\hat{H}_3 = \phi_{t+1} G(W^{t+1}) + \phi_{t+2} G(W^{t+2}) + \ldots + \phi_p G(W^p)$.

When this approximation formula is used, an error term [J] is involved. It is the difference between G_y, as defined in equation (10.27), and $\hat{G}_y$:

(10.31a) $J = G_y - \hat{G}_y = J_1 + J_2 - J_3$, where

(10.31b) $J_1 = \phi_1 d_1 + \phi_2 d_2 + \ldots + d_q d_q$,

(10.31c) $J_2 = \phi_{q+1}d_{q+1} + \phi_{q+2}d_{q+2} + \ldots + \phi_t d_t,$ and

(10.31d) $J_3 = \phi_{t+1}d_{t+1} + \phi_{t+2}d_{t+2} + \ldots + \phi_p d_p,$ where

(10.31e) $d_i = G(W^i) - G(\hat{W}^i).$ $(i = 1, 2, \ldots, p)$

In equation (10.31e) d_i is the difference between the Gini coefficient of the true factor component and that of the approximated factor component. Notice in equation (10.28a) that the difference between W^i and $\hat{W}^i$ is θ^i. When the absolute value of the correlation coefficient $[r_i]$ is close to 1, θ^i is close to a zero vector, leading to the fact that d_i is close to zero.

By comparing equation (10.30) and theorem 10.4, it can be seen that the approximation formula can be used even when the absolute values of the correlation coefficients $[r_i]$ are not close to zero. In other words, the fact that they are close to zero is a sufficient, but not a necessary, condition. In the monotonic model, G_y is equal to $\hat{G}_y$. Hence the linearity error vanishes—that is, $J = 0$—even though $d_1, d_2, \ldots, d_p$ may not vanish. [For a numerical example see equation (10.24).] Thus it is recommended in attempts to apply the linear model to empirical work that checks be made to ensure that the following conditions are fulfilled:

(10.32) $|r_i| = |r(Y, W^i)| \simeq 1.$ $(i = 1, 2, \ldots, p)$

In words, the linear correlation coefficient between W^i and Y should be close to 1 or -1.

Approximation of the Monotonic Model

Suppose that Y and W^i $(i = 1, 2, \ldots, n)$ are given as in equation (10.2) and that the monotonic conditions are only approximately satisfied. If the monotonic model is to be used, the equation of approximation is:

(10.33) $\hat{\hat{G}}_y = U_1 - U_2,$

where U_1 and U_2 are defined as in theorem 10.4. The difference between $\hat{G}_y$ and G_y, as defined in the exact decomposition equation (10.5), is the Gini error term:

(10.34a) $E = \hat{\hat{G}}_y - G_y = E_1 - E_2,$ where

(10.34b) $E_1 = \phi_1 g_1 + \phi_2 g_2 + \ldots + \phi_t g_t \geq 0$

for $0 \leq R_i \leq 1$, and

(10.34c) $E_2 = \phi_{t+1} g_{t+1} + \phi_{t+2} g_{t+2} + \ldots + \phi_p g_p \geq 0$

for $-1 \leq R_i \leq 0$, where

(10.34d) $g_i = G_i(1 - R_i)$ and $(i = 1, 2, \ldots, t)$

(10.34e) $g_i = G_i(1 - R_i)$. $(i = t+1, t+2, \ldots, p)$

The term E_1 includes all components $[W^i = (W_1^i, W_2^i, \ldots, W_n^i)]$ for which R_i is positive. This condition is interpreted as approximately satisfying the monotonic increasing condition $[W_1^i \leq W_2^i \leq \ldots \leq W_n^i]$. Similarly the term E_2 includes all W^i for which R_i is negative. This condition is interpreted as approximately satisfying the monotonically decreasing conditions $[W_1^i \geq W_2^i \geq \ldots \geq W_n^i]$.

It is easy to show that E_1 and E_2 in equations (10.34b) and (10.34c) are nonnegative. The Gini and pseudo Gini coefficients of a factor component $[W^i]$ may be written as they are in equations (10.7a) and (10.7b):

(10.35a) $G_i = s_i^+ + s_i^-;$ $(i = 1, 2, \ldots, p)$

[*factor Gini*]

(10.35b) $\bar{G}_i = s_i^+ - s_i^-.$ $(i = 1, 2, \ldots, p)$

[*pseudo factor Gini*]

When the total income pattern $[Y]$ is monotonically arranged $[Y_1 \leq Y_2 \leq \ldots \leq Y_n]$ for a particular factor component $[W^i = (W_1^i, W_2^i, \ldots, W_n^i)]$, the average supporting gap $[s_i^+]$ is the sum of all such terms satisfying $(W_u^i - W_v^i) > 0$ for $u > v$. In other words, if the total income is higher $(Y_u > Y_v)$, the factor income is also higher $(W_u^i > W_v^i)$. Conversely the contradicting gap $[s_i^-]$ includes all terms such that the factor income is lower $(W_u^i < W_v^i)$ if the total income is higher. Equations (10.34d), (10.34e), (9.12a), and (9.21b) give:

(10.36a) $g_i = 2s_i^-$ $(i = 1, 2, \ldots, t)$

when $W_1^i \leq W_2^i \leq \ldots \leq W_n^i$ is approximately satisfied and:

(10.36b) $g_i = 2s_i^+$ $(i = t+1, t+2, \ldots, n)$

when $W^i \geq W^i \geq \ldots \geq W^i$ is approximately satisfied. The fact that s^- and s^+ are nonnegative implies that E_1 and E_2 are nonnegative, as was to be demonstrated. Furthermore the underlying nature of the error terms is now known. For E_1 the error is traced to the violation of monotonically increasing conditions. For E_2 the error is traced to the violation of monotonically decreasing conditions.

Because E is the difference between two nonnegative terms E_1 and E_2, it can be seen that $\hat{\hat{G}}_y$ defined in equation (10.33) can either underestimate or overestimate the true G_y. If all values of R_i are positive, then E_2 vanishes and $\hat{\hat{G}}_y$ always overestimates G_y. This condition can be stated as:

THEOREM 10.5. *If all factor correlation characteristics are positive—that is, if $R_i > 0$ for $i = 1, 2, \ldots, p$—then the error of estimation $[E]$ defined in equation (10.34) is:*

$$E = E_1 = 2(\phi_1 s_1^- + \phi_2 s_2^- + \ldots + \phi_p s_p^-) \geq 0.$$

Hence $\hat{\hat{G}}_y = \phi_1 G_1 + \phi_2 G_2 + \ldots + \phi_p G_p$ *always overestimates* G_y.

Furthermore E is twice the weighted sum of contradicting gaps.

When the monotonic model is to be used for empirical work, equation (10.34) suggests that the following conditions should be verified after the correlation characteristics $[R_i]$ are computed:

$$|R_i| \approx 1. \qquad (i = 1, 2, \ldots, p) \tag{10.37}$$

In words, the absolute values of all R_i should be close to 1 to ensure that the monotonic conditions are approximately fulfilled.

CHAPTER 11

Applications and Extensions of the Models of Decomposition

THE CONSTRUCTION OF A GENERAL MODEL of additive factor components in chapter ten led to the exact decomposition equation (10.5). Construction of the monotonic model, a special case of the general model, led to the exact decomposition equation in theorem 10.4. Construction of the linear model, a special case of the monotonic model, led to the exact decomposition equation (10.20). These three models can be used both for theoretical purposes and for empirical applications.

The general model of equation (10.5) is most useful for empirical applications because of its generality. Precisely for that reason, however, the monotonic model or the linear model may be preferred for theoretical purposes. If there are a priori reasons, based on economic theorizing, for assuming that the monotonic conditions of expressions (10.22a) and (10.22b) are fulfilled, the monotonic model should be used. Similarly, if there are a priori reasons for assuming that the strong linear conditions of equation (10.16) are fulfilled, the linear model should be used. The monotonic model is less complicated than the general model, because the correlation characteristics can be neglected as a first approximation. The linear model can, in addition, identify three different types of income—types which help in reasoning about the distribution of income. In reality, the monotonic and linear conditions can only be approximately fulfilled. Thus the exact monotonic and linear models are used for theoretical purposes; the approximation models, for empirical work.

Remarks on Chapter Three

The approximation of the linear model was applied in chapter three. Because of the aggregated data, the conditions of equation (10.32) were judged to be fulfilled: $|r_i| = |r(Y, W^i)| \simeq 1$ (observe the values of r_w, r_π, and r_a in table 3.3). For the empirical application in that chapter, there was no type three income (observe that the values of a_w, a_π, and a_a are positive in table 3.3). Thus the terms H_3 and J_3 respectively vanish in the approximation equation (10.30a) and the error equation (10.31a), which reduce to:

$$\hat{G}_y = \hat{H}_1 + \hat{H}_2 \quad \text{and} \tag{11.1a}$$

$$J = J_1 + J_2. \tag{11.1b}$$

The value of J is denoted by θ in table 3.2 of chapter three. Notice that because the linear conditions are judged to be fulfilled, the values of θ are quite tolerable. The overestimation of the true G_y by $\hat{G}_y$, which the positive values of θ in table 3.2 indicate, is suggested by theorem 10.5: $\hat{\hat{G}}_y - G_y = E \geq 0$.

How do the formulations of chapter three relate to those presented in chapter ten? In the theoretical derivation of chapter three, equation (3.3b) is a special case of equation (10.30a): that is, $\hat{G}_y = \phi_w G_w + \phi_\pi G_\pi - \phi_N G_N$ is a special case of $\hat{G}_y = \hat{H}_1 + \hat{H}_2 - \hat{H}_3$. (Notice that the term $\phi_N G_N$ corresponds to a type three income.) Equation (3.5a) is a special case of equation (10.25f): that is, $W^i = b_i + a_i Y$ is a special case of $\hat{W}^i_j = \hat{b}_i + \hat{a}_i Y_j$. The definition of G_y in equation (3.8b) is the same as in equation (10.30): that is, $G_y = H_1 + H_2 - H_3$ is the same as $\hat{G}_y = \hat{H}_1 + \hat{H}_2 - \hat{H}_3$. Nevertheless θ, which corresponds to J in equation (10.31), was not explicitly discussed in chapter three. Theorem 3.1 corresponds to equation (10.27): that is, $G_y = \hat{H}_1 + \hat{H}_2 - \hat{H}_3$. Theorem 3.2 corresponds to equation (10.19): that is, $G(\hat{W}^i) = (a_i/\phi_i) G_y = G_i$ for type one and type two incomes, and $G(\hat{W}^i) = -(a_i/\phi_i) G_y = G_i$ for type three income. The statements in equations (3.12a) and (3.12b) are proved by equation (10.21): that is, $G_i \geq G_y$ for type one income, and $G_i \leq G_y$ for type two income. Equations (3.14a) and (3.14b) are suggested by theorem 10.5: that is, when there is no type three income, $G_y = \phi_1 G_1 + \phi_2 G_2 + \ldots + \phi_r G_r - \theta$, where $\theta \geq 0$, is suggested by $\hat{\hat{G}}_y =$

$\phi_1 G_1 + \phi_2 G_2 + \ldots + \phi_p G_p$, where $\hat{\hat{G}}_y$ overestimates G_y by an amount equal to the error term E.

Remarks on Chapter Six

Equations (6.3a) and (6.3c) of chapter six stated that:

(11.2a) $V = C_1 + C_2 + C_3 + S$ and

[*expenditure model*]

(11.2b) $Y = V + T_1 + T_2$.

[*tax model*]

In the expenditure model the pattern of income after tax $[V = (V_1, V_2, \ldots, V_n)]$ is the sum of three consumption components $[C_i = (C_{i1}, C_{i2}, \ldots, C_{in})\ (i = 1, 2, 3)]$ and a savings component $[S = (s_1, s_2, \ldots, s_n)]$. In the tax model the pattern of income before tax $[Y = (y_1, y_2, \ldots, y_n)]$ is the sum of V and the patterns of direct tax payments $[T_1 = (t_{11}, t_{12}, \ldots, t_{1n})]$ and indirect tax payments $[T_2 = (t_{21}, t_{22}, \ldots, t_{2n})]$. For these two models the exact decomposition equation (10.5) was applied: $G_y = \sum \phi_i R_i G_i$ [see equations (6.4a) and (6.4b) in chapter six].

The tax model is a good example of the way sound economic reasoning should guide the choice among decomposition models. When total income before tax is monotonically increasing $[Y_1 \leq Y_2 \leq \ldots \leq Y_n]$, any reasonable taxation system should approximately satisfy the conditions that V, T_1, and T_2 also are monotonically increasing—conditions described as "no reversal of rank" and "minimum progressiveness" in equation (6.8) of chapter six. Thus confidence in this reasoning should have led to the choice of the monotonic model, not the more complicated general model. As it turned out, the accuracy of exact decomposition associated with using equation (10.5) is spurious because all the correlation characteristics $[R_i]$ are close to 1, as would be expected in the first place (see the values of R_v, R_1^t, and R_2^t in table 6.3 of chapter six).

In the expenditure model, whether C_i should be monotonically increasing or decreasing is a matter of well-known theoretical speculation in the economic theory of consumption. The pattern of consumption $[C_i]$ is expected to be monotonically increasing if the commodity is a noninferior good; it is expected to be monotonically decreasing if the commodity is an inferior good. For this model it turns out that the correlation characteristics $[R_i]$ also are close to 1 (see the values of R_1^c, R_2^c, R_3^c, and R_s in table 6.2). Nevertheless the general equation (10.5) was used in chapter six, as it should be in such cases, because the strength of those correlations was uncertain until the values of R_i were calculated.

Additive Factor Components and Growth Theory

The models of additive factor components have been abstractly constructed to emphasize that these models can be applied to many problems once there is a classification of the sources of income. In a theoretical application, the models must be combined with additional theoretical notions, economic and noneconomic, to increase the understanding of the social and economic forces that determine the equity of family income distribution. When adopting such an approach, certain behavioristic assumptions usually must be added to the framework of additive components.

The analysis of equity in relation to growth in chapter three is an example of such an approach. But in that chapter the linear model was used as a first approximation: $G_y = \phi_w G_w + \phi_\pi G_\pi - \theta$. What if the basic decomposition equation (10.5) had been used instead? What would have been the added theoretical requirement associated with such a generalization? To illustrate with the urban family case of chapter three:

$$\text{(11.3)} \qquad G_y = R_w \phi_w G_w + R_\pi \phi_\pi G_\pi, \quad \text{where} \quad \phi_w + \phi_\pi = 1.$$

Equation (11.3) decomposes G_y into the wage income effect $[R_w \phi_w G_w]$ and the property income effect $[R_\pi \phi_\pi G_\pi]$. The decomposition now is exact. This exactness appears to be an advantage, because it now is unnecessary to worry about an error term in empirical applications. That advantage is not gained, however, without a cost. The theoretical requirement becomes greater because of the appearance of the correlation characteristics $[R_w$ and $R_\pi]$ in equation (11.3).

When these variables are functions of time, differentiating equation (11.3) gives:

$$\text{(11.4a)} \qquad \frac{dG_y}{dt} = B^o + D^o + R^o, \quad \text{where}$$

(11.4b) $$B^o = R_w\phi_\pi \frac{dG_w}{dt} + R_\pi\phi_\pi \frac{dG_\pi}{dt},$$

[*factor Gini effect*]

(11.4c) $$D^o = (R_wG_w - R_\pi G_\pi) \frac{d\phi_w}{dt}, \quad \text{and}$$

[*functional distribution effect*]

(11.4d) $$R^o = \phi_wG_w \frac{dR_w}{dt} + \phi_\pi G_\pi \frac{dR_\pi}{dt}.$$

[*correlation effect*]

Notice that the terms B^o and D^o are direct generalizations of the factor Gini effect [B] and the functional distribution effect [D] of equation (3.16) in chapter three. The term R^o is a newly added correlation effect. It indicates the impact of the variation of the correlation characteristic on total income inequality. It essentially captures the variations of the ways in which wage and property income are correlated with total family income: that is, the extent of exceptions to the rule that wealthier families tend over time to receive more wage and property income than poorer families. This simple example shows that at least three types of forces can affect G_y in the process of growth.

The endeavor to link growth theory with income distribution theory can proceed at the aggregate or disaggregate level. The framework of reasoning provided by equation (11.3), or equation (3.16) in chapter three, aims to link them at the aggregate level and to take advantage of the knowledge accumulated in the more developed branch of development theory. A good example of this link is the functional distribution effect; another is the reallocation effect in the more general all-households model. These effects constitute the focal points of analysis of aggregate growth theory in a dualistic economy and can now be incorporated into the framework of FID analysis.

It should be noted that very little is inductively known about R^o. Even less is known about a positive behavioristic theory of R^o. Thus, by focusing on the special case in chapter three and omitting R^o in the framework of reasoning, heavy costs are not incurred because not much is to be gained by including R^o. This is not to deny that future advances in understanding R^o would be helpful.

The obvious advantage of theoretical simplicity in the special case must be weighed against the disadvantage of imprecise results traceable to the omission of R^o. When aggregated data are used, as in the analysis in chapter three, θ/G_y is observed to be uniformly less than one percent. Thus the precision of analysis is not impaired by the use of the approximation formula. In fact, the use of equation (11.3) instead of $G_y = \phi_w G_w + \phi_\pi G_\pi - \theta$ would have led to an expensive search for spurious accuracy traceable to a factor $[R^o]$ about which not much is known.

By constructing a number of abstract models of additive factor components as frameworks for theoretical reasoning and empirical analysis, it has been shown that the choice of appropriate models is guided not only by the availability of statistical data, but by the complementary theoretical inputs which are currently or potentially available.

Income Components with Observation Error

In economic applications total family income $[Y_i]$ may be the sum of several components and an observation error $[\delta_i]$. Thus:

$$\text{(11.5a)} \quad Y_i = W_i^1 + W_i^2 + \ldots + W_i^p + \delta_i; \quad (i = 1, 2, \ldots, n)$$

$$\text{(11.5b)} \quad \delta_1 + \delta_2 + \ldots + \delta_n = 0;$$

$$\text{(11.5c)} \quad s_y = Y_1 + Y_2 + \ldots Y_n = S_1 + S_2 + \ldots + S_p;$$

$$\text{(11.5d)} \quad S_i = W_1^i + W_2^i + \ldots + W_n^i. \quad (i = 1, 2, \ldots, p)$$

In vector notation let $\delta = (\delta_1, \delta_2, \ldots, \delta_n)$. Then:

$$\text{(11.6a)} \quad Y = W^1 + W^2 + \ldots + W^p + \delta, \quad \text{where}$$

$$\text{(11.6b)} \quad \delta = (\delta_1, \delta_2, \ldots, \delta_n).$$

Notice that the sum of all elements in δ is zero by construction. All other vectors—that is, Y and W^i $(i = 1, 2, \ldots, p)$—are assumed to be nonnegative. Thus the only difference between equation (11.5) and the components problem introduced at the beginning of chapter ten is that one "factor component" may have negative entries: δ. Such a situation may arise, for example, when Y and W^i are independently estimated in empirical work.

The Gini coefficients G_y and G_i $(i = 1, 2, \ldots, p)$ can be defined as before. But a Gini coefficient cannot be defined for δ because it contains negative entries. To construct a decomposition equation, first construct a system of weights and define a weighted observation error, δ, in the following manner:

(11.7a) $j_i = i/g,$ where $(i = 1, 2, \ldots, n)$

(11.7b) $g = 1 + 2 + \ldots + n = n(n + 1)/n,$

(11.7c) $\delta = j_1\delta_1 + j_2\delta_2 + \ldots + j_n\delta_n,$ and

(11.7d) $\Delta = \delta/\bar{Y},$ where

(11.7e) $\bar{Y} = (Y_1 + Y_2 + \ldots + Y_n)/n$ and

(11.7f) $j_1 + j_2 + \ldots + j_n = 1.$

Thus $(j_1, j_2, \ldots, j_n)$ are the "rank weights"; δ is the rank-weighted observation error; and Δ is δ expressed as a fraction of the mean income of all families.

THEOREM 11.1. $G_y = \phi_1\bar{G}_1 + \phi_2\bar{G}_2 + \ldots + \phi_p\bar{G}_p + (n + 1)\Delta/n,$ *where* $\Delta = \delta/\bar{Y}.$

Proof: $u_y = (1/s_y) \sum Y_i \lambda_i = (1/s_y) \sum \lambda_i(W_i^1 + W_i^2 + \ldots W_i^p + \delta_i)$ by equation (11.5)

$$= (s_1/s_y)(\sum \lambda_i W_i^1/s_1) + (s_2/s_y)(\sum \lambda_i W_i^2/s_2) + \ldots + (s_p/s_y)(\sum \lambda_i W_i^p/s_p) + (1/s_y)\sum \lambda_i\delta_i$$

$$= \phi_1\bar{u}_1 + \phi_2\bar{u}_2 + \ldots + \phi_p\bar{u}_p + J, \quad \text{where}$$

$$J = (1/s_y)\sum\lambda_i\delta_i = (S_n/s_y)(\lambda_1\delta_1/S_n + \lambda_2\delta_2/S_n + \ldots + \lambda_n\delta_n/S_n)$$

$$= [n(n + 1)/2s_y][j_1\delta_1 + j_2\delta_2 + \ldots + j_n\delta_n]$$

by equations (11.7b) and (11.7c)

$$= (n + 1)\delta/2\bar{Y}$$

$$= (n + 1)\Delta/2.$$

Hence:

$$G_y = (2/n)u_y - (n + 1)/n$$

$$= (2/n)[\phi_1\bar{u}_1 + \phi_2\bar{u}_2 + \ldots + \phi_p\bar{u}_p + (n + 1)\Delta/2] - (n + 1)/n$$

$$= \phi_1\bar{G}_1 + \phi_2\bar{G}_2 + \ldots + \phi_p\bar{G}_p + (n + 1)\Delta/n.$$

This completes the proof.

Based on theorem 11.1, equation (10.5) can be modified as:

$$(11.8a) \quad G_y = \phi_1 R_1 G_1 + \phi_2 R_2 G_2 + \ldots + \phi_p R_p G_p + (n+1)\Delta/\text{n},$$

where:

$$(11.8b) \quad R_i = \bar{G}_i / G_i \quad \text{and} \qquad (i = 1, 2, \ldots, p)$$

$$(11.8c) \quad \Delta = \delta/\bar{Y} = (j_1\delta_1 + j_2\delta_2 + \ldots + j_n\delta_n)/\bar{Y}, \quad \text{where}$$

$$(11.8d) \quad j_i = 2i/n(n+1).$$

Theorem 11.1 is a direct generalization of the special case of equation (10.5).

Family Income with Negative Components

In empirical reality the net income of a family may have a negative component. For example, although gross income has such positive components as wage income and property income, tax payments must be subtracted from gross income to obtain net family income. The following equations formulate this problem conceptually:

$$(11.9a) \quad W^i = \text{col}(W_1^i, W_2^i, \ldots, W_n^i) \geq 0; \qquad (i = 1, 2, \ldots, p)$$

$$(11.9b) \quad Z^i = \text{col}(Z_1^i, Z_2^i, \ldots, Z_n^i) \geq 0; \qquad (i = 1, 2, \ldots, q)$$

$$(11.9c) \quad \delta_c = \text{col}(\delta_1, \delta_2, \ldots, \delta_n); \qquad (\textstyle\sum \delta_i = 0)$$

$$(11.9d) \quad Y = W^1 + W^2 + \ldots + W^p - Z^1 - Z^2 \ldots - Z^q + \delta_c$$
$$= \text{col}(Y_1, Y_2, \ldots . Y_n) \geq 0;$$

$$(11.9e) \quad X = Y + Z^1 + Z^2 + \ldots + Z^q = W^1 + W^2 + \ldots + W^p + \delta_c$$
$$= \text{col}(X_1, X_2, \ldots, X_n) \geq 0.$$

Thus W^i stands for the ith positive income component; Z^i for the ith negative income component. Net family income is Y; gross family income is X. As in the preceding section, δ_c stands for a column vector containing the elements δ_i with a zero sum. It is assumed that gross incomes are arranged in a monotonically increasing order:

$$(11.10) \qquad X_1 \leq X_2 \leq \ldots \leq X_n.$$

The purpose of the analysis is to find out the causation factors that explain G_y, the inequality of net income. Equation (11.9d) shows that this problem can be solved by investigating two components problems:

(11.11a) $$X = Y + Z^1 + Z^2 + \dots + Z^q;$$

(11.11b) $$X = W^1 + W^2 + \dots + W^p + \delta_c.$$

To apply equation (11.8) to these problems, the terms ϕ_i, R_i, and Δ must be defined. For ϕ_i, define:

(11.12a) $$\bar{X} = (X_1 + X_2 + \dots + X_n)/n,$$

(11.12b) $$\bar{Z}_i = (Z_1^i + Z_2^i + \dots + Z_n^i)/n, \qquad (i = 1, 2, \dots, q)$$

(11.12c) $$\bar{W}^i = (W_1^i + W_2^i + \dots + W_n^i)/n, \qquad (i = 1, 2, \dots, p)$$

(11.12d) $$\bar{Y} = (Y_1 + Y_2 + \dots + Y_n)/n;$$

(11.13) $$\bar{X} = \bar{Y} + (\bar{Z}_1 + \bar{Z}_2 + \dots + \bar{Z}_q) \quad \text{by equation (11.9e)}$$

$$= \bar{W}_1 + \bar{W}_2 + \dots + \bar{W}_p$$

by equations (11.9e) and (11.9c);

(11.14a) $$\phi_y = \bar{Y}/\bar{X},$$

(11.14b) $$\phi_i^z = \bar{Z}_i/\bar{X}, \qquad (\text{i} = 1, 2, \dots, q)$$

(11.14c) $$\phi_i^w = \bar{W}_i/\bar{X}, \qquad (i = 1, 2, \dots, p)$$

(11.14d) $$\theta_i^z = \phi_i^z/\phi_y = \bar{Z}_i/\bar{Y}, \qquad (i = 1, 2, \dots, q)$$

(11.14e) $$\theta_i^w = \phi_i^w/\phi_y = \bar{W}_i/\bar{Y}; \qquad (i = 1, 2, \dots, p)$$

(11.15a) $$\phi_y + \phi_1^z + \phi_2^z + \dots + \phi_q^z = 1 \quad \text{by equation (11.12b),}$$

(11.15b) $$\phi_1^w + \phi_2^w + \phi_3^w + \dots + \phi_p^w = 1 \quad \text{by equation (11.12b).}$$

In equation (11.12) the means are defined for all the column vectors of equation (11.9e), leading to the equalities in equation (11.13). The relative shares of the two components problems in equation (11.11) are defined in relation to these means. Observe that ϕ_y is net income as a fraction of gross income; ϕ_i^w is the ith income component as a fraction of gross income; ϕ_i^z is the ith payment as a fraction of gross income. In equation (11.14) the income and payment components are expressed as a fraction of net income: θ_i^w and θ_i^z. To apply equation (11.8), the following must also be defined:

(11.16a) $G_x = G(X)$,

(11.16b) $G_y = G(Y)$,

(11.16c) $G_i^z = G(Z^i)$, $(i = 1, 2, \ldots, q)$

(11.16d) $G_i^w = G(W^i)$; $(i = 1, 2, \ldots, p)$

(11.17a) $\bar{G}_y = \bar{G}(y)$,

(11.17b) $\bar{G}_i^z = \bar{G}(Z^i)$, $(i = 1, 2, \ldots, q)$

(11.17c) $\bar{G}_i^w = \bar{G}(W^i)$; $(i = 1, 2, \ldots, p)$

(11.18a) $R_y = \bar{G}_y/G_y$,

(11.18b) $R_i^z = \bar{G}_i^z/G_i^z$, $(i = 1, 2, \ldots, q)$

(11.18c) $R_i^w = \bar{G}_i^w/G_i^w$; $(i = 1, 2, \ldots, p)$

(11.19) $\Delta = (j_1\delta_1 + j_2\delta_2 + \ldots + j_n\delta_n)/\bar{X}$ by equation (11.8c).

In equation (11.16) G_x is the Gini coefficient of gross family income; G_y, of net family income; G_i^w, of the ith income component; G_i^z, of the ith payment component. The pseudo Gini coefficients are defined in equation (11.17). Notice that these pseudo Gini coefficients are defined relative to expression (11.10): the gross income ranking is used as the exogenous characteristic. The relative correlation coefficients are defined in equation (11.18); the relative rank-weighted error term is defined in equation (11.19).

Applying equation (11.8) to the two problems in equation (11.11) gives:

(11.20a) $G_x = \phi_y R_y G_y + \phi_1^z R_1^z G_1^z + \phi_2^z R_2^z G_2^z + \ldots + \phi_q^z R_q^z G_q^z$

by equation (11.16) and

(11.20b) $G_x = \phi_1^w R_1^w G_1^w + \phi_2^w R_2^w G_2^w + \ldots + \phi_p^w R_p^w G_p^w + (n+1)\Delta/n$

by equations (11.17) and (11.19).

It now is possible to solve for G_y and obtain:

(11.21a) $G_y = (A^+ - A^- + E)/R_y$, where

(11.21b) $A^+ = \theta_1^w R_1^w G_1^w + \theta_2^w R_2^w G_2^w + \ldots + \theta_p^w R_p^w G_p^w \geq 0$,

[*income effect*]

(11.21c) $A^- = \theta_1^z R_1^z G_1^z + \theta_2^z R_2^z G_2^z + \ldots + \theta_q^z R_q^z G_q^z \geq 0,$ and

[*payment effect*]

(11.21d) $E = (n + 1)\Delta/n\phi_y$

$= [(n + 1)/n](j_1\delta_1 + j_2\delta_2 + \ldots + j_n\delta_n)/\bar{X}\phi_y$

by equation (11.19)

$= [(n + 1)/n](j_1\delta_1 + j_2\delta_2 + \ldots + j_n\delta_n)\bar{Y}$

[*decomposition error*] by equation (11.14).

The inequality of net family income $[G_y]$ is therefore decomposed into an income effect $[A^+]$, a payment effect $[A^-]$, and an error term $[E]$. When an income component is positively correlated with gross income—that is, when $R_i^w > 0$—an unequal distribution of an income component, indicated by a large G_i^w, contributes to income inequality. When an income component is negatively correlated with gross income—that is, when $R_i^w < 0$—an unequal distribution of an income component contributes to income equality. The opposite relations are true for the payment effect. When a payment is negatively correlated with gross income, an unequal distribution of payment, indicated by a large G_i^z, contributes to net income equality. The error term $[E]$ tends to be small when net income accounts for a higher fraction of gross income and ϕ_y is large.

Computation Procedure

A numerical example will now illustrate the computation procedure for the problem described in the preceding section. For the five families shown in table 11.1, there are two types of income (wage and property), two types of payment (tax and transfer), and an error term. Net income $[Y_i]$ and gross income $[X_i]$ are also given. All families are arranged in a monotonically increasing order according to gross income, thereby satisfying expression (11.10). The pseudo Gini coefficients are computed relative to this family ranking. It should be noted in this example that the rankings

Table 11.1. *Numerical Example of Original Income Data*

Variable	*Notation*	*Family 1*	*Family 2*	*Family 3*	*Family 4*	*Family 5*	*Total*
Wage income	W^1	8	4	12	20	6	50
Property income	W^2	0	10	5	15	45	75
Tax payment	Z^1	−1	−3	0	−4	−7	−15
Transfer payment	Z^2	−2	−2	−2	−2	−2	−10
Error term	δ_i	0	1	0	1	−2	0
Net family income	Y_i	5	10	15	30	40	100
Gross family income	X_i	8	15	17	36	49	125

Source: Constructed by the authors.

Table 11.2. *Distributive Shares, Gini Coefficients, and Pseudo Gini Coefficients for Original Data in Table 11.1*

Variable	*Notation*	X	Y	W^1	W^2	Z^1	Z^2
Mean		25	20	10	15	3	2
Distributive share in X	ϕ_i	1.0	0.8	0.4	0.6	0.12	0.08
Distributive share in Y	ϕ_i	—	1.0	0.5	0.75	0.15	0.10
Gini coefficient	G_i	0.3296	0.3600	0.3040	0.5333	0.4533	0.0000
Pseudo Gini coefficient	$\bar{G}_i$	—	0.3600	0.0960	0.5066	0.3467	0.0000
Relative correlation	R_i	—	1.0000	0.3158	0.9499	0.7648	0.0000

— Not applicable.
Source: Calculated from table 11.1.

of families according to X and Y are the same. This relation nevertheless is just an accident leading to $R_y = 1$. Thus table 11.1 contains all the primary data needed for the decomposition problem. The computation procedure is set forth in tables 11.2 and 11.3.

Table 11.3. *Decomposition Analysis of Original Data in Table 11.1*

Variable	*Notation*	*Computation*	*Value*
Rank-weighted error term	Δ	$= \delta/\bar{X} = (j_1\delta_1 + j_2\delta_2 + \ldots + j_5\delta_5)/\bar{X}$ $= -(4/15)/25 =$	$-4/3$
Income effect[a]	A^+	$= \theta_1^w R_1^w G_1^w + \theta_2^w R_2^w G_2^w =$	0.4279
Payment effect[b]	A^-	$= \theta_1^z R_1^z G_1^z + \theta_2^z R_2^z G_2^z =$	0.0519
Decomposition error[c]	E	$= (n + 1)\Delta/n\phi_y =$	−0.0160
Decomposition analysis[d]	G_y	$= A^+ - A^- + E$ $= 0.4279 - 0.0519 - 0.0160 =$	0.3600
Relative weight	1	$= A^+/G_y - A^-/G_y + E/G_y$ $= 1.1886 - 0.1446 + (-0.0440) =$	1.0000

Sources: Calculated from tables 11.1 and 11.2.
a. See equation (11.20b).
b. See equation (11.20c).
c. See equation (11.20d).
d. See equation (11.20a).

CHAPTER 12

Regression Analysis, Homogeneous Groups, and Aggregation Error

THREE ADDITIONAL SUBJECTS require elaboration. The first is the manner in which regression analysis of variations in family income can be related to the analysis of additive factor components. The second is the analysis of the distribution of income by homogeneous groups of income recipients. The analysis of these groups could be so construed that the Gini coefficient is decomposed into intergroup and intragroup effects, as well as a crossover effect. That crossover effect will be shown to increase as the decisiveness with which ordinal rankings of groups affect earning power is perverted. The third subject is the error introduced when grouped data on the distribution of family income must be used because of the unavailability of primary data. It will be shown that the use of grouped data leads to the consistent underestimation of the index of inequality and hence the degree of that inequality.

Regression Analysis

One of the most popular methods used in attempts to explain the variation of family income is based on a linear regression model of the following form:

(12.1a) $Y = a + b_1X^1 + b_2X^2 + \ldots + b_qX^q + \delta,$ where

(12.1b) $X^i \geq 0.$

The family income is to be explained by independent variables $[X^i]$ which stand for various ordinal characteristics, such as education, age, and sex. The term δ represents a randomly distributed error term. The basic aim of regression analysis is twofold: first, to estimate the regression constant a and the regression coefficients b_i; second, to assess the reliability of these estimations once the observable data of n families are given:

(12.2a) $$Y = \mathrm{col}(Y_1, Y_2, \ldots, Y_n);$$

(12.2b) $$X^i = \mathrm{col}(X_1^i, X_2^i, \ldots, X_n^i) \geq 0; \quad (i = 1, 2, \ldots, q)$$

(12.2c) $$0 \leq Y_1 \leq Y_2 \leq \ldots \leq Y_n.$$

The total incomes of the n families and the values of the independent variables are shown as column vectors. Assume that the regression constant a and the coefficients b_i are already estimated and given as a starting point of the analysis—that is, the reliability of estimation, which is the focal point of traditional regression analysis, is not a concern. Once the values of equation (12.2) and the regression coefficients are given:

(12.3a) $$Y = a_c + b_1X^1 + b_2X^2 + \ldots + b_qX^q + \delta_c, \quad \text{where}$$

(12.3b) $$a_c = \mathrm{col}(a, a, \ldots, a),$$

(12.3c) $$\delta_c = \mathrm{col}(\delta_1, \delta_2, \ldots, \delta_n), \quad \text{and}$$

(12.3d) $$\delta_1 + \delta_2 + \ldots + \delta_n = 0,$$

and where δ_i is an error term defined to ensure equality for the regression equation of the ith family. Notice in equation (12.3d) that the sum of all values of δ_i is zero. It can now be seen that the vector of total family income is the sum of $q + 2$ components: the first component is the constant term a; the last component is the error term δ_i; the other q components are the independent variables.

Causation of G_y based on regression analysis

Traditional regression analysis emphasizes the causes of variation in family income $[Y]$; it is not concerned with the cause of variation in the inequality of family income $[G_y]$. Nevertheless, when the traditional regression analysis is done, it is possible to proceed with an analysis of G_y based on the technique developed in chapter eleven for factor component analysis. This possibility is seen from equation (12.3a), where the Y vector is the additive sum of $q + 2$ column vectors: that is, Y now has $q + 2$ components. In particular, equation (12.3d) shows that equation (11.9) is applicable. Consequently the decomposition result obtained in equation (11.18) can be applied.

The sign of the column vector b_iX^i is the same as that of the regression coefficient. The sign of the column vector a_c is the same as that of the regression constant. Therefore equation (12.3) can be rewritten in two ways, depending upon whether a_c is positive or negative:

$$(12.4a)\quad Y = a_c + b_1X^1 + b_2X^2 + \ldots. + b_pX^p - (c_1Z^1 + c_2Z^2 + \ldots + c_qZ^q) + \delta_c \quad \text{when } a_c \geq 0, \text{ and}$$

$$(12.4b)\quad Y = b_1X^1 + b_2X^2 + \ldots + b_pX^p - (a_c + c_1Z^1 + c_2Z^2 + \ldots + c_qZ^q) + \delta_c \quad \text{when } a_c < 0,$$

where:

$$(12.4c)\quad b_i \geq 0, \qquad (i = 1, 2, \ldots, p)$$

$$(12.4d)\quad c_i < 0, \qquad (i = 1, 2, \ldots, q)$$

$$(12.4e)\quad Y = \text{col}(Y_1, Y_2, \ldots, Y_n) \geq 0,$$

$$(12.4f)\quad X^i = \text{col}(X_1^i, X_2^i, \ldots, X_n^i) \geq 0,$$

$$(12.4g)\quad Z = \text{col}(Z_1^i, Z_2^i, \ldots, Z_n^i) \geq 0,$$

$$(12.4h)\quad a_c = \text{col}(a, a, \ldots, a), \quad \text{and}$$

$$(12.4i)\quad \delta_c = \text{col}(\delta_1, \delta_2, \ldots, \delta_n), \quad \text{where}$$

$$(12.4j)\quad \delta_1 + \delta_2 + \ldots + \delta_n = 0.$$

Use the notation $M(X)$ to denote the mean of the column vector X. Applying this notation to the column vectors of equations (12.4a) and (12.4b) gives:

$$(12.5a)\quad M(Y) = [a + b_1M(X^1) + b_2M(X^2) + \ldots + b_pM(X^p)] - [c_1M(Z^1) + c_2M(Z^2) + \ldots + c_qM(Z^q)] \quad \text{when } a \geq 0,$$

(12.5b) $$M(Y) = [b_1M(X^1) + b_2M(X^2) + \ldots + b_pM(X^p)] - [a + c_1M(Z^1) + c_2M(Z^2) + \ldots + c_qM(Z^q) \quad \text{when} \quad a < 0,$$

(12.5c) $$\phi_a = |\, a \,| / M(Y),$$

(12.5d) $$\phi_i^x = b_iM(X^i)/M(Y), \quad \text{and} \qquad (i = 1, 2, \ldots, p)$$

(12.5e) $$\phi_i^z = c_iM(Z^i)/M(Y). \qquad (i = 1, 2, \ldots, q)$$

For the case when $a \geq 0$ define:

(12.6a) $$U = \text{col}(U_1, U_2, \ldots, U_n) = Y + \sum_{i=1}^{q} c_iZ^i = a_c + \sum_{i=1}^{p} b_iX^i + \delta_c$$

by equation (12.4a),

(12.6b) $$\bar{U} = \sum_{i=1}^{n} U_i/n = \bar{Y} + c_1\bar{Z}_1 + c_2\bar{Z}_2 + \ldots + c_q\bar{Z}_q = a + b_1\bar{X}_1 + b_2\bar{X}_2 + \ldots + b_p\bar{X}_p, \quad \text{and}$$

(12.6c) $$\phi_y = \bar{Y}/\bar{U}.$$

For the case when $a < 0$ define:

(12.7a) $$U = \text{col}(U_1, U_2, \ldots, U_n) = Y + a + c_1Z^1 + c_2Z^2 + \ldots + c_qZ^q = b_1X^1 + b_2X^2 + \ldots + b_pX^p,$$

(12.7b) $$\bar{U} = \sum_{i=1}^{n} U_i/n = \bar{Y} + a + c_1\bar{Z}_1 + c_2\bar{Z}_2 + \ldots + c_q\bar{Z}_q = b_1\bar{X}_1 + b_2\bar{X}_2 + \ldots + b_p\bar{X}_p, \quad \text{and}$$

(12.7c) $$\phi_y = \bar{Y}/\bar{U}.$$

The definition of the column vector U corresponds to equations (11.9c) and (11.9d). Its components, given by $(U_1, U_2, \ldots, U_n)$, are assumed to be arranged in a monotonically increasing order as in expression (11.10):

$$(12.8) \qquad U_1 \leq U_2 \leq \dots \leq U_n.$$

All the pseudo Gini coefficients are defined relative to this ranking. Respectively use the notation $G(X)$ and $\bar{G}(X)$ to denote the Gini coefficient and the pseudo Gini coefficient, and define:

$$(12.9a) \qquad G_y = G(Y),$$

$$(12.9b) \qquad G(a_c) = 0,$$

$$(12.9c) \qquad G(b_iX^i) = G(X^i) = G_i^x, \qquad (i = 1, 2, \dots, p)$$

$$(12.9d) \qquad G(c_iZ^i) = G_i^z; \qquad (i = 1, 2, \dots, q)$$

$$(12.10a) \qquad \bar{G}_y = \bar{G}(Y),$$

$$(12.10b) \qquad \bar{G}(a_c) = 0,$$

$$(12.10c) \qquad \bar{G}(b_iX^i) = \bar{G}_i^x, \qquad (i = 1, 2, \dots, p)$$

$$(12.10d) \qquad G(c_iZ^i) = G_i^z; \qquad (i = 1, 2, \dots, q)$$

$$(12.11a) \qquad R_y = \bar{G}_y/G_y,$$

$$(12.11b) \qquad R_i^x = \bar{G}_i^x/G_i^x, \qquad (i = 1, 2, \dots, p)$$

$$(12.11c) \qquad R_i^z = \bar{G}_i^z/G_i^z; \quad \text{and} \qquad (i = 1, 2, \dots, q)$$

$$(12.12a) \qquad E = [(n + 1)/n](j_1\delta_1 + j_2\delta_2 + \dots + j_n\delta_n)/\bar{Y}, \quad \text{where}$$

$$(12.12b) \qquad j_i = 2i/n(n + 1).$$

Notice in equations (12.9) and (12.10) that the Gini coefficient and pseudo Gini coefficient for the column vector a_c obviously are zero. The Gini coefficient and pseudo Gini coefficient for the column vector b_iX^i obviously are the same as $G(X_i)$; those for the column vector c_iZ_i, the same as $G(Z_i)$. Hence the regression constant a and the regression coefficients b_i and c_i are not involved in the foregoing definitions. They nevertheless are involved in the definition of the relative shares in equation (12.5c). A direct application of equation (11.18) leads to:

$$(12.13a) \qquad G_y = (A^+ - A^- + E)/R_y,$$

where R_y is defined as in equation (12.11) and where:

$$(12.13b) \qquad A^+ = \phi_1^x R_1^x G_1^x + \phi_2^x R_2^x G_2^x + \dots + \phi_p^x R_p^x G_p^x,$$

$$(12.13c) \qquad A^- = \phi_1^z R_1^z G_1^z + \phi_2^z R_2^z G_2^z + \dots + \phi_q^z R_q^z G_q^z, \quad \text{and}$$

$$(12.13d) \qquad E = [(n + 1)/n](j_1\delta_1 + j_2\delta_2 + \dots + j_n\delta_n)\bar{Y}.$$

Table 12.1. *Numerical Example of Income Data and Regression Terms*

Variable	*Notation*	*Family 1*	*Family 2*	*Family 3*	*Family 4*	*Family 5*	*Total*	*Mean*
Independent variables	X_i^1	4	2	6	10	3	25	5
	X_i^2	0	2	1	3	9	15	3
	Z_i^1	1	3	0	4	7	15	3
Net family income	Y_i	5	10	15	30	40	100	20
Column vectors								
$a = -2$	a	−2	−2	−2	−2	−2	−10	−2
$b_1 = 2$	$b_1x_i^1$	8	4	12	20	6	50	10
$b_2 = 5$	$b_2x_i^2$	0	10	5	15	45	75	15
$c_1 = -1$	$c_1z_i^1$	−1	−3	0	−4	−7	−15	−3
Estimated net family income	$\hat{Y}_i$	5	9	15	29	42	—	—
Error term	δ_i	0	1	0	1	−2	0	0
Gross family income	U_i	8	15	17	36	49	125	25

— Not applicable.
Source: Constructed by the authors.

The terms in equations (12.13b) and (12.13c) were defined in equations (12.5c) and (12.11); those in equation (12.13d), in equations (12.6), (12.7), and (12.12).

Computation procedure

Table 12.1 gives for five families the family income [Y_i] and the values of the three independent variables [X^1, X^2, and Z^1]. From this set of data a regression equation of the following form is estimated:

(12.14a) $Y = a + b_1X^1 + b_2X^2 + c_1Z^1$, where

(12.14b) $a = -2, b_1 = 2, b_2 = 5, c_1 = -1.$

Table 12.2. *Distributive Shares, Gini Coefficients, and Pseudo Gini Coefficients for Original Data in Table 12.1*

Variable	*Notation*	a	X_1	X_2	Z_1	Y	U
Net family income weight $[\bar{Y}/\bar{U}]$	ϕ_y	—	—	—	—	4/5	—
Distributive share in Y	ϕ_i	−2/20	1/2	3/4	−3/20	1/1	—
Gini coefficient	G_i	0.0000	0.3040	0.5333	0.4533	0.3600	0.3296
Pseudo Gini coefficient	$\bar{G}_i$	0.0000	0.0960	0.5066	0.3467	0.3600	—
Relative correlation	R_i	0.0000	0.3158	0.9499	0.7648	1.0000	—

— Not applicable.
Source: Calculated from table 12.1.

When the values of X_i^1, X_i^2, and Z_i^1 in table 12.1 are substituted into this equation, the column vectors a, $b_1x_i^1$, $b_2x_i^2$, and $c_1x_i^1$ are obtained. The sum of those vectors is the estimated value of net family income $[\hat{Y}_i]$. The error term is the difference between $\hat{Y}_i$ and Y_i. Notice that the sum of the vector δ is zero. Notice also that the vectors a and $c_1x_i^1$ are both negative. The sum of nonnegative vectors—that is, $b_1x_i^1$, $b_2x_i^2$, and δ_i—is shown in the row for gross family income. The computation of pseudo Gini coefficients is carried out relative to this ranking (table 12.2). Notice that when the regression analysis is transformed into an income components problem, it takes on exactly the same numerical value as shown in table 11.2. Thus the decomposition analysis shown in table 12.3 merely is a repetition of that in table 11.3.

Remarks on chapter four

The analysis of inequality of family wage income in chapter four was based on the decomposition equation (12.13a) In table 4.6 of that chapter the regression coefficients a_1, a_2, a_3, and a_4 are positive; the regression constant a_0 is negative. This is a special case of equation (12.4b) in which the terms $Z^1, Z^2, \ldots, Z^q$ vanish. Equation (12.7) reduces to the special case:

$$\text{(12.15a)} \quad U = \text{col}\,(U_1, U_2, \ldots, U_n)$$

$$= Y + a_c = b_1X_1 + b_2X_2 + b_3X_3 + b_4X_4 + \delta_c;$$

Table 12.3. *Decomposition Analysis of Original Data in Table 12.1*

Variable	*Computation*	*Value*
Rank-weighted error term	$= \delta/\bar{Y} = (j_1\delta_1 + j_2\delta_2 + \ldots + j_5\delta_5/\bar{Y}$ $= (-4/15)/20 =$	$-1/75$
Income effect[a]	$A^+ = \phi_1^x R_1^x G_1^x + \phi_2^x R_2^x G_2^x =$	0.4279
Payment effect[b]	$A^- = \phi_1^z R_1^z G_1^z + \phi_a R_a G_a =$	−0.0519
Decomposition error[c]	$E = (n+1)\Delta/n =$	−0.0160
Decomposition analysis[d]	$G_y = A^+ - A^- + E$ $= 0.4279 - 0.0519 - 0.0160 =$	0.3600
Relative weight	$1 = A^+/G_y - A^-/G_y + E/G_y$ $= 1.1886 - 0.1446 + (-0.0440) =$	1.0000

Sources: Calculated from tables 12.1 and 12.2.
a. See equation (12.13b).
b. See equation (12.13c).
c. See equation (12.13d).
d. See equation (12.13a).

(12.15b) $U_1 \leq U_2 \leq \ldots \leq U_n$ implies that $Y_1 \leq Y_2 \leq \ldots \leq Y_n$ by expression (12.8);

(12.15c) $R_y = 1$ as $\bar{G}_y = G_y$ in equation (12.11a);

(12.15d) $\phi_y = \bar{Y}/\bar{U} = \bar{Y}/(\bar{Y} + a)$ in equation (12.7).

Thus equation (12.13) reduces to the special case:

(12.16a) $G_y = \phi_1 R_1 G_1 + \phi_2 R_2 G_2 + \ldots + \phi_p R_p G_p + E,$ where

(12.16b) $E = (\langle n+1\rangle/n)(j_1\delta_1 + j_2\delta_2 + \ldots + j_n\delta_n)/\bar{Y}.$

Equation (12.16a) is the decomposition equation (4.3) in chapter four. In that chapter ϕ_i is defined in equation (4.11e), G_i in equation (4.5b), R_i in equation (4.13a), and $E = \Delta$ in equation (4.12a).

In equation (4.18a) $\hat{W}$ is defined as the sum of the nonnegative components indicated on the right-hand side. Thus the decomposition equation (4.15) used in chapter four is the exact decomposition equation (10.5) of chapter ten.

Family Income Inequality with Homogeneous Groups

In the analysis of family income distribution, one popular approach is to identify homogeneous groups of income recipients. For example, the homogeneous groups in the urban sector may be capitalist families, blue-collar labor families, white-collar labor families, and civil servant families. For another example, the homogeneous groups in the rural sector may be landlord families, owner-cultivator families, and tenant families. When such groupings of families are accepted, the total family income of n families can immediately be classified into q mutually exclusive groups:

(12.17a) $$X^i = \text{col}(X_1^i, X_2^i, \ldots, X_{n_i}^i); \quad (i = 1, 2, \ldots, q)$$

(12.17b) $$n_1 + n_2 + \ldots + n_q = n;$$

(12.17c) $$\theta_i = n_i/n; \quad (i = 1, 2, \ldots, q)$$

(12.17d) $$S_i = X_1^i + X_2^i + \ldots + X_{n_i}^i; \quad (i = 1, 2, \ldots, q)$$

(12.17e) $$S_y = S_1 + S_2 + \ldots + S_q;$$

(12.17f) $$\bar{X}_i = S_i/n_i; \quad (i = 1, 2, \ldots, q)$$

(12.17g) $$\phi_i = S_i/S_y; \quad (i = 1, 2, \ldots, q)$$

(12.17h) $$\phi_1 + \phi_2 + \ldots + \phi_q = 1.$$

In equation (12.17c) θ_i is the fraction of families in the ith group; in equation (12.17g) ϕ_i is the fraction of total income earned by the ith group. The average income in the ith group is given by $\bar{X}_i$ in equation (12.17f). The value of $\bar{X}_i$ may be thought of as the income earned by a typical member of the ith group. Equation (12.17a) thus contains the primary data of this section.

Intuitive ideas associated with homogeneous groups

When a classification of families is given, the presumption is that the characteristic of each grouping is decisive in affecting total family income. More precisely two ideas are implied.

First, there is the presumption that the groups are ordinally ranked by their income-earning potential. Thus the q groups will be arranged so that:

$$\bar{X}_1 \leq \bar{X}_2 \leq \ldots \leq \bar{X}_q, \tag{12.18}$$

that is, typical incomes of the members of q groups are arranged in monotonically increasing order. As a further illustration of this point, suppose the n families to be cross-classified into six groups by education and sex (table 12.4). The integers in the six cells in this table indicate a particular ordinal ranking in which the lowly educated female contributes least in determining family income and the highly educated male contributes most. Altogether there are 720 (6!) possible ways to rank these cells ordinally. Ideally the acceptance of a particular ordinal ranking is the result of theorizing and constitutes a null hypothesis. In fact, the theorizing is informal, and the empirical ranking obtained in equation (12.18) thus is often taken to be indicative of the relative earning potential of the various groups.

Second, such a group ordering, when given as in expression (12.18), is decisive in two senses. One sense is that the variation of income within each group—that is, the variation of family income within each cell in table 12.4—should not be as great as the variation of income between the groups. Therefore the notions of intragroup and intergroup variation in incomes must be separated. The other sense is that no member of a group should receive an income higher than any member of a group with a higher ranking. When perversity is observed, it is to be regarded as evidence contradicting the hypothesis that groupings are decisive in affecting income. As an illustration of this idea, suppose in an apartheid society that the ordinal

Table 12.4. *Numerical Example of the Classification of Families by Education*

	Ordinal rank		
Sex	*Low education*	*Medium education*	*High education*
Female	1	2	3
Male	4	5	6

Source: Constructed by the authors.

ranking of white and nonwhite groups may be so decisive that no member of the nonwhite group receives an income higher than even the poorest member of the white group. If perversity of order is observed, the apartheid system will be regarded as incomplete. It follows that to measure this decisiveness a "crossover effect" should somehow be measured.

In summary, once family income is classified into homogeneous groups as in equation (12.17), an intergroup variation [G_r], an intragroup variation [A], and a crossover effect [C] should be defined.

Intergroup variation

The natural definition of G_r, the intergroup variation, is the Gini coefficient for the following set of n numbers:

$$(12.19a) \qquad R = \text{col}(\overbrace{\bar{X}_1, \bar{X}_1, \ldots, \bar{X}_1}^{n_1}; \overbrace{\bar{X}_2, \bar{X}_2, \ldots, \bar{X}_2}^{n_2}; \ldots; \overbrace{\bar{X}_q, \bar{X}_q, \ldots, \bar{X}_q}^{n_q});$$

$$(12.19b) \qquad S_y = n_1\bar{X}_1 + n_2\bar{X}_2 + \ldots + n_q\bar{X}_q.$$

Equation (12.19a) is constructed by replacing every X_j^i by the mean of the group [$\bar{X}_i$] to which it belongs. It is apparent in this set that there is no intragroup variation, because all families within each group receive a typical income. If the groups indeed are homogeneous and all members within each group cannot be distinguished from each other by their income, then equation (12.19a) represents the income pattern of idealized homogeneous groups. To define the Gini coefficient for this set, first define the following numbers:

$$(12.20) \quad C_i = n_1 + n_2 + \ldots + n_i; C_0 = 0. \qquad (i = 1, 2, \ldots, q)$$

where C_i is the cumulative number of families earning a typical income less than or equal to $\bar{X}_i$. The next theorem indicates the method of computing the Gini coefficient for the pattern of idealized homogeneous groups indicated by R in equation (12.19a):

THEOREM 12.1. $$G_r = G(R) = [\phi_1(C_0 + C_1 - n)/n] + [\phi_2(C_1 + C_2 - n)/n] + \ldots + [\phi_q(C_{q-1} + C_q - n)/n]$$

Proof: Theorem 8.2 gives:

$$G_r = \sum (\bar{X}_i - \bar{X}_j) n_i n_j / S_y n \quad \text{for } i > j$$

$$= g_1 \bar{X}_1 / S_y n + g_2 \bar{X}_2 / S_y n + \ldots + g_q \bar{X}_q / S_y n, \quad \text{where}$$

$$g_i = [(C_{i-1} - (n - C_i)] n_i.$$

The reason for this result is that $\bar{X}_i$ appears C_{i-1} times as the upper end in the definition of income gaps and $n - C_i$ times as the lower end in the definition of income gaps. Thus:

$$G_r = \sum (C_{i-1} + C_i - n) n_i \bar{X}_i / S_y n = \sum (C_{i-1} + C_i - n) \phi_i / n.$$

This completes the proof.

Intragroup variation and the crossover effect

In defining the intragroup variation [A] it is to be noted because there are q groups that A is by nature a weighted average of the intragroup variations of q groups. Therefore the intragroup variation can be heuristically defined as:

(12.21a) $A = \theta_1 \phi_1 G_1 + \theta_2 \phi_2 G_2 + \ldots + \theta_q \phi_q G_q$, where

(12.21b) $G_i = G(X^i)$. $\quad (i = 1, 2, \ldots, q)$

The intragroup effect [A] is defined to be the weighted average of the Gini coefficients of the q groups, where the weights are the product of the relative group size [θ_i] and the relative income share [ϕ_i] respectively defined in equations (12.17c) and (12.17g).

To define the crossover effect [C] it will first be assumed that the incomes of families within each group are arranged in a monotonically nondecreasing order:

(12.22) $X_1^i \leq X_2^i \leq \ldots \leq X_n^i$. $\quad (i = 1, 2, \ldots, q)$

Each of the n families so ordered will be assigned a natural ranking $(1, 2, \ldots, n)$. In other words, each family will be assigned a lexicographic ranking in the following way:

(12.23) The rank of X_j^i is $C_{i-1} + j$ (lexicographic rank).

$(j = 1, 2, \ldots, n_i)$

$(i = 1, 2, \ldots, q)$

This ranking can be illustrated by an example with seven families and three groups:

$$(12.24a)\quad (X_1^1 = 1 \leq X_2^1 = 3; X_1^2 = 1 \leq X_2^2 = 4 \leq X_3^2 = 7;$$
$$X_1^3 = 6 \leq X_2^3 = 10);$$

$$(12.24b)\quad (1, 2; 3, 4, 5; 6, 7);$$

$$(12.24c)\quad \bar{X}_1 = 2 \leq \bar{X}_2 = 4 \leq \bar{X}_3 = 8.$$

Thus the families in each group are arranged in a monotonically nondecreasing order, satisfying expression (12.22). Furthermore it can be seen from expression (12.24c) that the group means are also arranged in a monotonically nondecreasing order, thereby satisfying equation (12.18). The ranks assigned according to expression (12.23) are indicated in expression (12.24b). In order words, after the families are arranged in a lexicographic order, expression (12.23) simply is the first n integers arranged in the natural order. The ranking may be referred to as a lexicographic ranking conforming to the group decisiveness. The main idea is that members of the first group are ranked first, those of the second group second, and so on.

When the lexicographic ranking of expression (12.23) takes the place of the characteristic rank $[C]$ of equation (9.1) in chapter nine, the Gini coefficient $[G_y]$ of n families is the sum of two terms, s^+ and s^-, according to equation (9.18a). In this case the s^+ term is the average of the gaps that support the lexicographic ordering; the s^- term is the average of the gaps that contradict the lexicographic ordering. In the numerical example s^- is calculated as follows:

$$s^- = [(X_2^1 - X_1^2) + (X_3^2 - X_1^3)]/(7 \times 32)$$
$$= [(3 - 1) + (7 - 6)]/224 = 3/224.$$

Notice because of expression (12.23) that a term in s^- can only occur between two members belonging to different groups. Furthermore such a term exists when and only when a member of a lower income group earns more income than a member of a higher income group, thus perverting the lexicographic ranking. The s^- term may therefore be referred to as the crossover effect. Formally the crossover effect can be defined as:

$$(12.25) \quad s^- = \sum (X^i_p - X^j_q) \quad \text{for all} \quad X^i_p > X^j_q \quad \text{with} \quad i < j.$$

Decomposition of G_y

When the primary data on homogeneous groups are given as in equation (12.17), the intergroup variation $[G_r]$, the intragroup variation $[A]$, and the crossover effect $[s^-]$ can be defined. Now let G_y be the Gini coefficient for the n numbers X^i_j in equation (12.17a). The basic theorem to be proved is:

THEOREM 12.2. $G_y = G_r + A + 2s^-$.

The theorem states that the Gini coefficient $[G_y]$ can be decomposed into an intergroup variation term $[G_r]$, an intragroup variation term $[A]$, and twice the crossover effect $[2s^-]$.[1] All these terms are nonnegative. As a result, if homogeneous groups are postulated, the Gini coefficient of all families, when approximated by intergroup and intragroup effects, always leaves a nonnegative error $[2s^-]$. The magnitude of this error term is determined by the degree to which group decisiveness is perverted.

Theorem 12.2 can be illustrated by the numerical example in equation (12.24a) and tables 12.5 and 12.6, which classify the income of seven families into three homogeneous groups. The means of the three groups are arranged in a monotonically increasing order. With the lexicographic ordering, the supporting and nonsupporting gaps are shown by s^+ and s^-. The decomposition of G_y according to theorem 12.2 is given in the bottom row.

To prove theorem 12.2 all that is needed is to prove the following lemma:

LEMMA 12.1. $\bar{G}_y = s^+ - s^- = A + G_r$.

1. This three-way decomposition of the Gini coefficient to address the problem of homogeneous groups was first proved by Bhattacharya and Mahalanobis. It was rediscovered by Rao and reinterpreted, with simplified proofs, by Pyatt. Mangahas presented a two-way decomposition corresponding to intragroup and intergroup effects alone. In chapter five we worked with the variance, not the Gini coefficient, primarily because of the simplification caused by the disappearance of the G_r term for the particular problems tackled there. For the sources of studies mentioned here see note 1 to the introduction of part two.

Table 12.5. *Numerical Example of the Classification of Seven Families into Three Homogeneous Groups*

Variable	*Nota-tion*	*Group 1* $[x^1]$	*Group 2* $[x^2]$	*Group 3* $[x^3]$	*Total*
Family income	x_j^i	1,3	1,4,7	6,10	—
Group frequency	n_i	2	3	2	7
Group income	x^i	4	12	16	32
Mean of group income	$\bar{x}^i$	2	4	8	7/32
Relative group frequency	θ_i	2/7	3/7	2/7	—
Group income share	ϕ_i	1/8	3/8	4/8	—
Group Gini coefficient	G_i	1/4	1/3	1/8	—

— Not applicable.
Source: Constructed by the authors.

By using equation (9.15a) in addition to lemma 12.1, theorem 12.2 can be immediately derived. To prove this lemma, the Gini coefficients for every one of the q homogeneous groups are defined as:

$$(12.26a)\quad G_i = G(X^i) = G(X_1^i \leq X_2^i \leq \ldots \leq X_{n_i}^i)$$

$$= (2/n_i)u_i - (n_i + 1)/n_i, \quad \text{where} \quad (i = 1, 2, \ldots, q)$$

$$(12.26b)\quad u_i = (1)(X_1^i/S_i) + (2)(X_2^i/S_i) + \ldots + (n_i)(X_{n_i}^i/S_i)$$

by theorem 8.1.

The pseudo Gini coefficient ($\bar{G}_y$) takes on the following form:

$$(12.27a)\quad \bar{G}_y = (2/n)\bar{u}_y - (n+1)/n, \quad \text{where}$$

$$(12.27b)\quad \bar{u}_y = \phi_1 u_1 + \phi_2 u_2 + \ldots + \phi_q u_q + C_1\phi_2 + C_2\phi_3 + \ldots + C_{q-1}\phi_q,$$

where C_i is defined as in equation (12.20).

Proof: By theorem 8.3 and letting $S_y = \sum_{i=1}^{q} \sum_{j=1}^{n_i} X_j^i$:

Table 12.6. *Decomposition Analysis of Data in Table 12.5*

Variable	*Computation*	*Value*
Intergroup variation	$G_r = \Sigma(X_i - X_j)n_in_j/S_yn$ $= (4-2)(2)(3) + (8-2)(2)(2)$ $+ (8-4)(2)(3) =$	230/112
Intragroup variation	$A = \theta_i\phi_iG_i = (2/7)(1/8)(1/4)$ $+ (3/7)(3/8)(1/3)$ $+ (2/7)(4/8)(1/8) =$	9/112
Crossover effect	$s^- = (X^1_2 - X^2_1) + (X^2_3 - X^3_1)/(32)(7) =$	3/224
Supporting gap	$s^+ = (2+12+4+3+6+1+4+5+9$ $+3+7+5+9+2+6+3)/$ $(32)(7) =$	81/224
Pseudo Gini coefficient	$\bar{G}_y = A + G_r = S^+ - S^-$ $= 30/112 + 9/112$ $= 81/224 - 3/224 =$	39/112
Gini coefficient	$G_y = S^+ + S^- = 81/224$ $+ 3/224 = 84/224 =$	21/56
Decomposition of Gini coefficient	$G_y = A + G_r + 2S^-$ $= 9/112 + 30/112$ $+ 3/224 = 84/224 =$	21/56

Source: Calculated from table 12.5.

$$
\begin{aligned}
\bar{u}_y &= \sum_{i=1}^{n_1} iX^1_i/S_y + \sum_{i=1}^{n_2} (C_1 + i)X^2_i/S_y + \ldots + \sum_{i=1}^{n_q} (C_{q-1}+i)X^q_i/S_y \\
&= \sum_{i=1}^{n_1} i(X^1_i/S_1)\phi_1 + \sum_{i=1}^{n_2} (C_1 + i)(X^2_i/S_2)\phi_2 + \ldots \\
&\quad + \sum_{i=1}^{n_q} (C_{q-1} + i)(X^q_i/S_q)\phi_q \\
&= \phi_1u_1 + \phi_2u_2 + \ldots + \phi_qu_q + C_1\phi_2 + C_2\phi_3 + \ldots + C_{q-1}\phi_q.
\end{aligned}
$$

This completes the proof of equation (12.27b).

Substituting equation (12.27b) into equation (12.27a) gives:

$$\bar{G}_y = \frac{2}{n}(\phi_1 u_1 + \phi_2 u_2 + \ldots + \phi_q u_q)$$

$$+ \frac{2}{n}(C_1\phi_2 + C_2\phi_3 + \ldots + C_{q-1}\phi_q) - (n+1)/n$$

$$= \phi_1 \frac{n_1}{n}\left[\frac{2}{n_1} \times u_1 - \frac{n_1+1}{n_1}\right] + \phi_2 \frac{n_2}{n}\left[\frac{2}{n_2} \times u_2 - \frac{n_2+1}{n_2}\right]$$

$$+ \ldots + \phi_q \frac{n_q}{n}\left[\frac{2}{n_q} \times u_q - \frac{n_q+1}{n_q}\right]$$

$$+ \left[\phi_1 \frac{n_1+1}{n} + \phi_2 \frac{n_2+1}{n} + \ldots + \phi_q \frac{n_q+1}{n}\right]$$

$$- \left[\phi_1 \frac{n+1}{n} + \phi_2 \frac{n+1}{n} + \ldots + \phi_q \frac{n+1}{n}\right]$$

$$+ \frac{2}{n}[(C_1\phi_2 + C_2\phi_3 + \ldots + C_{q-1}\phi_q)]$$

$$= \phi_1\theta_1 G_1 + \phi_2\theta_2 G_2 + \ldots + \phi_q\theta_q G_q + B, \quad \text{where}$$

$$B = \phi_1 \frac{n_1 - n}{n} + \phi_2 \frac{n_2 + 2C_1 - n}{n} + \phi_3 \frac{n_3 + 2C_2 - n}{n} + \ldots$$

$$+ \phi_q \frac{n_q + 2C_{q-1} - n}{n}$$

$$= [\phi_1(n_1 - n) + \phi_2(C_1 + C_2 - n) + \phi_3(C_2 + C_3 - n) + \ldots$$

$$+ \phi_q(C_{q-1} + C_q - n)]/n$$

$$= G_r \quad \text{by equation (12.26).}$$

Hence:

$$\bar{G}_y = A + G_r \quad \text{by equation (12.21).}$$

This completes the proof of lemma 12.1, which also proves theorem 12.2.

Gini Error Arising from the Use of Grouped Data

One important problem relevant to the analysis in this volume was first brought to our attention by Professor Orcutt. As an illustration of that problem, which is associated with the use of grouped data on the distribution of family income, assume that an income survey has been conducted for ten families and that the results are processed as follows:

(12.28a) (4, 10, 14, 5, 12, 15, 6, 14, 16, 4)

[*survey returns*]

(12.28b) (4, 4, 5, 6, 10, 12, 14, 14, 15, 16)

[*ordered tabulation of primary data*]

(12.28c) [(4), (4, 5, 6), (10, 12, 14), (14, 15, 16)]

[*partitioned primary data*]

(12.28d)

	Family group			
Variable	1	2	3	4
Number of families	1	3	3	3
Total income	4	15	36	45
Mean income	4	5	12	15

[*published frequency distribution*]

(12.28e) [(4), (5, 5, 5), (12, 12, 12), (15, 15, 15)]

[*grouped data*]

The survey returns are first ordered into a tabulation: that is, they are computerized. Next some partitioning of the ordered tabulation is selected. In the example here the ten families are classified into four groups according to total income rank. In actual practice a decile partition is often chosen to enable international comparisons. Then a frequency distribution is computed. The frequency distribution presented here indicates the number of families, total income, and average income for each family group. In reality the number of families usually is very large, and the final tabulation of the frequency distribution is the only practical way in which data can be published and made available to the general user.

When the original survey returns (12.28a) are processed into a frequency distribution, all intragroup variations are suppressed. Published data almost always suppress intragroup variations when the sample size is large. One method a researcher can use to recover part of the suppressed information for empirical work is by interpolation—that is, by guessing or speculating about the intragroup variations with the aid of additional assumptions.[2] An ideal method, which we strongly advocate, obviously is to work with primary data—something which is becoming increasingly feasible in this age of computerization, but which was not possible for us.[3] The purpose in this section, however, is to investigate the seriousness of this suppression when the published frequency distribution is used to calculate the Gini coefficient.

The problem is not serious when grouped data are used for the computation of mean income. In grouped data every member belonging to the same group is interpreted as having the same income as the mean income of the group; those mean values essentially replace the primary data.[4] Suppose the incomes within each group to be randomly distributed around the group mean. Then the average income computed from grouped data will not differ much from the true mean of the primary data. But if grouped data are used to

2. Joseph L. Gastwirth, "The Estimation of the Lorenz Curve and Gini Index," *The Review of Economics and Statistics*, vol. 54, no. 3 (August 1972), pp. 306–16.

3. This method is especially advocated for any future research that involves the multidimensional cross-listing of data. Our work in chapter four has shown that the most serious deficiency of published data is the absence of cross-listing, not the suppression of intragroup variation. Consequently this section, as well as the interpolation method, may some day have only historical interest in the analysis of the distribution of family income.

4. This obviously is the only interpretation when the original survey data are not available and interpolations are not used.

compute the Gini coefficient, or for that matter any reasonable index of inequality, there will always be an underestimation of the degree of inequality. In the numerical example the true Gini coefficient computed from primary data is:

$$G_y^T = 0.256; \tag{12.29a}$$

the Gini coefficient computed from grouped data is:

$$G_y = 0.240. \tag{12.29b}$$

Thus G_y underestimates G_y^T by 0.016. By comparing the grouped data and primary data it is seen that G_y, when computed from grouped data, captures only the intergroup effect of G_y^T. Because the grouped data represent a consecutive partitioning of a monotonically increasing vector, there is no crossover effect in this case. Equation (12.21a) can be used to compute the intragroup effect in the numerical example as follows:

$$\theta_1 = 0.1,\ \theta_2 = 0.3,\ \theta_3 = 0.3,\ \theta_4 = 0.3; \tag{12.30a}$$

$$\phi_1 = 0.04,\ \phi_2 = 0.15,\ \phi_3 = 0.36,\ \phi_4 = 0.45; \tag{12.30b}$$

$$G_1 = 0,\ G_2 = 4/45,\ G_3 = 2/27,\ G_4 = 4/135; \tag{12.30c}$$

$$\begin{aligned} A &= (0.1)(0.04)0 + (0.3)(0.15)(4/45) \\ &\quad + (0.3)(0.36)(2/27) + (0.03)(0.45)(4/135) \\ &= 0.016. \end{aligned} \tag{12.30d}$$

That value of A is exactly the amount of underestimation. Thus, when grouped data are used, there always is a systematic downward bias in the estimation of the true degree of inequality.

Grouping Error in the Analysis of Additive Factor Components

When the pattern of total income has factor components, the use of grouped data presents additional problems, which can be illustrated by the numerical example in table 12.7. The total income $[Y_i]$, wage income $[W_i]$, and property income $[\pi_i]$ of six families constitute the primary ungrouped data for this example. Notice that Y_i is the sum of W_i and π_i. Furthermore, as in the tabulation discussed at the beginning of the preceding section, the primary ungrouped

Table 12.7. *Numerical Example of the Factor Gini Error in Grouped Data*

Family	Primary ungrouped data ($f = 1$)[a]			Wage income pattern in published data[b]		
	Total family income	Wage income	Property income	$f = 2$	$f = 3$	$f = 6$
1	$Y_1 = 12$	$10 = w_1$	$2 = \pi_1$	8	25.3	19.2
2	$Y_2 = 14$	$6 = w_2$	$8 = \pi_2$	8	25.3	19.2
3	$Y_3 = 64$	$60 = w_3$	$4 = \pi_3$	30	25.3	19.2
4	$Y_4 = 70$	$0 = w_4$	$70 = \pi_4$	30	13.3	19.2
5	$Y_5 = 80$	$0 = w_5$	$80 = \pi_5$	20	13.3	19.2
6	$Y_6 = 100$	$40 = w_6$	$60 = \pi_6$	20	13.3	19.2

Source: Constructed by the authors.
a. The symbol f stands for the number of families in each income class.
b. Of the type used for the model of additive factor components in this volume.

data for the six families are ranked according to total income: $Y_1 \leq Y_2 \leq Y_3 \leq Y_4 \leq Y_5 \leq Y_6$. As a result, the primary data on wage income $[W_i]$ and property income $[\pi_i]$ are not monotonically ranked. If the primary data are available, the values of W_i can be monotonically ranked, as in table 12.7, and used to compute the true wage Gini $[G^T(W)]$. The same holds for the values of π_i.

The published data available to the general reader do not, however, include the primary ungrouped data. According to the standard practice of data publication, some integer f is always chosen so that primary data are consecutively partitioned into classes of families and that f families are included in each income class. In the example here, f is a divisor of 6: $f = 1$, $f = 2$, $f = 3$, and $f = 6$. The primary data on wage income in table 12.7 correspond to the case $f = 1$. The cases $f = 2$, $f = 3$, and $f = 6$ correspond to different levels of aggregation of wage income patterns and are also given in table 12.7. Notice the difference between patterns based on published data, which are monotonically ordered by total income rank, and those based on primary data, which are monotonically ordered by

Wage income patterns based on original unpublished data and ranked by wage rank				*Published grouped data*[b] *(f = 2)*			*Property income pattern based on original unpublished data and ranked by property rank*			
f = 1	*f = 2*	*f = 3*	*f = 6*	*Total income*	*Wage income*	*Property income*	*f = 1*	*f = 2*	*f = 3*	*f = 6*
0	0	2.0	19.2	13	8	5	2	3	4.6	37.3
0	0	2.0	19.2	13	8	5	4	3	4.6	37.3
6	8	2.0	19.2	67	30	37	8	34	4.6	37.3
10	8	36.6	19.2	67	30	37	60	34	70.0	37.3
40	50	36.6	19.2	90	20	70	70	75	70.0	37.3
60	50	36.6	19.2	90	20	70	80	75	70.0	37.3

wage income rank. At each level of aggregation the group mean replaces the income of a particular family.

The numerical example's published data on total income $[Y_i]$, wage income $[W_i]$, and property income $[\pi_i]$ are grouped for $f = 2$ in table 12.7. Notice that total income is the sum of wage income and property income. In other words, the published grouped data satisfy the basic requirement of the additive factor-components problem: $Y_i = W_i + \pi_i$. The published data in this grouped form customarily are available only for a limited number of values of f—usually for 15 to 25 family groups. In the early chapters of this book, such as chapter three, the decomposition analysis is based on the use of grouped data in this form: following the decile convention, the value of f is equal to the total number of families divided by ten. Thus, when primary ungrouped data are not available on tape, researchers must use grouped data at a particular level of aggregation corresponding to a particular value of f.

The true wage Gini and the pseudo wage Gini can be computed from the primary data in table 12.7: $G_t(W) = 0.61$; $\bar{G}_t(W) = 0.09$. Based on different levels of aggregation, a set of wage Ginis $[G(W,f)]$ and a set of pseudo wage Ginis $[\bar{G}(W, f)]$ can also be computed. Notice that $G_t(W) = G(W, 1)$ and $\bar{G}_t(W) = \bar{G}(W, 1)$. In figure 12.1

Figure 12.1. *Behavior of Indexes of Inequality under Different Levels of Aggregation*

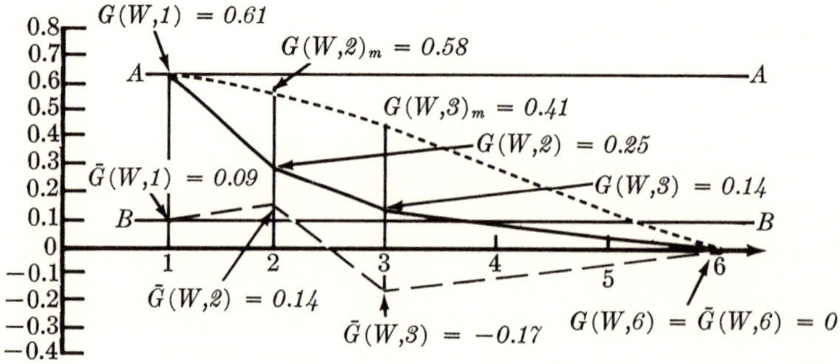

True wage Gini a———a′

True pseudo wage Gini b———b′

——— *Wage Gini for wage pattern ranked by total income rank*

– — — *Pseudo wage Gini for wage pattern ranked by total income rank*

-------- *Wage Gini for wage pattern ranked by wage rank*

Source: Calculated from table 12.7.

the values of the true wage Gini [$G(W, 1)$] and the true pseudo wage Gini [$\bar{G}(W, 1)$] are respectively indicated by the horizontal lines aa' and bb'. The values of the wage Ginis at different levels of aggregation are: $G(W, 2) = 0.25$; $G(W, 3) = 0.14$; and $G(W, 6) = 0$. The corresponding values of the pseudo wage Ginis are: $\bar{G}(W, 2) = 0.14$; $\bar{G}(W, 3) = -0.17$; and $\bar{G}(W, 6) = 0$. As the data become more aggregated—that is, as the values of f become higher—$G(W, f)$ decreases. Thus $G(W, f)$ implies an increasing underestimation of the true wage Gini as f increases from one. That underestimation is indicated by the vertical gap, $G_t(W, 1) - G(W, f)$, between the solid curve and the horizontal line aa'. Notice that the pseudo Gini [$\bar{G}(W, f)$] behaves more erratically as f increases.

When the wage pattern is monotonically ranked, a different set of wage Ginis can be computed: $G(W, 1)_m = 0.61$; $G(W, 2)_m = 0.58$; $G(W, 3)_m = 0.41$; and $G(W, 6)_m = 0$. These values are indicated in figure 12.1. Notice in this monotonic case that the underestimation of the true wage Gini represents the intragroup effect discussed in conjunction with equations (12.29) and (12.30).[5]

By comparing the two error terms, it can be seen that $G(W, 1) - G(W, f)_m$ generally is smaller than $G(W, 1) - G(W, f)$ for every f. The reason is that the wage patterns associated with the second error are not monotonically ranked. Thus, in addition to the intragroup effect, there are other sources of underestimation. It should now be clear that two distinct problems, both associated with the Gini error, arise from the use of grouped data.

The first problem is related to the size of the Gini error when the income pattern is monotonically arranged. It has been shown that this error $[G(W, 1) - G(W, f)_m]$ corresponds to the intragroup effect, which can be calculated when the primary ungrouped data are available.[6] When the primary data are not available, this error can be estimated by an interpolation method which has already been developed.[7]

The second problem is conceptually more complicated. It is associated with the Gini error $[G(W, 1) - G(W, f)]$ when a factor income component is not monotonically ranked. Our discussion should have made it clear that this constitutes a special problem which arises when the grouped data are used for the analysis of additive factor components—that is, when the arrangement of factor incomes is by total income rank and for this reason is not monotonic. For this new problem the Gini error is larger than the intragroup effect, but its precise nature remains to be investigated from a

5. Exchanges with Graham Pyatt of the World Bank indicate that two additional words of clarification may help to avoid further confusion. First, if only published grouped data are available, as often is the case, the values of $G(W, f)_m$ cannot be computed. Second, $G(W, f)_m$ is irrelevant to the additive factor-components method of Gini decomposition. This is true despite the fact that $G(W, f)_m$ is a better approximation of the true wage Gini than is $G(W, f)$ for each value of f. The reason is that the patterns of wage and property income must add up to the pattern of total income, as is illustrated by the published data in table 12.7, if this method is to be applied. But when wage and property income respectively are monotonically ranked according to wage and property rank, the patterns of factor income do not add up to the pattern of total income.

6. Of course, it is preferable to use primary data, when available, and thus avoid this error. The interpretation of this error nevertheless is conceptually important.

7. See Gastwirth, "The Estimation of the Lorenz Curve and Gini Index."

theoretical standpoint.[8] Thus the intrinsic interpretation of the error term, as a property of the primary ungrouped data, remains to be studied. Furthermore no method has yet been developed, at least to our knowledge, to estimate upper and lower bounds of this error when primary data are not available—that is, a method comparable to the interpolation method for the simple case when the income pattern is monotonically arranged.

This second problem is serious for all users who must rely, as we have in this volume, on published grouped data to implement the additive factor-components approach. Future research can be expected to proceed along three fronts: theoretical research on the nature of the Gini error as a property of ungrouped data; empirical research using ungrouped data to determine the seriousness of underestimation associated with each level of aggregation[9]; the design of interpolation methods when primary data are not available. The empirical results in this volume will no doubt require reassessment as further work in these areas comes to fruition.

8. For certain special cases it can be shown that the Gini error has two components: an intragroup effect and a crossover effect. See theorem 12.2.

9. The purpose of that research ultimately is to determine safe levels of aggregation $[f]$ so that the error falls within tolerable limits.

Index

The World Bank and the Yale Economic Growth Center supported the research leading to the publication of this volume. Established as an activity of the Department of Economics in 1961, the Economic Growth Center is a research organization whose purpose is to analyze the economies of developing countries and their relations with economically advanced nations. Its current program of research is focused on six principal areas: basic processes of economic development; agriculture and rural development; technology choice and change; economic demography and labor markets; poverty, employment, and the distribution of income; and international economic interdependence, including North-South problems. Publications of the Center include book-length studies and journal reprints by staff members. For more information, write to the Economic Growth Center, Box 1987, Yale Station, New Haven, Connecticut 06520, U.S.A.

The full range of World Bank publications, both free and for sale, is described in the *Catalog of World Bank Publications;* the continuing research program is outlined in *World Bank Research Program: Abstracts of Current Studies.* Both booklets are updated annually; the most recent edition of each is available without charge from the Publications Unit, World Bank, 1818 H Street, N.W., Washington, D.C. 20433, U.S.A.